Thinking Life with Luce Irigaray

SUNY series in Gender Theory

Tina Chanter, editor

Thinking Life with Luce Irigaray

Language, Origin, Art, Love

Edited by

Gail M. Schwab

Cover art: *Elemental Congruence* by Marcie Van Auken

Published by State University of New York Press, Albany

For information, contact State University of New York Press, Albany, NY
www.sunypress.edu

Library of Congress Cataloging-in-Publication Data

Names: Schwab, Gail M., editor.
Title: Thinking life with Luce Irigaray : language, origin, art, love / edited by Gail M. Schwab.
Description: Albany : State University of New York, 2020. | Series: SUNY series in gender theory | Includes bibliographical references and index.
Identifiers: LCCN 2019014127 | ISBN 9781438477817 (hardcover : alk. paper) | ISBN 9781438477824 (pbk. : alk. paper) | ISBN 9781438477831 (ebook)
Subjects: LCSH: Irigaray, Luce.
Classification: LCC B2430.I74 T548 2020 | DDC 194—dc23
LC record available at https://lccn.loc.gov/2019014127

10 9 8 7 6 5 4 3 2 1

With immense gratitude to Neil, who even attended the conferences,
and to Julien, Allison, and Wolfie

Contents

Acknowledgments

First and foremost, on behalf of all contributors to this volume, I wish to thank Luce Irigaray for the beauty and the amplitude of her work. She has been, and continues to be, a daring and inspiring philosophical, political, and spiritual leader for those who desire change in the world.

Thinking Life was the title of the Luce Irigaray Circle conference held at the University of Bergen, in Bergen, Norway, in June of 2013, directed by Professor Ellen Mortensen of the University of Bergen. Many of the chapters in this volume were presented initially at the Thinking Life conference, and I, along with the Luce Irigaray Circle, am grateful to Ellen and her team at Bergen for a great conference. I am also grateful to Ellen for her initial work on the volume, work that allowed me to complete the editing.

Many thanks to the Luce Irigaray Circle, a labor of love that has borne fruit. I would also like to thank Tina Chanter, editor of the SUNY Series in Gender Theory, whose ongoing support for the Irigaray Circle has been invaluable.

The Luce Irigaray Circle extends its thanks to Hofstra University for funding Luce Irigaray's contribution and to Stony Brook University and Mary C. Rawlinson for their generous support over the years.

I wish to express my gratitude and appreciation for the generosity of Marcie Van Auken, senior graphic designer at Columbia University, who created the cover image, *Elemental Congruence I* (2019).

Peg Rawes and I thank Bloomsbury Publishing Plc. for permission to reprint in Peg Rawes's "Building Sexuate Architectures of Sustainability" a short extract from "Biopolitical Ecological Poetics," chapter 1 of *Poetic Biopolitics: Practices of Relation in Architecture and the Arts*, Peg Rawes, Timothy Mathews, and Stephen Loo, eds. London: I.B. Tauris, an imprint of Bloomsbury Publishing Plc., 2016.

Acknowledgments

PART I

THINKING LIFE WITH LUCE IRIGARAY

Introduction

Thinking Life with Luce Irigaray: Language, Origin, Art, Love

GAIL M. SCHWAB

In the first chapter of *Between East and West: From Singularity to Community* (2002), in a critique of what she considers Schopenhauer's (mis)reading and (mis)representation of Indian philosophy and spirituality, Irigaray writes that "philosophy is a matter of death," and she goes on to quote Schopenhauer: "Death is the real inspiring genius or Musagetes of philosophy, and for this reason Socrates defined philosophy as *thanatou mélétè* (preparation for death; Plato, *Phaedo*, 81a). Indeed, without death there would hardly have been any philosophizing" (Schopenhauer, *The World as Will and Representation* cited in *Between East and West* 23). Irigaray further notes: "A philosopher living and thinking life is *a priori* suspect in our philosophical culture" (ibid.). Nevertheless, she will forcefully declare in the introduction to *Between East and West*: "I love life, and I have searched for solutions in order to defend it, to cultivate it" (4), and ask: "How to go against the current? To stop the exploitation, in particular through a simple inventory, of the human and of his or her environment? How to return to where death has taken place because of the cessation of becoming, mistaking what we are? How to renew a cultivation of life, and recover our energy, the path of our growth?" (viii). Many thinkers and theorists are currently pursuing answers to these questions.

The contributors to *Thinking Life with Luce Irigaray*, the latest in a series of volumes resulting from ten conferences of the Luce Irigaray Circle, which took place between 2006 and 2019, attempt to address these questions and to "think life" through the multifarious strands of Irigaray's philosophy, including, of course, the foundational strand of sexuate difference, and to show how the possibility of life in sexuate difference, far from freezing up into a rigidly codified binary of "two sexes," might blossom rather into a living continuum of ever-evolving change(s) and difference(s) in language, culture, art, spirit, nature, human relations, and politics. The philosophy of Man, of the Universal and the One, as Schopenhauer understood (without understanding), is rooted, grounded, in death. However, as Mary C. Rawlinson, feminist philosopher of life and Irigaray Circle co-founder, has written in her 2016 book, *Just Life: Bioethics and the Future of Sexual Difference*, "Man has had his day" (13). It is time to move on, to try something different—to try difference. Life is never One, as Irigaray frequently reminds us; in fact, life is always at least two, and always generating the diverse and the multiple. The chapters that follow Irigaray's both explore and illustrate what it might mean to think life in all of the above-mentioned domains, and in others besides.

Origin, Maternity, and Relationality

Part 1: "Thinking Life with Luce Irigaray," in addition to this introduction to the entire volume, includes an essay by Irigaray, "How Could We Achieve Women's Liberation?," presented via video link at the third conference of the Luce Irigaray Circle in the Fall of 2008. Irigaray began her brief but densely rich remarks by questioning the discouraging failure of twentieth-century women's movements to have achieved women's "evolution" at either the personal or the collective level—beyond, that is, a certain undeniable economic and social progress, both the importance of which and the limits of which Irigaray went on to acknowledge. Urging women to take control of their own liberation and to cultivate freedom for themselves and for their own becoming, "How Could We Achieve Women's Liberation?" ranges over many of the themes that have formed the foundation of Irigaray's major works and thought—themes that are integral to her life-centered philosophy. Particularly important in Irigaray's essay is the problem of the noncompetitive and nonconflictual, but also nondependent and nonfusional, ethical relation to the other, a relation defined by respect for limits and by the creation of the "threshold," or the "interval," a space-between that allows two human beings to cultivate and maintain their own subjectivity while creating a living relation between them. This has been a particularly rich area of exploration in Irigaray scholarship, as we shall see in many of the chapters that follow, which include a piece by Rebecca Hill, whose book on the interval has been highly influential (see Hill 2012).

Relationality could be said to constitute the main thrust of works like *The Ethics of Sexual Difference* (1993), *To Be Two* (2001), *I Love to You* (1996), *Sharing the World* (2008), and *Teaching* (2008). More specifically in the area of ethical relations, "How Could We Achieve Women's Liberation?" has some interesting things to say about desire and sexuality—ideas that look back to, and substantially develop, Irigaray's call for the cultivation of desire in, for example, "Spiritual Tasks for Our Age" in *Key Writings* (2004, 171–85), where she emphasized the connection between sexuality and spirituality; in "How Could We Achieve Women's Liberation?," she underlines the link between sexuality and freedom:

> Sexuality is, in a way, unnecessary with respect to our own life. As such, sexuality is also the place where the question of our human freedom is most critical. Sexuality can lead us to stay at or fall back into the mere elementary or material level of our instincts, or it can help us to overcome our native human belonging towards aiming at spirituality. Sexuality is the part of our body of which the function is almost only relational. [. . .] Sexuality attracts us beyond ourselves, and provides us with energy for this going beyond. (33)

Several of the chapters that follow develop the themes of love, eroticism, and sexuality—concepts/experiences that are obviously of central importance to the problem of "thinking life."

Another Irigarayan theme in the area of relationality that appears in "How Could We Achieve Women's Liberation?" concerns the urgent need to "return to our birth, with its bodily and contextual dimensions—that is, to our natural origin and identity" (27), and to acknowledge our debt to the mother and recognize our birth as the originary truth, not only of our own life, but as that of all of civilization. The relation to the mother is one of the pillars of Irigarayan ethics, and she has written about it extensively, in essays like "Body against Body: In Relation to the Mother," "Belief Itself" (*Sexes and Genealogies* 1987, 7–21, 23–53); "When the Gods Are Born" (*Marine Lover of Friedrich Nietzsche* 1991, 121–90); "The Forgotten Mystery of Female Ancestry" (*Thinking the Difference* 1994, 89–112); "On the Maternal Order" (*Je Tu Nous* 1993, 37–44); and "Spiritual Tasks for

Our Age," to name only a few examples. In "How Could We Achieve Women's Liberation?," Irigaray reaffirms that the way to women's liberation does not follow the male path of "emergence from the natural origin that is generally confused with the maternal body and world," in order to enter "a culture in the masculine" (26); such a trajectory is not only unsuitable to female subjectivity, but also actively "opposes it" (ibid.), as Irigaray writes. We shall see that the rethinking of the relation to and the debt owed the mother—conceptual problems that, like sexuality and love, are indispensable to thinking life—figure as prominent themes in many of the chapters in this volume. This is also a fruitful area of current research in Irigaray studies, as philosophers like Rachel Jones and Fanny Söderbäck, for example, continue to develop Irigaray's thinking on the maternal relation, natality, and placental ethics (see Jones 2011, 2012, 2013; Söderbäck 2016).

Of course, Irigaray continues, woman "has a natural origin that she has to consider and cultivate, but she herself is also a natural origin" (28), and "she has to preserve the transcendence of the one to whom she gives birth as being another human with an origin different from hers. This requires the ability to distance herself from the work of her own body" (29). Being an origin goes beyond procreation, however, as "each woman, independently of giving birth to a child, is a place from which an origin can and must spring. This presupposes a certain way of dealing with life, with breathing, with energy, with language" (29). A woman, while acknowledging her maternal debt and cultivating a spiritual and ethical relation to the mother, must also take responsibility for and forge her own origin as a free human being, creating her self, her own spirit, and a language or medium appropriate both to express that self and to reach out to others. In some of her most recent work, Irigaray develops this concern for "being an origin" far beyond the concept of "women's liberation" into an ontology of human becoming and urges us to give birth—through breathing, through the assumption of sexuate difference, and through appropriate relations to others—to an entirely new humanity (see, for example, *To Be Born* 2017). Irigaray's emphasis on the becoming of the species has inspired the thought of Elizabeth Grosz, whose work on the ontology of sexual difference is foundational to current feminist thought on evolution, change, transformation, and becoming, or on "becoming undone," to use Grosz's term (See Grosz 2011, 2013, and 2016), and Grosz's work in this area has influenced many contemporary thinkers and writers, including Rebecca Hill, Rachel Jones, Cheryl Lynch-Lawler, Kristin Sampson, Peg Rawes, Ellen Mortensen, and myself, to name only a handful of those who read her.

Logic, Language, Art

Regarding the need to transform language as a medium, Irigaray has been questioning, studying, and analyzing language across the entire breadth of her oeuvre, in addition to (re)creating it (revitalizing it—that is, reinfusing it with life) herself in the highly original style of her writing, where she seeks, as she writes in "How Could We Achieve Women's Liberation?," "to think while being faithful to myself as a woman and not to submit myself to a culture that [is] not appropriate to me" (30). She began her own research and writing with sociolinguistic studies in *Le Langage des Déments* (1973) and with the essays in *To Speak Is Never Neutral* (2002), carried on with this work in her major essay "Représentation et auto-affection du féminin" in her edited collection *Sexes et genres à travers les langues* (1990, 31–82), and used the data and the insights she had acquired in her social-scientific studies to create important syntheses in several of the essays in *I Love to You* and in her pedagogical investigations with Italian schoolchildren in *Le Partage de la parole* (2001, partially published in *Key Writings* as "Towards a Sharing of Speech" [77–94]). Language and linguistics constitute one of the five principal themes of *Key Writings,* and, perhaps unexpectedly, language is also what is at stake in the *Way of Love*, whose title seems to promise something quite different, but whose execution demonstrates that finding the way of love requires a new language. The rethinking and remaking of language make up a vein of scholarship that has been central in my own work on Irigaray over the years (see Schwab 1998, 1998, 2016).

"How Could We Achieve Women's Liberation?" calls for a commitment to creative exploration enabling women to connect to our own subjectivity and energy, to express difference and plurality rather than oneness and sameness, and to enter into communication with (the) other(s). It is incumbent upon us to develop new language(s), new logic(s), and new cultural forms; in an interesting comment that she (regrettably) does not pursue any further, Irigaray proposes that we move beyond our long preoccupation with the difference between metaphor and metonymy, and, instead, consider "another way of expressing the real that perhaps has to do with diaphor" (31), a type of metaphorical expression emphasizing, not similarities but rather differences (diaphora), creating the possibility of something new, leading "to a greater potential for living, growing, coexisting, and sharing with the whole of the real" (ibid.).

Irigaray writes in "How Could We Achieve Women's Liberation?" that western logic and culture have used words

> to duplicate the real and construct a world parallel to the living world. This constructed world is in a way finished, closed, just as a chessboard is limited, and the words—that is, the pieces that move on the chessboard—are also limited and defined, as is the case for their movements. There is no longer life in such a world but only a representation of the living world that aims to put it at man's disposal. (30–31)

The binary oppositions structuring language and thought in our Western tradition have transformed the "living real into dead realities" (32) cut off from nature. In the contemporary moment, the chess board has become a violent video game, where the "pieces"—more obviously representations of humans than the kings, queens, knights, bishops, and so on on a chess board, but no more alive—would seem to enjoy more freedom of movement and choice than their chess counterparts, but whose movements take place only in the representation of space, and whose choices are exercised only in the representation of freedom—the "choices" lying invariably between the "freedom" to overpower and to kill or the "freedom" to be overpowered and killed. Death is in either case the goal and the result. Many of the chapters in this book take up Irigaray's critique of death-dealing Western either-or binary logic and seek to find another path, or paths, rather—multidirectional, winding, intertwining paths of expression and becoming—of life and lives.

Nature

Finally, in Irigaray's essay, we also take note of her expressions of concern about the state of our planet and her ongoing involvement in ecological and environmental issues, which first became explicit in her well-known, now-classic piece inspired as a response to the disaster at Chernobyl, "A Chance for Life" (*Thinking the Difference* 1–35), where she demonstrates her passionate advocacy for a nonexploitative, nonextractive relation to nature and the earth, and for a respectful relation to all that lives. As we begin to consider the ways that "our culture has damaged and endangered our planet" and come to recognize that "we have to rethink our behavior with respect to nature" ("How Could We Achieve Women's Liberation?" 27), we move beyond the human-centered concerns of relationality and self-expression and communication and begin to attend to life in the nonhuman, including animal and vegetal life, and the life of the earth itself—its water, soil, rock, air, and climate—that is, all of organic and inorganic nature, all that sustains all that sustains us; we move from human life to Life. (I would mention in this context the collection of essays edited by Peg Rawes, *Relational Architectural Ecologies: Architecture, Nature, and Subjectivity* [2013], that deals with the ecology and the economy of the built and natural environments, as well as with human subjectivity and a politics of community and care. For further development of these issues by Irigaray, see *In the Beginning She Was* [2013] and *Through Vegetal Being: Two Philosophical Perspectives*, written with Michael Marder [2016].)

Life in and through Nature, Desire, Freedom, and Love

In Part II: "Life in and through Nature, Desire, Freedom, and Love," several of the contributors, in particular Rebecca Hill, Cheryl Lynch-Lawler, Kristin Sampson, Erla Karlsdottir and Sigridur Thorgeirsdottir, and Ellen Mortensen seek new ways of thinking that would open up "chessboard logic" in support of a fluid vitality. Cheryl Lynch-Lawler, Erla Karlsdottir and Sigridur Thorgeirsdottir, and Kristin Sampson re-examine some of the traditional binaries of Western thought—that is, nature-culture, male-female, mind-body, reason-emotion, sense perception-cognition, and life-death—and Rebecca Hill broadens the dialogue they establish with contemporary and classical Western thinkers to include philosophers and artists of the First Nations peoples of Australia. Ellen Mortensen, Fanny Söderbäck, Louise Burchill, Phyllis H. Kaminski, and I then shift the focus of thinking life onto problems of relationality and of life with (the) other(s), and consider the cultivation of love and desire through sexuate difference.

In "The Reenchanted Garden: Participatory Sentience and Becoming-Subject in 'Third Space,'" Cheryl Lynch-Lawler, working with the insights gained in her psychoanalytic practice, seeks sense-based and emotional pathways to the reintegration of the mind, body, and spirit, as she takes up Irigaray's challenge to the Western logic of solids and urges us to seek in the natural world, as well as within our psyche, a fluidity of thought and a connectedness to our own inner wellspring of creativity, all of which we have come perilously close to losing in our capitalist-consumerist world of overly mediatized digital images and networks—representations of life that are cut off from living, breathing life, as Lynch-Lawler shows. Irigaray writes in "How Could We Achieve Women's Liberation?" that we have begun to "act, experience, and even feel as an element of a more or less huge machine in which the relations between two elements are regulated by the whole without any freedom, responsibility, or even personal experience" (36), and her call for spiritual and artistic endeavor allowing us to connect to the whole of our being, as well as to others, vibrates here in Lynch-Lawler's rejection of traditional Western philosophico-scientific logic and her search for the wholeness of human subjective becoming in new ways of "doing" science, in sensory immersion in nature, and in a more holistic relation to self, others, and the world.

Irigaray has ceaselessly mined the canonical Western tradition, and in particular, the stories, tragedies, and philosophy of the Greeks, and her relationship to the Greek heritage has inspired many thinkers; I note here, in particular, the major collection edited by Elena Tzelepis and Athena Athanasiou, *Rewriting Difference: Luce Irigaray and "the Greeks,"* which includes important essays by Dorothea Olkowski, Mary Beth Mader, Lynne Huffer, Judith Still, Tina Chanter, and Luce Irigaray herself (see Tzelepis and Athanasiou 2010). *Thinking Life with Luce Irigaray* continues to develop this line of thought in the chapters by Rebecca Hill, Fanny Söderbäck, Kristin Sampson, and Alison Stone. Looking back beyond Aristotelian metaphysics, as well as beyond the pre-Socratics, to Homer and to the poets of antiquity she labels the "pre-pre-Socratics," in "Thinking Life through the Early Greeks," Kristin Sampson, in a further critique of the either-or logic of Western culture, examines the philological roots of the concepts of "life" and "nature," removing both terms from the binary oppositions of metaphysical thought, where "life" came to mean the "opposite of death" and "nature" the "opposite of culture." Sampson demonstrates the complexity and the amplitude of the concepts of "life" and "nature," whose pre-pre-Socratic meanings vary according to the vicissitudes of concrete situations and life experiences, and she opens up the possibility of rereading both pre-Socratic and pre-pre-Socratic Greek thought in order to come to greater clarity regarding the contemporary structuring of our concepts of nature and of life and to develop potentialities for future becoming.

Emphasizing, as do Lynch-Lawler and Sampson, the place of humans within and with respect to nature, Rebecca Hill looks at many literary topoi and strands of Western culture through the dystopian, post–environmental-disaster lens of Australian First Nations writer Alexis Wright's 2013 novel *The Swan Book*, in "Between Her and Her: Place and Relations between Women in Irigaray and Wright." Philosophers and feminist scholars will undoubtedly follow the direction taken by Rebecca Hill in her reading of the resonances between Irigaray's work and that of Alexis Wright, as they move away from criticism of Irigaray's thought (or lack thereof) on differences other than sexual/sexuate difference and as they begin to grapple with the potential of her work to illuminate intersectionality in useful ways—as Hill does in her chapter. Intersectionality was one of the principal themes of the ninth Irigaray Circle conference entitled Horizons of Sexual Difference, directed by Athena Coleman at Brock University in June of 2018. Work by, among others, Rebecca Hill herself, Sabrina Hom (see 2013), and Emily Anne Parker (see 2014, 2018), who all made presentations at the 2018 conference, has already begun to open Irigaray studies in the direction of intersectional and decolonial thought. In this context, we should note the importance of striking a balance between ontological concerns and the demands of intersectionality. This balance will be crucial for the future of Irigaray studies. Australian feminist philosopher and activist Laura Roberts's new book, *Irigaray and Politics: A Critical Introduction* (2019), deals with ontological questions of space and time, as well as with the problematics of intersectionality and differences beyond sexual difference; Roberts's work may point to a path forward (see also Roberts 2015).

In her chapter, Rebecca Hill reads a "double matricide" in the systematic sacrifice of nature in the Western economic model coupled with the exploitation of the sexuality and the fertility of women in the reproduction of patriarchal society. The problem of matricide, and of the excessive violence against women in general, that lies at the foundation of Western culture is one of the principal themes in the chapters by Ellen Mortensen, Phyllis H. Kaminski, Alison Stone, and Emily Holmes. Rebecca Hill contrasts the dereliction—the placelessness—of women in the West with the ontology of space and time of the Indigenous peoples of the Australian continent, whose "country never leaves its people" and whose time is multidimensional—where "all times exist together" and no times "cease to be." Hill then goes on to discuss Irigaray's "interval," or "sensible transcendental," as the basis for the ethical relation to the other, as well as to all that lies beyond the human scale within both the temporal and the spatial universe. The interval will appear again and again in the chapters that follow; Fanny Söderbäck's, Louise Burchill's, Phyllis H. Kaminski's, Eva Maria Korsisaari's, Tomoka Toraiwa's, Karen Schiler's, Britt-Marie Schiller's, Caroline Godart's, and mine all grapple with the problems of relating ethically to the other in various domains, including the erotic, the spiritual, the pedagogical, and the political.

In their collaborative essay, "Nature, Culture, and Sexuate Difference in Luce Irigaray's Pluralist Model of Embodied Life," Erla Karlsdottir and Sigridur Thorgeirsdottir critique, like Kristin Sampson, the hierarchizing binary logic of the Western cultural tradition, particularly the closed-off and static model of sexual identity as a male/female binary. Karlsdottir and Thorgeirsdottir, following Ellen Mortensen, read Irigaray's relationship to Nietzsche and her awareness of his longing to reconnect with a premetaphysical conception of embodied life, as a source for her model for thinking life—where nature and culture; self and other; and male and female (along with other potential sexuate identities) interact and intertwine in a nonagonistic way, in a way that is fruitful and creatively generative of multiplicity, pluralism, diversity, and asymmetricality, establishing the foundation for the creation and/or renewal of democracy through civil identities based on the interplay of sexuate differences.

In "Between Heidegger's Poetic Thinking and Deleuzian Affect: Irigaray's *The Way of Love,*" Ellen Mortensen's reading of *The Way of Love* illustrates Irigaray's engagement with Heidegger and her critique of his too-exclusive focus on a language "steeped in death, nothingness, and sameness" (Mortensen 120), as Mortensen writes, reminding us of Irigaray's, Lynch-Lawler's, Sampson's, Hill's, Karlsdottir's and Thorgeirsdottir's calls for a renewal of thought in a language that would be a "fluid, incomplete, and ever-changing language of difference and becoming, one that is energized by the elements of fire, earth, air, and water" (ibid.). Mortensen ultimately finds that Irigaray's way of love requires a mode of speech that would lay the foundation for relationality—a language, as Irigaray writes in "How Could We Achieve Women's Liberation?," that "uses forms, but living forms, forms that are not fixed, closed, defined once and for all [. . .], words which reveal something of the living real" (31)—a language "that tries to express our whole being and speak to the whole being of the other" (35).

The Way of Love is not exclusively a book about a path toward a new language; considerations regarding the transformation and renewal of desire and sexual energy are prominent within it, as they are in so many places in Irigaray's work. In "How Could We Achieve Women's Liberation?" she writes that

> if our needs generally concern us at a mere individual level, it is not the case with regard to sexuality. [. . .] Sexual attraction, in fact, has nothing to do with our individual needs, but rather with overcoming them. Sexual attraction can transform our needs into a component of our being at the service of our relational existence. [. . .] This presupposes training our immediate attractions in order that they become a desire that can be shared. To establish and respect limits is especially decisive. [. . .] Sexuate desire compels us to transcend ourselves, and it is maintained by the respect of the transcendence of the other in relation to ourselves. (34)

The next group of essays—comprising, in particular, Fanny Söderbäck's, Louise Burchill's, and my own—deals extensively with ethical erotic relations, and anticipates the further development of this theme we shall see in the chapters by Eva Maria Korsisaari, Britt-Marie Schiller, and Caroline Godart in part 3.

With an emphasis on the interval that both recalls, and contrasts with, Rebecca Hill's reading in "Between Her and Her," in "Time for Love: Plato and Irigaray on Erotic Relations," Fanny Söderbäck considers Irigaray's call for a new space-time in erotic love that would allow for the possibility of two irreducibly different subjectivities being "co-present" to each other in a ceaseless temporal becoming, across the interval created by love figured as the daimon Eros, as described in the beginnings of Diotima's discourse reported by Socrates in Plato's *Symposium.* Söderbäck urges us to read the *Symposium* with renewed focus on the form of the platonic dialogue, a form that creates complexities and ambiguities that carry us far beyond the traditional readings of professors of philosophy, who tend to find a quest for eternity, oneness, and universality in what they call "Diotima's ladder." Indeed, attentiveness to the dialogue form reveals that it actually models the concept of love as the interval "between." We might then consider—extrapolating from Söderbäck's argument—that the literary form and style of the Platonic dialogue present us with an exemplar of one of those "new" languages, or of those "new" artistic forms to which Ellen Mortensen's essay refers and Irigaray calls for in "How Could We Achieve Women's Liberation?"

Focused, like Fanny Söderbäck, on sexuate identity and on the erotic relation to the Other, Louise Burchill, in "Life-Giving Sex versus Mere Animal Existence: Irigaray's and Badiou's Paradoxically Chiasmatic Conceptions of 'Woman' and Sexual Pleasure," brings another perspective to bear on desire, sexuality, and love, as she looks at the work of French philosopher Alain Badiou and contrasts his concept of sexual difference to Irigaray's position. Burchill's detailed analysis shows that although Badiou, until 2011, denied sexual difference to have any real effectivity, or importance for thought, outside the specific field of love, he nevertheless defines "sexual disjunction" in such a way that the philosophy of Irigaray could well qualify, within his own terms, as "feminine," since Irigaray not only claims primacy for the relation between two in love and eroticism, but also views the between-two as both ontologically and epistemologically foundational. Thus, we see here that philosophy is both the love of wisdom and the wisdom of love, as Irigaray reminds us on the first page of the first chapter of *The Way of Love.*

Irigaray opened "How Could We Achieve Women's Liberation?" with a consideration of the problem of freedom, asking in her first subtitle, "At

What Freedom Do Women Aim?," questioning an energy that "when it exists, has not yet found a manner of investing itself that allows it to be kept, to be cultivated, and to be shared," and calling for the cultivation of an energy and a freedom that would be appropriate to "a woman herself" (26). My essay, "Freedom, Desire, and the Other: Reading Sartre with Irigaray," connects to Irigaray's essay, as well as to Cheryl Lynch-Lawler's, Kristin Sampson's, and Ellen Mortensen's, in its emphasis on the renewal of freedom in subjectivity through the opening of closed networks in human thought, and like Fanny Söderbäck's and Louise Burchill's, it foregrounds relationality. In a close reading of Irigaray's discussion of *Being and Nothingness* (1966) in *To Be Two*, I attempt to show that, unlike Sartre, who found that conflict between free individuals was inevitable, Irigaray rejects conflict/competition as foundational in human relations and sees a sharing of the world, or of worlds, as the only possible path to the individual's freedom. The way of love is also ultimately the way of freedom.

Phyllis H. Kaminski also looks at Irigaray's critique of Sartre's analysis of human relations in "Daughters, Difference, and Irigaray's Economy of Desire." Her focus, however, is the concept of "daughterness"—the structural position occupied by all women within the various international patterns of familial, social, and economic exchange. In her opening essay, Irigaray emphasizes that women's liberation cannot be measured solely in economic and social terms: "[G]oing no further makes us productive machines or social products without the creative ability that characterizes humanity as such. Indeed, a human being is a being which can transcend itself through its creation" (27). Kaminski similarly argues that beyond economic and social progress, it is the development, the self-creation, of the potential sexuate subjectivity of the Daughter, "making it blossom with respect for [her] own life, the life of the other" (28), that constitutes the way forward to "women's liberation" and to renewed human relations in all types of settings, including social, political, and spiritual. Kaminski also takes up Irigaray's insistence on the cultivation of an energy appropriate to female becoming and explores spiritual paths that we might once again name the way of love. She thus connects *Thinking Life with Luce Irigaray* to studies in the wider field of Irigarayan spirituality, an area in which she is herself a leader (see Kaminski 2013, 2013, among others), along with Emily Holmes, whose "The Age of the Spirit" is the next essay in the volume, and whose co-edited collections, *Breathing with Luce Irigaray* (see Holmes and Škof 2013) and *Women, Writing, Theology: Transforming a Tradition of Exclusion* (see Holmes and Farley 2011), constitute major contributions to religious studies. Phyllis H. Kaminski and Emily Holmes are, of course, indebted to the previous work in this area by Morny

Joy (see 2003, 2006), Amy Hollywood (see 2002), and Grace Jantzen (see 1999), as are many others, including myself.

Revitalizing History, Philosophy, Pedagogy, and the Arts

Thinking life requires a transformation of the truth traditions of Western thought, and in Part III: "Revitalizing History, Philosophy, Pedagogy, and the Arts," contributors consider some of the ways in which "life-thinking" has creative potential—in the weaving of new narratives in literature and in the documentation of history, as we see in the essays by Emily Holmes and Alison Stone, as well as in the rereading of traditional philosophical analyses, including those of the twentieth-century pragmatists, phenomenologists, and postmodernist theorists, as we see in the chapters by Anne van Leeuwen, Eva Maria Korsisaari, Tomoka Toraiwa, and Karen Schiler.

In "The Age of the Spirit: Irigaray, Apocalypse, and the Trinitarian View of History," Emily Holmes examines Irigaray's metaphorically trinitarian orientation toward Christian history and her reading of the contemporary spiritual moment as the inauguration of sexuate difference into Christianity, in an "age of the breath"—an age of "the spirit and the bride." Holmes shows that Irigaray is not the first to read history with such "spiritual optimism," as she takes us back to the narrative of the medieval Christian sect of the Guglielmiti, a group of thirteenth-century religious (mostly) women united in love and admiration for Guglielma, a saintly abbess they believed incarnated a third age of the spirit, wherein God in the form of a woman would redeem us all. Thinking life will require the recasting of the entirety of Western history in new and unexpected terms, focusing on those whose stories have been neglected, repressed in the official versions of events, official versions that have been the necessarily incomplete and misleading story of the hegemony of the One. A life-centered reading of History will render the stories of many others like the Guglielmiti, who—it should be noted here—were condemned to silence and to the stake, along with their own original versions of church and world history. Emily Holmes, co-editor of *Women, Writing, Theology*, is doing the work required to find their voices and their words.

In "Tragedy: An Irigarayan Approach," Alison Stone returns, with Kristin Sampson and Fanny Söderbäck, to Greek culture; her focus, however, is the tragedians, and she marshals Aristotle's, Freud's, and Irigaray's readings of Greek tragedy and myth in order to emphasize tragedy's potential to document historical change and to inspire political action. Stone thus supports Irigaray's claims, if not to an actual matriarchy that would have preceded the institution of the patriarchy, at least to a time before patriarchal social structures were fully entrenched in Greek society, a time "documented," as it were, in the great tragedians and in the earlier myths. Stone's interpretation of the *Oresteia* recalls Rebecca Hill's reading in "Between Her and Her"; Hill also emphasizes the way that Irigaray, among others, has unearthed the originary matricide(s) that underlie(s) the parricide that was read by Freud as the founding moment of culture and civilization. Freud's reading is, of course, explicitly rejected by Irigaray in her opening essay and elsewhere, and Stone maintains, following Irigaray, that the cause of women's dereliction in culture lies in damaged mother-daughter relations—a problematic that also resonates with the work of Ellen Mortensen and Phyllis H. Kaminski, as well as with mine.

In "The Ethics of Elemental Passions in Eugène Guillevic and Luce Irigaray," Eva Maria Korsisaari also contextualizes Irigaray's thought, but within twentieth-century secular philosophy, rather than Christian or ancient history. Like Cheryl Lynch-Lawler, Korsisaari explores the importance of the cultivation of life through the senses and sensory experience, although she places significantly more emphasis on the erotic relation to and desire for the other than on the relation to nature and to the self, a perspective recalling the essays of Ellen Mortensen, Louise Burchill, Fanny Söderbäck, and myself. Like many contemporary feminist scholars, and several prominent philosophers in Irigaray studies from the Nordic countries (see in particular Heinämaa 2006, 2011, and Lehtinen 2014), Korsisaari works in the phenomenological tradition, and she reads the work of Maurice Merleau-Ponty and Emmanuel Levinas through the twentieth-century love poetry of Eugène Guillevic and through Irigaray's meditations on love and sexuality, as expressed principally in her *Elemental Passions* (1992). Korsisaari finds that Irigaray and Guillevic take Merleau-Ponty's and Levinas's phenomenology to a new depth as they "describe the primordial dimensions of subjectivity and intersubjectivity, that affective and sensible level where our relations with the world or others are not analyzable in instrumental or practical terms," as well as "an eroticism where [. . .] lovers would recognize each other as different" (Korsisaari 251), as Korsisaari writes.

Anne van Leeuwen's "Deconstruction, Defiguration, Disconcertion: Reading *Speculum de l'autre femme* with Derrida and Lacan" also contextualizes Irigaray's thought within twentieth-century philosophical debates, specifically in relation to Lacan's and Derrida's critiques of difference, identity, and representation in linguistics, phenomenology, and psychoanalysis. Van Leeuwen, while emphasizing the similarity in the projects of Lacan, Derrida, and Irigaray, shows that it is only Irigaray for whom "originary difference refers to sexual difference" (van Leeuwen 258); thus, we note that for Irigaray, constitutive difference is grounded in and inseparable from life and growth. Neither strictly cognitive-symbolic nor strictly unconscious-imaginary, sexual difference requires becoming—that is, living, changing embodiment.

Historical narratives and philosophic debates can result in life-affirming real-world praxis and applications, as we see in the essays of Tomoka Toraiwa and Karen Schiler. In "Dewey and Irigaray on Education and Democracy: The Classroom, the Ineffable, and Recognition," Tomoka Toraiwa establishes a striking and unexpected parallel between the American pragmatist John Dewey and Irigarayan philosophy, as she examines their respective approaches to the theory and practice of education and of its relation and importance to democracy. Toraiwa emphasizes both the need for and the difficulty of establishing ethical horizontal relations among students and between teacher and students in the classroom where authoritarian vertical relations have traditionally predominated. Rejecting prescriptive and formulaic solutions to the problem, Toraiwa, following Dewey and Irigaray, concludes that the student-teacher relation can only thrive ethically as "between two"—that is, as a particularized face-to-face relation—and that it is only on that same basis of "between-two" that education can be said to form the foundation for true democracy. We might further emphasize here that pedagogy is an increasingly fruitful area of inquiry both for Irigaray and Irigarayans, as demonstrated by *Teaching* and by *Building a New World: Luce Irigaray Teaching II* (2015), collections of essays edited by Irigaray with, respectively, Mary Green and Michael Marder, as well as by her earlier *Partage de la Parole* reporting on her linguistic research with Italian schoolchildren (see Schwab 2016).

Karen Schiler's "Discursive Desire and the Student Imaginary," as it lays out some of the current issues and controversies in college composition theory, clearly illustrates and provides concrete examples of the very types of vertical classroom relations that Toraiwa theorizes and shows how such relations can be harmful to students' development as thinkers and writers. Schiler cautions professors to be aware of the complexities of student desire and of the student imaginary as they seek to "liberate" students and effect political change through their classrooms. She further challenges educators to beware the imposition of their own desires and their own imaginary on students, potentially practicing a type of politics in education that is precisely "nonliberating" and decidedly *not* the apprenticeship in democracy called for by Dewey.

Aesthetics has been an important area of exploration for Irigaray herself and in Irigaray studies, and I would note Elaine Miller's thought in this context (see Miller 2007, 2016), as well as Helen Fielding's (Fielding 2001, 2004, 2008, 2015). *Thinking Life with Luce Irigaray* includes a focus on Irigaray and the arts, beginning with "How Could We Achieve Women's Liberation?," where Irigaray calls for a renewal of creative artistic expression. She even claims that

> we have to reverse the traditional hierarchy between philosophy and art here. Of course, the matter is not only one of granting superiority to art with respect to philosophy; rather it is of considering that art—at least in our epoch—could express our whole being better than philosophy, and can more easily overcome the dichotomies of our past logic. [. . .] No doubt art, then, no longer amounts to works of art that some artists create in order to be exhibited in an art gallery or somewhere else. Art refers to a language that tries to express our whole being and speak to the whole being of the other. (34–35)

This volume's chapters on the arts by Peg Rawes, Britt-Marie Schiller, and Caroline Godart all heed Irigaray's call as they consider the radical potential of the arts—that is, specifically, architecture, sculpture, and film, (and it would make sense here also to note the Platonic dialogue as explored in Fanny Söderbäck's essay, poetry as in Eva Maria Korsisaari's, and theater as in Alison Stone's)—to inspire political transformation and renew and recreate life. Whereas Peg Rawes focuses on problems of sustainability and its interface with economic and social issues of equality and inequality, justice and injustice, Caroline Godart and Britt-Marie Schiller explore visual and spatial metaphors in film and sculpture that express the development of intersubjectivity and underline ambiguities of separation and closeness, distance and intimacy that recall Rebecca Hill's work on spatiality, Fanny Söderbäck's on temporality, and Phyllis H. Kaminski's on "daughterness."

In her essay in part 1 of this volume, Irigaray confirms the importance of economic equality for women, while also maintaining that a new energy appropriate to female sexuate identity is required in order to move forward in women's liberation. In "Building Sexuate Architectures of Sustainability," Peg Rawes looks at different materials and structures for the built environment, as well as at stable and renewable energy sources that would both power and sustain future communities around the planet; in Irigarayan terms, we might consider such sustainable materials, forms, and energy sources "open structures" that "can conform to a living growth" ("How Could We Achieve Women's Liberation?" 32). While the emphasis in Irigaray's essay is mainly on the cultivation of an interior energy required for the growth of sexuate subjectivity, Rawes clearly shows, in readings of "The Mechanics of Fluids" (*This Sex Which Is Not One* 106–18), "A Chance for Life," and *The Way of Love*, the imbrication of all forms of earthly (including personal and individual) energy, while demonstrating that the form and mechanism of male sexual energy have determined, and limited, the types of energy we have available to us, and that the forms and mechanisms of female sexual energy offer alternative structural models for future energy sources, thereby bringing an important new perspective to current debates on the economics and politics of sustainability.

In "Habitats for Desire: Sculptural Gestures Toward Sexuate Living," Britt-Marie Schiller explicitly takes up Irigaray's challenge to seek artistic outlets as a means to found a new logic, to "transform the real," as Irigaray wrote in "Fecundity of a Sexuate Art," the introduction to part 3 of *Key Writings* (98). In a psychoanalytic reading of sculptures by Louise Bourgeois and Richard Serra, Schiller develops the possibility of creating appropriate spaces for female and male subjects living in sexuate difference. Along the way, Schiller—like Ellen Mortensen, Phyllis H. Kaminski, Alison Stone, and I—also delves into the mother-daughter relation as both the origin of conflict and suffering among women and the potential source of new ways of living and relating. Schiller has some very interesting things to say about the "aggressivity" of daughters and mothers, as illustrated by Bourgeois's massive sculptural spiders, and she creates an important counterpoint to Irigaray's critique of female aggressiveness in "How Could We Achieve Women's Liberation?"

Scholars of cinema have begun to mine Irigaray's thinking on female identity and subjectivity for film studies, and this has proven to be a successful excavation. I would here mention only two of the most interesting recent books in this area: Caroline Bainbridge's *A Feminine Cinematics: Luce Irigaray, Women, and Film* (2008) and Lucy Bolton's *Film and Female Consciousness* (2015). I anticipate many more intersections between film and Irigarayan theory as women, and as feminism, come to play a more important role in cinema studies. The final essay of this volume, Caroline Godart's "The Feminist Distance: Space in Luce Irigaray and Jane Campion's *The Piano*," takes us back to Rebecca Hill's and Fanny Söderbäck's thinking on the erotics of space and time, as she undertakes a new and highly detailed rereading of the Irigarayan lips, looking at female sexuality as she examines the interval through an analysis of the character of Ada in Jane Campion's *The Piano*. The lips here illustrate an eroticism "more or less internal and porous in relation to the outside world, to the other," a morphology which can "close while remaining open," requiring "open structures and meanings which can conform to a living growth," as Irigaray writes in "How Could We Achieve Women's Liberation?" (32). Godart's methodology demonstrates the power of the filmic medium to address questions of desire, identity, and relationality, as she teases out the erotic spatial complexities of Campion's film by looking at Ada as a woman seeking to experience her own desire, and yet ultimately finding jouissance in an at least partly phallocentric relationship, and as a woman who "settles down" into spoken language and into a quasitraditional heterosexual relationship within the domesticized space of white Victorian colonial society—even as she reserves, in her dreams, a special place/space/time for herself under the waves, alone, anchored to her abandoned piano, listening (along with us) to its language, that which was her own. As Irigaray maintains, "language as art will never be universal nor permanent, but at the service of the embodiment of each one in their own singularity. This presupposes that this sort of language aims to express and share our complete energy [, . . .] discovering another manner of entering into communication that gives voice to our whole being in the present and allows the respect for our differences" (35).

In *Thinking Life with Luce Irigaray: Language, Origin, Art, Love,* readers of Irigaray, along with and led by Irigaray herself, occupy a living environment that is dense, fertile, rich, and diverse, variegated in tone, color, shape, direction, and intention—a creative space of/for thinking and writing. May this fecundity continue to bear fruit in language, in art, in love, and in politics into a living future, sustaining individual freedom in subjectivity and collective freedom in democracy.

Notes

In attempting to create a context for *Thinking Life with Luce Irigaray: Nature, Origin, Art, Love,* I have discussed, or merely mentioned, the work of many fine scholars whose work I respect and admire, but there are just as many and more whose work I was unable to recognize due to space constraints. I ask for understanding from those whose names don't appear here.

Works Cited

Bainbridge, Caroline. 2008. *A Feminine Cinematics: Luce Irigaray, Women, and Film.* Basingstoke: Palgrave MacMillan.

Bolton, Lucy. 2015. *Film and Female Consciousness.* London: Palgrave MacMillan.

Cimitile, Maria C., and Elaine P. Miller, eds. 2006. *Returning to Irigaray: Feminist Philosophy, Politics, and the Question of Unity.* Albany: State University of New York Press.

Fielding, Helen. 2001. "Only Blood Would Be More Red: Irigaray, Merleau-Ponty, and the Ethics of Sexual Difference." *Journal of the British Society of Phenomenology* 32:2, 147–59.

———. 2004. "Luce Irigaray: To Paint the Invisible, Translation and Interview." *Continental Philosophy Review* 37:4, 389–405.

———. 2008. "A Phenomenology of the 'Other World': On Irigaray's 'To Paint the Invisible.'" *Chiasmi International: Trilingual Studies concerning Merleau-Ponty's Thought* 9, 518–34.

———. 2015. "Dwelling and Public Art: Serra and Bourgeois." In *Merleau-Ponty: Space, Place, Architecture,* edited by Patricia M. Locke and Rachel McCann. Athens, Ohio: Ohio University Press.

Grosz, Elizabeth. 2011. *Becoming Undone: Darwinian Reflections on Life, Politics, and Art.* Durham, NC, and London: Duke University Press.

———. 2013. "Sexual Difference as Sexual Selection: Irigarayan Reflections on Darwin." In *Relational Architectural Ecologies,* edited by Peg Rawes.

———. 2016. "Irigaray and Darwin on Sexual Difference." In *Engaging the World,* edited by Mary C. Rawlinson.

Heinämaa, Sara. 2006. "On Luce Irigaray's Phenomenology of Intersubjectivity: Between the Feminine Body and Its Other." In *Returning to Irigaray,* edited by Maria C. Cimitile and Elaine P. Miller.

———. 2011. "A Phenomenology of Sexual Difference: Types, Styles, and Persons." In *Feminist Metaphysics: Explorations in the Ontology of Sex, Gender, and the Self,* edited by Charlotte Witt. Dordrecht: Springer, 2011.

Hill, Rebecca. 2012. *The Interval: Relation and Becoming in Irigaray, Aristotle, and Bergson.* New York: Fordham University Press.

Hollywood, Amy. 2002. *Sensible Ecstasy: Mysticism, Sexual Difference, and the Demands of History.* Chicago: University of Chicago Press.

Holmes, Emily A. 2008. "Writing the Body of Christ: Each Flesh Becoming Word." In *Teaching,* edited by Luce Irigaray and Mary Green.

Holmes, Emily A., and Wendy Farley, eds. 2011. *Women, Writing, Theology: Transforming a Tradition of Exclusion.* Waco: Baylor University Press.

———, and Lenart Škof, eds. 2013. *Breathing with Luce Irigaray.* London and New York: Bloomsbury.

Hom, Sabrina. 2013. "Between Race and Generations: Materializing Race and Kinship in Moraga and Irigaray." *Hypatia* 28:3.

Irigaray, Luce. 1985. *This Sex Which Is Not One*. Translated by Catherine Porter. Ithaca, New York: Cornell University Press.

———, ed. 1990. *Sexes et genres à travers les langues*. Paris: Grasset.

———. 1991. *Marine Lover of Friedrich Nietzsche*. Translated by Gillian C. Gill. New York: Columbia University Press.

———. 1992. *Elemental Passions*. Translated by Joanne Collie and Judith Still. New York: Routledge.

———. 1993. *An Ethics of Sexual Difference*. Translated by Carolyn Burke and Gillian C. Gill. Ithaca, New York: Cornell University Press.

———.1993. *Je, Tu, Nous*. Translated by Alison Martin. New York and London: Routledge.

———. 1993. *Sexes and Genealogies*. Translated by Gillian C. Gill. New York: Columbia University Press.

———. 1994. *Thinking the Difference*. Translated by Karin Montin. New York: Routledge.

———. 1996. *I Love to You*. Translated by Alison Martin. New York and London: Routledge.

———. 2001. *Le Partage de la parole*. Oxford: Legenda.

———. 2001. *To Be Two*. Translated by Monique M. Rhodes and Marco F. Cocito-Monoc. New York: Routledge.

———. 2002. *Between East and West: From Singularity to Community*. Translated by Stephen Pluháček. New York: Columbia University Press.

———. 2002. *The Way of Love*. Translated by Heidi Bostic and Stephen Pluháček. London and New York: Continuum.

———. 2002. *To Speak Is Never Neutral*. Translated by Gail Schwab. London and New York: Continuum.

———. 2004. *Key Writings*. London and New York: Continuum.

———. 2008. "How Could We Achieve Women's Liberation?," included in this volume.

———. 2008. *Sharing the World*. London and New York: Continuum.

———, and Mary Green, eds. 2008. *Teaching*. London and New York: Continuum.

———, and Michael Marder, eds. 2015. *Building a New World: Luce Irigaray Teaching II*. London: Palgrave MacMillan.

———, and Michael Marder. 2016. *Through Vegetal Being: Two Philosophical Perspectives*. New York: Columbia University Press.

———. 2017. *To Be Born*. Cham, Switzerland: Palgrave MacMillan.

Jantzen, Grace. 1999. *Becoming Divine: Towards a Feminist Philosophy of Religion*. Bloomington: Indiana University Press.

Jones, Rachel. 2011. *Luce Irigaray: Toward a Sexuate Philosophy*. Cambridge, UK: Polity.

———. 2012. "Irigaray and Lyotard: Birth, Infancy, and Metaphysics." *Hypatia* 27:1 (Winter).

———. 2013. "Lyotard and Irigaray on Eros, Infancy, and Birth: The Dissymetrical Horizons of Being Between." In *Jean-François Lyotard: New Encounters*, edited by H. Bickis and R. Shields. Farnham: Ashgate.

Joy, Morny, Kathleen O'Grady, and Judith L. Poxon eds. 2003. *Religion in French Feminist Thought*. London and New York: Routledge.

Joy, Morny. 2006. *Divine Love: Luce Irigaray, Women, Gender, and Religion*. New York: Manchester University Press.

Kaminski, Phyllis. 2013a. "Desire and Contemplative Silence: A Feminist Exploration of Transformation within and beyond Tradition." In *The Shaping of Tradition*, edited by Colby Dickinson, L. Boeve, and Terrence Merrigan. Leuven, Belgium: Peeters.

———. 2013b. "Holy Mary, Holy Desire: Luce Irigaray and Saintly Daughters." In *The Postmodern Saints of France*, edited by Colby Dickinson. New York: Bloomsbury.

Lehtinen, Virpi. 2014. *Luce Irigaray's Phenomenology of Feminine Being*. Albany: State University of New York Press.

Miller, Elaine P. 2007. "Reconsidering Irigaray's Aesthetics." In *Returning to Irigaray*, edited by Maria Cimitile and Elaine P. Miller.

———. 2016. "Irigaray and Kristeva on Anguish in Art." In *Engaging the World*, edited by Mary C. Rawlinson.

Mortensen, Ellen. 1994. *The Feminine and Nihilism: Luce Irigaray with Nietzsche and Heidegger*. Oslo: Scandinavian University Press.

———. 2003. *Touching Thought: Ontology and Sexual Difference*. New York: Lexington.

Parker, Emily Anne. 2014. "Beyond Discipline: On the Status of Bodily Difference in Philosophy." *philoSOPHIA* 4:2, 222–28.

———, and Anne van Leeuwen, eds. 2018. *Differences: Rereading Beauvoir and Irigaray*. Oxford: Oxford University Press.

Rawes, Peg, ed. 2013. *Relational Architectural Ecologies: Architecture, Nature, and Subjectivity*. London and New York: Routledge.

Rawlinson, Mary C. 2016. *Just Life: Bioethics and the Future of Sexual Difference*. New York: Columbia University Press.

Rawlinson, Mary C., ed. 2016. *Engaging the World: Thinking After Irigaray*. Albany: State University of New York Press.

Roberts, Laura. 2015. "Cultivating Difference in Luce Irigaray's *Between East and West*." In *Building a New World: Luce Irigaray Teaching II*,. edited by Luce Irigaray and Michael Marder.

———. 2019. *Irigaray and Politics: A Critical Introduction*. Edinburgh: Edinburgh University Press.

Sartre, Jean-Paul. 1966. *Being and Nothingness: An Essay on Phenomenological Ontology.* Translated by Hazel Barnes. New York: Philosophical Library.

Schopenhauer, Arthur. 1966. *The World as Will and Representation.* Translated by E. F. Payne. New York: Dover.

Schwab, Gail. 1998a. "Sexual Difference as Model: An Ethics for the Global Future." In *Irigaray and the Political Future of Sexual Difference*, edited by Pheng Cheah and Elizabeth Grosz. *Diacritics* 28:1 (Spring).

———. 1998b. "The French Connection: Luce Irigaray and International Research on Language and Gender." In *Untying the Tongue: Gender, Power, and the Word*, edited by Linda Longmire and Lisa Merrill. Westport, CT: Greenwood.

———. 2016. "Creating Inter-Sexuate Inter-Subjectivity in the Classroom? Luce Irigaray's Linguistic Research in Its Latest Iteration." In *Engaging the World*, edited by Mary C. Rawlinson.

Söderbäck, Fanny. 2016. "In Search for the Mother through the Looking-Glass: On Time, Origins, and Beginnings in Plato and Irigaray." In *Engaging the World*, edited by Mary C. Rawlinson.

Tzelepis, Elena, and Athena Athanasiou, eds. 2010. *Rewriting Difference: Luce Irigaray and "The Greeks."* Albany: State University of New York Press.

How Could We Achieve Women's Liberation?

LUCE IRIGARAY

At What Freedom Do Women Aim?

If women have not achieved a more important evolution either at an individual or collective level, it may be because they wanted to overcome a certain state in their way of being and existing without succeeding in carrying out this undertaking. They have too often waited for an evolution that would happen through men—either rebelling against them or becoming like them, amongst other things by entering a culture in the masculine. They have also imagined that men ought to carry out some change before or instead of they themselves doing so. Now their aspiration for evolution requires going beyond themselves, and no one if not them can take such a step forward. Waiting for the other to achieve such a gesture instead of oneself does not correspond to an autonomous behavior, but to a claim for subjecting or submitting oneself to the other. Many women have probably not yet perceived what freedom means and, in a way, do not claim freedom, except at a social level. This is not irrelevant, but it is not sufficient to take advantage of the freedom then gained. In fact, many women think of freedom as something to win in *spite of* or *against* the other, or others, and not something to be gained *by* and *for* themselves. The kind of energy needed is not the same in both cases.

To free oneself in order to accomplish oneself, or a task of one's own, needs an energy that is more cultured and responsible than merely freeing oneself from or against the other, others. The energy that resulted from cultural revolution, from women's liberation, has too often remained at the stage of freeing oneself *against* and not by and *for*, and has thus turned into aggressiveness, mere sensitive immediacy, unless it has become formalism or some moralistic repression, some political correctness without a real positive content. In all that, it is not yet a question of a culture appropriate to woman herself, that is, of an alternative culture that has arisen from women's emancipation from past tradition, from women's liberation. It is not yet a question of a new way of being, nor even of a greater happiness.

The liberated energy, when it exists, has not yet found a manner of investing itself that allows it to be kept, to be cultivated, and to be shared. This energy is still too often spent in rebelling against the other, against others—including other women—instead of becoming a personal or collective strength at the service of a feminine evolution, and even beyond: a human evolution that is needed. Freedom, then, is still thought of as freeing oneself *from* or *against*, and energy does not remain available for a becoming of one's own.

Another way in or by which the liberated energy is trapped is through the entry into a culture in the masculine that does not suit it, and which is instead elaborated against the maternal or the feminine world. In reality, the freedom of man in our culture is conceived as resulting from an emergence from the natural origin that is generally confused with the maternal body and world. At least it is the case in Western tradition in which masculine subjectivity has not yet gained a freedom of its own. Entering a culture in the masculine, woman then enters a construction that aims to render man independent with respect to her, a culture that somehow is built against the specificity of her sexuate identity. The process that man needs for his individuation as man is adopted by woman against her own individuation. Women then become split between a female belonging that remains at the stage of sensitive immediacy and a culture and development that not only do not suit their female belonging, but also oppose it.

Many women today have not overcome such a state, and this explains both their unhappiness and their aggressiveness, amongst other things between themselves, if not to say against all the world. In fact, this aggressiveness is the only way through which they can bind their energy and provide it with a certain unity.

Of course, the fact that women have gained an economic and even a social status that was previously refused to them could be objected to my words. It is true. And it is also true that the economic and social aspects seem to represent the whole of humanity in our times, but they correspond only to a part of our human identity. And we are mistaken when we consider that the liberation of woman can stop at an economic or social level. This can only provide us with a framework thanks to which reaching freedom can happen, and no more. Going no further makes us productive machines or social products without the creative ability that characterizes humanity as such. Indeed, a human being is a being which can transcend itself through its creation. Neither as economical beings, nor as social beings, can we really reach our humanity, nor when going no further than sensitive immediacy, or imitation of the other, notably because of the fear of differentiating ourselves from that which already exists.

Not Only Having but Also Being an Origin

How thus to become ourselves as woman? In other words: how can we transcend our female being towards becoming a woman? How to create ourselves starting from what or who we are by birth? How to cultivate our natural belonging in a way that suits it?

First, by freeing ourselves from what or who we are not. Not from the other as such, but from all we have become through taking part in a culture that is not our own. In a sense, this requires us to return to our birth, with its bodily and contextual dimensions, that is, to our natural and original identity. Today we know how much we have to rethink our behavior with respect to nature. We discover that our culture has damaged and endangered our planet. The same is true concerning our human natural belonging, to which we have to go back in order to cultivate it in a more adequate way. This is not an easy undertaking. We have to leave behind our way of behaving, of speaking, of relating to and with ourselves, the world, the other, and others. Yet we do not have any instruction about the manner of changing. We are in some ways in a desert without markers that give us the right directions. Now we are accustomed to searching for the direction to be taken in front of ourselves. It is there that it is generally indicated to us what we have to do or to think in our culture based on representation. We are not used to seeking within ourselves why, and how, we come to the right decision. Modifying our usual way of thinking, of acting, is really difficult. And many women are still in search of their own identity and subjectivity outside themselves, in some representation or other before them, instead of searching within themselves for the source of what or who they have to be. As I recently answered a researcher who asked me for instructions about feminine subjectivity: "You are still living; thus, you must first question yourself about the way of developing the living energy of the one you are, the living energy that is your own." She was really surprised by my words, but, from this moment, she looked and manifested herself in a very different way. She has discovered that the source of her subjectivity has first to be within her, and not in some representation external to her. Of course, the matter is not one of expressing all that we feel in an immediate and uncultured manner, but of becoming able to question the source of the unity of our self, and the way of developing it, of making it blossom with respect for our own life, the life of the other, of others, and of the world which we inhabit.

The perception of what structures our own self is particularly difficult, but it is part of our task in order to liberate feminine subjectivity and give birth to ourselves as feminine subjects. In our tradition, the masculine subject has generally not had a clear awareness of what or who he was. He projected his wanting or desire to be onto what he was doing or thinking. And deciphering the structure of his subjectivity became possible only in a sort of afterwards, most of the time through the interpretation of another subject who was capable of exceeding such a structure and reading it. This process could somehow correspond, in our history, to the insistent and mythic figure of the murder of the father by the son, notably in relation to the domination of mother as nature. The winner was the one who was able to attain a more perfect awareness, while remaining inside a given framework. The figures of awareness were thus in competition, a blind competition, because those who were defining a new configuration did not know what was really at stake: freeing oneself from a lack of differentiation with respect to the maternal world as one's natural origin.

The undertaking of a woman with regard to the development of her subjectivity is not the same. Of course, she has a natural origin that she has to consider and cultivate, but she herself is also a natural origin. And to remain unaware of this different position with respect to origin deprives us of a critical means to affirm and develop the singularity of our own culture. While man has constructed his culture, and in particular his relation to transcendence, against his maternal origin, woman can find, in her position to natural origin, a way to discover another relation to the transcendental. This presupposes that she relinquishes any contiguity, fusion, and possession with regard to the one to whom she gives a natural origin. She has to preserve the transcendence of the one to whom she gives birth as being another human with an origin different from hers. This requires the ability to distance herself from the work of her own body. However, nature itself carries out such a gesture, when it separates the maternal body and the foetus by means of the placenta, the first home in which a human life can dwell. Being careful not to mix up her life with that which she provides with an origin, a woman becomes able to gather her own energy and to cultivate it, not against the natural origin, as does man, but, on the contrary, in order to respect the natural origin: her own and that of another living being.

This must not remain dependent on a mere physical order—that is, it must have a margin of freedom not only *against* generation or reproduction, but render it *truly human* by respecting the origin of the other—one could say the transcendence of the other—and, as a sort of afterwards, safeguarding one's own. If women reach such a behavior with respect to procreation, the relation to origin, which determines an important part of our tradition, will be modified. Man will no longer have to struggle to distance himself from his maternal beginning or origin; he will be confronted with the task of elaborating his own origin, an origin both singular and living that he must cultivate in faithfulness to his life as unique, and with respect and gratitude towards the one who provided him with this life.

In this case, man is endowed with a human destiny from the very beginning, and he does not have to emerge from a mere natural belonging in order to affirm himself as a human being. The relation between mother and son is then, from the very beginning, a human relation.

Of course, there is a continuity between delivering a simple bodily birth and a spiritual birth. And the two ought to exist from the beginning, to be granted by the mother. But each woman, independently of giving birth to a child, is a place from which an origin can and must spring. This presupposes a certain way of dealing with life, with breathing, with energy, with language. Before considering this question, I would like to stress how much we are still unable to recognize a woman as a place from which an origin can arise. In order not to dwell on this for a long time, I will just quote my own example and allude to all the origins, often the masculine origins and preferably hidden origins, that are attributed to my work, notably on the part of women, as if a woman could not be at the origin, could not be the cause of herself, the creator of herself and of her work.

No doubt this entails the capability of an aware and transcendental attitude with respect to one's own natural belonging and immediate experience, and also the intention of liberating oneself in order to accomplish oneself and one's own task, and not merely in order to free oneself against something or someone. I would like to add that I always quoted the authors to whom I referred, but if they compelled me to think and argue with rigour, they did not provide me with the original source from which I could question them and develop my own work. On the contrary, it is through being faithful to my own relation to origin that I could fulfill all that I carried out, and never through imitating men's culture with respect to origin nor simply rebelling against it, against them: neither at the theoretical level nor at the empirical level, as some imagine. If you permit me to clear up another misunderstanding concerning my work: mimicry has always represented a partial and selective strategy to which I alluded but which I almost never used.

Discovering and Expressing Faithfulness to the Self

My choice in thinking results from a decision that I made during my early academic studies: I decided to try to think while being faithful to myself as a woman and not to submit myself to a culture that was not appropriate to me. It was, in a way, a decision of a transcendental nature—a transcendental which no longer amounted to an end to be reached but to a means to be followed—that did not result from some harm that I suffered from a particular man or men. Rather, I suffered from what I had to learn to gain enough qualifications—that is, from a culture that did not correspond to the development of my feminine belonging. I could not tolerate subjecting myself to a culture or a tradition that did not suit me and, moreover, destroyed my own relation to transcendence.

And I would like to specify, on this occasion, that my thought is not the outcome of a traditional fruitful imagination that, for example, would fill some voids in masculine culture, as can be observed through Western literature; rather, my thought results from a faithfulness to that which I experienced and which I considered as needing criticism and another cultural elaboration. I thus discovered that the conceptual construction of my tradition in some way harmed life itself, and that it was necessary to invent new means of thinking and saying based on what I experienced and which I desired to pass on and share.

Our Western culture uses words to duplicate the real and construct a world parallel to the living world. This constructed world is, in a way, finished, closed, just as a chessboard is limited, and the words—that is, the pieces that move on the chessboard—are also limited and defined, as is the case for their movements. There is no longer life in such a world but only a representation of the living world that aims to put it at man's disposal. This logical economy has paralyzed life in fixed forms and structures, even if a certain mobility remains between them. But this movement is extraneous to the growth of what or who is living. Our logic, the logos, does not traduce, does not express, the reality and the growth of life that I, as a woman, wanted to convey through my words, including when relating to the other, to others. I had thus to discover a language that uses forms, but living forms, forms that are not fixed, closed, defined once and for all. I had to resort to words that reveal something of the living real that I experienced, without intending to duplicate it, without interrupting its original link with life itself. I had to help the living real to manifest itself without breaking a living original energy, either that of the world or my own, without immobilizing life and its sap in definitive forms and meanings.

My desire was, and still is, to discover a means to give form to my living energy in relation to myself, to the world, to the other or others, to discover a means that is able to gather my energy in a certain situation and at any present moment in order to keep it, express it, and perhaps share it. Instead of naming and ordering the real to appropriate it and communicate through such an appropriation, I wanted to express the real as it was at a certain moment, including the real that I experienced, that I was, with a keeping and a sharing in mind—not thanks to a definitive expression, but rather as a stage that can lead to a growth, a development. I could say that I did not want to reach a metareal—as one speaks about metaphysics—but to work out an elaboration of the real towards a coexistence and sharing with all living beings with respect for their particular origin and growth—that is, with respect for their difference(s) in being and existing.

I think that the question here is not only to contrast metonymy with metaphor, but also to invent another way of expressing the real that perhaps has to do with diaphor—that is, with a transformation of the real which remains faithful to its origin and leads it to a greater potential for living, growing, coexisting, and sharing with the whole of the real. In this connection, I consider today that the most important problem I had to face regarding the academic world resulted from my way of passing on meaning. Of course, it was difficult for this world to agree with criticism. But it has finally succeeded in adopting even criticism towards its own traditional culture as a method. What this world cannot accept and recognize is the possibility of another logic to express and convey truth, a living truth.

And many academic women do not yet understand, even in our time, that they need another logic to keep, cultivate, and share their own life, their own energy, their own work. They appropriate some of the content of the feminine discourse through our past logic, but this is not sufficient for the cultivation of a feminine subjectivity.

Our past logic transforms living real into dead realities. This does not suit a feminine relation to origin, but it can help man to differ from the living maternal world. Instead, being faithful to our feminine relation to life needs open structures and meanings which can conform to a living growth. Besides, such open structures and meanings fit better with the morphology of a woman's body, which can close while remaining open. Which allows her to pass from one level of perception to another and even to simultaneously experience various levels, more or less internal and porous in relation to the outside world, to the other. The fact that the body of a woman remains open obeys certain necessities of life but also determines certain ways of relating to life, to the world, and to the other, that require a specific cultivation. Because of a lack of caring about that, the discourse of women runs the risk of being still more formal than that of man, a formalism that does not result from necessity for women, contrary to men. Instead of being at the service of a becoming of their own, entering the chessboard of a masculine logic cuts them more and more off from their own life and prevents the discovery of a culture that suits them from happening.

Limits and Forms Provided by Life Itself

Of course, meaning needs limits in order to be expressed, kept, and shared. But these limits can be given or imposed in a different manner from that at work in our past Western logic. Limits can be provided by respect for our own life, the world in which we live, the other whom we are meeting or with whom we are coexisting. Limits can also be provided by the space and time in which we are now, by our present intention, rather than by a permanent order imposed on us from the outside. The limits that allow meaning to exist and to be shared could be at the service of our living energy, instead of repressing it in the name of some abstract ideal. Limits are necessary and must be respected in order to keep, cultivate, and share life: limits to our self, to each living being, and to other humans.

There are limits which little by little transform a body as a corpse into living flesh. I think that to resort to a mere body, as is too often done today, especially on the part of women, could trap them inside a logic that has thought of the body and the mind as divided and somehow in opposition. We then stop at the pairs of opposites thanks to which our tradition has tried to dominate the living real, amongst which can be found the pairs of opposites boy and girl, man and woman. We must give up this way of constituting meaning. Body and thought cannot be kept separate: a body from the very beginning is animated by the spiritual matter and process that air and breathing potentially are, but also by the cultural network of relations with others, in particular with the mother. The morphology of the body also presupposes a certain relational economy. We have to consider and take charge of this real and transform the mere materiality of a body into the spiritual matter of the flesh.

Our sexuate belonging is especially crucial in this process, notably because sexuality transcends the process relative to a mere bodily survival. Sexuality is, in a way, unnecessary with respect to our own life. As such, sexuality is also the place where the question of our human freedom is most critical. Sexuality can lead us to stay at or fall back into the mere elementary or material level of our instincts, or it can help us to overcome our native human belonging towards aiming at spirituality. Sexuality is the part of our body of which the function is almost only relational. With regard to sexuality, our body is a mediation or the mediator which allows us to enter into presence and relations with the other at various levels: from the most public to the most private, from the most external to the most intimate, from the most visible to the most invisible, and so on. Sexuality also gathers together different states of matter, but also of spirit. In reality, it is probably the human dimension that is most able to collect our whole being. At least it would be the case if we were taught to value all the properties of our sexuality, in particular, the fact that it includes the ability to transcend our own body and self towards the other, towards the world. Sexuality attracts us beyond ourselves and provides us with energy for this going beyond.

Our tradition did not take enough account of the importance of this relational energy and the necessity of developing it. Rather, this tradition repressed sexuality as a mere natural dimension that we have to keep hidden in the family home as something a little shameful, as an aspect that could be redeemed only through procreation. Now, procreation as such amounts to the most natural aspect of sexuality, which, on the contrary, can have a really important function in our spiritual becoming. We remain unaware of the transcendental properties of sexuality, and, instead of cultivating them towards our individual or collective blossoming as humans, we have concealed them through a so-called neuter transcendence that would exist beyond our human existence. Now, before thinking of or believing in a superhuman divinity, it would be fitting to develop our humanity and our human relations as far as it is possible, and not to use, for example, God himself to prevent us from doing that. The lack of cultivation of our sexual attraction towards sharing our human desires is partly due to a presumed conflict between "God" and the development of our sexuate belonging. This implies an idea of God that is badly transcendental and has not helped us to become truly human thanks to a cultivation of our relational energy. If our needs generally concern us at a mere individual level, it is not the case with regard to sexuality, if not as an issue of some misunderstanding and repression. Sexual attraction, in fact, has nothing to do with our individual needs, but rather with overcoming them. Sexual attraction can transform our needs into a component of our being at the service of our relational existence. It can be used for putting our individual needs at the service of our relational belonging.

This presupposes training our immediate attractions in order that they become a desire that can be shared. To establish and respect limits is especially decisive in succeeding in such a training. And first we have to respect the radical otherness of the other, the transcendence of the other. Sexuate desire compels us to transcend ourselves, and it is maintained by the respect of the transcendence of the other in relation to ourselves. As soon as our attraction is reduced to a need—a need to discharge our energy or to procreate, to dominate or possess the other, to merge with the other in order to regress to the maternal world, or even to a need to stay only with what is familiar to us, the same as us—desire vanishes, and our sexual attraction no longer achieves our human destiny.

Art as Means towards a New Logic

Our tradition has not yet taken desire into consideration enough. And a logic based on concepts or on the same-as and the identical-to cannot be of help in carrying out such an undertaking. Thus, we have to resort to another logic in order to go further towards the accomplishment of our humanity. It is the case for that which concerns our relation to origin, thus to genealogy; it is also at stake when it is a question of our horizontal sexual attraction. We lack the means to cultivate our human belonging at both these levels. I think that we have to reverse the traditional hierarchy between philosophy and art here. Of course, the matter is not only one of granting superiority to art with respect to philosophy; rather, it is of considering that art—at least in our epoch—could express our whole being better than philosophy and can more easily overcome the dichotomies of our past logic. This implies that we interpret the partial character of Western logic with regard to humanity, and that we use art in a different way from that which we are accustomed to—that is, as a manner of conveying and sharing our whole being and truth in a more appropriate manner than our past philosophy could do.

No doubt art, then, no longer amounts to works of art that some artists create in order to be exhibited in an art gallery or somewhere else. Art refers to a language that tries to express our whole being and speak to the whole being of the other. The matter and the medium can vary, and can even be words themselves, but used in a different way from that which is agreed in our Western tradition, because its logic does not aim at expressing and sharing our whole being, but instead at preventing this from happening. Neither does using the words towards an artistic language any longer mean resorting to a traditional poetic discourse which is somehow complementary and secondary with respect to our Western logical discourse. The undertaking is quite different. It is now one of discovering another manner of entering into communication that gives voice to our whole being in the present and allows the respect for our differences—a thing that our traditional logic does not permit because we must communicate through a third world and codes already defined and presumed valid for all. Instead, language as art will never be universal or permanent, but at the service of the embodiment of each one in their own singularity. This presupposes that this sort of language aims to express and share our complete energy and is not limited to or does not focus on a mental level. Thus, we no longer have to discharge our sexual energy, as Freud wrote, but we must keep it to communicate with the other, and, furthermore, this energy must not remain at only an immediate sensitive level. The transformation of this immediate energy into a shareable language cultivates it without, for all that, repressing or destroying it. The first immediate sexual attraction becomes a material available for cultivating one of the most crucial dimensions of humanity: being in embodied relations with the other as other.

Such a process helps us to keep ourselves, and not to spend our energy for nothing. The elaboration of this energy in order to express our desire to the other, and to try to share it, needs this energy to turn back to ourselves, and us to become aware of this energy as ours, even if it is aroused in relation to the other. In some way, this energy belongs to the two and already takes part in the third world that we have to create together. So that this third world will exist, each of us has to take charge of the part that is incumbent upon us. Thus, I have to keep and cultivate my own energy, but without forgetting its origin. I cannot cultivate this energy only for my own benefit or the benefit of a third who, or which, is not the cause of the energy. If we do that, as is often the case, we make the relation with a particular other impossible, and we lose any experience of the difference between us. We all merge or fall back into a lack of differentiation where the relation in two cannot exist, because we have become only a piece of the mass within which perception and behaviour are determined by purposes external to each one and most of the time unconscious. We then act, experience, and even feel as an element of a more or less huge machine, in which the relations between two elements are regulated by the whole without any freedom, responsibility, and even personal experience.

Our tradition too often led us to such a situation. And if I lay the stress on the relation in difference between two, it is in order to return to our humanity, even when we are many. I am not inviting people to remain in the traditional private relation in two, as has been said. Instead I propose a path to recover, and, furthermore discover, our whole humanity in any situation or context.

Notes

Author: This text was written on the occasion of my participation in a conference on the philosophy of Luce Irigaray, organized by Gail Schwab at Hofstra University in 2008, in collaboration with Stony Brook University. I heartily thank Mary Green for rereading my English version of the text.

Editor: The 2008 Hofstra conference was organized by the Luce Irigaray Circle, of which Gail Schwab and the collaborators from Stony Brook University—Mary C. Rawlinson, Sara McNamara, and Danae McCleod—were all members.

PART II

LIFE IN AND THROUGH NATURE, DESIRE, FREEDOM, AND LOVE

The Re-Enchanted Garden

Participatory Sentience and Becoming-Subject in "Third Space"

CHERYL LYNCH-LAWLER

> Two privileged dimensions allow us to open the structure of the world in which we are included from the very beginning: relations with nature as an autonomous living world and relations with the other. . . . Nature represents possible inter-worlds [and] ought to serve as a space of mediation between all. The living environment is necessary to . . . survival, but also to their culture or cultivation.
>
> —Irigaray 2008, 66

Introduction

As a clinical psychoanalyst, I think a lot about psychic structure, and when thinking through an Irigarayan lens, I become interested in the interplay between the inner and outer worlds, between culture and human subjectivity, and in the ways in which each is reflected in the other. Irigaray describes the process of human becoming as it necessarily unfolds within a "confusion of networks [. . .] which exist before, [. . . and in which] one's first opening to the world is, in part, an unrecognized apprehension of a confinement" (72–73). She suggests that the longing for a beyond, or an outside, to this primordial experience of confinement is deferred to a transcendence to be found in another world, rather than in this life or in this world. She argues, however, that it is in creating openings within the fabric of *this* world that we can cultivate a beyond in the here and now and thereby actualize our subjectivity. It is also in this manner that human subjects transform the pregiven nature of the world in which they were born into something new, creating a breathable porosity in the otherwise stifling enclosures of reified cultural structures. In her essay, "The 'Mechanics' of Fluids," Irigaray assails the "dichotomous oppositions" characteristic of unconscious language structures and processes of "symbolization that grant *precedence to solids*" (Irigaray 1985b, 110). In this either/or logic, fluidity is lost between different modes of consciousness, and instead, we find the hegemony of the solid product that is the *result* of a preconscious fluidity of thought, a fluidity that she suggests constitutes the disavowed foundation of logical discourse. Similarly, Henri Bergson in *Matter and Memory,* refers to a "gulf . . . between two consecutive verbal images" and to "the constant tendency of discursive intellect to cut up all progress into *phases* and afterwards to solidify these phases into *things*" (Bergson 159–60).

In *Saving the Appearances: A Study in Idolatry* (1988), Owen Barfield brings another useful lens to the possibilities for what we might conceptualize as *living thinking*, or co-creative engendering of self and world, which he refers to as "participation," an experience which, he claims, we in the West have almost completely lost. While Irigaray (2013) views as a "wrong turn" the nearly idolatrous valorization of abstracted rationality as it has been priviledged over the corporeal, the maternal-feminine, and nature, Barfield sees it as part of a larger evolutionary trajectory required for what he refers to as "final participation." His participatory theory, which, briefly stated, claims that in what was once an "original participation," human consciousness was more immersive and less differentiated from the natural world. This immersive state evolved/devolved into a self-conscious loss of participatory consciousness and an increasing development of the abstract rational mind. He theorized what he referred to as "final participation," as the next turn of a cycle in which humans become self-conscious participants in the cosmos (Barfield 1988).[1] However, Barfield also claims that collective representations arising out of cultural figurations can be faulty, encoding and promulgating mistakes as a reality in a given culture, and that these mistakes may continue unabated for centuries. This is congruent with Irigaray's notion of a "wrong turn." Barfield, like Irigaray, insists that we must excavate the faulty logic that is buried in our prehistory if we are to evolve Western consciousness. For him, in order to proceed with this task, we must "have firmly grasped the fact that the phenomenal world arises from the relation between a conscious and an unconscious and that evolution is the story of the changes that relation has undergone and is undergoing" (136). Barfield views our current evolutionary task as one in which we need to develop the capacity for self-conscious participation with the living world that, I argue, following Irigaray, could reopen the confinement of the overly rational mind, healing and transforming the logical errors, or "wrong turns," that have continued to be perpetuated within the cultural fabric.

In this essay I explore the formation of subjectivity, as it unfolds within the parameters of a hierarchical binary logic of solids that refuses to acknowledge its moorings in the movements of a fluid, living universe. Within this paradigm, we experience the foreclosure of possibilities for subjective awareness of sentient participation with the living world and, concurrently, of the movement within the subject between two modes of consciousness: the abstract rational and the holistic intuitive. In *The Wholeness of Nature*, the late philosopher of science Henri Bortoft deconstructs what he refers to as the "analytical" or "verbal-intellectual" mode of consciousness, which he sees as resulting from our "technical-scientific culture [and] develop[ing] in conjunction with our experience of perceiving and manipulating solid bodies" (Bortoft 61). He argues that there are at least two modes of human consciousness, and that what he refers to as the "holistic" mode has been eclipsed by our internalization of the logic of solids, where everything is separate and external to everything else. This predisposes a form of thinking that is focused externally, given that "the fundamental characteristic of the world of solid bodies is *externality—i.e.*, everything is external to everything else . . . , [and] it is also necessarily sequential and linear, proceeding from one element to another in piecemeal fashion [as in] the principle of mechanical causality" (ibid.).

In the holistic intuitive mode, based on the Goethean scientific notion of "active seeing," in which one attunes to the interior depth and fluid liveliness of the phenomenon—what Goethe referred to as the practice of exact "sensorial imagination"—a bridge or copula is formed between the concrete sensory detail and an experience of the wholeness inherent *within* the phenomenon. This type of comprehensive seeing is nonmetaphysical and nondualistic and is a higher cognitive achievement than the abstract and analytical, with its emphasis on gathering external details in order to form a generality from which meaning and connections are subsequently abstracted. In holistic seeing, sensory perception occurs simultaneously with the recognition of the interior and transmutes the opposition interior/exterior. We are able to comprehend two registers simultaneously rather than merely one, as in abstract analytical thought (302–03). Bortoft posits this as an alternative mode of thinking that can " 'short-circuit' the linear logic of the analytical mind" (59). In a similar vein, G. William Barnard (2008) elaborates on what he refers to as Bergson's "participatory vision of the universe," which he sees as a redemptive alternative to an "atomistic . . . mechanistic universe" (Barnard 321). He posits a subject that is "integrally connected to wider, deeper dimensions of dynamic, multileveled, and open-ended reality . . . , [a reality] that is enriched and creatively shaped, moment by moment, by our experiences, choices, and behavior" (ibid.). It is the capacity of the human subject to actively engage with the phenomenal world that has the power to open what remains closed to the purely analytical mind. This position is congruent with Irigaray's when she posits that, as human subjects, our becoming is integrally embedded within the fabric of the living world. It is also quite resonant with her notion of a sensible transcendental in which both corporeality and knowledge—two different registers—are experienced simultaneously (Irigaray 1993).

Based on my clinical experience, I argue that the capacity of human subjects to open the pregiven world into which we are thrown, becoming active participants, is increasingly threatened by our extreme saturation within the confines of a hypermediated existence. Even our relations with others are being commandeered by media experts and digital networks, each of which extends the reach of this pregiven world, such that the longing for an outside is mediated and medicated. The longing of the nascent subject for connection is met with an overwhelming array of glamorous and titillating deterrents, substitutes, and remedies that disorient and distract. Given our increasing distance from the living world of nature, human sexuality and food are virtually all we have left of our once rich immersion in the diversity of life. It is therefore not surprising that they have come to be the locus of hypercharged emotions and cathexes—that is, of crazed pathologies such as food and sexual addictions and perversions that eclipse the human capacity for connection within the self, with human others, and with all sentient life.[2] What is at stake here is our very existence as sentient beings. When we become alienated from the immediacy of intimacy with one another, when we have no concern for the land and animals that we depend upon for our food supply, we are not able to nurture future generations. Hence, longing for becoming and connectivity is circumvented, and the nascent subject is transformed into an increasingly passive and spellbound but sophisticated consumer of pregiven ideologies, commodities, and expert solutions, even when those commodities are other nascent human subjects—well branded and packaged for mutual consumption. For instance, what Bauman (2003) refers to as "liquid love," which is a by-product of the commodification of relationships, is exemplified in internet dating practices which offer "termination on demand [. . . and a] reduction of risks coupled with the avoidance of option-closing[, . . .] unlike the awkward negotiation of mutual commitments" (65).

It is against this backdrop of crisis in our relationships to the human other that I turn my attention toward that other dimension that Irigaray claims is necessary for human survival. It is engagement with the living world around us with its fluid[abil]ity to surprise us with its originality that holds the promise of an opening beyond the confines of an increasingly claustrophobic enclosure in a hypermediated world. The engagement with the extra-discursive fluidity of living nature, or what I call "participatory sentience," awakens the intuitive capacity for an internal ternary process in which we are able to move into the gap between nature and culture, actively enlivening and sustaining the passage in-between, and allowing us to "speak corporeal" (Irigaray 1991, 43) from within that "third space" that *we are*. Awakening our capacity for participation transmutes the boundary between two realms which we, as living beings, inhabit—nature *and* culture—reopening the enclosure of the world of abstracted cultural artifacts by ceasing to abnegate our role as an enabling *third*. As clinical case narratives presented below will show, the *active* apprehension of *natural* interiority, of open-ended sentient life, opens nascent subjects to an awareness of inner fluidity and ongoing becoming that otherwise gets hardened in consumption of overly mediated cultural caricatures of life. Bergson discusses the limitations of static images and discursive abstractions when he states that "speech can only indicate by a few guideposts placed here and there the chief stages in the movement of thought. [. . .] *For images can never be anything but things, and thought is a movement*" (Bergson 159) (emphasis mine). In reorienting attention toward the fluid aspect of thought, the possibility arises for a participatory encounter with the fluid sentience of the living world, which is further elaborated within the subject, creating the copulative link between the mutually enlivening capacities for abstraction and immersion. With a viable bridge linking the intuitive and the discursive, the natural and the cultural, and a *recognition of ourselves as an embodiment of that bridge*, fresh experiences are alchemized into new discursive abstractions, and new language patterns evolve to create openings in an otherwise closed inscriptatory system.

Disoriented Subjects

With the exponential expansion of digital technologies that both extend and magnify the reach of a Western cultural mindset, it is important to consider how human consciousness is evolving (or perhaps devolving) in response. In *The Decadence of Industrial Democracies* (2011), Bernard Steigler writes that consumption and the consumerist model were taken to a new level with the creation by the United States of the worldwide digital network—the internet—based on the binary system and linked to telecommunications and computer systems and—via barcodes, credit cards, and cell phones—able to compile immense stores of information, culminating in a vast empire of globally integrated production and consumption. This digitalization amounts to what Steigler refers to as a "mutation of the global technical system" of such huge proportions as to override the capacity of individuals and/or governing bodies to articulate meaningful parameters within which human subjectivity can continue to exist or to create new ways of life compatible and coevolving with technological innovations (Stiegler 10). Instead, he argues, we are witnessing a failure of this process, and "in place of the necessary creation of these new modes of existence, there is substituted an *adaptive* process of *survival,* in which possibilities for existing disappear, being reduced instead to simple modalities of subsistence." (12). The dynamism of this system penetrates psychic space, which is increasingly colonized by the constant onslaught of media (9–10).

Clinically, I have noted a sense of what I would characterize as a state of "functional dissociation" in patients who seem to be functioning well but are emotionally numbed. Their subjectivity is overlaid by a collage of images and ideas that are loosely woven together in a seeming coherence that is reshuffled according to current trends in thought and fashion. In psychoanalytic theory, this phenomenon could be classified as the "as-if personality," a term first used by Helene Deutsch in "Some Forms of Emotional Disturbances and Their Relationship to Schizophrenia" (1942), in which she describes this phenomenon as one of "mimicry . . . with a highly plastic readiness to pick up signals from the outer world and to mold oneself and one's behavior accordingly . . . , [and] a lack of real warmth" (Deutsch 304). Further, "all the expressions of emotion are formal, [and] all inner experience is completely excluded. It is like the performance of an actor who is technically well trained but who lacks the necessary spark to make his impersonations true to life" (303). I suggest this character structure is becoming the norm in highly techno-capitalist societies. Patients may report feeling depressed and/or anxious, but often what they are experiencing is a disconnect from the active dynamism of a healthy inner world and the lack of a sense of meaning in their existence. It is as though their capacity for *living thinking* has been lulled to sleep, and yet their sleep is filled with disturbing dreams.

Another prevalent clinical theme that continues to emerge has to do with the reporting of dreams and associations to bridges that are either not passable or are in a state of disrepair. In general, I have begun to understand this as a deepening disconnection between two essential modes of consciousness—the capacity for rational abstraction and the capacity for intuitive reflection. As Bortoft's analysis above suggests, in the former mode, one moves away from an object of interrogation, severing the parts from the whole in a process of rational analysis in which they are viewed as a series of externalities. When the parts are retroactively fitted together to form a system, the living, dynamic whole that is integral, and integrative of the parts, is lost, resulting in a counterfeit whole. In contrast, in integrative, living, intuitive thinking, consciousness is holistic in nature and opens to a participatory encounter that grasps the whole within the parts themselves and also includes the observer as integral to the apprehension of authentic wholeness. "In a moment of intuitive perception, the universal is seen within the particular [. . .] as a living manifestation of the universal [, rather than] a generalization [. . .] produced by abstracting from different instances something that is common to them [and producing] an abstracted unity with the dead quality of a lowest common denominator" (Bortoft 22). Both of these modes, the analytical and the intuitive, are important to subjective becoming, and together they create a synergy that is the *sine qua non* of what it means to be human and to cultivate a living bridge between the two modes within ourselves. However, the capacity for participatory intuition and living thinking is being eclipsed further and further with the technological expansion that has, as Stiegler has noted, colonized psychic space. While this disconnect is inherent in Western binary thought, which separates the privileged subject interrogator from the abjected object of interrogation, the sheer ubiquity and reach of digital and abstracting technologies ups the ante, such that we are becoming further and further exiled from the living world in which we dwell and which enlivens and renews an inner fluidity, a capacity for living thinking.

Participatory encounters can, by definition, only occur within the context of sentience to sentience. While contemporary subjects may have ongoing interactions with digital simulacra of life, these interactions are not participatory according to the meaning I assign the term. These digitally rendered images are nonliving, nonfluid, and nondynamic, while giving the illusion that they are all of this. Hence, they can be very libidinally stimulating and titillating, creating a closed-circuit, ecstatic union with a virtual *representation* of the other and further compromising a relationship with the *sentient other*. The lack of satisfaction in these virtual "encounters" creates and sustains a market for always "fresh" digital images with which to "interact" and transports an increasingly passive consumer into a virtual realm emptied of anything other than solipsistic projections of an increasingly lonely self. Writing about the loss of the middle voice—that which underwrites the capacity for self-reflective circuitry between one's own interiority and the interiority of the other—Irigaray worries about the building of a world in which humans would lack this capacity, a world "which little by little substitutes itself for us. A world in which historians will be in search of some traces, some 'skins,' as testimonies of humanity's passage on earth" (Irigaray 2010, 259).

In striking contrast to silicon-based fabrications, carbon-based sentience is characterized by its utter originality and continuous, living becoming *on its own terms*. For example, one may stand in the same landscape each day, and each day—indeed, each moment—will be different. It will be visited by different creatures: hummingbirds in summer, monarch butterflies a little later, cardinals in winter, and so on. The wind and weather patterns as they play in the sky and rustle through the greenery are always changing from fog to rain to sunshine, and cloud formations change continuously. While all roses have petals and stems, no rose is exactly like any other. Nor can the uniqueness of human sentience be any more than superficially described by statistical analysis, diagnostical categories, demographics, and discourses. Sentience, human and other, cannot be reduced and captured in these ways, and yet, as our interactions with commodities and digital media proliferate, our inner lives come to reflect the lifeless solidity of metadiscourses and fabricated environments that capture and fetishize the living. Just as in any given discourse/discipline we find a proliferation of categories and concepts that we are told represent an advancement of knowledge, so we simultaneously find subjectivity increasingly fracturing and a sense of inner integrity more and more difficult to experience. We begin to relate to both ourselves, and to other human subjects, as nothing more than an externality defined by a litany of labels such as those perpetually proliferating in contemporary identity politics.

Undoubtedly, there is much at stake for us as we reflect on our concept of the human with regard to the nature/culture debate. For Lena

Gunnarsson (2014), whose critical realist lens overcomes the opposition between poststructuralist and new materialist feminism, the social and the biological are two levels of interconnected reality articulated in terms of temporal "emergence," in which "nature not only temporally precedes the humanity that emerged from it; it is also the causal foundation of humanity in any moment in time, this being revealed by the fact that nature can exist without humanity while humanity cannot exist without nature" (75). In her dialectical approach, she labors to think the two—biology and culture—together in what she refers to as "unity-in-difference" and what I refer to as corporeal-culture. Similarly, Vicky Kirby (2008) views the relationship of nature and culture as one of *consubstantiality* in which nature is already culture with a language of its own and "whose collective expression . . . *we are*" (229). Linguistic abstractions sublimated into digital simulacra distract from the dynamism and diversity of sentience and undermine the process of living thinking that accompanies participatory sentience. Nature is never finished, and by extension, neither are human beings. In restricting ourselves more and more to "encounters" with the worlds of pregiven discourse and image, in abnegating our ternary role as the embodiment of consubstantial nature/culture, we must wonder if we are, in essence, *becoming* dead.

In what follows, I will discuss what I think of as a dual bridge-building process—first, between the sentient self and the sentient other, which I have referred to as participatory sentience, and second, within the self between intuitive/participatory consciousness and abstract/conceptual consciousness. The first is essential to the second—that is to the creation of a bridge within the subject between the two modes of abstract rationalism and holistic intuition. If the inner intuitive and participatory fluidity is not nurtured, the subject is left stranded in culture without a means of appropriating pregiven discursive abstractions and imbuing them with lived meaning or of opening pathways into new realms yet to be elaborated discursively. It is when both modes are working in unison that our uniquely human capacity to transmute corporeal sentience into shared discursive patterns is able to go on creating.

Abstract Rationalism Wed to Consumer Capitalism

Mariano Artigas has argued that science is not value-free but is widely compromised by the influence of social factors (Artigas 2000). Irigaray has spoken of science as a form of "imperialism without a subject" [in which] "the subjective is prohibited" (Irigaray 2002, 248, 247). In this logic, subjectivity privileges the *one* of a hierarchical binary "imposing a model on the universe in order to appropriate it . . . , claiming that one is rigorously exterior to the model . . . to prove that the model is . . . *objective* . . . [and] not dependent on the senses. . ." (250). She traces this progressively distancing logic, in which the subject is severed from its own subjectivity and ultimately becomes merely another object of investigation, back to the failure of Western culture to symbolize the child's relationship with the maternal in any way other than as that muted and abjected ground of their being, from which they must distance themselves if they are to become autonomous subjects. She finds this theme exemplified in psychoanalytic discourse in Freud's discussion of the *fort-da* game, which "requires the absence of the mother as interlocutor, and the presence of the grandfather as observer and regulator of 'normal' language" (258). This leads her to ponder what is missing from symbolization that might elaborate "an *exchange between* mother and son" (ibid.). She further challenges psychoanalysts to look beneath Freud's *Totem and Taboo*, which posits the foundation of Western society as a parricide, to an earlier matricide, reflected in earlier Greek myths and tragedies. This partial symbolization amounts to "the murder of the mother in her cultural dimension" (257) and has left us—both women and men—essentially motherless subjects without a symbolic bridge between ourselves and the living world in which we are immersed.[3] What scientists fail to interrogate in their axiomaticization of the living world is their own internal psychic split and the resulting blindness to "all intuitions not already programmed in the name of science" (254). Intrinsic to this logical blind spot is the mapping of the foreclosure with regard to the maternal relationship onto the entirety of the living world—hence—mother/nature.

This blindness in the midst of the seeming advancement of science is discussed by Michael Marder in his book *Plant Thinking: A Philosophy of Vegetal Life* (2013), where he argues that the manner in which science has approached botany exemplifies the predominating scientific worldview in which, for example, the "plant cannot become a scientific object without getting irretrievably lost, transformed into dead matter, dissipated in cellular activity and in the larger anatomical (or phytotomical) units, prepared in advance for vivisection" (19). This approach is an example of human abstraction gone amuck, without an appreciation of the living whole within the parts. Marder's insight is congruent with that view expressed by Goethe in "The Metamorphosis of Plants" in which he asserts, against the science of his time, a sense of living nature as dynamic; regarding the plant, for example, one could never see the completed plant in full form but rather as the ongoing metamorphosis and continuous elaboration of organs that appear as separate when viewed from the purely analytical mode, but when seen intuitively through a participative lens, appear as being embedded in an organic and unfolding movement that attests the wholeness of the living plant (Goethe 76–97). According to Bortoft, Goethe's concept of metamorphosis was his attempt to elaborate the intensive, "non-physical, yet real, movement, [in which] the movement itself appears as primary, [and . . .] organs serve as markers which make the movement visible" (Bortoft 279). As mentioned above, opening one's perception to actively apprehend the interior depths of the living phenomenon in the process of metamorphosis is an exercise in that higher cognitive function termed *sensorial imagination,* in which we are able to perceive in two registers simultaneously. It is that capacity that is crucial if we are to comprehend the living process that characterizes the authentic whole,[4] which is the hidden, yet active, absence that is present within the phenomenal appearance of all sentient life, including our own. "What is entailed is really an intensive step within consciousness, so that we are conscious in the *seeing* of the seen instead of the seeing of the *seen*" (281). In becoming aware of the movement of metamorphosis, there is no new factual data, and yet there is a subtle change in what is seen. "*The movement of metamorphosis is in the way of seeing,* and a change in the way of seeing *transforms* what is seen without *adding* to the content" (282).

Abstract rationalism seeks to break down objects into constituent parts, whereas Goethe began with the living form as it is observed or perceived within the participant observer. Albert Linderman, elaborating on Goethe's insight, notes that one never sees the plant in a completed form unless it is dead. It is always in flux, changing at every moment in time. It is a whole, yet in a process of becoming, and "the only way to understand its fullness is to understand it as a totality of ever-changing forms" (Linderman 156). From Bortoft's Goethean perspective, one might say that the plant is an unfinished dynamic unity, which starkly contrasts with the retroactive unification of severed parts into a (dead) system. Marder argues that what is at stake for human subjects immersed in this scientific worldview is "the very meaning of life, handed over to extreme objectification and treated as though it were a plastic image of death" (Marder 19). When one living partner in any exchange, even when this partner is a plant, has been reduced to such abjection, both partners partake of this dereliction, and the co-generative process between the two is foreclosed. In psychoanalytic theory, this type of co-relation is referred to as "parallel process." The ultraobjectification of the living world by the predominating scientific worldview has come back full circle and enclosed the human subject within the prison of this necrophilic logic, and in "exercising a domination over the environing world, man has been damaging life itself, including his own" (Irigaray 2008, 67).

The active process of perception is inherently synesthetic and participatory (cf. Merleau-Ponty 1962), guaranteeing the perpetual opening of otherwise closed systems. When it is overrun with mass-produced images and expert advice, a psychic paralysis can develop in which the active subject is converted into a passive consumer (and performer) of goods, services, images, information, and so on. The rich inner life is foreclosed and replaced by the eerily "as if" quality described by Deutsch. When wed to the Western mode of consciousness that places the subject as a priviliged interrogator external to the world, that world becomes objectified and emptied of sentience, and the rational subject ironically succumbs to a state of devitalized abjection that reflects the abjection of the living world he has dissected and tragically turned into a corpse for his investigation, mastery, and consumption—a consumption that eventually consumes him.

Robert Pogue Harrison, in *Gardens: An Essay on the Human Condition*, notes a "tragic discrepancy between the staggering richness of the visible world and the extreme poverty of our capacity to perceive it" (Harrison 114). As a professor on the Stanford campus, he has witnessed what he refers to as a "wholesale desertion of the visible world by the young," for whom that world seems to "have disappeared behind a cloaking device" (115). He attributes this to a "transmutation" *within* the human subject that is a feature of this historical epoch, in which human vision is being mediated primarily through screen images rather than "appearances." The distinction he makes is significant: appearance "intimates" and therefore requires *active participation,* which does not foreclose a synesthetic grasp of the world, while image "merely indicates" and leads toward passive consumption of static representations (ibid.). For example, for living phenomena such as one discovers within a garden to make an appearance, a beholder is required. But when the human beholder is supplanted by a nonliving digital beholder (such as a camera or computer screen), the living subject is placed outside the garden, which is then given to them via algorithmic coding of digital mechanisms in the form of screen images and information. With the increasing sophistication of digitally enhanced media, the Western predilection for privileging the gaze (and the solid product that is the end result of the movement of thought) is taken to an extreme, and vision is extracted from an otherwise synesthetic immersion with other sensual modalities. The sequestering of vision within digitally captured sequences forecloses any possible synesthetic appreciation of the living world. The implications for subjectivity and consciousness are profound and need to be thought through, especially since, as Harrison points out, our mode of being is intricately bound up with our mode of vision (ibid.).

We are witnessing not only the perversion of democracy but also the shriveling of our capacity to see the world—and ourselves—apart from its digital mediation. As I have argued, life is not a series of petrified images offering a simulacrum of life, but a dynamic, unpredictable, nonuniform, and continuous process. In the same way, *human* life is a continuous process that becomes lost to the subject whose life is "given" to them in a steady stream of images, scripts, statistical analyses, diagnostical categories, ideological positioning, and information bits and bytes. For example, a patient recently told me that he could identify with the character on a popular television show—a sociopath who leads a double life and seems quite human, although his "humanity" is just an act. My patient stated that he, too, "knows how to *act* human and to mimic the behaviors that are purported to be human, but it is a mere mental abstraction and does not have any inner coordinate." This patient presents well, is highly functional, is in a prestigious career, has an intact family life with spouse and children, and yet has come to treatment desperate to connect his outer life—his image, his brand, his persona—with a sense of an authentic inner life that would no longer "feel machine-like, feel dead." He can "go through the motions," but he is not there. He feels he is "being lived" rather than living.

The Originary Error in the Split Subject

A related dimension that poses a challenge to our capacity for living thinking is articulated by Irigaray in *Spiritual Tasks for Our Age,* when she refers to the nature of the God we have inherited, who "functions as a kind of idol of the spirit, resistant to perception by the senses" (Irigaray 2004, 172), and in whom the "dialectic between nature and culture is interrupted" (176). In the space of this interruption, Irigaray locates "the nearly idolatrous over-valorization of nature in procreation, and its annihilation in culture, where the historically male subject appropriates nature, and attempts to dominate it in order to bend its will to his [. . .] technological projects" (ibid.). Freud's theorizing on the subject of God and Nature exemplifies what Irigaray refers to above as the idolatrous God split off from the sense world. He says of

Nature that *she* is "cruel" and that, "she has her own particularly effective method of restricting us. She destroys us—coldly, cruelly, relentlessly, as it seems to us, and possibly through the same things that cause satisfaction" (Freud 1961, 15, emphasis mine). God is understood by Freud as the "rampart . . . which will not suffer us to become a plaything of the over-mighty and pitiless forces of Nature" (19). Freud's notion of the divine as external to the living sense world, which is assimilated to the feminine, and further characterized as destructive and cruel, and for whom humans are mere playthings in need of rescue, could not contrast more starkly with Irigaray's project to cultivate a bridge between nature and culture, between human and divine. Freud's project, whether diagnostical or prognostical, represents the splitting of the immanent living world, characterized as "cruel Mother Nature," from a cultural notion of a God that is severed from the world. A mutually coevolving and participatory cocreativity between the sentience of nature, including human nature, and the conceptual realm of cultural discourse, including spiritual discourse, requires a bridge and not a rampart.

Parallel to the split between nature/culture and human/divine, we find the devitalization of subjectivity severed from its living roots and elaborated within the psychic structure of human subjects who, within the confines of this logic, must experience their inner liveliness as potentially cruel and dangerous—certainly not partaking of a sacred dimension. The splitting of nature and culture is a projection of the split in subjectivity that results from, and in return validates, a logic of abstraction, alienation, and even outright hostility towards the living world. But, more importantly, it interferes with our capacity to create an inner alignment with our authentic and metamorphosing wholeness as it is embedded in the wholeness of a living, evolving, cocreative cosmos. In this split is housed an error writ large—a flaw in our logic—as it is taken up into our collective cultural representations, our language, our science, and our technology. As such, it becomes constitutive of our world. Within this logic, we are unable to recognize our fluid participation in the relational matrix of life. Lacking this insight, the subject is free to strive to capture the living world in a series of discourses and algorithims—a world of robot and AI simulacra and reified images that mimic life. The subjects of this logic are mesmerized into thinking themselves gods in a transcendental kingdom. Within this mindset, there is no sense of limitation; these demigods can continue to create *stuff* seemingly endlessly, whereas nature, while being endlessly creative and evolving, also sets a co-creative limit on human subjectivity, given that we are truly *only part* of Life and not separate, omnipotent entities. Life *will* have its way with us, and we can choose to become active dance partners with the dynamic cosmos—or not. But it is pure omnipotent delusion to believe that we can go on forever disavowing our immersion in the wholeness of life and continue treating Earth as a never-ending consumer's delight. *Natural* resources are not infinite, and we, therefore, are not without limitation. As Gunnarsson claims, in denying the real constraints of the natural world, "our conception not only of nature but also of the social dynamics that it underpins will prove incoherent" (Gunnarsson, 71).

Bortoft refers to the refocusing of attention away from percepts and into mental abstractions that occurs in the analytical mode of consciousness characteristic of the verbal-intellectual and technological mind of the West as "automatization," a term he elaborates and borrows from Arthur Deikman (Deikman 1973, cited in Bortoft 65). Automatization results from turning attention away from the living world and toward mental abstractions. In these mental abstractions, what we typically experience is merely "a process of associating . . . abstractions via the medium of language which encapsulates them" (ibid.). It is possible to so sever participatory immersion in the sensory world from our mental abstraction as to become "tuned out altogether—so that what we 'experience' is only an abstraction, in which case we are completely automatized and in fact no longer different from any complex machine" (ibid.). As mentioned above, in his elaboration of Goethe's notion of "active seeing," Bortoft posits that a holistic mode of consciousness is "concerned more with relationships than with the discrete elements that are related. [. . .] It is important to realize that this mode of consciousness is a way of seeing, and as such, it can only be experienced in its own terms" (63). It is difficult for the analytical mind, with its focus on discrete elements, to grasp the reality of the unifying field or relationship—the authentic whole. But this shift can occur when we allow our attention to open to an intuitive participation with nonlinear and infinitely varied sentient life. Turning to this mode of consciousness promotes "de-automatization"—that is, liberation from the stifling uniformity of the pregiven abstractions of the intellectual mind—and results in "a restructuring of consciousness itself" (ibid.).

Bridge Building: Participatory Embodiment of "Third Space"

Barfield suggests that the way to transform an existing paradigm is to seriously engage it to its logical ends; for him, "the way out [is] through and not back" (Barfield 57). He discusses the process by which error is introduced into conceptual systems and by which our solid world of concepts—our collective representations—has emerged. Basically, collective representations are the result of human interaction with what Barfield terms "the unrepresented." The process is participatory in nature, but, for the most part, our participation remains unconscious. Thus, we assume that these representations exist independently of us. They form the parameters of our cultural world—our house of language representations—determining what we are able to see and not see, know and not know. Hungarian philosopher Georg Kuhlewind also sees the processes of consciousness (including thinking, perceiving, and making mental pictures) as "superconscious" processes that remain unconscious, making "the *results* of these processes appear much more real than the processes themselves" (Kuhlewind 50). Additionally, "while the *production* of consciousness is not conscious, not experienced, the *product* becomes all the more distinct. The finished, lifeless picture is clearly outlined because it is no longer animated by anything living" (38). Bergson, too, spoke of the retroactive construction of solid, discursive "things" and saw the process of arriving at that finished product as being "born *a priori* from a kind of metaphysical prepossession [which is not capable] of following the movement of consciousness" (Bergson 159).

The reach of this logic of abstraction is exponentially extended with the ubiquitous intervention of digital technologies and creates the urgent necessity for conscious participation, in which the subject reappropriates the capacity to actively and willfully engage with life and the living, not as a transcendent subject, but as co-emergent and consciously active participant. This recalls Gunnarsson's temporal "emergence" of culture from/with nature. Thus, when Irigaray offers up her provocative, "but what if the 'object' started to speak?" (Irigaray 1985a, 135), we might extend this question to our relationship with all forms of life and allow ourselves to ponder what we might experience in a genuinely participatory encounter, not only with the human other but also with the *other* that we perceive in all forms of sentience.

I offer a brief clinical vignette to illustrate this process. Upon seeking psychoanalytic treatment, a patient reported:

> I had been feeling depressed and despondent for a long time. I went out for a walk in the woods and came upon a pond. I was thinking, "Why go on? . . . life is so flat and meaningless . . ."

> At that moment, two dragonflies came right up to my face and did a little dance. They got my attention, and I followed them with my vision. I looked out over the pond to see hundreds or more of these beautiful creatures just glistening in the sunshine reflected on the water. [. . .] And I thought, "How can I not say *yes* to this beauty?" It was that day that I picked up the phone to call you.

Several dreams occurring during the opening phase of this person's analysis had, as an organizing theme, desolate cityscapes populated with tall steel buildings and manufactured debris, void of any signs of life but characterized by a menacing eeriness. I understood the steel buildings to represent both the stability *and* the inflexibility of a reified psychic structure. The lifeless, manufactured debris represented a lack of inner vitality. The self-structure was capable of *survival* but severely lacking in a dynamic liveliness.

The patient was depressed but highly functioning. We discussed the fact that she seemed to "manage" herself rather than live. She had an *image* in her mind corresponding to what a good mother should be, and any time she failed to behave according to the logic of this image she began to berate herself mercilessly. During one session, she reported feeling mortified when her second-grade daughter brought home a drawing in which were depicted her two daughters on bikes in the driveway and their mother, the patient, standing back and looking at her smartphone rather than at her children. This image did not fit with her image of a good mother, but, paradoxically, it also enabled her to reflect on how compelled she was by images in general. She recollected that she had stopped looking into the mirror around the age of thirty-seven because the changes she saw there did not gel with her static image of herself as a "fresh face with taut skin." She felt images were reliable in that they were not subject to the "messiness of real life," but they were a cause of deep concern and guilt when her real life failed to measure up. She reported that in a subsequent dream:

> I was riding a donkey, and we were in a kind of race. I knew that I had the capacity to win, and we were well on our way when we came to a bridge, but the bridge was blocked by a solid wall. Somehow, my donkey and I were communicating telepathically, and he told me that he could get me to the end of the race, but I would have to tell him which way to get across

> to the other side. He seemed to believe that I was able to figure this out. I felt so disheartened and unsure, but somehow I knew I had to find a route to the other side.

The patient was becoming aware of the ideological distortions she had imposed on herself and the need to find a way "across the bridge" to a more life-enhancing way of thinking and being. Given the above discussion, I find that this dream represents the need for a copula—a bridge between, on the one hand, her overly developed analytic ability to think in terms of a solid logic filled with pregiven images imposed upon her body and mind, and on the other hand, her fluid intuitive self, which was being challenged to find a creative path through a *solid* wall. Much of the work that followed had to do with an analysis and deconstruction of what I refer to as "thinking in terms of solids," which, in this context, connotes a way of conceiving the self in terms of an image—of a finished product or a commodity. As an image, it is devoid of life; it is petrified, perfected, and completed. It is, however, humanly unattainable; the living are finished only in death—as corpses or, perhaps, as rational automatons.

More than two-thirds of the way through a three-year treatment, this patient's psychic structure began to shift. What emerged was a more fluid interweaving between her inner, nonlinear life and her "manager." Rather than a stern taskmaster perpetually measuring how well she fit the image, this "manager" continued to provide perspective and stability, effected through participatory immersion in the ever-changing messiness of the real person that she was becoming. She was becoming aware of the amazing potential of a fluid movement of thought, a living thinking, and a unifying field behind all real life. Her thought processes in general became more fluid. She reported the following dream segment:

> I was on a horse and we crossed a bridge. I was absolutely enraptured with what I saw on the other side. There seemed to be more dimensions; for example, blades of grass seemed thicker and rounder and multi-dimensional. The colors were so rich, and everything glowed from within. It was like a different world; everything was so alive.

The bridge in this dream represented the bridge, now traversed, between two modes of consciousness. She was finding her way to another side of herself that grasped things intuitively and holistically, and she had been freed to participate in the meaning and creation of her own life. She began to embody a "third space" of becoming; a participatory sentience in which there was an apprehension of interiority; an interiority found within the living world and within the self. We saw that her entrapment in a solid world of images and oppositional logic began to open when she encountered the dragonflies, felt something inside herself resonate with their visit, and took steps to begin therapy; she began to look for something more—something beyond the deadened existence she was experiencing, exemplified by the picture of herself focused on her smartphone screen and away from the life inside herself and her daughters. The interior life in the dragonflies had awakened a fleeting glimpse of something more—life had beckoned to life—and in seeking psychotherapy, she began to turn her gaze elsewhere and discover the resonant aspect of her own interiority. Likewise, her sense of the analyst transformed. She began to *see* me as embodying an interiority with its own mystery that was captivating to her. She wondered how she had previously not thought of me as a real person but only as a function—there to help her feel less anxious. She struggled with her burgeoning awareness that she is "not 'finished' and never will be." In this way, her personal quest, along with the personal quests of others who are able to build bridges to connect two distinct and yet mutually vital modes of consciousness within themselves, to perceive in two registers at once, offers the best possibility for creating openings in an otherwise necrophilic enclosure within the structure of a logic of solids that is easily captured and perpetuated via digital simulacra.

Conclusion: Human Ternary Process

Technological augmentation that extends the abstract rational dimension of consciousness can enhance our innate human capacity to know our world. But when wed to a consumerist commodity-driven paradigm that breeds passive consumption and submission to pregiven images and products, it also leads subjects to devolve to the status of finished products, and it threatens to destroy the fluid movement across a bridge between two essentially human modes of consciousness—the abstract rational and the participatory intuitive. As I have shown, the abstract rational dissects the phenomenal world through an analytical lens into more and more component parts and then retroactively aggregates them into systems that Bortoft refers to as a counterfeit whole. The living thinking that I refer to as participatory sentience begins with an awareness of subjects' integral co-emergence within the fabric of the living world of which they are a part and a re-opening to their intuitive participation in its fluid movement. This type of active *seeing* of the seen, partaking of the Goethean sensorial imagination, involves what Bortoft refers to as a higher cognitive achievement that occurs as a result of an open bridge between two fully human modes of consciousness. This way of apprehending in two registers simultaneously transforms both the seer and the seen. Both modes of consciousness are essential to human becoming subject. Participatory immersion allows us to intuit the fluid, unifying relational field in which all of our knowledge is grounded and in which we are integrally planted. However, when our ternary participation with the living matrix becomes threatened by over-mediatized simulacra of life, in which cultural representations become our reified and deified creators, our capacity for opening the structure of the world is stifled. I have argued that one way of opening the closure of the given world is by engaging with what Irigaray refers to as the "inter-worlds" of nature, with a sense of conscious participation—what I have called participatory sentience. It is when we engage the sentient world in which we are immersed with our own inherent sentience that we breathe new life into abstracted interrogation and open the passage within our psychic space between the capacity to conceptualize and the capacity for intuitive immersion in life. When that happens, the liveliest life in us awakens to the life all around, and we find, as Harrison suggests, that "the penumbral depths . . . belong as much to the garden as to the mind or soul of the beholder" (Harrison 118).

Notes

1. In an analysis of Barfield, Robert McDermott (2008) explains the loss of "participation consciousness" as integral to Barfield's overall theory, in which "devolution is simultaneously a progression toward the possibility, and to some extent the realization, of individuality, freedom, and love" (297).

2. There are many current and ongoing clinical studies investigating the link between addictions to internet pornography and sexual dysfunction, isolation, and incapacity for intimacy. For example, Duffy et al. (2016) found that self-perceived pornography addiction "is reported to affect users and their partners in similar ways, such as increased feelings of isolation and relationship breakdowns." Likewise, Park et al. (2016) found that "sexual arousal to aspects of internet pornography use . . . [does] not readily transition to real-life partners, such that sex with desired partners may not register as meeting expectations, and arousal declines."

3. For a discussion of the implications of cultural matricide for individual psychic structure, see Lawler 2011.

4. It is important to keep in mind that Bortoft is not referring to a completed, metaphysical whole but to an always-unfinished, metamorphosing whole*ness*.

Works Cited

Artigas, Mariano. 2000. *The Mind of the Universe: Understanding Science and Religion.* Philadelphia and London: Templeton Foundation Press.

Barfield, Owen. 1988. *Saving the Appearances: A Study in Idolatry.* Middletown, CT: Wesleyan University Press.

Barnard, G. William. 2008. "Pulsating with Life: The Paradoxical Intuitions of Henri Bergson." In *The Participatory Turn: Spirituality, Mysticism, Religious Studies,* edited by Jorge N. Ferrer and Jacob H. Sherman. Albany: State University of New York Press.

Bauman, Zygmunt. 2003. *Liquid Love.* Cambridge: Polity.

Bergson, Henri. 1911. *Matter and Memory.* Translated by Nancy Margaret Paul and W. Scott Palmer. London: George Allen and Unwin LTD.

Bortoft, Henri. 1996. *The Wholeness of Nature: Goethe's Way toward a Science of Conscious Participation in Nature.* Great Barrington: Lindisfarne Books.

Deikman, Arthur J. 1973. "Bimodal Consciousness" and "Deautomatization and the Mystic Experience." In *The Nature of Human Consciousness,* edited by Robert E. Ornstein. San Francisco: W. H. Freeman.

Deutsch, Helene. 1942. "Some Forms of Emotional Disturbance and Their Relationship to Schizophrenia." *The Psychoanalytic Quarterly,* 11: 301–21.

Duffy, Athena, David Dawson, Roshan das Nair. 2016. "Pornography Addiction in Adults: A Systematic Review of Definitions and Reported Impact." https://www.ncbi.nlm.nih.gov/pubmed/27114191. *J Sex Med.* 13, no. 5 (May): 760–77. doi: 10.1016/j.jsxm.2016.03.002.

Freud, Sigmund. 1961. *The Future of an Illusion, Civilization and Its Discontents, and Other Works.* In *The Standard Edition of the Complete Psychological Works of Sigmund Freud,* vol. 21 (1927–1931), edited by J. Strachey. London: Hogarth.

Goethe, Wolfgang von. 1988. "The Metamorphosis of Plants." In *Goethe: Scientific Studies,* edited by Douglass Miller. New York: Suhrkamp.

Gunnarsson, Lena. 2014. *The Contradictions of Love: Towards a Feminist-Realist Ontology of Sociosexuality.* Oxford/New York: Routledge.

Harrison, Robert P. 2009. *Gardens: An Essay on the Human Condition.* Chicago: University of Chicago Press.

Irigaray, Luce. 1985a. *Speculum of the Other Woman.* Translated by Gillian G. Gill. Ithaca: Cornell University Press.

———. 1985b. *This Sex Which Is Not One.* Translated by Catherine Porter. Ithaca: Cornell University Press.

———. 1991. *The Irigaray Reader.* Edited by Margaret Whitford. Oxford: Blackwell.

———. 1993. *An Ethics of Sexual Difference.* Translated by Carolyn Burke and Gillian C. Gill. Ithaca: Cornell University Press.

———. 2002. *To Speak Is Never Neutral.* Translated by Gail Schwab. New York: Routledge.

———. 2004b. *Key Writings.* London: Continuum.

———. 2008. *Sharing the World.* London: Continuum.

———. 2010. "The Return." In *Rewriting Difference: Luce Irigaray and "the Greeks,"* edited by Elena Tzelepis and Athena Athanasiou. Albany: State University of New York Press.

———. 2013. *In the Beginning She Was.* London: Bloomsbury Academic.

Kirby, Vicky. 2008. "Natural convers(at)ions: Or, What if Culture Was Really Nature All Along?" In *Material Feminisms*, edited by Stacy Alaimo and Susan Hekman. Bloomington: Indiana University Press.

Kuhlewind, Georg. 1988. *From Normal to Healthy.* Translated by Michael Lipson. Stuttgart: Lindisfarne Books.

Lawler, Cheryl. 2011. "Orestes with Oedipus: Psychoanalysis and Matricide." In *Thinking with Irigaray*, edited by Mary C. Rawlinson, Sabrina L. Hom, and Serene J. Khader. Albany: State University of New York Press.

Linderman, Albert. 2012. *Why the World Around You Isn't As It Appears: A Study of Owen Barfield.* Great Barrington: Lindisfarne Books.

Love, Todd, Christian Laier, Matthias Brand, Linda Hatch, Raju Hajela. 2015. "Neuroscience of Internet Pornography Addiction: A Review and Update." *Behavioral Sciences* 5, no. 3: 388–433. https://www.ncbi.nlm.nih.gov/pubmed/26393658.

Marder, Michael. 2013. *Plant Thinking: A Philosophy of Vegetal Life.* New York: Columbia University Press.

McDermott, Robert. 2008. "Participation Comes of Age: Owen Barfield and the Bhagavad Gita." In *The Participatory Turn: Spirituality, Mysticism, Religious Studies.*

Merleau-Ponty, Maurice. 1962. *Phenomenology of Perception.* Translated by Colin Smith. London: Routledge and Kegan Paul.

Park, Brian Y., Gary Wilson, Jonathan Berger, Matthew Christman, Bryn Reina, Frank Bishop, Warren P. Klam, and Andrew Doan. 2016. "Is Internet Pornography Causing Sexual Dysfunctions? A Review with Clinical Reports." *Behavioral Sciences* 6, no. 3. http://doi.org/10.3390/bs6030017.

Stiegler, Bernard. 2011. *The Decadence of Industrial Democracies: Disbelief and Discredit,* vol. 1. Translated by Daniel Ross and Suzanne Arnold. Cambridge: Polity.

Thinking Life through the Early Greeks

KRISTIN SAMPSON

In her 2013 *In the Beginning, She Was*, Luce Irigaray returns to the Pre-Socratics, the early Greek thinkers before Plato and Aristotle, and asks what it means "to begin with the Greeks" (Irigaray 2013, 139). As she states in the very first sentence of her book: "It is probably necessary to return to the world of the Pre-Socratic philosophers in order to understand something about the between-us today" (1). Making a return to the past in order to understand ourselves today might be understood in (at least) two ways; on the one hand, we need to go back to the past as a part of our history and as what has made our culture and ways of thinking what they are today. The past considered in this light can then be questioned critically in terms of what went wrong. At what point was a wrong turn made in the path of our history? That Irigaray partly considers the early Greek thinkers from this perspective becomes apparent when she writes that "the Pre-Socratic philosopher somehow prepares our tradition for nihilism" (4); the context of the Pre-Socratics thus emerges as a crossroads. This is a view espoused by Judith Still, who writes that Luce Irigaray "insists on the crucial importance of Greek mythology to our understanding of sexual difference; we need to return to Greek culture in an attempt to find the crossroads where we took the wrong path" (Still 2010, 150). Furthermore, as Claire Colebrook states:

> To look back at the Greek world is to open the closure of the present. If certain decisions, divisions, and occlusions were effected

> in the Greek past, then our entire metaphysical vocabulary will determine the structure of our present thinking. And this determination and orientation in thinking will not only dominate metaphysics in the narrow sense, as a quite specific branch of academic philosophy; it will also orient our everyday relations to the world. (Colebrook 2010, 177)

If our present situation is determined by conditions—"decisions, divisions, and occlusions," as Colebrook says—that were laid down in "the Greek past," then it is important to go back to that past in order to open up the closure of the present and to ask: What if things were different? What if different ways of thinking had unfolded?

On the other hand, the past can also be considered as something that diverges from contemporary notions and conceptions that are so obvious to us they have become invisible. In this sense, the past opens up an outside to our own ways of thinking. The past then emerges as something against which we can contrast the present. Irigaray writes of a remembrance of a previous time that can be found in the earliest Greek thinkers: "At that time, a memory still exists of an unsaid, of a beyond in which wonder, magic, ecstasy, growth, and poetry mingle" (Irigaray 2). Considered in this light, going back to the distant past of early Greek thinking can appear as a project where the aim is to bring out something of the strangeness and "foreignness" of the early Greek context. In this chapter I, together with Irigaray, return to the early Greeks to ask what conceptions of life can be found in early Greek thinking in the contexts of the Pre-Socratic thinkers and of the period prior to the Pre-Socratics, that I have termed "pre-Pre-Socratic."

I will start by looking at Irigaray's description of what happens at the crossroads where the thinking of the Pre-Socratic philosophers occurs—the moment that may be thought of as the beginning of the wrong turn. I will subsequently investigate Irigaray's claim that there was a different way of thinking prior to these thinkers. Here I attempt to provide further background for her views by looking at conceptions of life and corporeality in a pre-Pre-Socratic context, where among others, the texts of Homer belong. I argue that there is an "outside" to be found by making a return to Homer, an outside representing a way of thinking that is different from and resides beyond that of the later Greek philosophical tradition, which has had such an important influence up until our own time.

Irigaray's Reading of the Pre-Socratic Thinkers

According to Irigaray, the Pre-Socratic thinkers are positioned at the crossroads where a wrong turn is made. Something goes astray with them; a way of thinking is instituted that is not compatible with or amenable to a fruitful way of conceptualizing life. She explicitly mentions Heraclitus in this regard, noting that "discourse closes upon itself through strategies of conflicting oppositions" (3). This constitutes the beginning of a dichotomous way of thinking, where there is no room for real difference to emerge. This dichotomous logic also closes thinking off from life: "The house of language has become a kind of tomb to which it is necessary to give back a semblance of life. The closure of logos, of the world, calls for contraries, oppositions, conflict" (5).

In her previous work, the Pre-Socratic thinker that Irigaray refers to and uses perhaps the most frequently is Empedocles, above all, his thinking concerning the four elements. *In the Beginning, She Was*, however, is also critical of Empedocles, especially of his conception of strife, thought as an opposition to love (13–15, 25–26). With allusions to both Anaximander and Parmenides, Irigaray connects the opening—*apeiron*, "the limitless"—together with living growth; however, with the Pre-Socratic thinkers it is this very opening that begins to be closed off into a logic of opposition and dualism. "Against becoming over time, against growing, man will oppose Being and not-Being in the present. The *apeiron* related to becoming is thus kept in a logical economy" (12). Already with the Pre-Socratics, things start moving in the wrong direction; living, moving, growing life is beginning to be thought in terms of a static, dichotomous hierarchy, one that in the end will prove disastrous, according to Irigaray.

However, in some of the Pre-Socratic thinkers a remnant and a remembrance of something prior and different are still present, and Irigaray finds in them what she considers an earlier way of thinking. This she relates to the Goddess, and she mentions, for example, Parmenides and Empedocles as thinkers who allude to this female deity (2–3). Throughout her book, Irigaray writes again and again of what has been lost, using the terms "the Goddess" or "nature." She also sometimes inserts a third term—"woman," as in "Goddess, nature, woman" (36 and 55). Irigaray also speaks of living nature in relation to the mother—a mother who was there in the beginning (111). Later, this goddess/mother is forgotten, appropriated, and reduced to an entity defined through a dualistic, hierarchical way of thinking. It is true that Parmenides invokes the Goddess in his poem, and that this unnamed Goddess teaches the young man about being. However, to claim that this is evidence of an earlier culture devoted to the Goddess—a culture where women and the female were placed in a position of reverence, respect, and authority—is highly controversial and something that most scholars of ancient Greek philosophy and history would reject. Nevertheless, I will argue that Irigaray is correct in noting that a change does happen, or begins to happen, with the Pre-Socratics—a change in the concept of life. I will, however, argue this point in a way that differs from Irigaray's line of argument.

Early Greek Conceptions of Life

Irigaray clearly alludes to a time prior to the earliest Pre-Socratic thinkers when the feminine has not been appropriated, forgotten, or rendered invisible—the time Irigaray calls "the beginning," a time when "discourse still grows starting from the same depths as vegetal growth" and is connected to what she calls "the roots of life" and to its becoming (27). This pre-Pre-Socratic beginning takes place prior to, for instance, Parmenides's conception of thinking and being, when thinking and perception are still closely linked. Irigaray writes, with an obvious allusion to Parmenides: "In the beginning, to perceive and to think are the same" (29). Thinking here emerges as something bound to a situation, to a surrounding landscape, and to what Irigaray again terms the "roots of becoming" (ibid.). The rootedness of thought is a link to the real, and when it is lost, "the words no longer adhere to the real, no longer transmit a living energy" (31). The real is life, according to Irigaray, and she sometimes uses "the real" and "life" synonymously (23).

According to Irigaray, "life is what grows; it is not considered as a completed totality to which death is opposed" (23). This negative definition of what life is not—that is, *not* the opposite of death—is indicated by *zôê*, an early concept that pre-dates the conception of life as something opposed to death. After Homer, *zôê*, the most common word for life in classical Greek, means "life" or "existence"—that is, the opposite of death. However, if we go back to Homer, the word emerges in a different, and more concrete, manifestation.[1] In Homer, *zôê* carries meanings such as "(a) living," that is to say, one's "substance" or "property." For example, in the *Odyssey* (14.96) Homer says: "Verily his substance (*zôê*) was great past telling, so much has no lord either on the dark mainland or in Ithaca itself; nay, not twenty men together have wealth so great."[2] He also says (16.429): "Him, then, they were minded to slay (*fthisai*), and take from him his life (*hêtor*, that is 'heart') by violence, and utterly to devour his great and pleasant livelihood (*zôên*)." What is striking in this passage is that the word that later in Greek will come to mean "life" here means "livelihood," while the expression that is translated into English as "take from him his life" literally means "bereave him of his beloved heart." My point is that there is not one word designating life as such in Homer, but there are several ways of expressing what we would gather together into one word, namely "life." We do not find a conception of life—*zôê*—as an entity that constitutes the opposite of death. This meaning emerges later in Antiquity, after the time of Homer.[3]

According to Bruno Snell, in Homer, "abstractions are as yet undeveloped, while immediate sense perceptions furnish [the living human being] with a wealth of concrete symbols" (Snell 1982, 1).[4] If we go back to Homer, a few centuries before Plato, the distinction between, for example, body and soul is not conceptualized in the same way as it will be some centuries later.[5] In Homer, we do not find a clear distinction between the corporeal, spiritual, and emotional aspects of the living human being. According to Hermann Fränkel, "there are no boundaries, there is no cleavage between feeling and the corporeal situation" (Fränkel 1975, 79). And, as James M. Redfield argues: "Homer is pre-Cartesian and, for that matter, pre-Socratic. He does not make a sharp distinction between body and soul" (Redfield 1975, 175). Or, as Michael Clarke puts it: "Homeric man does not *have* a mind; rather his thoughts and consciousness are as inseparable a part of his bodily life as are movement and metabolism. [. . .] By the same token, he will not *have* a body" (Clarke 1999, 115). What can be found in Homer is what I have elsewhere called a "corporeality without body."[6]

The very words connoting "the body" and "the soul" are not yet thought as components of a living human being. Instead, in this pre-Pre-Socratic context, the words *sôma* and *psuchê* name the dead body and the dead soul. These are the very words that later will become the names for the living body and the soul within a living human being. Brooke Holmes points out that "the physical body is something new in the late archaic and classical periods" (Holmes 2010, xi). Furthermore, she argues that this body is so entrenched "in modern Western culture that it is difficult to conceive of its absence" (Holmes 2010, 4). One way to overcome this difficulty is to go back to a time prior to this conception of the physical body. Homer, belonging to a historical context that is prior to this introduction of the body, never uses words like "body" and "soul" when referring to a living human being. Instead, the Homeric Greeks have a variety of different words for various aspects of meaning that the body (that is, what we would call the body) can express.

Irigaray studies the language of the early Greeks as a source for something different that existed prior to the culture she criticizes. For instance, she looks at early meanings of *heteros* ("a different other," "of another kind, different") and *genos* ("race, stock, kin" or "lineage," "family") (145–47 and 160 ff.).What she is seeking to regain is a "cultivation which asks us not to separate spirit from body, mind from affect" (154). In light of this project, going back to the way of conceptualizing corporeality that can be found in Homer is useful. Irigaray does mention Homer; nonetheless, she appears to be uncertain how to view the Homeric epos, where, as she writes, "love is already becoming an institution bound to the *polis*" (141). She admits, however, that "the hero still bears witness to self-affection" (ibid.). In my view, Irigaray could find much more support for her depiction of something prior to the Pre-Socratics by looking at conceptions of corporeality within the Homeric textual material. Furthermore, the Homeric conception of corporeality and the living predates the concept of the subject. Irigaray argues: "In those ancient Greek times, specular or speculative reflection did not yet exist, nor a subject as such who may be concerned by them" (113). According to Holmes, the emergence of the subject is conditioned on the materialization of the physical body, and the physical body materializes both within what was called "inquiry into nature" (Holmes 2010, 4)—that is, within Pre-Socratic thought—and within the development of classical Greek medicine, both dating to around the fifth century BCE.

Life as Growth

The Pre-Socratic thinkers are known as the philosophers of nature: *phusis*. The ancient Greek word *phusis* carries meanings like "origin" and "growth," and it stems from the verb *phuô*—"to bring forth," "to beget," and "to engender," and also "to become" and "to grow" (Liddell and Scott 1996). According to Irigaray, the growth that is life, and that she also calls natural growth, is without limits (*apeiron*). She makes a comparison to vegetal life to illustrate this, using a plant as an example: "The plant appears with borders, with a form, but to express it as such amounts to having already deprived this plant of its vegetal life. Indeed its life is never definitive: it evolves according to the hour, the day, the season, the year" (57). The concept of life as limitless growth can be understood in terms of temporality. *Aiôn* carries meanings related to both temporality and life. On the one hand, *aiôn* can mean "eternity" and is used when referring to something that lasts forever. On the other hand, *aiôn* can be used to refer to something that lasts a lifetime, like a living being. As Emile Benveniste points out, *aiôn* in Homer still retains its full meaning related to human life. Here, the word not only indicates the lifetime of a human being; it expresses the force of life or the source of life and vitality (Benveniste 1937, 107). The transition from "lifetime" to "eternity" seems surprising, considering that these two concepts are usually considered to be mutually exclusive and that *aiôn* does not give expression to a meaning such as "eternal life." Rather, it is used to refer to a transient lifetime—a limited existence.[7]

Benveniste points to a plurality of meanings related to the word *aiôn* in Indo-European languages, including Greek from Homer onwards. According to Benveniste, when *aiôn* becomes the term for eternity, it indicates the reproduction on a cosmological level of a structure in the human *aiôn*. Between these two—the human *aiôn* and the cosmic *aiôn*—there is an accordance; the force of life is thus to be understood as reproduction, where something new is constantly replacing the old. We might imagine something upholding itself never-endingly, always appearing as fresh and new. Within the universe, there is constant reproduction; thus, the universe itself might be conceived as an entity in constant and continuous reproduction. Everything in the universe has a beginning and an end: whatever is born must die. This can be considered a law of nature. However, this law itself need have neither beginning nor end. Benveniste writes: "Everything recommences except the law of recommencement. As regards time, every element of the universe is at the same time limited and unlimited: limited insofar as it belongs to a limited duration, unlimited because it reinstates without stop its limited duration" (Benveniste 1937, 112).[8] That is to say, it regenerates itself constantly, and, in this way, it achieves unlimited existence.

We observe in this transference of meaning—from lifetime to eternity—a movement away from a more concrete and toward a more abstract way of thinking, a move similar to the one I noted above in relation to corporeality. This movement toward increasingly abstract thinking is what Irigaray criticizes in the emergence of philosophy in Greece. As Irigaray claims, with reference to the Pre-Socratics and their approach to *phusis*, "*phusis* is already cut off from its living roots by the logos" (Irigaray 28). That is to say, the *phusis* that the Pre-Socratic thinkers attempt to discover is already separated from the real, from life.

With the philosophical tradition initiated by the Pre-Socratics, a world is invented "without change, a mechanism with neither life nor breath" (42). Life as growth cannot be grasped simply through a logos, or through logos. Irigaray states: "Life never speaks simply. It shows itself in its flower, hides itself in its roots" (33). The world as it was unfolded and understood by the Pre-Socratics is a world where "the flower is only perceived through the idea of flower" (32), as she puts it. It is important to note that Irigaray emphasizes the idea of flower as something perceived. Thinking in terms of ideas is still a form of perception, but it is a perception of a frozen image of a flower, not a blossoming, living flower. What Irigaray calls life, or the real, has become distant and displaced by the idea.

Life as Cosmic

Life, according to Irigaray, is an extensive concept that encompasses more than living beings. The rhythms related to the transitions between night and day, and the changes of the seasons from spring, to summer, to autumn, to winter, for example, also belong to what Irigaray calls "a rhythm of life" (92). The early Greeks understood the earth (*Gê* / *Gaia*) as a living corporeal entity, with pulsations, flows, and rhythms. Irigaray speaks of air, water, light, warmth, and the earth in terms of what she calls "generational order" (126–27). These are all elements that provide conditions for life to grow, for living growth. Life then emerges as encompassing both living beings and cosmic elements like earth, water, air, and fire, as well as the cyclic movements of the seasons and of night and day. Life appears as connected to *phusis*, understood as life, nature, and world. This world Irigaray contrasts with another, which begins with the Pre-Socratic thinkers, a world created by man, which is characterized as a world of dualistic binary oppositions, hierarchy, and lack of life and becoming. This is a world of the immoveable and the static.

Irigaray opposes what she calls "natural engendering" to this artificially created world—"a world created outside of natural engendering, a world in which creatures are organized in a hierarchical manner in relation to an absolute model" (106). This hierarchical and absolute model is a model of opposites and dualism. Natural engendering, on the other hand, belongs to a different model of conception. Or, as Irigaray puts it, "Conceiving is never the fruit of an opposition except within a world parallel to the real and living world, a world elaborated by a single part of humanity" (108). Nature is not hierarchical, or, at least, natural differences are "less hierarchical because each remains faithful to its own origin, growth, and blossoming and is not standardized through its submission to one unique world that knows only quantitative differences. [. . .] Nature is not lacking in differences [. . .]. Nature is more differentiated than the world built by man [. . .]" (131).

Does Irigaray's distinction between a real and living world and a world created by man imply that she draws a simple distinction between nature and culture? Is there, on the one hand, a given world, nature, and, on the other hand, a created world, culture? My answer would be "no." It is not the distinction between nature and culture as such that Irigaray is evoking. Rather, she presents a critique of a certain creation of a world that in turn implies a specific distinction between nature and culture. At the end of *In the Beginning, She Was,* she explicitly criticizes the divisions both between body and mind and between nature and culture when she writes: "It is through a division into body and mind, nature and culture, sensible and intelligible that masculine subjectivity has tried to emerge from an undifferentiated link with the first other" (148). The distinction between nature and culture belongs to the world, or worldview, of dualistic oppositions and hierarchies, which Irigaray explicitly criticizes. She censures the way that the concept of "world" has been placed in opposition to the living world that she calls nature. She calls for different ways of thinking that do not imply a conception of the real that stands in opposition to life, growth, and nature.

What is ultimately broken in the transformation that begins with the Pre-Socratics is the in-between: "This between-them is annihilated if it is appropriated by the One, the Unique—truth or God—or neutered as a neither-the-one-nor-the-other rather than both-the-one-and-the-other" (7). According to Irigaray: "This between-two takes place in the opening of the difference between the one and the other, but it is in no way proper to the one or the other—it arises from the two" (8). The in-between is not only something that "takes place"; it is something that lives, and it is something to be kept alive. The problem with the culture of today is that this in-between is no longer living: "There is no longer any between-us that is free, available, still silent, still alive" (11). Irigaray emphasizes the importance of respecting and cultivating what she calls "natural life," which involves remembering the relational aspect of life between "two different human beings, man and woman" (111).

Thinking Life

The title of this chapter is "Thinking Life through the Early Greeks." So how are we to think life? The problem with thinking as it exists in the philosophical tradition starting with the Pre-Socratics is that it separates itself from life and the real. Irigaray wishes to reunite thinking with life. Irigaray writes: "The logos does not take into account the relationship with her, which, in man, can evolve from elementary vitality to a culture of listening, of speech, of love, of thought" (58). Or, as she also writes, emphasizing the importance of life, breath, and a relation in difference: "Speech, unanchored from its origin, searches for weight in rhetoric or logic, which become sophistic strategies if they no longer obey the economy of life, of breath, of the relation in difference" (79). The attempt to transcend what Irigaray calls the natural world—the real, life, or growth—is an impossible and futile task: "Neither the logos nor an only masculine God have really transcended the natural world. They have artificially replicated it for lack of having found how to express a movement of natural growth" (82). Thinking life must move beyond the dualisms and dichotomous oppositions between life and death, body and soul, and nature and culture, in order to ground itself in real difference, and for Irigaray sexual difference is crucial to such a project. Furthermore, man and woman need to be thought differently, not as a dichotomy where one defines the other, but as grounded in a difference that renders them incommensurable.

Can a detour to a distant past be useful in thinking life differently? In what way can a detour back into the conceptual world of the Homeric texts be of value? The early Greek examples in Homer point to conceptions that lie beyond a later philosophical tradition; thus, they shed light upon that tradition by evoking a thinking that predates it and is placed outside of it. Furthermore, what the conceptions of life and living corporealities found in Homer make obvious is that the later dualistic conceptions of—to take one example—life as the opposite of death, that belong to our Western conceptual horizon, are dependent upon, and embedded within a specific culture and tradition. They are neither self-evident nor unavoidable. There was a time when these conceptions were thought differently.

Moreover, a detour and a return to a distant past can be useful in opening up new possibilities to create different ways of thinking in the future. The nongeneralized, concrete conceptions of life and of living corporeal existence in Homer are characterized by a variety of different words that all indicate specific ways of acting and perceiving. They are all inherently relational in the sense that they indicate different relations toward a concrete situation or context. A nongeneralized notion of existence is more emphatically open for difference than are more generalized notions. It is a conception of reality that focuses not on generalities and functions, but rather on specificities and difference(s).

In Homer, we find a view of human life where the distinction between body and soul is not yet thought. This implies that a concept of, for example, a sexed body and a soul devoid of sexual characteristics would be imposible. A clear distinction between nature and culture would also be difficult to conceptualize. Consequently, there cannot be a body, given as a natural entity—that is, as sexed, in the sense of something biologically given—that is clearly distinguishable from a culturally constituted gendered aspect. The distinction between sex and gender that we operate with today cannot be found in any similar way in Homer. However, and I would like to emphasize this point, in going back to Homer, I am not arguing that there is an Irigarayan form of sexual difference to be found there. The exclusion of woman and the feminine in the earliest Greek textual material is well documented by a number of scholars.[9] My aim is thus not to describe how sexual difference was thought historically in the period of the Homeric Greeks, but it is rather to attempt to investigate how a Homeric conception of living existence can be used as a source of inspiration in an attempt to think and create something new within a contemporary context. In my view, Homeric conceptions of life and living corporeality open up the possibility of conceiving of living existence as differentiated, including sexually. Going back to this distant past may thus, hopefully, provide conceptual tools that can be useful in creating new ways of thinking life.

Notes

I owe a debt of gratitude to Ellen Mortensen and Gail Schwab for useful and instructive comments to an earlier version of this chapter.

1. In the present chapter, I do not go into the question of who Homer was, or whether there is one author or several poets composing the *Odyssey* and the *Illiad*. For a discussion of the so-called "Homeric question," see Rutherford (1996).

2. See also the *Odyssey* (14.208): "But the fates of death bore him away to the house of Hades, and his proud sons divided among them his substance (*zoê*), and cast lots therefor."

3. In ancient Greek there is also the word *bíos*. In Homer this word can mean livelihood or means of living. It is used also to denote the manner in which

one lives. See the *Odyssey*, 15.491: "thou livest well (*zôeis d'agathon bion*)"; *Odyssey*, 18.254 and 19.127, where Penelope in both places speaks of "this life of mine (*ton emon bion*)."

4. Snell's seminal work, *The Discovery of the Mind in Greek Philosophy and Literature*, first published in 1953, has been widely discussed. I follow those who consider Snell to be on to something important—for example, E. R. Dodds (1951, 15–17); Fränkel (1975, 75–85); Redfield (1975, 175); Clarke (1999, 115–119); Holmes (2010, 1–41).

5. See Sampson 2013.

6. See Sampson 2015.

7. See my doctoral thesis, Sampson 2006.

8. My translation of: Tout recommence, sauf la loi du recommencement. Au regard du temps, chaque élément de l'univers est à la fois fini et infini: fini, parce qu'il se meut dans dans une durée limitée; infini parce qu'il réintègre sans trêve sa durée finie (Benveniste, 112).

9. See Zeitlin 1996, especially chapters "Figuring Fidelity in Homer's *Odyssey*" and "Signifying Difference: The Case of Hesiod's Pandora." Vernant 1990 investigates marriage in pre-classical Greece (see chapter "Marriage"); Vernant 1991 looks at femininity and death. See chapters "Feminine Figures of Death in Greece" and "Death in the Eyes: Gorgo, Figure of the *Other*." See Loraux 1993 and 1991 on feminine figures and women in early Greek mythology and tragedy. See Laqueur 1992 on conceptions of sex in early Greek medical texts, especially chapter "Destiny Is Anatomy."

Works Cited

Benveniste, Emile. 1937. "Expression indo-européen de l' 'éternité.' "*Bulletin de la Société de linguistique,* vol. 38, 103–39. Paris: Klincksieck.

Clarke, Michael. 1999. *Flesh and Spirit in the Songs of Homer: A Study of Words and Myths*. Oxford: Clarendon.

Colebrook, Claire. 2010. "Dynamic Potentiality: The Body That Stands Alone." In *Rewriting Difference: Luce Irigaray and "the Greeks,"* edited by Elena Tzelepis and Athena Athanasiou, 177–91. Albany: State University of New York Press.

Dodds, E. R. 1951. *The Greeks and the Irrational.* Berkeley: University of California Press.

Fränkel, Hermann. 1975. *Early Greek Poetry and Philosophy: A History of Greek Epic, Lyric, and Prose to the Middle of the Fifth Century.* Oxford: Basil Blackwell.

Holmes, Brooke. 2010. *The Symptom and the Subject: The Emergence of the Physical Body in Ancient Greece*. Princeton and Oxford: Princeton University Press.

Homer. 1984. *Odyssey*, vols. 1 and 2. Translated by A. T. Murray. Cambridge, MA, and London: Harvard University Press.

Irigaray, Luce. 2013. *In the Beginning, She Was*. London and New York: Bloomsbury.

Laqueur, Thomas. 1992. *Making Sex: Body and Gender from the Greeks to Freud.* Cambridge, MA and London: Harvard University Press.

Liddell, H. G., and R. Scott. 1996. *Greek-English Lexicon*. Oxford: Oxford University Press.

Loraux, Nicole. 1991. *Tragic Ways of Killing a Woman*. Cambridge, MA, and London: Harvard University Press.

———. 1993. *The Children of Athena*. Princeton: Princeton University Press.

Redfield, James M. 1975. *Nature and Culture in the Illiad: The Tragedy of Hector*. Chicago and London: University of Chicago Press.

Rutherford, Richard. 1996. *Homer*. Cambridge: Cambridge University Press.

Sampson, Kristin. 2006. *Ontogony: Conceptions of Being and Metaphors of Birth in the* Timaeus *and the* Parmenides. Bergen, Norway: Fagbokforlaget.

———. 2013. "*Sôma, technê* and the Somatechnics of Sexual Difference." In *Somatechnical Figurations: Kinship, Bodies, Affects,* edited by Nikki Sullivan, Jane Simon, Ulrika Dahl, and Jenny Sundén. In *Somatechnics*, vol. 3 (2). Edinburgh: Edinburgh University Press, 233–50.

———. 2015. "Beyond the Subject: Early Greek Conceptions of Corporeality." *Agalma* 30 (October). Rome: Mimesis edizioni.

Snell, Bruno. 1982. *The Discovery of the Mind in Greek Philosophy and Literature.* New York: Dover.

Still, Judith. 2010. "Hospitality and Sexual Difference." In *Re-Writing Difference*, edited by Tzelepis and Athanasiou, 149–65.

Vernant, Jean-Pierre. 1990. *Myth and Society in Ancient Greece*. New York: Zone Books.

———. 1991. *Mortals and Immortals*. Princeton: Princeton University Press.

Zeitlin, Froma I. 1996. *Playing the Other: Gender and Society in Classical Greek Literature*. Chicago and London: University of Chicago Press.

Between Her and Her

Place and Relations between Women in Irigaray and Wright

REBECCA HILL

> Only heaven knows, there were millions of people throughout the world who either offered pigs as sacrifices to their Gods, or flowers, or the first grain of the new season's crop. There were even others who offered up their own people to the Gods. Now the day had come when modern man had become the face of the God, and he simply sacrificed the whole Earth.
>
> —Wright 2013, 12

> I started to learn that protecting and valuing the earth's ingenious systems of reproducing life and the fertility of all of its inhabitants may lie at the center of the shift in worldview that must take place if we are to move beyond extractivism. A worldview based on regeneration and renewal rather than domination and depletion.
>
> —Klein 2014, 424

> Can a society live without sacrifices, without aggression? Perhaps, if it obeys the moment of cosmic temporality. The sacrificial order overlays the natural rhythms with a different and cumulative temporality that dispenses and prevents us from attending to the moment. Once this occurs imprecisions multiply and grow. A catharsis becomes necessary.
>
> —Irigaray 1993b, 77

This chapter strives to trace a path away from the nihilism of "the global death project" of modernity towards a different ethics, an ethics that recognizes nature as fundamentally nontotalizable.[1] The excessiveness of nature is not to be mourned or dreaded; it is in relation to this overwhelming mystery that human beings must build an ethics that respects the fecundity of life. I take up Luce Irigaray's critique of the instrumentalist framing of nature as a resource and her suggestions for moving beyond this reductive framework in order to elaborate a new relationship with what is called "nature." Famously for Irigaray, this can only take place through the articulation of a nonhierarchical ethics of sexuate difference. Her recent articulations of the theory of sexuate difference are grounded upon the relationship between two kinds of human being who are irreducible: woman and man. The heterosocial relationship that founds the ontology of sexuate difference is widely written about in scholarship on Irigaray, but there is another aspect of her philosophy that has received far less attention—her rethinking of the status of the relationship between women.[2] The generation of a woman-to-woman sociality in which women are situated as subjects who are irreducible to one another is essential to the ethics of sexuate difference. For Irigaray, this requires the elaboration of relations between women as "sisters" (a horizontal axis of relationships), a maternal genealogy (a vertical axis of relationships between women-subjects), and the establishment of respect for the evolving "whole" of "nature" which can never be totalized—or for what I call in this chapter the "Common Mother." The elaboration of woman-to-woman sociality, of maternal genealogy, and of respect for the Common Mother has decisive significance that goes beyond the anthropocentric challenge of engendering intersubjective relations between women; it is fundamental to dismantling the instrumental framing of "nature" as a resource, a framework that is sacrificing the Earth as such.

My discussion of Irigaray is situated alongside a reading of the relationship between the two central women characters in the Waanyi writer Alexis Wright's novel, *The Swan Book* (2013). It's impossible to describe the plot of Wright's complex, sprawling, philosophical, and poetic novel, which operates at multiple levels of reality. This is because what is central to *The Swan Book* is an Indigenous sense of Being, and Aboriginal ontologies are not premised on the metaphysics of presence. In my view, Irigaray's thought has some striking resonances with Aboriginal ontology.[3] Her thinking on intersubjectivity is also resonant with aspects of the relationship between the central women characters in *The Swan Book.*

The two women characters at the heart of this novel are an old white climate-change refugee called Bella Donna of the Champions and an Aboriginal girl Bella Donna "rescues" from the bough of a sacred tree and names Oblivia Ethylene (20). I am not arguing that Wright's depiction of Oblivia and Bella Donna in *The Swan Book* is influenced by Irigaray (or that Irigaray is influenced by Wright). Nonetheless, there is a striking resonance between Irigaray's ideas about the difficulty for women to articulate intersubjective relationships with one another and the way in which Bella Donna and Oblivia interact.

These characters have profoundly different senses of their relationship to the milieu or place in which they live. This is most pronounced in their diverging conceptions of the relationship between place and language, especially speech. Bella Donna's view of speech is congruent with the dominant western sense of language as something that can be used to make intelligible arguments "across the world" (23). Through her refusal to speak, and in her mind, Oblivia criticizes this Western conception of language as rootless. She prefers to remain silent (23). I argue that Oblivia's decision to remain silent can be read in resonance with Irigaray's "concept" of the sensible-transcendental, which Irigaray also calls a "space of silence" (Irigaray 2008). The sensible-transcendental is a mysterious and excessive "concept" that designates place as a relation between bodies that exceeds presence. This strange threshold, which cannot strictly be named, is fundamental to Irigaray's ontology of sexuate difference; the sensible-transcendental is the groundless ground of the nonhierarchical relationship between woman and man and the basis of a relationship of difference between women; "it" is also coextensive with all of life. The sensible-transcendental is the basis of a new ethics. As we shall see, this strange "concept" has some commonality with the Indigenous relational sense of Being articulated vividly in Wright's *Swan Book*.

The Founding Matricide

Irigaray's critique of phallocentrism is a critique of the denigration and exploitation of "nature" in the broadest sense. For her, the instrumentalization of nature in the ongoing project of colonialization-globalization has roots in ancient thought that is credited with founding the Western tradition.

My use of the phrase "Western tradition" should not be read as an endorsement of the idea of "the West" as some kind of exclusively European tradition birthed by the so-called Greek miracle. The Western tradition is a body of texts drawn from a mixture of sources, many of which are not European, and it mingles and overlaps with other traditions. Like Édouard Glissant, I understand "the West" as a project and not a place (1989, 2). For instance, the state of Australia is not located in the West (of Europe), and yet the dominant frames of thought, affect, and governance in that nation-state are Western ideas that have been imposed through the ongoing project of settler colonialism. In this sense, Irigaray's Eurocentric philosophy is valuable for thinking about the Australian context (among other places).

In *Sexes and Genealogies*, Irigaray argues provocatively that "our society and culture operate on the basis of an original matricide" (1993b, 11). For Irigaray, the ancient murder of the woman-mother is necessary to the establishment and maintenance of patriarchal order. This is a claim about the immense violence done to women and girls; it is also a claim about the immense violence done to what is called "nature." Irigaray's engagement with the canonical trilogy *The Oresteia* by the ancient Greek tragedian, Aeschylus (2008), is one of the touchstones of her argument for the foundational status of matricide.

In the first play, the *Agamemnon*, when King Agamemnon returns from Troy after a ten-year absence, waiting for him is his wife, Queen Clytemnestra, who welcomes her husband home and then kills him. Clytemnestra justifies the killing of Agamemnon on the basis that her husband had sacrificed their daughter Iphigenia at the command of the goddess Artemis in order to obtain favorable winds for the Greek fleet. In *The Libation-Bearers*, Orestes, the son of Clytemnestra and Agamemnon, returns to avenge his father. He tricks his way into the palace of Argos, and, in an erotically charged confrontation, kills his mother. The second play concludes with Orestes being hounded into madness by the chthonic goddesses of vengeance, the Furies, because he has killed his own "blood" relation. In the third play, *The Eumenides*, Apollo represents Orestes at his trial in Athens. Apollo defends Orestes's matricide as a just act of revenge against Clytemnestra for what he interprets as the heinous crime of murdering her husband. When the jury's decision is split, the judge, the goddess Athena, breaks the tie by casting a vote in Orestes's favor. The Furies then threaten to wreak destruction on the city of Athens, but Athena persuades them to give up vengeance against those who kill their own "flesh and blood" and to become deities of the city, honored with sacrifices by the citizens of Athens. The final play ends with Athena and the Furies (now called the Eumenides or "Kindly Ones") celebrating Athens and Athenian justice.

This play cycle is traditionally read as a grand narrative of progress in which opposed forms of social and divine order do battle and are "resolved" in the conclusion of the final play into a "harmony" (Fagles 1977, 16). On a feminist reading, the "progress" of the trilogy can be read as justification for patriarchal rule (Irigaray 1993b, 12–13; Zeitlin 1978). More specifically, the judgment of Orestes's matricide as justifiable by the men of Athens, and their patron goddess can be read as a condemnation of Clytemnestra's revolutionary violence against patriarchal order. Clytemnestra has valued the life of her sacrificed daughter and her own sexual autonomy over her husband's life.

Froma Zeitlin draws attention to the way that *The Oresteia* progressively displaces Iphigenia's sacrifice by her father (1978, 159–60). While Iphigenia's killing is explicitly related by the chorus of elders (Aeschylus 2008, 195–250) and invoked by Clytemnestra in the first play (1418–20), the second play only alludes to her death once. Electra, the surviving daughter of Clytemnestra and Agamemnon, speaks of "the sister who was piteously sacrificed" (241), although she does not name her father as her sister's killer. In the third play, Iphigenia and the circumstances of her death receive no mention. Arguably, there is an implicit reference to the sacredness of the mother-daughter bond, though this is expressed in violent negation. In a laughably misogynist speech at Orestes's trial, Apollo discounts the mother-child bond by claiming that the father is the sole origin of the child and that the "so-called mother" is merely a "stranger" who houses the father's "seed" (657–74). He even invokes the birth of his half-sister, Athena, from the head of Zeus to affirm that the father does not need a woman to beget a child. Apollo's speech is explicitly directed at discounting the significance of Orestes's matricide. Implicitly, we can also read his speech as a way of nullifying the importance of Clytemnestra's claim in the first play of the trilogy that she killed Agamemnon to get justice for her murdered daughter. In a remark directed at Aristotle's metaphysics that can apply equally to Apollo's account of the cause of reproduction, Irigaray writes: "Every utterance, every statement, will thus be developed and affirmed by covering over the fact that being's unseverable relation to mother-matter has been buried" (1985a, 162).

For Irigaray, one of the senses of "original matricide" is that the love relationship between mother and daughter cannot be symbolized or respected in patriarchal culture (1993b, 11). To do so would threaten the order of things; it would allow for a relationship between women in which men have no direct role. Apollo's account of the origin of the child as exclusively masculine, which anticipates Aristotle's account of reproduction, also betrays, through its inversion of the facts of reproduction, just how threatening maternity is to the patriarchal order of things.[4] It is unspeakable.

Stepping back from the specific context of *The Oresteia*, Irigaray's critique of phallocentrism shows us that woman is not a subject in her own right. Woman functions as a use-value to male subjects; she is the provider of the free labor of maternity (even though the mother is disavowed as a primary cause of human offspring) and of sexual service to men (which, for Irigaray, is not clearly distinguished from the maternal function) (1993a, 41). As she argues, the only proper position for woman in the patriarchal order is as mother (as the place for the father's seed to grow and as the caregiver of "his" children) (10). Woman is denied the very possibility of autonomous subjectivity. Furthermore, in monotheist traditions, woman is also denied a specific relationship to the divine; God is always written in the masculine and women's relations to God are mediated by men (1993a, 6–7; 1993b, 61–62, 64, 78).

For Irigaray, woman is left in a state of placelessness or dereliction—abandoned by God and homeless. She is homeless because woman gives place to man (the intrauterine place during pregnancy, the vagina as a sexual place in heterosexual coitus) but has no place of her own as a subject and no place to share with other women (as friends or as lovers). This makes woman-to-woman sociality or relations between women very difficult. Margaret Whitford explains that "women suffer from an inability to individuate themselves, 'from confusion of identity between them,' from lack of respect for, or more often lack of perception of, the other woman as different" (Whitford 1991, 79).

The Sacrifice of Natural Fertility

How is the founding matricide related to the argument that nature is instrumentalized as a resource for man? In "Women, the Sacred, and Money," Irigaray makes explicit that she reads the founding matricide as a sacrifice of natural fertility (1993b). The fertility of women is harnessed to reproduction of patriarchal society; procreation and maternal labor are enacted for free and yet in a real way uphold the very functioning of patriarchal cultures (81–82). More obliquely, patriarchal societies are founded on the sacrifice of the natural fertility of life on earth–of animals and plants, of the oceans, of the air (80). For instance, in Genesis, plants and animals are placed by God under the dominion of man (Gen. 1:26). Along with women, the extraordinary variety and multitude of life forms are conflated into functioning as resources for man's benefit and use.

I suggest that this is why Irigaray often deploys "nature," "natural fertility," "life," and "woman" interchangeably in her corpus. This gesture is evident from her early work to her most recent publications. For example, in *Speculum of the Other Woman*, some of her inscriptions of "woman" can be read as a synecdoche for the nontotalizable multiplicity of nature (1985a, 227–29). In her recent book, *In the Beginning, She Was*, Irigaray deploys the phrase "nature, woman, or Goddess" (2013, 3) to designate natural fertility prior to and in excess of "its" instrumentalization in the evolution of Western phallocentric thought and social relations. In homage to Irigaray and as a gesture of revaluing the feminine aspects of existence, in contrast to the misogynist denigration of the hegemonic formation of Western thought, I call nontotalizable nature the Common Mother.[5]

The sacrifice of natural fertility is occluded by Western systems of representation that function to cover over man's debt to the fertility of the earth and to the human mother who gave birth to him. Irigaray writes: "The race of men lays a second ground underfoot, creates a meaning substance that supposedly knows no gender. This substance is almost tautologically opened up toward heaven, man's heaven, which he believes to be the source of things" (1993b, 121). In the capitalist economies of modernity, words such as "growth" and "creation" are deployed to describe the generation of jobs by industries such as mining. In contrast, the creativity of life and the growth of living beings have no value, except in being harnessed to the projects of man.

In short, the Western tradition valorizes a conceptual and social architecture that is isomorphic with phallic masculinity, while traces of the feminine, the maternal, and the Common Mother are devalued. This cover-up is not entirely successful, and traces of the awesome and inhuman power of life are legible in culture, though they are often denigrated and attacked as a way to ward off the acknowledgment of what has been covered up. We see this today in acts of misogynist violence by some (many) men against women and in the wanton destructiveness toward what is called "nature" in various industrial practices (such as fracking and the clear-fell logging of old-growth forests). For Irigaray, we need a revolution in thought and ethics in order to engender human societies that are respectful of natural fertility (1993a, 6; 1993b, 81).

For Country Never Leaves Its People

I deploy the terms "Aboriginal," "Indigenous," and "First Nations peoples" in this chapter to designate collectively the First Nations peoples of Australia. In doing so, I am following the writing practices of many Indigenous writers, especially the Goenpul/Nunukul scholar Aileen Moreton-Robinson of the Quandamooka First Nation (2013); Irene Watson, a woman of the Tanganekald and Meintangk peoples (2015); and Wright, who is of the Waanyi Nation (2002; 2013). The First Nations peoples of Australia are not a homogenous group; as the legal theorist and philosopher Watson explains, the idea of Australian Aboriginal people as being "one big mob" is a colonial myth (Watson 2015, 20). Before the British Empire's colonization began in 1788, there were over five hundred language groups in the place that is now known as Australia (Moreton-Robinson 2013, 340). Each of these groups had sovereign relations to tracts of land or "country" (340). While these civilizations are distinct from one another, they also share a fundamental sense of their being as emanating from their relation to "country." The word "country" derives from Aboriginal English and expresses a living relationship. For Jay Arthur:

> The words that Aboriginal people use about country express a living relationship. The country may be mother or grandfather, which grows them up and is grown up by them. These kinship terms impose mutual responsibilities of caring and keeping upon the land and people . . . For many Indigenous Australians, person and place, or "country," are virtually interchangeable. (Arthur in Nicholls 2014, 4)

Sovereign relations to country were established during the origin time in which the form of social living was created by ancestral beings. "The ancestral beings created animals, plants, humans, and the physiographic features of the country associated with them" (Moreton-Robinson 2013, 340). They also established the Indigenous ways of life: laws for its social institutions and patterns of activity (340; Watson 2015, 12–13).

> From Kaldowinyeri [origin time], Nungas have lived as sovereign peoples, respecting and recognizing the sovereignty of others and having independent authority over a territory. Hundreds of First Nations in existence at the time of colonization (many of

> them surviving post-invasion) are evidence of this respect and recognition for each other. (Watson 2015, 152)

Aboriginal sovereignty is nothing like the Western conception of sovereignty. Where the Western sense of sovereignty designates the exclusive ownership of a territory or of some thing or some one that I have mastery over, Indigenous sovereignty emanates from relationality. For Watson, this relationality "is embedded in Indigenous knowledge systems; 'knowledge belongs to a people and the people belong to a landscape' " (13). Australian Indigenous ontologies elaborate an interconnectedness of country, ancestors, totems, people, animals, plants, rivers, oceans, the wind—that is, an interconnectedness of all "things." Strictly speaking, there are no "things" that can be isolated and counted in quantitative terms. The Aboriginal sense of country is not a mass that can be carved up into pieces of property or instrumentalized through the technologies of man; country is the common spirit-body to which a people belong. For instance, in *The Swan Book,* when the lake people listen to Bella Donna's stories of the destruction of her homeland in the northern hemisphere, they say that "country can never leave its people" (Wright 2013, 26). Their relationship to country continues even in the face of hundreds of years of the genocidal practices of settler colonialism. In the lake people's understanding, Bella Donna's mutilated country still lives in her stories, in her imagination, in her relationships with others.

The sense in which country can never leave its people must be understood in terms of the Aboriginal sense of time. Time in Indigenous ontologies is starkly different from the chronological time of "progress." What do I mean by chronological time? Chronological time is a linear figuration which orders events into a sequence and privileges the present. In this focus on the present, there is a displacement of the past. For instance, in the late 1990s, the then prime minister of Australia, John Howard, refused to apologize to the Stolen Generations—generations of children subjected to cultural genocide by being taken from their Aboriginal families and forced into government- and church-run orphanages and foster homes where they were forced to assimilate into white Australian culture. The prime minister justified his refusal to apologize for the genocide by saying "the past is the past" (as though lived experience in the chronological present is not inhabited by the past!).

Wright speaks about the Aboriginal concept of time in an essay written in the aftermath of the Howard government's refusal to apologize to the Stolen Generations (Wright 2002, 20). In stark contrast to the former prime minister's reductive and denialist figuration of time, Wright says:

> All times are important to us. No time has ended and all worlds are possible. [. . .] The world I try to inhabit in my writing is like looking at the ancestral tracks spanning our traditional country which, if I look at the land, combines all stories, all realities from the ancient to the new, and makes it one—like all the strands in a long rope. Our stories are like the music which feeds the soul and the heart, which sometimes flies above the bitterness of pure logic and rational thought and soars like an eagle, as a friend of mine would say, above the turkeys below. (Ibid.)

Wright is describing a nonlinear way of understanding time in which all times exist together and do not cease to be. All worlds are possible, which is to say that there are infinite possibilities in coexisting and overlapping dimensions. This multidimensional time is the origin time, which is often called the Dreaming (Nicholls 2014). It is the time in which the ancestors or Spirit Beings make land and laws. Time is place; country "itself" is made by the tracks of the ancestors, and events can be seen by looking at the land. The Dreaming is not exiled into the inaccessible past; it is immanent to the process of living. As Watson explains the ontology of her people: "Kaldowinyeri [the Dreaming], or a long time ago, in the beginning, is also the time now, and time into the future. The beginning, the present, and the future encircle the place of Kaldowinyeri" (Watson 2015, 16).

Nowhere Special

In chronological terms, much of *The Swan Book* is set at the end of the twenty-first century. Climate catastrophe is devastating the planet, and human civilizations are embroiled in catastrophic wars and famines. In the novel, chronological time is conceptualized as the time of nihilism. "In every neck of the woods people walked in the imagination of doomsayers and talked the language of extinction" (Wright 2013, 6). The novel is set mainly in and around a lake in northern Australian where an Aboriginal community lives. In her mind, Oblivia calls this place "Nowhere Special" (2013, 54). This can be read to suggest that nowhere is special *and* that now, here, is special. Perhaps this is a way of saying that all is sacred. The people of the lake live in abject poverty and the lake is heavily polluted. Early in the novel, the place gets turned into a detention center for the processing of refugees and displaced Aboriginal people from other parts of the continent of Australia.[6] A coercive and racist government-led intervention in which the army controls the lives of Aboriginal people is ongoing.[7] The army is also involved in carrying out military tests on the ancestral country of the lake people.[8]

Bella Donna of the Champions is an old white woman from the northern hemisphere, a refugee of the climate-change wars (23). She arrived at the lake before the detention center was built, and the local Aboriginal community, while wary of her, let her stay on their country (32). She lives on a wrecked boat hull that floats in the water, rather than among the shanties of the local people at the edge of the lake. She tells extraordinary stories and believes that she has the power to call swans. She attributes her survival in the climate-change wars to a white swan that guided her and other refugees away from catastrophe when her country was destroyed (17).

Oblivia is a local Aboriginal girl who was lost for ten years after being gang-raped by a group of youths who were high from petrol-sniffing (82). She is found by Bella Donna in the bowel of a giant and ancient eucalyptus tree. Bella Donna sees herself as Oblivia's savior: "Remember who it was who rescued you with her bare hands" (20). Oblivia lives with Bella Donna on the wrecked ship hull in the lake. Where Bella Donna has an affinity with the white swans of the northern hemisphere, the girl is related to black swans of the southern hemisphere. Oblivia does not acknowledge herself as kin to the lake people, and her Aboriginal parents no longer recognize her as their child (11). But she is nonetheless of the tree, of the ancestors:

> There was a story about a sacred tree where all the stories of the swamp were stored like doctrines of Law left by the spiritual ancestors, of a place so sacred, it was unthinkable that it should be violated. [. . .] When the girl was found though, the tree was destroyed by the Army on the premise that this nexus of dangerous beliefs had to be broken, to close the gap between Aboriginal people and white people. Those stories scattered into the winds were still about, but where, that was the problem now. It made us strong and gave us hope that tree. The kinspeople of the tree had believed this since time immemorial. [. . .] They were too speechless to talk about a loss that was so great, it made them feel unhinged from their own bodies, unmoored, vulnerable, separated from eternity. They had been cut off. They called themselves damned people who felt like strangers walking around on their country. (78–79)

When Oblivia lives in the bough of the tree, she writes or is written by an ancient sacred language (7–8). The tree took her in and nursed her; she is of the tree. Later in the book, Oblivia yearns for the tree, especially in the wake of Bella Donna's death.

Muteness and Silence

After Bella Donna pulls her out of the tree, Oblivia is mute. The idea of woman going mute in the aftermath of rape is canonical in the Western literary tradition. In book 6 of Ovid's *Metamorphoses*, Philomela is raped by her brother-in-law, Tereus, the king of Thrace. In an attempt to evade the discovery of his crime by his wife, Philomela's sister Procne, Tereus cuts out Philomela's tongue and confines her to a remote castle. Philomela weaves a tapestry that narrates her violation and gets a servant to smuggle the tapestry to her sister (Ovid, 423–674).[9] Modern versions of the trope of the raped mute woman can be found in the fiction of, for example, the nineteenth-century French writer Honoré de Balzac and in the contemporary South African writer J. M. Coetzee. In Balzac's short story "Adieu," Stephanie is reduced to a near-mute stupor after being gang-raped by French soldiers during the Napoleonic army's disastrous retreat from Russia in the campaign of 1812 (2012). When Stephanie is found years later by her former lover, Philippe, she does not recognize him, and he tries to "cure" her by getting her to recognize him as her beloved. Stephanie does finally recognize Philippe; she says his name, declares her love for him, and, immediately upon uttering her declaration, dies.[10] The status of sexual violence and its silencing in phallocentrism is a central concern of J. M. Coetzee's postapartheid novel, *Disgrace* (2000). The main character, David Lurie is dismissed from his position as a university professor after he is reported for coercing a woman student into a sexual relationship. At the university hearing into the incident, David refuses to listen to the written testimony of the student he has assaulted. Later in the novel, after David's daughter, Lucy, is gang-raped on her farm, she refuses to report the attack to the police and largely refuses her father's demands to tell him about her experience.[11]

In Wright's feminist novel, Oblivia does not speak. The lake people regard her as a "dumb girl" (Wright 2013, 11). But Oblivia's speechlessness is not a stupor, nor is it a symptom of passivity. She has *decided* not to speak, that it is not worth speaking.[12] "She would rather be silent since the last word she had spoken when scared out of her wits, the day when her tongue had screeched to a halt with dust flying everywhere, and was left screaming Ahhhhhh! Through the bushland, when she fell down the hollow of a tree" (19).

An important aspect of woman's usefulness in phallocentrism is to perform heterosexual service for men. Rape renders this heterosexual service incoherent in many circumstances, since according to the terms of patriarchal logic, rape is premised upon the question of whether a particular man has the right to fuck a particular woman, and that boils down to his relations with other men, rather than to the woman's desire or lack of desire to fuck the man. This is one of the senses in which we can read Irigaray's remark that "woman is never anything but the locus of a more or less competitive exchange between men, including the competition for Mother Earth" (1985b, 31–32). Western thought devalues and disregards woman's voice. This emanates from woman's lack of agency as a subject; how can a woman choose to make love or not to make love if she has no autonomy as a woman subject? To give a famous example, Paris of Troy's infraction against the Spartan king Menelaus is Paris' failure to respect the king's exclusive right to his "property," his wife, Helen. Paris disrespects his homosocial bond with his host, Menelaus; Helen's voice we do not hear.

As readers of *The Swan Book,* we hear what's going on in Oblivia's head. And while she does not speak in words, she utters low-frequency noises and "copycats" Bella Donna's "nicely spoken words," though she "prefers the tempo of the local dialect, to interpret like a local [. . .] with her tongue tapping around behind closed lips" (22). Oblivia also engages in what I read as psychic communication with the black swans, with other spirits, with the Harbour Master, and with Bella Donna. Bella Donna, who is something of a white crusader, both in her claim to interpret Oblivia's thoughts and in her image of herself as Oblivia's rescuer (20), often hears what she wants to hear. She claims to know that "the girl had never recovered from being raped" (19), and she is frustrated by the girl's silence. She tells Oblivia:

> "You must use the voice."
> The girl thought that she should be silent if words were just a geographical device to be transplanted anywhere on earth. Then if that were possible: Was it possible for her voice to be heard by imaginary people too? (23)

Bella Donna's attitude to speech is congruent with the Western idea that using the voice is a way to influence people and action (23). Silence in the dichotomous logic of Western culture is conflated with passivity and absence. While Oblivia's decision to stop speaking is provoked by the trauma of gang rape, her continued resistance to human speech has a philosophical and ethical basis. Where Bella Donna thinks that words can be used to influence people "across the world," Oblivia does not want to use words if they are "merely a geographical device to be transplanted anywhere on earth" (23). *The Swan Book* does not say why she thinks this, though I read it as a fidelity to the tempo of the place in which she lives and to the sacred tree, which nursed her. She lives in fidelity to her milieu. Whereas Bella Donna says of herself that "she is not really here and not really there" (24), Oblivia belongs to country. According to the swamp people, she lives as "though she had by-passed human history, by being directly descended from their ancestral tree" (11).

Irigaray, Sexuate Difference, and the Sensible-Transcendental

Irigaray makes an ontological argument for the primacy of life and the need for human beings to respect life in the broadest sense, something which the death project of modernity fails to do. Since life cannot be negotiated with, we, as human beings, must work out a way to cultivate a respectful relationship to life (Irigaray and Marder 2016, 19). For Irigaray, all of life is sexed (Irigaray1993b, 108). She argues that building an ethics that foregrounds the sexually differentiated nature of human being is a necessary step in affirming ourselves as living aspects of non-totalizable nature (Irigaray 2015, 105).

> Sexual difference would constitute the horizon of worlds more fecund than any known to date—at least in the West—and without reducing fecundity to the reproduction of bodies and flesh. For loving partners this would be a fecundity of birth and regeneration, but also the production of a new age of thought, art, poetry, and language: the creation of a new poetics. (Irigaray 1993a, 5)

In Irigaray's corpus, sexuate difference is primarily theorized as the difference that engenders two human subjects in relation to one another who remain irreducible to each other: woman and man. She distinguishes three different modes of relation that are specific to the two human sexes. First, both sexes are born of woman, but their respective relationships to the mother are different. A little girl learns that she is like her mother and has the capacity, at least potentially, to give birth to an infant. The little boy, in contrast, is in the space of an unfathomable mystery. He learns that he is a different sex from his mother and can never engender from within himself (1995, 12–13). Second, Irigaray distinguishes the way in which women and men relate to one another in heterosexual coitus. Woman's experience of carnal contact with the other occurs from a cavity folded within her own body. Man's contact with woman occurs outside of his body through the envelopment of his penis by a vagina (1993b, 51).[13] Third, Irigaray suggests that there are differences between the sexes in the use of language. Through linguistic research she has conducted with children and adolescents, Irigaray claims that she found that male subjects tend to form sentences that favor subject-object formulations, while female subjects tend to create sentences that privilege intersubjective relationships. For instance, when Irigaray asked adolescents to use the words "with" and "together" in sentences, the girls created sentences such as "I'll go out with him tonight" and "we will always be together," while the boys formed sentences such as "I wrote this with my pencil" and "Me and my guitar are good together" (1995, 15–16).[14]

These sexuate relations are both embodied *and* conceptual; for Irigaray, they describe the very conditions of human being. The relations are not added to an existing world and a sexed subject (woman or man); they engender the very possibility of being a sexuate subject and having a world. For Irigaray, the giving of world to a woman is not substitutable with the giving of world to a man; world and subject are sexed. As conditions of being and becoming sexuate human beings, these relational formations are inhuman. Irigaray is dismissive of the legitimacy of trans subjectivities (Irigaray 1996, 61–62). In my view, this is a significant limitation in her thinking. A philosophy of sexuate difference should affirm woman and man *and* the living becoming of trans and what are called "nonbinary" sexes.[15] The task of becoming woman, the task of becoming man, the task of becoming trans is something that each woman and each man and each trans person must accomplish. This emerges in the most intimate and immediate aspects of human life.

Central to the tasks of becoming woman, becoming trans, and becoming man is the affirmation of the sensible-transcendental or interval. This strange "concept" is a synecdoche for something that remains essentially in excess of symbolization and cannot be said. As I read Irigaray, the sensible-transcendental designates the relationship of a sexed subject to the nontotalizable becoming of "nature" (the Common Mother). The Common Mother is not a thing, nor something "we" get a grip on, for it is the whole of time-space (of infinite dimensions) that is beyond our understanding or even of a super-human understanding. The Common Mother remains open and in becoming. The sensible-transcendental is a threshold to this mysterious "whole" of which we are tiny aspects. This threshold is embodied in my flesh, in the rhythm of my breath, in the myriad relationships I have with other bodies surrounding me (male, female or trans, human or inhuman, living or nonliving). Acknowledging the sensible-transcendental is what situates me in place, in a specific milieu.[16]

In Irigaray's thought, the sensible-transcendental is a relational threshold from which I as a woman exist and become. This interval establishes me as an embodied and spiritual being in relation to the community of women who are my sisters (contemporaries) and to a genealogy of women who precede me and will come after me (to figure this in linear terms). As women, we are different from one another *and* we share a gender. These relations of difference must be cultivated and affirmed if I am not to confuse myself with the subjectivity of another woman. The sensible-transcendental also establishes me in relation to the other sex—the male sex, and each man is situated in the horizontal community of men and the vertical genealogy of men.[17] For Irigaray, the sensible-transcendental between the two sexes is the fundamental ontological difference. Irigaray believes that it is in acknowledging the sexed other of the other sex (woman for a man and man for a woman) that the irreducibility of the outside is sensed and an ethics of respect for life can be articulated. The sensible-transcendental is also the sexually specific threshold of the milieus which nourish me as a woman such as the air, other nonhuman animals, and plants. And I would add that the sensible-transcendental also places me in a relation of sexed difference from a trans subject, who has a specific passage of becoming in the articulation of their subjectivity that is different from me as a cis woman and different from the becoming of a cis man.

Irigaray deploys a variety of "words" for the sensible-transcendental or interval. Strictly speaking, they are neither words nor concepts, but are, rather, finite figures. The intervals that she describes are not reducible to one another. Each modality of interval has a sense that emerges in the context of describing relationships that come to be in specific milieus. Many of her figurations of the interval designate relations between the two human sexes (the angel, love, the approach, the space of silence) (Irigaray 1993a;

1996; 2008). Some are modalities that are peculiar to woman (the lips, the mucous) (1985b; 1993a). There is at least one instance in which she posits an interval to describe the openness of an oeuvre to future readings that cannot be anticipated (the remainder) (1993a, 8).

There are, furthermore, inscriptions of an explicitly posthumanist thinking of the sensible-transcendental in Irigaray. For instance, she posits air as a fundamental condition of life on earth (Irigaray 2000). To avow air as an interval is to avow that air is not only material; air is permeated with the transcendental. The affirmation of air as sensible-transcendental—a substance that is enmeshed in the milieus of many animal and plant species on this planet—takes the postulation of the interval beyond sexual difference and beyond human being. While Irigaray does not spell it out in didactic terms, we must affirm the transcendental permeating the entire extent of sensible being and insensible being.

Toward Articulations of Language and Gestures That Respect Place

In *The Swan Book*, the character of Bella Donna believes in the power of the voice being used to influence people across the world (Wright 2013, 23). In contrast, Irigaray emphasizes the power of silence in relation to speech. She is explicit regarding the fact that words cannot say everything and should not try to (Irigaray and Marder 2016, 7). Her thinking on the interval is precisely an effort to articulate "what" eludes the metaphysics of presence, without destroying it by claiming to say "what it is" (7). In the context of relations between two women, the very mystery of the sensible-transcendental grounds their situation as a relationship between two different subjects. It is my sense that Oblivia's decision to remain silent in the face of Bella Donna's demand that Oblivia use her voice can be read in resonance with Irigaray's "concept" of the sensible-transcendental, which, as I have indicated, Irigaray also calls a "space of silence" (Wright 2013, 23; Irigaray 2008).[18]

Irigaray articulates multiple modalities of the sensible-transcendental, and each figure of the sensible-transcendental has a specific sense, albeit an allusive and mysterious sense. For instance, the mucous is especially related to woman's subjectivity (Irigaray 1993a, 110–11). Insofar as a woman is a living universal subject, the mucous can be conceived, at least potentially, in relation to a woman anywhere on earth. And yet, as material, mucous only emerges in relation to a woman in a concrete situation; "it is only in an *act* that the mucous perceives and loves itself without thesis, without position outside itself. The potency achieves 'its' act which is never set in a finished piece of work" (111). When there is a passage to the mucous, "its" advent is singular.

For Irigaray, the thought of the interval emerges from a place (or milieu), and respect for that milieu in which the subject experiences the sensible-transcendental is fundamental to "what" "it" "is." Spirituality has its roots in the natural environment and is not separate from living matter (Irigaray, 1993b, 191).[19] For Irigaray, the task of cultivating a relational ontology is a matter of daily practices of "art" in gestures taken up by every woman and every man. This involves an attentiveness to the moment of becoming, an effort not to sacrifice anything or anybody (Irigaray 2013, 22). The writing of the interval—which can never be presented as such—and the articulation of gestures which respect the sensible-transcendental are central to this task.

I have suggested that Oblivia's open mental question on whether her voice can be heard by imaginary people be read to suggest that spoken language can only have meaning when connected to place (Wright 2013, 23). I do not want to claim that Oblivia's thinking on the voice and words articulates a coherent philosophical and ethical position; she is struggling with the trauma of sexual violence and settler colonialism or what is referred to in *The Swan Book* as "the virus" (1–5, 329–34). Sometimes her affects towards others are hostile—for instance, in her relationship towards the Harbour Master when he comes to visit Bella Donna (38). And while Oblivia's hostile thoughts can be read as resistance to the colonizing acts of Bella Donna or the dismissive attitude of the Harbour Master, I am not suggesting these affects should be celebrated as ethical gestures of conduct from which we should learn. I do think that Oblivia's fidelity to the tree and to the black swans is attentive to her living milieu in a way that resonates with Irigaray's call for a relational ethics and practice of sexuate difference.

In *The Swan Book*, Oblivia and the local people live in cyclical time, in spite of the genocidal incursion of modern chronological time. "It was hell to pay to be living the warfare of modernity like dogs fighting over the lineage of progress against their own quiet whorls of time. Well! That just about summed up the lake people, sitting for all times in one place" (Wright 2013, 12). To be sitting for all times in one place is to live place as the quiet whorls of time. Irigaray's thinking on the sensible-transcendental is also a cyclical figuring of time. To be attentive to the moment without sacrifice is to be in place without pulverizing events into a linear chain in which the present displaces the past. "The interval always remains in play as place or the possibility of place" (Irigaray 1993a, 48).

In the effort to challenge global nihilism, Irigaray rethinks the frames of thought and perception in a way that strives to be faithful to life. Her claim that this requires an ethics of sexuate difference is crucially important. But perhaps it is not necessary that the primary orientation of a relational philosophy be turned towards the sexuate human other, woman or man. For Oblivia's character, the primary challenge would seem to be in her attentiveness to the black swans and to the sacred tree. Where Bella Donna believes in the power of rescuing vulnerable others, a philosophy that is fundamentally relational would be one which recognizes that we are all tiny aspects of larger milieus. Our ethics and thoughts should emanate from a respect for what is larger than us, the common-spirit body to which we all belong, in which we all are and become in the quiet whorls of time. Then we are not saviors (or killers) but aspects of a larger, nontotalizable nature—the Common Mother.

Notes

1. The phrase "global death project" is drawn from Seely 2017, 44.

2. There are a few texts focused on the importance of woman-to-woman sociality in Irigaray's thought. See Muraro 1994; Schwab 1998, 2010; and Whitford 1991.

3. Irene Watson also argues that Irigaray's thinking on cyclical time is similar to Aboriginal philosophical thought. See Watson 2015, 25. And see Seely, who finds important common ground between the ontology of the Kogi people of South America and Irigaray's thought (2017).

4. Irigaray elaborates a brilliant deconstruction of Aristotle's account of reproduction in "How to Conceive of a Girl" (See 1985a 160–67). I read her text with Aristotle in chapter 1 of Hill 2012.

5. In relation to the term "mother earth," Naomi Klein writes: "The gender essentialism of the term still makes some people uncomfortable. But it seems to me that the specifically female nature is not of central importance. Whether we choose to see the earth as a mother, a father, a parent, or an ungendered force of creation, what matters is that we are acknowledging that we are not in charge, that we are part of a vast living system on which we depend. The earth, wrote the great ecologist Stan Rowe, is not merely 'resource' but 'source' " (Klein 2014, 443–44).

6. Since 1992, successive Australian governments have incarcerated asylum seekers in detention centers for processing their asylum claims. The government specifically targeted asylum seekers who tried to arrive in Australia on boats. At the time of writing, most of these people have been found to be refugees but many of them remain imprisoned in offshore detention on Nauru and on Manus Island in Papua New Guinea. For a brief history of Australian government policy towards refugees and asylum seekers, see the Refugee Council of Australia Timeline.

7. The "Intervention" depicted in *The Swan Book* is a clear allusion to the Australian Federal government's Northern Territory Emergency Response Act, which is known colloquially as "the Intervention" into remote Aboriginal communities in the Northern Territory. For an analysis and critique of the "Intervention," see Watson 2009 and 2011.

8. This can be read as a reference to the atomic tests conducted by the British military with Australian government and military backing at Maralinga in the South Australian desert between 1953 and 1963. Many Aboriginal people died or were injured, and vast swatches of country were heavily polluted by the fallout from these bombs. British and Australian servicemen also contracted, and died from, illnesses related to the tests (see Tynan 2016).

9. For a reading of this gruesome myth, see Klindienst-Joplin's "The Voice of the Shuttle Is Ours" (1991). Joplin's outstanding essay attends to the double violation of Philomela in suffering rape and the severing of her tongue by Tereus and to the way that masculinist literary criticism has occluded this sexed violence by appropriating the story for other purposes.

10. For a classic feminist reading of the sexual violence of Balzac's story and of the illegibility of sexual violence in realist literary criticism, see Felman 1993.

11. For a feminist analysis of the central status of sexual violence in the novel *Disgrace*, see Graham 2003.

12. In *Disgrace*, Lucy also decides on silence, but the narration of the novel is focalized around her father's character, which leaves Lucy's experience and her decision to remain silent largely beyond our horizon of knowing (see Graham 2003, 44).

13. While Irigaray's presentation of the experience of carnal contact is heteronormative, she is making an important claim about the physical and morphological irreducibility of experiencing carnal contact through a vagina or experiencing carnal contact through a penis (see Hill 2012, 81, 163 n26).

14. For a detailed account of Irigaray's research on the problem of language and relational identity, see Schwab 2016.

15. The use of the term "nonbinary" is often left vague in trans and queer discourses. In Irigarayan terms, a binary model of sex only elaborates features of the male sex and figures the female as lacking the features that define maleness. Sexuate difference is not a postulation of binary sexes because each sex has "its" own specificity which is not reducible to the other sex. For a more detailed discussion of this point, see Hill 2017, 39. A philosophical elaboration of the status of trans subjectivities in the thinking of sexual difference is an important task, but it lies beyond the scope of the present essay to address this problem in any detail.

16. For Irigaray and for me, place designates a relationship between bodies that cannot be reduced to presence. The sensible-transcendental or interval is what makes place, and place is always open. For a detailed elaboration of this point, see chapters 2 and 3 of Hill 2012.

17. For a detailed elaboration of Irigaray's concepts of vertical and horizontal relations, see Deutscher 1994 and Schwab 2011.

18. Irigaray deploys the "space of silence" in *Sharing the World* to indicate the sensible-transcendental between woman and man (2008). As I read her, this modality of interval is also a threshold in relations between women. In the context of her recent writing on the profound significance of the vegetal, the space of silence must be safeguarded in the nonhierarchical relation of woman to vegetal being. She speculates that this is the case for Michael Marder, her male collaborator on their book *Through Vegetal Being* (2016, 6–7).

19. See Irigaray's remarks on the importance of composing *Speculum of the Other Woman* in the woods and by the sea (Irigaray and Marder 2016, 12).

Works Cited

Aeschylus. 2008. *Oresteia: Agamemnon, Libation-Bearers, Eumenides*. Edited and translated by Alan H. Sommerstein. Cambridge, MA, and London: Harvard University Press, Loeb Classical Library.

Balzac, Honoré de. 2012. *Adieu*. Translated by Katharine Prescott Wormeley. La Verne: Ingram.

The Book of Genesis. http://www.vatican.va/archive/bible/genesis/documents/bible_genesis_en.html.

Coetzee, J. M. 2000. *Disgrace*. Harmondsworth: Penguin.

Deutscher, Penelope. 1994. " 'The Only Diabolical Thing about Women': Luce Irigaray on Divinity." *Hypatia: A Journal of Feminist Philosophy* 9: 88–111.

Fagles, Robert. 1977. "A Reading of *The Oresteia*: The Serpent and the Eagle." In Aeschylus, *The Oresteia*. Translated by Robert Fagles. Harmondsworth: Penguin.

Felman, Shoshana. 1993. "Women and Madness: The Critical Phallacy." In *What Does a Woman Want? Reading and Sexual Difference*. Baltimore and London: Johns Hopkins University Press.

Glissant, Édouard. 1989. *Caribbean Discourse*. Translated by J. Michael Dash. Charlottesville: University Press of Virginia.

Graham, Lucy. 2003. "Reading the Unspeakable: Rape in J. M. Coetzee's *Disgrace*." *Journal of Southern African Studies* 29, no. 2: 433–44.

Hill, Rebecca. 2012. *The Interval: Relation and Becoming in Irigaray, Aristotle and Bergson*. New York: Fordham.

———. 2017. "At Least Two: The Tendencies of Sexual Difference." *Australian Feminist Law Journal* 43, no. 1: 25–40.

Irigaray, Luce. 1985a. *Speculum of the Other Woman*. Translated by Gillian C. Gill. Ithaca, NY: Cornell University Press.

———. 1985b. *This Sex Which Is Not One*. Translated by Catherine Porter. Ithaca, NY: Cornell University Press.

———. 1993a. *An Ethics of Sexual Difference*. Translated by Carolyn C. Burke and Gillian C. Gill. Ithaca, New York: Cornell University Press.

———. 1993b. *Sexes and Genealogies*. Translated by Gillian C. Gill. New York: Columbia University Press.

———. 1995. "The Question of the Other." *Yale French Studies* 87: 12–13.

———. 1996. *I Love to You: Sketch of a Possible Felicity in History.* Translated by Alison Martin. New York and London: Routledge.

———. 2000. *The Forgetting of Air in Martin Heidegger.* Translated by Mary Beth Mader. Austin: University of Texas Press.

———. 2008. *Sharing the World.* Translated by Heidi Bostic and Stephen Pluháček. London: Continuum.

———. 2013. *In the Beginning, She Was*. London and New York: Bloomsbury.

———. 2015. "Starting from Ourselves as Living Beings." *The Journal of the British Society of Phenomenology* 46, no. 2: 101–08.

Irigaray, Luce, and Michael Marder. 2016. *Through Vegetal Being: Two Philosophical Perspectives*. New York: Columbia University Press.

Klein, Naomi. 2014. *This Changes Everything: Capitalism vs. the Climate.* Harmondsworth: Penguin.

Klindienst-Joplin, Patricia. 1991. "The Voice of the Shuttle Is Ours." In *Rape and Representation*, edited by Lynn A. Higgins and Brenda R. Silver. New York: Columbia University Press.

Moreton-Robinson, Aileen. 2013. "Toward an Australian Indigenous Women's Standpoint Theory." *Australian Feminist Studies* 28, no. 78: 331–47.

Muraro, Luisa. 1994. "Female Genealogies." In *Engaging with Irigaray*, edited by Carolyn Burke, Naomi Schor, and Margaret Whitford. New York: Columbia University Press.

Nicholls, Christine. 2014. " 'Dreamings' and dreaming narratives: What's the relationship?" *The Conversation* February 6. http://theconversation.com/dreamings-and-dreaming-narratives-whats-the-relationship-20837.

Ovid. 1955. *The Metamorphoses of Ovid.* Translated by Mary M. Innes. Harmondsworth: Penguin.

Refugee Council of Australia Timeline. https://www.refugeecouncil.org.au/getfacts/timeline/.

Schwab, Gail. 1998. "Sexual Difference as Model: An Ethics for the Global Future." *Diacritics* 28, no. 1: 76–92.

———. 2010. "Mothers, Sisters and Daughters: Luce Irigaray and the Female Genealogical Line in the Stories of the Greeks." In *Rewriting Difference: Irigaray and "the Greeks,"* edited by Elena Tzelepis and Athena Athanasiou. Albany: State University of New York Press.

———. 2011. "Beyond the Vertical and the Horizontal: Spirituality, Space, and Alterity in the Work of Luce Irigaray." In *Thinking with Irigaray*, edited by Mary Rawlinson, Sabrina Hom, and Serene Khader. Albany: State University of New York Press.

———. 2016. "Creating Inter-Sexuate Inter-Subjectivity in the Classroom? Luce Irigaray's Linguistic Research in Its Latest Iteration." In *Engaging the World: Thinking after Irigaray*, edited by Mary Rawlinson. Albany: State University of New York Press.

Seely, Stephen D. 2017. "Irigaray between God and the Indians: Sexuate Difference, Decoloniality and the Politics of Ontology." *Australian Feminist Law Journal* 43, no. 1: 41–65.

Tynan, Lyz. 2016. "Sixty Years On, the Maralinga Bomb Tests Remind Us Not to Put Security over Safety," *The Conversation*, September 26. https://theconversation.com/sixty-years-on-the-maralinga-bomb-tests-remind-us-not-to-put-security-over-safety-62441.

Watson, Nicole. 2009. "Of Course It Wouldn't Be Done in Dickson! Why Howard's Battlers Disengaged from the Northern Territory Emergency Response." *Borderlands e-journal* 8.1. http://www.borderlands.net.au/vol8no1_2009/nwatson_dickson.htm.

———. 2011. "Northern Territory Emergency Response–Has It Really Improved the Lives of Aboriginal Women and Children?" *Australian Feminist Law Journal* 35, no. 1: 147–63.

Watson, Irene. 2015. *Aboriginal Peoples, Colonialism and International Law: Raw Law*. Oxford and New York: Routledge.

Whitford, Margaret. 1991. *Luce Irigaray: Philosophy in the Feminine*. London: Routledge.

Wright, Alexis. 2002. "The Politics of Writing." *Southerly* 62, no. 2: 10–20.

———. 2013. *The Swan Book*. Sydney: Giramondo.

Zeitlin, Froma. 1978. "The Dynamics of Misogyny: Myth and Mythmaking in the *Oresteia*." *Arethusa* 11, no. 2 (Spring): 149–84.

Nature, Culture, and Sexuate Difference in Luce Irigaray's Pluralist Model of Embodied Life

ERLA KARLSDOTTIR AND SIGRIDUR THORGEIRSDOTTIR

Over the last decade, scholars have shown increased interest in the concept of nature in Luce Irigaray's work; several have expressed concerns about it, fearing that Irigaray's philosophy of nature harbors tendencies towards essentializing a binary of sexual difference. Ann V. Murphy, for example, notes the increased emphasis on nature in Irigaray's works and speaks of the "troubled employment of nature in [her] later texts," claiming that it is not a "benign" development in her work (Murphy 2002, 79, 81). The emphasis on nature has been seen by, among others, Judith Butler in *Gender Trouble*, as consolidating Irigaray's philosophy of sexual difference into a core ontological distinction in life; Butler also finds that her idea of nature yields a heterosexist, essentialist notion of sexual difference, excluding multiplicity (Butler 1990, 39).[1] More recent interpretations have, however, challenged this negative view and seized the opportunity to depict Irigaray's philosophy of nature as a novel and important aspect of her later philosophical development. Her distinctive conception of nature is seen as being intertwined with culture, and Alison Stone claims that Irigaray "avoids reinstating the traditional culture/nature hierarchy" (Stone 2006, 128).

In this essay, we suggest that Irigaray's philosophy of nature offers a pluralist philosophy of embodied life that undermines the charge of dualistic essentialism. Irigaray is interested in a rapprochement of the sexes that have in our philosophical and psychoanalytical traditions been interpreted as opposites. A pluralist model of life, based on asymmetricalities fruitful for generating multiple differences out of encounters between two who transcend confinement to dualities, allows us to surpass static opposites. As Rosi Braidotti claims, "Irigaray's notion of sexual difference rests on the idea that there is no symmetry between the sexes" (Braidotti 1994, 121). Asymmetry is a precondition for the multiple becomings of sexual difference—that is, the generation of plurality that Irigaray discusses as a natural as well as a cultural and political phenomenon.[2] Silvia Stoller has noted that the notion of ontological asymmetry 'still lacks theoretical grounding within the context of a feminist philosophy of difference" (Stoller 2005, 8); however, we find that within contemporary feminist philosophy, Irigaray's philosophy of sexual difference offers an important contribution to an understanding of asymmetricality. Here we will mainly discuss this asymmetricality in terms of masculine and feminine sexuate difference; however, we find Irigaray's philosophy of sexual and sexuate differences compatible with queer theory as developed by, for example, Lynne Huffer (Huffer 2013).

For Irigaray, asymmetricality stems from the different forms of self-affection that characterize the sexes, forms that she explicates according to a psychoanalytic understanding of sexual difference and her notion of embodiment. The morphology of the lips is the privileged place of women's self-affection (Irigaray 2013, 156), whereas the possibility of self-affection lies in men's reconnecting with their maternal source (150–52). Women need to connect more effectively with themselves and with the creative sources of thought within themselves, while men as embodied beings need to connect with their maternal source as an other outside themselves.[3] These forms of self-affection create a new ground for the relation between the sexes; the connection with the maternal source, for example, implies a different material and spiritual disposition towards life and nature.

Regarding nature, Irigaray's pluralist ontology is, as we shall argue in a first step, based on Friedrich Nietzsche's philosophy of life as will to power. Second, we will show how Irigaray modifies a vulgarized (mis)understanding of Nietzsche's schema of antagonistic wills in favor of asymmetrical wills that transform each other through their encounter. It is Irigaray's notion of sexual difference as embodied reality that allows her to interpret Nietzsche's philosophy of life in this productive manner. By introducing asymmetrical dualities, Irigaray offers a totally new and original interpretation of Nietzsche's pluralist ontology of wills as a theory of change, growth, and transformation. Third, we will show how this pluralist ontology is a useful model for civil life and for democratic politics. We note that hegemonic political power creates antagonisms and simplifies reality in order to sustain itself; it instrumentalizes and exaggerates opposites, in order to overpower the other/s who is/are portrayed as a monolithic adversary, or to polarize a population around issues that distract and blind it to the workings of hegemonic power. Such oppositional thinking stifles transformations since it does not open up an "interval," and thus hinders the process of a vibrant politics of difference and pluralism.

Irigaray's emphasis on a transition from a static culture of opposites to a culture of two becoming subjects relies on an interval in the sense of a pause, a new and neutral space where two subjects meet. We argue that the concept of the interval enables an intersubjective becoming, a transformative encounter that encourages diversity and has as its precondition a deeply rooted respect for the other as a sexuate subject. This respect for the other is based on respect for one's own *sexuate* identity—an identity that Irigaray distinguishes from the narrower notion of *sexual* identity, which has to do with sexual orientation. Taking one's own sexuate identity seriously is the precondition for recognizing others in their otherness on the level of natural and civil life. This encounter is, therefore, much stronger than mere tolerance, which does not really take others seriously in their otherness, and more vibrant than simplified opposition, which essentially reduces the other to an other of the same. This respect for self and other creates a ground for openness to the possibility of self-transformation through the other. This is where democracy needs to begin, according to Irigaray, since so many problems of global culture have to do with oppositions that have feminine and masculine connotations. The conception of nature we find in recent writings by Irigaray allows us to think nature, life, democracy, and politics together.

Life and Nature: Irigaray and Nietzsche

Helen Fielding argues persuasively that the criticism of Irigaray's concept of nature as essentialist is misconceived insofar as it is based on a traditional conception of nature, according to which it is either understood as "unchanging organism" or as "matter that can be ordered, manipulated, and inscribed upon" (Fielding 2003, 1). She subsequently analyzes Irigaray's concept of nature against the backdrop of Heidegger's philosophy of Being, in order to shed light on Irigaray's notion of nature's dynamic character. Ellen Mortensen, however, has argued for the ways in which Irigaray's meditation on the ontological ground of Nietzsche's thinking departs from Heidegger's notion of Being (Mortensen 1995, 141). She maintains that Nietzsche's doctrine of the will to power is important for feminist readings of Irigaray because the ontological problematic is attuned to questions of freedom (Mortensen 2006, 65). We will follow Mortensen's thread and demonstrate that Irigaray's conception of embodied life is, in important respects, articulated in dialogue with Nietzsche's philosophy of life as becoming, which calls dualist ontologies into question. Nietzsche's notions of rhythms of life and the body, and of life as becoming, are taken up by Irigaray, notwithstanding her criticism of his appropriation of feminine elements for an expansive masculinity—that is, of his matricide (Thorgeirsdottir 2010).

Fielding, Murphy, and other interpreters such as Alison Stone have focused on the notion of nature, while leaving aside the concept of life in Irigaray's later texts (Stone 2003). However, the concept of life is central to Irigaray's reflections on nature in *In the Beginning, She Was* (2013), and it is a pluralist conception of life that provides the framework for her understanding of nature in this work. The book aims to show how Western philosophy, from its beginnings in ancient Greek thought, has abandoned, due to its logic of binary oppositions, a pre-Socratic notion of life as self-organizing processes of growth (Irigaray 2013, 58). Western logic and Western metaphysics have alienated us from life and from the real, and we are currently in dire need of a different culture of life and nature. For this purpose, Irigaray contrasts, on the one hand, life and the real that are bound up together, and, on the other hand, a nature that has turned against itself by generating an "anti-natural, ecologically destructive culture" (Stone 2003, 415).

With the concept of life developed in *In the Beginning, She Was*, Irigaray returns to Nietzsche's philosophy of life, long after having dedicated one of her earlier works, *Marine Lover of Friedrich Nietzsche* (1991), to him. Although Irigaray rarely mentions Nietzsche, except at a crucial point where she discusses the need to overcome metaphysics in order to be able to recover our natural belonging (Irigaray 2013, 142), she sees Nietzsche as her predecessor and his criticism of a dualist metaphysics as marking the beginnings of a return to a pre-Socratic notion of life. Irigaray's concept of life, thought as a substratum of her philosophy of nature and of culture, is not only indebted to Nietzsche's philosophy of life; the pluralist ontology of the Nietzschean concept also forms the basis on which Irigaray undermines the supposed binary opposition of nature and culture. As already mentioned, interpreters who have criticized essentialism in Irigaray's concept have actually subscribed to notions of nature that Irigaray herself has surpassed. An adequate understanding of the pluralist model conveyed by her concept of life shows that the core aspect of her ontology—sexual difference—does not reinstate the binary oppositional structure that she detects in Western metaphysics.

Sexual duality as a core structure of life, prior to lived experiences of it, is the very dynamic that engenders multiplicity and a plurality of differences. The distinction we make here between general core structures of life and lived experiences of sexual difference is based on a distinction that Irigaray makes between a prediscursive or pre-representational structure and its worldly expressions in lived experiences. The philosophical anthropology involved in this conception of life is sexually differentiated; yet this conception of sexual difference as a natural duality is not comparable to a logical binary of metaphysics because it is part of a pluralist ontology that is devoid of oppositional structures. Life and death, Irigaray writes, are not opposites but rather in a dialectical relation "which transforms both their meaning and their lived experience" (Irigaray 2013, 102). Her philosophy of life is a pluralist model of asymmetricalities and differences of degree rather than of hierarchical oppositions. Although we will not address this issue in detail in this chapter, it is worth mentioning here that Irigaray's philosophy of the elements (air, water, fire, earth) is important in this respect. Penelope Deutscher argues that "though Irigaray would not make this suggestion herself, an elemental genealogy contains the possibility of reflecting on a 'prior' to sexual difference" (Deutscher 2011, 71). If sexual difference generates plurality, expressions of sexual difference must also be the product of a plurality that generates difference. In this sense, there can be no original symmetrical opposition or binary at the center or at the outset—only differences that emerge and that enter into contest with each other, differences which in turn allow them to be transformed.

Philosophy of Life, Organization, and Meaning

Needless to say, the concept of life is highly debated, not only within philosophy, where it is often met with scepticism based on the concern that a philosophy of life is necessarily biologically reductionist and that such biological reductionism can, moreover, have troubling political implications.

Thus, it is imperative to demonstrate that Irigaray's concept of life is not tainted with biological determinisms or with questionable ideologies derived from them. While neovitalist philosophies, such as that developed and represented by Elizabeth Grosz (who, in regard to vitalism is influenced by Bergson, Nietzsche, and Irigaray), do not offer any dubious (i.e., fascist) connotations of Nietzsche's philosophy of life (Grosz 2004), philosophers like Grosz are nonetheless criticized for advocating a vitalist conception that makes life the higher agency, and humans puppets on the string of life, bereft of agency (Lettow 2011, 145–48). Since Irigaray's notion of agency challenges the traditional dualist opposition activity/passivity, and since she does make a distinction between nonhuman and human life as regards agency, such allegations are not especially relevant to her concept of life. Her notion of agency is deeply relational and contextual compared to traditional, androcentric, one-sidedly individualistic, and disembodied notions of "Man." The relation to the human other is, as she writes, "no doubt the dimension most specific to humanity" (Irigaray 2013, 58). Irigaray claims that nonhuman nature is different and other (Irigaray 2004) and tries to avoid humanizing nonhuman life by attempting to project humanistic ideals onto it. From the perspective of posthumanist philosophies, Irigaray's philosophy of life offers tools to transcend anthropocentrism, while remaining humanistic in its emphasis on recovering a belonging to nature with the purpose of strengthening humanity.

Irigaray's philosophy of sexual difference, based on a materialist notion of embodiment, has motivated a rethinking of distinctions between sex and gender by challenging clear-cut divisions between the two. This, in turn, calls into question any clear-cut opposition between the natural and the cultural—a concept certain materialist and phenomenological feminist thinkers have taken to heart—thinkers like Karen Barad, for whom humans are part of the nature we seek to understand (Barad 2007). In a similar vein, Tina Chanter writes (quoting Merleau-Ponty) that we have been mistaken to think that the "body is 'in' the world and we are 'in' our bodies, as the water is in the glass" (Chanter 2000, 222). Hence, the body is to be understood as an interaction where there is no clear distinction between inside and outside, as is apparent in the inhalation and exhalation of air in breathing. From the point of view of Irigaray's philosophical anthropology, we are part of nature and part of the world, and forces of both run through us—intersect in us—just as we as human beings are a force that affects nature and makes worlds. World and nature are thus intertwined. In this regard, Irigaray's conception of life as an intertwining of world and nature is often compared to Merleau-Ponty's notion of the flesh, which combines the worldly and the natural (Chanter 2000).

Irigaray's philosophical anthropology can be seen to be in alignment with Nietzsche's program of re-establishing humans in nature as sensing beings. It also undertakes to describe the common features of what it means to be human; for Nietzsche, as well as for Irigaray, these features include embodiment as both temporal and spatial being. For Irigaray, a distinction needs to be made between, on the one hand, the level of philosophical anthropology, where we are spatiotemporal, relational beings, and, on the other hand, the level of lived experiences that can be described phenomenologically, where we are not tuned to the more general level of existence. Logocentric thinking has caused a separation from this general, prediscursive level, diminishing our capability for mining it for knowledge and philosophy. Thus, Irigaray, as well as Nietzsche, calls for cultivating sensitivity to bodily rhythms and towards our environments. Irigaray also places major emphasis on breathing to undermine sharp divisions between outside and inside, between self and self, and between self and other.

Relationality is part of what it means to be embodied, and Irigaray gives interpersonal relationality more weight than Nietzsche does. Whereas Nietzsche reflected on sexual difference mostly within the individual, as a means of becoming a wider and deeper (male) philosophical knower, Irigaray reflects more on sexual difference in interpersonal terms as a major potential for growth in philosophical thinking. Both of them are thinkers of difference, wanting to maintain sexual difference (Thorgeirsdottir 2017), although Nietzsche did not wish to follow it through by granting women rights, in the way that Irigaray does with her concept of embodied, sexuate rights.[4] Nietzsche did not see women's rights as a preconditon for the transformation and change from a logocentric culture to a culture more attuned to life. We should also note in this context that the relational idea of the subject Irigaray develops with her placental economy is more radical than Nietzsche's reflections on otherness within the self, in friendship, or in relations with significant others. Therefore, Irigaray considers Nietzsche's Dionysian concept of life as lacking the feminine ethics of care exhibited in her placental economy.

In forging her concept of life, Irigaray takes over Nietzsche's Dionysian idea of life as overabundance of vital force, as well as his idea of the need to organize and channel this force productively. Thus, on the one hand, she discusses life as a natural force and natural growth, and on the other hand, claims that it is the human capacity to organize this force that is precisely the mark of this force itself. Hence, she distinguishes between life as vital force and the "mere survival" that we must transcend through the cultivation of a sharing of life that harnesses the power of difference (Irigaray 2017, viii). Vital force becomes vital for us in the very capacity to organize it; where there is chaos and disorganization, there is no energy (Irigaray 2013, 25). The background for this idea is to be found in Nietzsche's description of the strong will that gains the upper hand in a will organization composed of a multiplicity of will quanta (Müller-Lauter 1999). This idea is taken up by Deleuze in his notions of assemblage and of the power of the assemblage to sustain itself (Deleuze 1987, xvi). The notion of agency comes in here, in the capacity and the effort it takes to give an organization a direction, notably through an empowered will that has gained ascendancy through battle with other wills, or will-formations, within the organization. This battle can be agonistic, but it is more generally to be understood as an encounter of wills that mutually interpret and subsequently transform each other.

In the case of human beings, Irigaray claims that men reproduce *phusis* or nature by "encircling it" with their sayings (Irigaray 2013, 58). This saying or meaning-giving is what has in patriarchal culture alienated us from nature. A different kind of meaning-giving is required, and that is what Irigaray attempts to offer with her own model of *phusis.* When discussing movement as a natural growth, Irigaray makes yet another distinction between the human and the nonhuman; the human being is more complex and rapid in its mobility since, as Irigaray writes, "it evolves not only as a body but also as spirit" (ibid.). It is therefore not surprising that she associates the idea of the organizing will with love; she writes that the opposition of love is not hate, but nonlove. Nonlove means that "energy does not exist or is not organized as such" (25). When there is no energy and no organizing will, "chaos [. . .] reigns [, . . .] [like] uncoordinated impulses that destroy the whole" (ibid.).

From the War of Opposites to Transformative Encounters

When we are in tune with the real and the natural—and for Irigaray that means to be in tune with our experiential knowledge and reflected emotions—we can understand that love and hate have been constructed as opposites (Schoeller and Thorgeirsdottir 2019). Irigaray refuses such couplings of opposites, which she claims that logocentric "philosophy needs in order to surmount the living" in the name of symmetry (4). In her view, love and hate cannot be totally symmetrical; they cannot be laid out "as antagonists." Viewing love and hate as opposites is required by the need to substitute a *polemos*—a war, or a "conflict between entities already artificially constructed [—] for a moment of natural growth" (26). Irigaray here seems to fall into the same fallacy she accuses the phallogocentric tradition of—namely, that of establishing the natural and the artificial as opposites. However, this is the kind of obvious trap we typically encounter in reading Irigaray's texts, where she *seems* to merely reproduce the duality of the tradition that she objects to. In this instance, she *seems* to re-establish the opposition or the hierarchy of the natural and the artificial. However, she is not merely reversing the duality; she is also undermining it as such. The duality of the natural and artificial does not form a binary opposition in her thought because the natural and the cultural are intertwined. Traditional dualistic thinking is artificial in the sense that it is alienated from the real or the natural, as Irigaray writes.

Logical binarism has thus hindered us from seeing the real, where, according to Irigaray, there are no opposites. Binary oppositions have been used to cover over the living (56). What is detrimental about this logocentric operation is that its symmetric dualities have been substituted for the "multiple composition" that characterizes life (ibid.). In the final instance, such logical binarism is based on a repression and displacement of the feminine, and that means cutting us off "from [. . .] birth, from flesh, from desires" (ibid.). Irigaray replaces the traditional, logically construed binary of the sexes (where man has represented culture and woman nature in a hierarchical order, subsuming nature to culture) with a natural duality of the sexes. This may lead to the false conclusion that Irigaray reverses this binary by privileging the natural over the cultural. That is precisely not her intention, given her attempt to bridge the gap between nature and culture. What she intends to convey is a more profound understanding of the natural duality of the sexes, given that, in her view, logical binarism has been based on a logic of opposition whereby the masculine has been posited as the one, while the feminine has been thought as the other.

According to Irigaray, the two sexes form a duality, but they are not opposites conditioning each other by being in a hierarchical relation to one another. The two genders have in the logocentric tradition become frozen, static entities. The masculine gender has lost or covered over its relation to what has generated it—its maternal origin, the she who was in the beginning, as Irigaray's title would have it. Shutting themselves off from her, cutting themselves off from their carnal source, logocentric religious and philosophical thinkers have hindered an encounter. Consequently, the cultural fecundity of the encounter of the sexes—the space between the sexes where multiplicity is actualized as a transformative encounter—has not been realized. The utopian part of Irigaray's project aims to create a philosophical space for the sexes to meet each other on new grounds. Each needs to look at itself through the eyes of the other, and that requires each to face its own localization, its privileges or lack thereof, its power or lack thereof, all of which are hugely important in the encounter between the sexes. It requires them to negotiate power in a different understanding of power as an interactive dynamic. This place, from which a real "beyond the dichotomy Being/non-Being could spring, has been neglected" (53).

The encounter of the sexes represents Irigaray's rendering of Nietzsche's Dionysian overabundance as the living or the real. In the terminology of Irigaray's philosophical anthropology this means that man has lost contact with his prediscursive condition as an embodied, spatiotemporal being. To reunite himself with himself, he needs to reunite with the feminine from which he has alienated himself, in order to activate the creative potential of difference. This understanding of duality, not as an opposition but as a creative dialectic, is echoed in Irigaray's understanding of other dualities. She argues that dualities have been displaced or perverted, precisely by being structured in a logic derived from symmetrical oppositions. She thus claims, in line with Nietzsche's philosophy of life, that life and death are not opposites. Life as perpetual birth or becoming is also life as perpetual or continuous dying (Thorgeirsdottir 2010).

Accordingly, Irigaray replaces a structure of binary oppositions with a more dialectical structure in which the duality is mediated through an encounter in which both parties are transformed. This is where her interpretation becomes relevant for contemporary Nietzsche studies. Nietzsche's idea of the will to power is frequently either associated solely with dominance and subservience (although there are milder versions of will to power to be found in his thought) or it is taken to the other extreme as a repudiation of the will. By taking dualities out of oppositional structures and instead placing them in a dynamic in which both parties condition one another, a much more interesting idea of conflict and tension emerges. Irigaray overcomes the idea of "conflictual oppositions in which the strongest wins." Respect for the "mystery—for the other" needs to substitute for this perpetual war (Irigaray 2013, 94–95). With her idea of a productive encounter between the sexes, she also steers clear of the repudiation of the will that amounts to solipsistic withdrawal.

Regarding the pluralistic ontology of wills, it is important to note that duality generates multiplicity by enabling both parties to grow. Their encounter is, however, not merely an organization that comes into being; it is, rather, an encounter of different organizations that are required to mutually interpret each other. This renders detectable the multiplicity of the preconditions that preceded the encounter, which brings about a reorganization that transforms all parties involved. This complex model accounts for the multiple beginnings that are presupposed in the duality and that are intensified and magnified in the encounter.[5] It is, moreover neither idealist nor materialist, since the opposition between idea and matter is also dissolved, as is the opposition between organic and non-organic, insofar as both are part of a dynamic continuum.

The idea of love and attraction that Irigaray introduces displays the greatest difference from Nietzsche in her rendering of his pluralist ontology of the will-organization. Love stands for her at the beginning. In the beginning there is "the attraction" (109). This attraction precedes the one and the other as separated. There are pre-Socratic sources for the idea of attraction, as well as concepts of sympathy in philosophies of life.[6] Nietzsche and Hölderlin are for Irigaray examples of an attempt to return to the pre-Socratic world, prior to the establishment of the binary-based metaphysical tradition. Both of these thinkers have a "feeling of nostalgia for an impossible return. Both of them have been removed from their own self by Western culture," and both of them have been unable to return (142). Instead of relating to the maternal within him, Nietzsche remained ensconced within the model of a mental mastery of the world. Nietzsche was, in Irigaray's view, not able to establish a self-affective connection either with the maternal source within himself or through a relation with another woman (Irigaray 1991, 2016). This, then is the point where Irigaray discovers a possibility of moving further, of moving beyond the thinking of Nietzsche and Hölderlin towards a culture of sexual difference. She also goes further with her philosophy of natural and civil life, because she insists on the intertwining of nature and culture. Irigaray refuses to conceive natural and civil life as opposites and puts forward a dynamic and pluralist ontology in all her projects, be they political or personal.

Irigaray's Philosophy of Natural and Civil Life

Throughout her work, Irigaray emphasizes that our culture is deeply constrained by logocentric thinking and that the only way to overcome alienation from nature is to rethink our relation to it. Irigaray does this through her theory of sexual difference; one of the reasons that she tirelessly weaves this theory into all of her work comes from her notion of the entrapment of the body (not exclusively the female body) in a fixed hierarchical culture. What began as criticism of damaging, hierarchical, outdated, male-biased psychoanalytic and philosophical theories has led to a proposal for a possible reinvention of human relations in the elaboration of a culture which may result in a different understanding of nature. For Irigaray, altered relations between the two different sexes should serve as a starting point for building a new culture of two subjects. This new culture of two subjects would in turn be a precondition for generating multiplicity. In that sense, each culture of two subjects is transitory—a new beginning and an end.

Irigaray believes that one way to begin the transition away from ancient behavioral patterns and thought processes is to introduce embodied rights into our culture. A culture of embodied rights effects a transition towards a material nature by acknowledging two natural subjects. Although Irigaray sticks with two natural subjects, it would be in line with her thought to require embodied rights for more than two natural subjects. In the last few years, laws that move in such a direction have been issued in Germany, Australia, New Zealand, and other countries—laws that recognize a third gender, an indeterminate sex; these laws make accommodation for intersex individuals born with a combination of male and female chromosomes or genitalia, who have characteristics of both genders. Even though feminist politics have consisted in a battle for equal rights based on the idea of symmetry, Irigaray contends that there need to be specific rights based on asymmetrical differences among persons. This form of civil identity opens up new possibilities in light of a multiplicity and plurality of differences that would be inclusive of alternative family structures. More complex families, like single-parent families or same-sex marriages, can in this light gain truer and fuller acceptance. Irigaray does not renounce the family as an institution, but she suggests that it is time for us to let go of the old patriarchal family structure and acknowledge the existence of diverse family structures. "As men and women, we have to protect the form of alliance that the family offers, not by regressing to a state of natural unity, an instinctual contract, or an emotional pact, but by taking a step forward towards winning a civil identity for ourselves, as human individuals" (Irigaray 2000, 97).

In order to create conditions for a different culture, we need to begin by admitting and squarely facing the continued influence that hierarchical and patriarchal thought has on us. Present-day feminist revolutions such as #Me Too illustrate the ways in which this type of thinking still permeates culture and clearly demonstrate that we need new perspectives and new ways to detect and fight it. Irigaray shows us that this influence continues to manifest itself in many different ways and always resurfaces in new guises. Irigaray believes that if we were protected by a civil code, which emphasized the individual's right to identity, we would be able to enjoy our rights to exist in a nonhierarchical manner. Such a right would then enable us to develop our singularity and individuality (Irigaray 2000, 95–105).

The Interval

How would a culture that would enable both sexuate subjects to grow become possible? It is not enough to be liberated from the constraints of phallogocentric culture. There has to be an encounter of the sexes for there to be an interval in which there is the possibility of a transformation for both sexes. Through such an interval, plurality and difference are generated. An intersubjective becoming of the two sexes is the mark of a transition from patriarchal culture to a culture of two subjects. In her book *The Interval: Relation and Becoming in Irigaray, Aristotle, and Bergson* (2012), Rebecca Hill has shown what a complex and multifarious concept the interval is.[7] Hill emphasizes the relational and communicative aspect of the interval as intersubjective becoming. In line with this argument, the interval is depicted as a relationship, not only between the two sexes, but also between friends, between mothers and daughters, and—we would like to add—between different cultures. The interval can thus function as way out of patriarchal confinement and as an opening into a culture of two subjects that generates new ideas about nature and hence different relations with it.

In *Sharing the World* (Irigaray 2008), Irigaray takes this idea of intersubjective becoming between the two sexes and extends it to an intersubjective becoming of all living beings. Intersubjective becoming is thus a motor for multiplicity as it allows each sex, as well as each type and species, to come into its own negatively and positively so to speak, in the sense of natural growth. We come to ourselves by growing through an encounter with a different subject. Therefore, the concept of nature is for Irigaray apt to describe this process of intersubjective becoming:

> Nature represents possible inter-worlds—it belongs to all living beings and to none. It ought to serve as a space of mediation between all, but that requires it to be subjected by, or to, none. Unfortunately, this is not the case. [. . .] Behaving like a master towards nature that surrounds him, man has appropriated that which could be used as a space of meeting between all living beings, between all that exists. (Irigaray 2008, 66)

This statement is indicative of how Irigaray has in her recent writings decentered the human being by placing her among other companion species that she shares the world with, although she continues to emphasize the importance of the interhuman relationship. The concept of sharing as intersubjective becoming is not to be equated with sharing in the sense of dividing limited goods between us, in the way that we would share a loaf of bread in a group and each of us would receive only a tiny piece. Sharing in the Irigarayan context is a sharing that entails a growth. Sharing ourselves with others and with the other does not diminish what is shared but rather increases it. By coming to ourselves, we come to new singularities, which add up to new multiplicities. Although Irigaray speaks in the passage above about the meeting of all living beings, she claims that the point of departure is the culture of two subjects. The human being is in her view first and foremost focused on other human beings, and we must get this relation right in order to enter into a better relationship with our internal and external nature.

The task at hand is to create new cultures of nature. As has become apparent in her recent writings, Irigaray is very skeptical of biotechnologies because she fears they endanger nature and reinforce patriarchal control and mastering of nature. Her idea of a culture of nature entails a supple relation to nature, as compared with one that would be technologically mediated. She is fundamentally pessimistic in her approach to technology, and she fails to acknowledge how technologies can and do help us in establishing a better relationship with nature. Perhaps there is another reason for her simplistic view of biotechnologies. The patriarchal tradition has devalued nature, "depicting it as secondary to the cultural, spiritual realms" (Stone 2006, 154). Irigaray insists that nature regain its dignity, in order to, among other reasons, remain a source for spiritual experiences. Her view on the restoration of nature's dignity becomes apparent in her depiction of the culture of two subjects as an erotic encounter of love and breathing.

Nature and Democratic Politics: From Opposites to Difference and Pluralism

Why has Irigaray in her recent works focused increasingly on nature and democratic politics? Is there a link between the two? Both are endangered, she claims. Our internal nature is threatened by biotechnological mastery. Furthermore, our erotic nature as two sexes cannot thrive because of the constraints of patriarchal culture that force the sexes to relate to one another as opposites, generating conflict and discord. We cannot speak to each other as sexuate beings. This state of affairs is, in her view, one reason for the problems of democratic politics, which are likewise constrained by oppositional thinking. The powers that exist—that is, ruling financial elites—have the means to control politics, direct the media, and influence public debates. These elites divide and rule populations by forming binary oppositions that generate clear-cut adversaries, which make them fight each other instead of joining hands in fighting the real powers. Again, it is important to bear in mind that opposites in this context differ from sexual difference, and Irigaray claims that it is sexual difference—that is, two sexes and not two opposites—we need for democratic politics to thrive.

In *Democracy Begins Between Two*, Irigaray discusses how rights have been articulated as the rights of man, disregarding our differences as two different sexes; taking these differences into account is a prerequisite for protecting the rights of individuals (Irigaray 2000, 1–20). Therefore, we have to link civil and natural life in our laws. We are embodied beings dependent on a socionatural environment; this environment, as part of our being, becomes an aspect of our embodiment, to be reckoned with in the area of rights. As natural beings, we do have commonalities, but acknowledging our nature is also a part of respecting our singularities, as becomes apparent in the fact that we are different in age, in sex, in capacities, and so on. Irigaray speaks of this difference in several of her works, not least in *I Love to You* (Irigaray 1996), where she writes that we must respect the other and accept the other as transcendent to ourselves. Respect is in itself a kind of interval and *not* a knowledge that we possess. In Irigaray's own description of a meeting between two sexuate subjects, she never grows tired of emphasizing the importance of a space between the two subjects: "Recognizing you means or implies respecting you as other, accepting that I draw myself to a halt before you as before something insurmountable, a mystery, a freedom that will never be mine, a subjectivity that will never be mine, a mine that will never be mine" (104). The interval can be seen as an emancipating relief from patriarchal confinement, enabling an opening for a different culture, a culture of two subjects. Intersubjective becoming can act as a motor for multiplicity where each sex's, each subject's, singularity becomes apparent. Thus, the interval is a space where multiplicity is actualized through a transformative encounter with the other, in which we are transformed and grow as individual selves. The encounter with the other depends on and, at the same time, enables connecting with ourselves in a more profound way.

Notes

1. Butler modifies this view in *Undoing Gender*, where she claims that for Irigaray sex is neither a biological category nor a social one, but rather a linguistic category that exists on the divide between the social and the biological (see Butler 2004, 43).

2. For a detailed discussion of sexual difference as asymmetrical and irreducible difference, see Stoller 2005, 7–26.

3. This is a topic of Irigaray's book *To Be Born* (2017).

4. For detailed discussions of Irigaray's idea of sexuate rights, see Deutscher 2000 and Schwab 1996. Deutscher is quite negative on Irigaray's sexuate rights, whereas Schwab has a more positive take on this.

5. For posthumanist interpreters of Irigaray, her philosophy of sexual difference may ultimately reach a point where it can be thought and lived beyond gender binaries. Claire Colebrook writes that we have

> achieved whatever could be achieved via gender politics and we now need to move on to more complex terrain, acknowledging complexities of class, sexuality, ethnicity and culture. Becoming-woman would be a post-feminist concept, a way of thinking the transition from molar women's movements to a micro-politics in which both man and woman would be abandoned as basic political units. (Colebrook 2013)

We argue that there is no need to abandon the Irigarayan position in favor of Colebrook's. They are not mutually exclusive. The process of diversification is ongoing on the levels of sexes, classes, ethnicities, and cultures. We nevertheless agree with

Irigaray about the necessity of philosophy and culture in the feminine. In light of how male-centric philosophical and religious traditions in different parts of the world are, how economic and financial systems are driven by masculine values, and how widespread gender-based violence is, we find that there is still a need for feminine values to oppose patriarchal values in the name of sexuate difference.

6. Irigaray is also inspired by Henri Bergson's and Arthur Schopenhauer's ideas of sympathy.

7. Irigaray's concept of the interval has also been studied by Anne-Claire Mulder (2010) and Margaret E. Toye (2012).

Works Cited

Barad, Karen. 2007. *Meeting the Universe Halfway*. Durham/London: Duke University Press.

Butler, Judith. 1990. *Gender Trouble*. London/New York: Routledge.

———. 2004. *Undoing Gender*. New York/London: Routledge.

Braidotti, Rosi. 1994. "Of Bugs and Women: Irigaray and Deleuze on the Becoming-Woman." In *Engaging with Irigaray: Feminist Philosophy and Modern European Thought*, edited by Carolyn Burke, Naomi Schor, and Margaret Whitford. New York: Columbia University Press.

Chanter, Tina. 2000. "Wild Meaning: Luce Irigaray's Reading of Merleau-Ponty." In *Chiasms: Merleau-Ponty's Notion of Flesh*, edited by Fred Evans and Leonard Lawlor. Albany: State University of New York Press.

Colebrook, Claire. http://quod.lib.umich.edu/o/ohp/12329363.0001.001/1:8/--sex-after-life-essays-on-extinction-volume-two?rgn=div1;view=fulltext;q1=irigaray.

Deleuze, Gilles, and Felix Guattari. 1987. *A Thousand Plateaus: Capitalism and Schizophrenia*. Minneapolis: University of Minnesota Press.

Deutscher, Penelope. 2000. "Luce Irigaray's Sexuate Rights and the Politics of Performativity." In *Transformations: Thinking Through Feminism*, edited by S. Ahmed, J. Kilby, C. Lury, M. McNeil, and B. Skeggs, 92–108. London, New York: Routledge.

———. 2011. "Animality and Descent: Irigaray's Nietzsche, on Leaving the Sea." In *Thinking with Irigaray*, edited by Mary C. Rawlinson, Sabrina L. Hom, and Serene J. Khader. Albany: State University of New York Press.

Fielding, Helen. 2003. "Questioning Nature: Irigaray, Heidegger and the Potentiality of Matter." *Continental Philosophy Review* 36:1–26.

Grosz, Elizabeth. 2004. *The Nick of Time: Politics, Evolution, and the Untimely*. Durham, NC: Duke University Press.

Hill, Rebecca. 2012. *Interval: Relation and Becoming in Irigaray, Aristotle, and Bergson*. New York: Fordham University Press.

Huffer, Lynne. 2013. *Are the Lips a Grave? A Queer Feminist on the Ethics of Sex*. New York: Columbia University Press.

Irigaray, Luce. 1991. *Marine Lover of Friedrich Nietzsche*. New York and Oxford: Columbia University Press.

———. 1996. *I Love To You: Sketch of a Possible Felicity in History*. New York: Routledge.

———. 2000. *Democracy Begins Between Two*. London: Athlone.

———. 2004. "Animal Compassion." In *Animal Philosophy: Ethics and Identity*, edited by Matthew Calarco and Peter Atteron. London: Continuum.

———. 2008. *Sharing the World*. New York: Continuum.

———. 2013. *In the Beginning, She Was*. London and New York: Bloomsbury.

———. 2017. *To Be Born*. Cham, Switzerland: Palgrave Macmillan/Springer Nature.

Lettow, Susanne. 2011. *Biophilosophien*. Frankfurt and New York: Campus.

Mortensen, Ellen. 1995. *The Feminine and Nihilism: Luce Irigaray with Nietzsche and Heidegger*. Oslo: Scandinavian University Press.

———. 2006. "Nietzsche in the Feminine: Questioning Nietzsche's Will to Power." In *Sex, Breath, and Force: Sexual Difference in a Post-Feminist Era*, edited by Ellen Mortensen, 59–70. Lanham, MD: Lexington Books.

Mulder, Anne-Claire. 2010. "An Ethics of the In-Between: A Condition of Possibility of Being and Living Together." In *New Topics in Feminist Philosophy of Religion*, edited by Pamela Sue Anderson, 297–318. Dordrecht, Heidelberg, London, and New York: Springer.

Müller-Lauter, Wolfgang. 1999. *Nietzsche: His Philosophy of Contradictions and the Contradictions of his Philosophy*. Chicago: University of Illinois Press.

Murphy, Ann V. 2001. "The Enigma of the Natural in Luce Irigaray." *Philosophy Today* 45:75–82.

Schoeller, Donata, and Thorgeirsdottir, Sigridur. 2019. "Embodied Critical Thinking: The Experiential Turn and Its Transformative Aspects." *PhiloSOPHIA* 9(1): 92–109.

Schwab, Gail M. 1996. "Women and the Law in Irigarayan Theory." *Metaphilosophy* 27 (1 and 2): 146–77.

Stoller, Silvia. 2005. "Asymmetrical Genders: Phenomenological Reflections on Sexual Difference." *Hypatia* 20, no. 2:7–26.

Stone, Alison. 2003. "Irigaray and Hölderlin on the Relation between Nature and Culture." *Continental Philosophy Review* 36: 415–32.

———. 2006. *Luce Irigaray and the Philosophy of Sexual Difference*. Cambridge: Cambridge University Press.

Thorgeirsdottir, Sigridur. 2010. "Nietzsche's Philosophy of Life." In *Birth, Death and Femininity: Philosophies of Embodiment*, edited by R. M. Schott, 157–210. Bloomington: Indiana University Press.

———. 2017. "Love of the Sexes in Nietzsche's Philosophy: From Opposition to Transformative Interaction." In *Nietzsche Studien 2017*, 105–13.

Toye, Margaret E. 2012. "Donna Haraway's Cyborg Touching (Up/On) Luce Irigaray's Ethics and the Interval Between: Poethics as Embodied Writing." *Hypatia* 27, no. 1: 182–200.

Between Heidegger's Poetic Thinking and Deleuzian Affect

Irigaray's *The Way of Love*

ELLEN MORTENSEN

In *The Way of Love* (Irigaray 2002), Luce Irigaray resumes her engagement with Martin Heidegger, a conversation that she initiated in the early 1980s while writing *Marine Lover of Friedrich Nietzsche* (Irigaray 1983) and *The Forgetting of Air in Martin Heidegger* (Irigaray 1999). In the preface to *The Way of Love*, Irigaray is quite explicit in her attempt to enter into a dialogue with the German philosopher, albeit not exclusively with him: "Reading *The Way of Love*, the reader enters in any case into an interweaving of exchanges: the dialogue that the book tries to stage between two subjects, the discussion that the writer holds with Heidegger, the exchanges between the writer and the translators" (Irigaray 2002, x).

Irigaray's poetic gesturing towards a new language pays heed to fundamental differences between the (two) sexes, all the while safeguarding a relation to the self, to the other, and to the world. In part, she follows Heidegger's path of ontological thinking on the four-fold, that is, the crossing of the sky and the earth, mortals and divinities. And like Heidegger, Irigaray attempts to be receptive to the event, notably the opening or clearing from whence something *new* might emerge—in language as well as in the world where mortals dwell. For Irigaray, the opening is an interval space from which a path of speech might spring forth, one that may allow for a veritable conversation between sexually different subjects. But whereas Heidegger's call of language emerges from the abyss of nothingness, Irigaray's language of the flesh emerges from the elemental, from love and passionate bodies, as well as from the spirit and the heart of living human beings.

Such a speech does not yet exist, she claims, and this becomes henceforth the task that she undertakes in *The Way of Love*. It is possible to claim that Irigaray's thinking on the question of sexual difference throughout the last four decades has been a labor towards clearing a path for such a language. She envisions a sharing of speech, in which differently sexed subjects may partake. It will necessarily be a limited speech, one that is circumscribed by the perspective and horizon of each sexed subject. For Irigaray, both the feminine and the masculine subject share this condition of limited perspective, and accordingly, neither subject may claim a totality in their perception and understanding of what *is*. *The Way of Love* represents yet another attempt in preparing a path for such a future speech, where the mode of communication between the sexes will be love and attraction, not hate and opposition.

Irigaray envisions a future speech that will reach beyond the horizon of Heidegger's language, which she claims is steeped in death, nothingness, and sameness. Thus, she searches for another saying, one that occurs in the present and is animated and in touch with the living forces; a fluid, incomplete, and ever-changing language of difference and becoming, one that is energized by the elements of fire, earth, air, and water. In my assessment, Irigaray's search for the vital forces in language and life moves her thinking into the vicinity of Deleuze and Guattari's understanding of *affect* (Deleuze and Guattari 1987), which speaks to the intensities that permeate and mobilize, not only the language of philosophy, but also the world in which we dwell.

Hence, in my reading of *The Way of Love*, I will attempt to touch upon not only the Heideggerian legacy of Irigaray's ontological thinking, but also her experimental thinking on the affective interconnectedness between the ontic and the ontological in her projection of a *sensible transcendental*. Affects traverse and intensify all that emerges in the four-fold, including what has been forgotten and what is yet to come. She thus attempts to find a path of thinking—by way of love and poetic musings—that is in touch with the elemental ground that may engender a language of sexual difference. Such a speech would secure a space or an interval of silence, a silence that is *not* nothing, as Heidegger claims, but a silence that is steeped in flesh and immanence and thus holds the promise of future becomings. For Irigaray, only a language to come, where true listening and poetic speaking might occur, could affectively bridge the worlds of two different sexes.

Irigaray and Heidegger's Poetic Thinking

In *On the Way to Language* (Heidegger 1971a), a work that Irigaray repeatedly invokes throughout her book, Heidegger explores a path of poetic thinking, as opposed to metaphysical thinking. Likewise, in *Poetry, Language, Thought* (Heidegger 1971b), he delves into the poetic language of a host of German poets, such as Friedrich Hölderlin, Rainer Maria Rilke, Georg Trakl, Stefan George, and Gottfried Benn. These poets are, Heidegger argues, able to dwell poetically in language in such a way that they are receptive to that which has been hidden or forgotten in metaphysical language—namely, the question of Being. Unlike philosophers, whose thinking is guided by metaphysics, these poets are attuned to this hidden and ancient wisdom. By being attentive to their poetic language, Heidegger claims to gain access to a forgotten way of Being-in-the-world, where Thinking and Being are the Same.

In this sense, Heidegger attempts to uncover, through a meditation on the poetic sayings of these poets, that which our metaphysical tradition has prevented us from discovering, above all our ontological indebtedness to language. According to Heidegger, language is not something that man creates and masters; on the contrary, language is devoid of human intention and will. Language speaks us, not the other way around, and mortals and gods alike find their Being in this language. Thus, for Heidegger, language is the house of Being, where mortals and gods dwell between earth and sky. Throughout centuries, metaphysical language has given authority to the knowing subject, authority to grant Being to beings, and we have come to understand the world instrumentally through the appropriating grasp of the subject-object framing of what *is*. What is granted being in metaphysics is what appears as an object for an appropriating subject.

Heidegger objects to this way of conceiving of human beings and their being in the world. Neither Being, which he understands ontologically, nor beings as ontic entities, can be adequately understood through metaphysical language, he claims. What grants beings Being, is *the* forgotten question in Western philosophy. Thus, in *Being and Time* (Heidegger 1962), Heidegger lays out the existential problematic concerning Dasein, this Being-towards death, which he understands within a complex existential problematic involving, above all, time. For Heidegger, the Being of the subject is implicated in this existential problematic and thus cannot serve as that which grants Being to itself, nor to any other beings. Both Heidegger's later works on poetic thinking and his early work on the hermeneutic circle and the ontological difference between Being and beings can be read as attempts to undermine the dominance of the language of metaphysics, which he claims understands Being instrumentally within the framework of the subject-object opposition and accordingly has forgotten the Being question. Furthermore, in *The Question Concerning Technology and Other Essays* (Heidegger 1977), Heidegger postulates that the state of affairs in the twentieth century is that we are living under the sway of technological thinking, which is likewise founded upon instrumental thinking, based on the subject-object opposition. In the age of technology, Heidegger argues, we have come to understand Being as beings, that is, as something "ready-at-hand" and as "standing reserve" for humans to exploit.

In *The Way of Love*, Irigaray by and large accepts Heidegger's overall analysis of the state of affairs with regard to metaphysical thinking and what she perceives to be the dominant mode of thought in the age of technology. She also seconds Heidegger's poetic approach to these questions, and throughout the text, she mimics his poetic language in search of another path of thinking, where sexual difference may come into play. To my knowledge, few feminist scholars have engaged with Irigaray's "Heideggerian" texts, be it *The Way of Love* or *The Forgetting of Air*. Anne van Leeuwen serves as an exception, and in her reading of these two works (van Leeuwen 2013), she highlights what she understands to be Irigaray's persistent commitment to Heidegger's transcendental phenomenology. As for *The Way of Love*, van Leeuwen focuses on Irigaray's metatheoretical commitment in this text, and she writes:

> If sexual difference is the fundamental philosophical principle, it operates through the *epoché* of its own operative logic. The metatheoretical commitment to the remembrance of this constitutive forgetting is thus instantiated in the articulation of a philosophy whose guiding principle resists any unequivocal expression. Irigaray thus invokes sexual difference not as a transcendent given but as the genesis of difference within a transcendental inquiry that does not forget the constitutive withdrawal of its own conditions. Sexual difference, in other words, names the emergence of difference within those incarnations of transcen-

> dental phenomenology that eschew the logic of the specular. (van Leeuwen 2013, 461)

I can only second van Leeuwen's astute analysis of Irigaray's relation to the Heideggerian legacy, and I have elsewhere, in my books *The Feminine and Nihilism* (Mortensen 1994) and *Touching Thought: Ontology and Sexual Difference* (Mortensen 2002), dealt in depth with the intricacies of the Irigaray-Heidegger nexus.

As I see it, the main difference between Irigaray and Heidegger is that, for Irigaray, language is not fundamentally nonhuman or inhuman the way it is for Heidegger—a hidden or forgotten saying from the past that we can only access through a poetic passivity, notably through poetic sayings. This is where her ontological thinking diverges most radically from Heidegger's. For Heidegger, Dasein enters into and receives language; language is the house of Being, the groundless ground that grants Being to all beings, which emerge in time through its *epoché*. By contrast, Irigaray does not understand language as devoid of life but instead as energized and mobilized by the forces of life, both negative and affirmative. Hence, language is alive and perpetually changing; it has a past (which may or may not be forgotten), a present, and a possible future. As indicated in the title, *The Way of Love*, the language that Irigaray seeks finds its engendering source in love, and the power of love may effect change in language, including the language of philosophy. For in the very name of philosophy, in its Greek origin, lies hidden the word "love"—*philia*—as well as the word "wisdom"—*sofia*. In the introduction to *The Way of Love*, she writes:

> If the human is divided into two, always open and in interaction [. . .], the one and the other interpenetrate and transmute each other such that the dichotomy between them no longer exists. The fixed polarities of one, of the One, return to the duality of subjectivities which, with a view to their human becoming, and in the name of the wisdom of love, renounce all completed personal fullness in order to work toward a more accomplished advent of humanity. (Irigaray 2000, 10–11)

Irigaray moves in *The Way of Love* in and out of Heidegger's texts as he meditates on the various German poets, among others, Stefan George, and on his poem "Words," where Heidegger's position on language becomes clearer to her. For Heidegger, Irigaray claims, communication between the two subjects does not exist. Rather, it becomes a question of the poet "reaching, in the relation to the word, an intimacy beyond measure" (28). According to Irigaray, the clearing of language that Heidegger hears in the intimacy between the poet and "the vastness without measure," actually means "beyond the representational rule of the word" for Heidegger. The clearing that safeguards the secret of the word, thus allowing for the intimacy between the poet and the word beyond representational thinking, is an aspect of Heidegger's thinking that Irigaray finds most appealing. His thinking can therefore be said to clear the path for her own thinking in her search for a sharing of speech between differently sexed subjects.

However, this passage also allows Irigaray to allude to the marked sexed difference between the two philosophers, namely Heidegger and herself, when it comes to what the "secret" of the word might entail, and she writes that "Heidegger invokes here the secret of the word, I would think rather–because of a misunderstanding? or because the philosopher stays already and always in the logos?–about the secret of the thing, or of the other, of their resistance to the logos. Relinquishing would then be recognition and gratitude" (152).

> What deepens through the absence of a proper saying according to Heidegger, would be recognition and gratitude toward the saying itself. Secret of the thing and of the other to me; secret of the word, according to Heidegger. Word called into question by the thing and by the other, in my opinion; thing called into question by the word for Heidegger. Would this not correspond to a fetishism of the word and of language? (29–30)

In the above passage, we get to the crux of Irigaray's skepticism toward Heidegger's understanding of language. For her, he becomes yet another representative of male philosophers who continue the tradition of language, which only allows for *one* voice, *one* horizon, a language which primarily speaks to itself, and where authentic language is thought to reside outside the realm of the living, in a non-sensuous space, permeated by the nothing. Irigaray projects another way of perceiving language, which is *not* characterized by "idolatry of the means," and she writes: "Idolatry of the means? In place of respect for the matter in which the thing—and the other—is made, matter above all elementary or elemental, open and thus resistant to the form of the idol, which is never indefinite but claims to take the infinite in the finite" (30).

She asks if Heidegger in fact does not go further than Plato in idealism when he submits the thing to the word, and she asks: "Does he not subjugate not only looking but all the senses, in particular hearing, to the power of language" (31)? Heidegger's speaking partner, like the poet's, is speech itself, which he claims speaks only with itself. This is expressed in Heidegger's famous dictums: *Die Sprache spricht* og *Es gibt* ("Language speaks" and "There is"). For Irigaray, this amounts to the following: "He interweaves, interlaces with the speaking of speech caring little about interweaving, interlacing when speaking with someone, at least someone living and present. He is on the way toward the call of speech, not toward the call of another subject" (ibid.). Heidegger's clearing, the opening up of a way toward a language, can therefore only partly serve as a guiding path for Irigaray. Her search will have to move beyond Heidegger's fetishizing of impersonal, in-human language, devoid of life. At the same time, Irigaray resides in the neighborhood of Heidegger's thinking on the silence and the interval of the opening, where the possibility of another language might emerge. But what Irigaray hears in this silence is not the withdrawal of Being into the Nothing, but rather a "return to the noises of nature, no more than that. Or a gathering in oneself without any saying?" (32).

For Irigaray, the initial silence, which safeguards things and the other in their withdrawal, alludes to Heidegger's account of the double veiling that occurs when Being withdraws in order for beings to be. Heidegger posits that the veil of mystery, which shields things in their innocence, is different from the veil that re-covers them because of their submission to the word. But Irigaray understands this veil of mystery in a different way than Heidegger does, and she interjects:

> In the first case, the veil is woven in the air in which every living being lies; is born, lives, grows. In the second case, the veil is already an artifice that submits every living being to the same—dwelling and being—preventing it from unfolding in accordance with its roots. The first veil is also related to a voluntary withdrawal in which the subject, if not the thing, would take refuge in order to respect what lives, what grows, without claiming to say its Being and assigning a shelter to it. In such a withdrawal, what is still to come from a becoming, particularly of or in speaking, is also preserved. The future is saved—still, partially at least, to be said. Not already trapped in

> the interlacings of language. If some permanence exists, it is, in part, fluid: it safeguards, and even gives, silence. (33)

Thus, Heidegger's poetic thinking can only take her so far. In order to explore a sharing of speech and being with the other in difference, Irigaray has to orient herself in a different terrain of thought, one that takes the *relational* and *the forces of life* into account. She searches for a saying that pays heed to life, to the becoming of life in a four-fold, where humans and divinities might dwell between earth and sky, and flourish in a breath of air, while being able to communicate with one another. Irigaray yearns for another path "where a space for a descent of each one into oneself is open, where body and spirit are mingled, and where the materiality of breath, of an energy, of a living being is still virgin" (53). Instead of turning towards Heidegger, she therefore orients herself, it seems, towards thinkers such as Deleuze and Guattari, whose material ontology proves more fertile than does Heidegger's poetic language of death, nothingness, and the Same.

Irigaray and Deleuze and Guattari

Philosophical connections between Irigaray and Deleuze and Guattari have been addressed before by, among others, feminist theorists such as Rosi Braidotti, Elizabeth Grosz, and Tamsin Lorraine. Albeit in different ways, they have all explored interesting points of convergence and productive differences between these thinkers. None of the three above writes explicitly about *The Way of Love*, but they all address important aspects of Irigaray's work in light of Deleuze and Guattari's thinking.

Braidotti, for her part, addressed the interconnections between Irigaray and Deleuze and Guattari in *Patterns of Dissonance* (Braidotti 1991), and she has repeatedly argued for a productive relation between Irigaray's thinking on sexual difference and the philosophies of the two French philosophers, be it in *Nomadic Subjects* (Braidotti 1994) or in *Metamorphoses* (Braidotti 2002). Likewise, in her article "Becoming Woman: or Sexual Difference Revisited" (Braidotti 2003), Braidotti explicitly favors Irigaray's early works while arguing for a reading of her work that not only highlights her reactive or critical thinking, but also the affirmative aspects of her oeuvre. In her reading of Irigaray, Braidotti emphasizes the way in which Irigaray's thinking on sexual difference might strengthen and supplement Deleuze and Guattari's thinking on body materiality. She also senses important resonances between Irigaray's writing on the feminine, as a vision projected onto the future, and Deleuze and Guattari's thinking on the virtual. In addition, Braidotti explores the connection between the two French thinkers' writing on the minoritarian/majoritarian and Irigaray's thinking on the position of women in Western patriarchal culture.

One of the concepts that Braidotti finds worth elaborating on is precisely the concept of *affect* as it relates to both Irigaray and Deleuze and their respective understandings of the body. She writes:

> A body is, spatially speaking, a slice of forces that have specific qualities, relations, speed, and rates of change. Their common denominator is that they are intelligent matter, that is: endowed with the capacity to affect and be affected, to interrelate. Temporally speaking, a body is a portion of a living memory that endures by undergoing constant internal modifications following the encounter with other bodies and forces. In both cases, the key point is the embodied subject's capacity for encounters and interrelation. As such, desire and yearning for interconnections with others lie at the heart of Deleuze's vision of subjectivity. (Braidotti 2003, 57)

Braidotti does not engage with *The Way of Love* explicitly in this article, but she might just as well have done so, since the major impetus in Irigaray's book is precisely to articulate—in poetic speech—the yearning and desire to interconnect with another, a differently sexed subject, and with the world. Irigaray's poetic vision of love in *The Way of Love* can thus be productively understood in terms of Deleuze and Guattari's concept of affect.

When Irigaray tries to be concrete about what "Being with the Other" in a mode of love entails in *affective* terms, she nevertheless starts by making a negative statement:

> This will not happen solely through designating the affects by a name nor through limiting oneself to simple interjections, exclamations. Neither will a recourse to the language of a people suffice, except for the relinquishing of singular experience, thus of one's own intimacy—a subjective core irreducible to collective familiarity. (Irigaray 2002, 57)

In addition to ironically alluding to Heidegger's appeal to the German language, the German people, and the dangers involved in such a privileging of a "people," Irigaray seeks other means and ways, where inventions of "indirect ways of advancing" (58) are to be preferred. She does not embrace

Heidegger's mode of poetic passivity, where the poet/philosopher is but a recipient of past "aletheic" insights. Irigaray instead insists on subjective action in the present, yet not in a mode of aggressive appropriation.

We are here reminded of the persistent linguistic meditation that Irigaray has pursued alongside her philosophic endeavors throughout her career. Works such as *I Love to You* (Irigaray 1996) come to mind, where she calls for a reinvention of love, one that is not performed in a mode of objective appropriation of the other, but rather as an approach in the indirect mode, which emphasizes the act of creating an interval space that allows for a *relation* between two differently sexed subjects.

Love has thus to be reinvented and rebuilt, Irigaray claims in *The Way of Love*, and speech can help change the way we understand love, both vertically (as between humans and what she understands as the divine) and horizontally (as between women and men, women and women, etc.). In this context, she prefers verbal constructions to nominalizations; verbal action is involved in "sketching perspectives, outlining horizons" (Irigaray 2002, 59), a process whereby something *new* might occur: "The verb of which the act sometimes will be assumed by a subject, sometimes left in the infinitive form—witness to the work of nature or to a still undifferentiated, sometimes common, energy" (ibid.).

In the slow and careful process of building a world and a speech where "Being with the Other" will thrive and grow, Irigaray invokes a notion of *affect* akin to that of Deleuze and Guattari. For Deleuze and Guattari, as for Irigaray, affect is not confined to a personal feeling; it is an affective force that is cosmic in scope, yet it involves also the smallest entities, down to the tiniest molecules. According to Deleuze and Guattari, affect is "the incredible feeling of an unknown Nature," and they write:

> For the affect is not a personal feeling, nor is it a characteristic; it is the effectuation of a power of the pack that throws the self into upheaval and makes it reel. Who has not known the violence of these animal sequences, which uproot one from humanity, if only for an instant, making one scrape at one's bread like a rodent or giving one the yellow eyes of a feline? A fearsome involution calling us toward unheard-of becomings. (Deleuze and Guattari 1987, 240)

It is possible to read into Irigaray's projection of a *sensible transcendental* an invocation of Deleuze and Guattari's thinking on the ontological primacy of the forces of life. Like the two French philosophers, in her ontology, Irigaray privileges *immanence*, the *sensuous*, or *the elemental*, and she projects a vision where the ontic and ontological act in constant interrelation and where the finite (mortals) and the transcendental (gods, ideas, the elements) are mutually affected by each other, in a continuous, sensuous exchange:

> Air is what is left common between subjects living in different worlds. It is the elemental of the universe, of the life starting from which it is possible to elaborate the transcendental. Air is that in which we dwell and which dwells in us, in varied ways without doubt, but providing passages between—in ourselves, between us. Air is the medium of our natural and spiritual life, of our relation to ourselves, to speaking, to the other. And this medium imperceptibly crosses the limits of different worlds and universes, sometimes giving the illusion of a gained intimacy while we are only sharing a common element. Air can permit us to be in communication if we are going on the way toward each other rather than believing ourselves near because of communion through or immersion in a third. (Irigaray 2002, 68)

This passage harkens back to *The Forgetting of Air in Martin Heidegger* (Irigaray 1983), the text where Irigaray most explicitly challenges the German philosopher's thinking on the ontological difference. However, in *The Way of Love*, she elaborates in more detail on the porous boundaries and the *affective* interconnections between the ontic and the ontological, between the elements thought as invisible and transcendental, yet permeating all living beings. The elemental affects all that appears in the world, the ontic as well as the ontological. Claire Colebrook's take on the status of "the sensible" in Irigaray's thinking is instructive in this context; she writes: "The sensible is proximate. Neither the full presence of experience, nor the radical anteriority of a transcendental condition, the sensible is given as the other body whom I recognize as another form of becoming, as a 'concrete universal' " (Colebrook 2000, 123).

According to Irigaray, it is not only the elemental that has been forgotten in Western philosophy. Likewise, the act of engendering, which to her constitutes the most crucial grounding act for life on earth, has been consigned to oblivion. In metaphysics as well as in most ontotheological accounts of engendering, the mother has been forgotten. In order to rectify this problem, in Irigaray's visionary world of "between-two," the mother is thus granted her rightful place:

> What is then reached as ground is a relational world where the other takes a decisive place, an always evaded stage particularly in the ontotheological foundation. Without the mother, there is no engendering, no birth, no survival, nor awakening of consciousness. This ground constitutive of subjectivity has remained unthought or reduced to facticity, to the empirical. Now its role, in Being and in thinking, is not nothing, including through its unconscious effects. (Irigaray 2002, 74)

There is a relation of fundamental affectivity between the origin of Being (which for Irigaray is invisible and elemental) and our existential condition of being-in-relation-with and being-born-of (the mother). In this sense, Irigaray creates both a critique of and a bridge to: first, what has been forgotten in Heidegger's understanding of the ontological difference; second, ontotheological accounts that silence the indebtedness of the transcendental God to the elements; and third, Deleuze and Guattari and their silence regarding the question of sexual difference and the creative act of giving birth in their material ontology.

Affect in Deleuzian-Guattarian terms is (following Spinoza) above all "the capacity to affect and to be affected" (Deleuze and Guattari 1987, 261):

> To every relation of movement and rest, speed and slowness, grouping together an infinity of parts, there corresponds a degree of power. To the relations composing, decomposing, or modifying an individual there correspond intensities that affect it, augmenting or diminishing its power to act: these intensities come from external parts or from the individual's own parts. Affects are becomings. (256)

In the process of "becoming intense," which marks a process of deterritorialization in different stages, Deleuze and Guattari include the notion of "becoming-woman" as a necessary stage. They thus acknowledge that the molar identity of "man" is being invested with oppressive power, notably through patriarchal-capitalist assemblages. Molar, masculine identity must therefore be deterritorialized on the plane of organization in order for life forces to be liberated, allowing for affects to circulate freely, which again might allow new becomings on the plane of consistency or immanence.

Affects, as intensive forces, are to them crucial for the capacity to act, notably in order to undermine the stability of molar identities and their oppressive assemblages. They therefore propose diverse strategies of deterritorialization in order to undo the patriarchal gender and sexuality regime, which serves the interest of man in capitalist societies. In their material ontology, "becoming-woman" is the first stage, and one that all processes of de-territorialization have to pass through. They ask:

> Why are there so many becomings of man, but no becoming-man? First, because man is majoritarian par excellence, whereas becomings are minoritarian. When we say majority, we are referring not to a greater relative quantity but to the determination of a state or a standard in relation to which larger quantities, as well as the smallest, can be said to be minoritarian: white-man, adult-male, etc. Majority implies a state of domination, not the reverse. [. . .] In this sense, women, children, but also animals, plants, and molecules, are minoritarian. It is perhaps the special situation of women in relation to the man-standard that accounts for the fact that becomings, being minoritarian, always pass through a becoming-woman. (291)

Affects likewise mobilize all further processes of deterritorialization, which start with "becoming-woman" and move via "becoming-child," "becoming-animal," and "becoming-molecular," and finally reach, "becoming-imperceptible," which constitutes the final stage of deterritorialization on the plane of consistency or immanence, from whence new becomings may spring forth. Deleuze and Guattari advocate in this context for a continuous, dynamic self-production of multiple sexes and poly-sexualities in the war machine against the tyranny of the molar identities of patriarchal-capitalist assemblages.

In their view, feminism, as an ideology of stable gender and sexuality categories, is implicated in this power dynamic and may contribute to solidifying power in this oppressive state of affairs. As such, feminist critique may function as reactionary and reactive forces in capitalist society. Furthermore, when Deleuze and Guattari propose ways of undermining patriarchal, molar power regimes on the plane of organization, they advocate for a dynamic self-production of multiple, unnatural and perverse assemblages, where the human body enters into productive relations with other affective entities—human, animal, machinic, or artificial—in order to create "unheard-of becomings."

Feminist theorists like Grosz, Lorraine, and Braidotti all address the concept "becoming-woman" in Deleuze and Guattari. Although all three agree that this marks a "feminist" stance in their philosophy, all of them have an ambivalent view of the concept when it comes to thinking sexual difference. Grosz devotes a chapter in *Volatile Bodies* (Grosz 1994) to the concept and returns to the problematic in all of her books. Braidotti includes a chapter, entitled "Becoming Woman, or Sexual Difference Revisited," in her book *Metamorphoses* (Braidotti 2002). Similarly, Tamsin Lorraine identifies in her book, *Irigaray and Deleuze: Experiments in Visceral Philosophy*, some of the differences between the two schools of thought. She writes: "Whereas Irigaray attempts to give a positive characterization of a feminine subject able to continually incorporate fluid transformations in concert with others, Deleuze and Guattari seem to assume a stable standard against which war machines must continually be launched" (Lorraine 1999, 186).

Grosz, for her part, continues to embrace Irigaray's understanding of sexual difference as a crucial point of reference in her readings of male philosophers and theorists, be it Deleuze and Guattari, Darwin, Bergson, or Nietzsche. Characteristically, in *The Incorporeal* (Grosz 2017), Grosz opens up a possible charge against Deleuze, similar to the one Irigaray articulates in her critique of Nietzsche in *Marine Lover*. Grosz writes:

> Irigaray could repeat the charge of matricide that she addresses to Nietzsche and Spinoza now to Deleuze: to place one's natural birth, from a maternal body, with a birth through one's own self-production, whether it is through the advent of culture or the creation of a second nature, or as here, through the endless adoption of events, is among the long-prevailing philosophical tactics for an evasion of the ineliminable debt to the mother's body and the event of one's birth, the event in which the subject is never a participant but only an effect. (Grosz 2017, 281, n.33)

Grosz here accepts Irigaray's insistence on the indebtedness to the mother, whether we understand the mother in terms of the sex that has the bodily capacity to give birth to another being, or we understand the mother in ontological terms, that is, as the ineliminable elemental ground that secures all forms of life on earth. In either case, Grosz seems to align herself with

Irigaray in her skepticism towards all forms of thinking that deny an indebtedness to this engendering capacity of the feminine.

While all the feminist scholars cited above are partially skeptical of Deleuze and Guattari's analysis of feminism and question the radical potential in the notion of "becoming-woman," none of them seems to think that one school of thought should be debunked in favor of the other. What they all emphasize is the salience of a continued productive dialogue between the Irigarayan philosophy of sexual difference and Deleuze and Guattari's philosophy of radical immanence and affectivity.

Irigaray's Poetic Rebuilding of the World

In the poetic speech between two that Irigaray envisages for the future, there will be a rebuilding, a clearing of a space and an interval that allows for human dwelling, not only in language, as Heidegger purports in his essay "Building, Dwelling, Thinking" from *Poetry, Language, Thought* (Heidegger 1971b), but above all in a world for and among the living:

> To construct only in order to construct does not suffice for dwelling. A cultivation of the living must accompany a building of that which does not grow by itself. For a human, the two do not seem separable. To cultivate human life in its engendering and its growth requires the elaboration of material and spiritual frameworks and constructions. These should not be opposed to the becoming of life, as they have too often been, but provide it with the help indispensable for its blossoming. (Irigaray 2002, 144)

Building a world for the future, Irigaray argues, must be done in a manner that activates all the senses and safeguards not only that which appears in the present, but also that which touches upon what is absent and forgotten, as well as that which is yet to come. This future dwelling place for humans must also find "gestures or words which will touch the other in his, or her, alterity" (151). This rebuilding will by necessity touch the elemental: that which grants us breath (air), engenders, nurtures and sustains our being and dwelling (earth), provides us energy and life force, both material and spiritual (fire), and offers the liquid element without which we could not survive (water). In her musings on the promises of such a speech, she projects another language, animated by the forces of life:

"A Nothingness which is not nothing" (174). Irigaray writes: "Touch which allows turning back to oneself, in one dwelling of an intimate light. But which also goes to encounter the other, illuminated-illuminating, overflowing one's own world in order to taste another brightness. In order to give and receive what can enlighten mortals on their path" (ibid.).

To conclude, in my reading of *The Way of Love*, I have shown that Irigaray's text reveals affinities, not only with Heidegger's poetic thinking, but also with Deleuzian *affect* in her vision of what is needed to rebuild the world in an act of love. She embraces Deleuze and Guattari's imperative to act, but not exclusively in a dynamic, affirmative mode of action, conceived as a continuous self-generation and refiguring of the self. Nor does she accept Heidegger's call of language, which implies a stance of poetic passivity and pure receptivity of past aletheic truths. Instead, Irigaray's call for action is by way of love and indirection in a relation between two. Her way of love requires a new mode of speech, a poetic language that allows for proximity, of the one to her/himself, to the other, and to the world, while dwelling *affectively*, that is, while being in touch with the elemental, which safeguards the silence and the interval that will let beings be in their difference and free becoming.

Works Cited

Braidotti, Rosi. 1991. *Patterns of Dissonance: An Essay on Women in Contemporary French Philosophy*. Cambridge: Polity.

———. 1994. *Nomadic Subjects: Embodiment and Sexual Difference in Contemporary Feminist Theory*. New York: Columbia University Press.

———. 2002. *Metamorphoses: Towards a Materialist Theory of Becoming*. Cambridge: Polity.

———. 2003. "Becoming Woman: Or Sexual Difference Revisited." *Theory, Culture and Society* 20, no. 3.

Colebrook, Claire. 2000. "Is Sexual Difference a Problem?" In *Deleuze and Feminist Theory*, edited by Ian Buchanan and Claire Colebrook. Edinburgh: Edinburgh University Press.

Deleuze, Gilles, and Félix Guattari. 1987. *A Thousand Plateaux: Capitalism and Schizophrenia*. Translated by Brian Massumi. Minneapolis: Minnesota University Press.

Grosz, Elizabeth. 1994. *Volatile Bodies: Towards a Corporeal Feminism*. Bloomington: Indiana University Press.

———. 2017. *The Incorporeal: Ontology, Ethics, and the Limits of Materialism.* New York: Columbia University Press.

Heidegger, Martin. 1962. *Being and Time.* Translated by John Macquarrie and Edward Robinson. New York: Harper & Row.

———. 1971a. *On the Way to Language.* Translated by Peter D. Herz and Joan Stambaugh. New York: Harper & Row.

———. 1971b. *Poetry, Language, Thought.* Translated by Albert Hofstadter. Cambridge: Cambridge University Press.

———. 1977. *The Question Concerning Technology and Other Essays.* Translated by William Lovitt. New York: Harper & Row.

Irigaray, Luce. 1991. *Marine Lover of Friedrich Nietzsche.* Translated by Gillian C. Gill. New York: Columbia University Press.

———. 1996. *I Love to You: Sketch for a Possible Felicity with History.* Translated by Allison Martin. London: Routledge.

———. 1999. *The Forgetting of Air in Martin Heidegger.* Translated by Mary Beth Mader. Austin: University of Texas Press.

———. 2002. *The Way of Love.* Translated by Heidi Bostic and Stephen Pluhâĉek. London: Continuum.

Lorraine, Tamsin. 1999. *Irigaray and Deleuze: Experiments in Visceral Philosophy.* Ithaca: Cornell University Press.

Mortensen, Ellen. 1994. *The Feminine and Nihilism: Luce Irigaray with Nietzsche and Heidegger.* Oslo: Scandinavian University Press.

———. 2002. *Touching Thought: Ontology and Sexual Difference.* Lanham: Lexington Books.

van Leeuwen, Anne. 2013. "An Examination of Irigaray's Commitment to Transcendental Phenomenology in *The Forgetting of Air* and *The Way of Love.*" *Hypatia* 28, no. 3 (Summer).

Time for Love

Plato and Irigaray on Erotic Relations

FANNY SÖDERBÄCK

Love is space and time made perceptible to the heart.

—Marcel Proust, 1982, 392

Introduction

How can I say "I love you" without reducing you to an object? How can I express my love to you while respecting your difference from me—the fact that you will always remain (at least partially) unknown to me? How love you without defining you, without trying to make you mine? These questions echo through the work of Luce Irigaray, who has devoted much of her thought to the ethics of erotic relations. In *I Love to You*, she notes that "making you my property, my possession, my *mine* does not accomplish the alliance between us. This act sacrifices one subjectivity to another" (Irigaray 1996, 111). What Irigaray is seeking to articulate is the possibility of *two* subjectivities and a nonpossessive and nonappropriating relationship between them. Due to the logic of sameness that, in her view, has shaped our culture, the subject exists only in relation to an object—be it an object of love—and this in turn reduces love to a possessive relation. You who are mine. You whom I can know and name. You whose alterity I can annihilate.

How, then, can we approach the other *as other*? How love in a way that respects and cultivates difference? Irigaray, who describes love as the "safeguard of life and time" (Irigaray 1996, 150), shifts the focus of the problem: "All too often," she writes, "sacramental or juridical commitment and the obligation to reproduce have compensated for this problem: how construct a temporality between us? How to unite two temporalities, two subjects, in a lasting way?" (111). Or, as she notes in a more recent contemplation on erotic relations, if we want to establish subjectivity in terms of intersubjectivity, if we want to be two in the proper sense of the term, and approach the other without appropriating him or her, "another relation to space and to time becomes necessary" (Irigaray 2002, 81). Each subject, to remain a subject without being reduced to—or reducing the other to—an object, must respect the space-time that opens up as an abyss between subjects irreducible to one another, at the same time as it unites the two and holds them together. Only if we cultivate this space-time between us can we foster closeness and intimacy without collapsing one subject into the other. Only if we "reconsider the whole problematic of *space* and *time*" (Irigaray 1993, 7) can we establish an ethics of sexual difference, and an ethics of erotic relations.

This chapter is an attempt to think through the relationship between time and love. I argue that temporality and relationality are inseparable, and that an ethics based on respect for the other as irreducibly other must take as its point of departure an understanding of love in temporal terms. It is important, however, that time not be understood in linear-teleological terms (this would preserve the subject-object-dynamic that I am trying to challenge here) but that it be articulated, instead, in terms of open-ended becoming in difference. I hope to shed light on the way in which love can be used as a model for an ethics of sexual difference, where woman is no longer reduced to lack and negativity but where each sex—and each individual, regardless of sex—can cultivate its own subjectivity, as lovers irreducible to one another.

To accomplish this task, I will turn not only to Irigaray but also to Plato, who placed love—or eros—at the heart of his own philosophical project. If philosophy since Plato has been understood as a love of wisdom (from the Greek terms *philia* and *sophia*), Irigaray has stressed the need to view it instead as a wisdom of love. Following Irigaray in this regard, I argue that philosophy indeed is an inherently erotic practice but that it all too often has been grafted onto a model of love that takes the erotic to be a one-way movement between lover and beloved (subject-object relation), as opposed to the temporal movement that unfolds between two lovers, irreducible to one another, and subjects in their own right. By inscribing temporality (understood not as linear-causal trajectory but as perpetual and unpredictable becoming) into the very structure of love and subsequently philosophy, I hope to sketch the contours of an ethics and a philosophy of erotic relations.

The Genesis of Love: Originary Wholeness or Primary Difference?

At the heart of Plato's celebration of love, the *Symposium*, we find an account of the genesis of love, as told by Aristophanes (Plato 1993, 189a–93d).[1] Love is described as the result of a fundamental split—the gods punishing the humans for their hubris by cutting them in half and dooming them to the eternal effort to reunite and become whole again. If humans were once "completely spherical, with their backs and sides making a complete circle" (189e), we now look the way we do because of this divine intervention, and it is because of this split that we spend our lives looking for our other half. This search is what we call love. While the speech is framed as a story about the genesis of love, it is evident that it has wider implications. Aristophanes, in fact, gives an account of the origins of human nature as we know it: desiring, imperfect, and finite. We learn that once Zeus has cut all humans in half, Apollo turns their heads around, forcing them to gaze at their scars so as to be constantly reminded of their sinful past and of their own vulnerability. Stanley Rosen has noted that "man first becomes human through the erotic awareness that is dependent upon looking downward, and not at the stars"—as in Socrates's account of the upward gaze of philosophic wonder—"but at himself" (Rosen 148). The human condition, we might say, is to be in a state of perpetual mourning, and it is this grief that drives us toward one another.

Initially, this downward-backward gaze of nostalgia poses a threat to human survival. The newly formed people of the Aristophanic myth cling to one another, and in this state of entwinement, they neglect the necessities of life and die from hunger and lack of sleep. Originally, their genitals had been placed "on the back side, and they fathered and conceived, not in each other, but in the ground like cicadas" (Plato 1993, 191b–c). In order to save the human race, Zeus shifts their genitals around so that they can procreate while embracing one another, securing future generations and, in a sense, allowing humans to overcome their finitude. Love is henceforth understood as a generative force. Their downward-backward glance is thus, ironically, what moves them forward—toward one another and, through their offspring, toward the future. Love becomes the condition of possibility for futurity, for regeneration.[2]

Aristophanes offers a series of variations on the theme of love as our longing for a long-lost past marked by originary wholeness. He describes love as that which "collects the halves of our original nature, and tries to make a single thing out of the two parts so as to restore our natural condition" (191d), and he claims that if given the choice, people would likely opt for being joined and welded together with their beloved: "The explanation of this is that our original nature was as described above and we were once whole beings. So, the name 'love' is given to the desire for wholeness. Before the current situation, as I explained, we were one whole, but now, because of our misdeed, we have been made by the god to live in a separated state" (192e–93a). Human separateness is thus understood in derivative terms. Difference is secondary and follows from an original state of wholeness.

Irigaray would surely take issue with Aristophanes's understanding of difference as derived from sameness. In her own writing, she consistently argues for the ontological status of sexual difference, and her own understanding of human subjectivity is grounded in the conviction that we are divided from the start, always two, not one plus one, but irreducibly two.[3] Contrary to Aristophanes's account—where oneness has ontological status and difference is a result of our disobedience and therefore a feature of human culture—Irigaray maintains that we are ontologically two, but culturally one. Sexual difference is for her a fundamental fact, albeit one that has been covered over to the point of erasure by a patriarchal culture privileging male subjectivity while reducing woman to a lacking (castrated) object. Oneness, or sameness, is for her a result of that very culture. If love for Aristophanes was an attempt at overcoming difference through fusion, for Irigaray love should instead aim at acknowledging and embracing our originary difference. For her, to love someone is exactly to acknowledge their irreducible difference from us.

For the Plato of the Aristophanic myth, love is thus our striving to overcome difference, and whether this is possible or not in reality, it is the primary driving force of desire. The lover longs for fusion with his or her other half, and the very object of love is understood as a previously lost part of the self. If desire is temporal, time is here construed as a line moving from singular origin to future offspring. Such a temporal model is likely to reproduce an erotic relation that seeks to annihilate rather than celebrate difference. It fails to maintain the becoming of two subjects who are different, and separate. Stanley Rosen has noted that if "Eros were to succeed in making one from two, he would not heal human nature, but destroy it. Aristophanes's real teaching is that cure and ailment constitute a perpetual cycle wherein human genesis gives birth to disease in the act of quenching it" (Rosen 150). Rosen highlights the impossibility of such a return to the origin: "The origin is not only imperfect but altogether inaccessible. Man is a contradiction balanced precariously between two forms of oblivion" (150).

In *Questioning Platonism*, Drew Hyland argues that the Aristophanic description of erotic desire is similar to the Socratic *aporia*. Incompleteness is followed by recognition thereof, which, in turn, is followed by the impossible quest to overcome this incompleteness (Hyland 144–45). We may say that philosophy begins with love but, as such, first and foremost is a reaction to a crisis, namely, the crisis of our inherent separateness. Philosophy is thus a response to the impossibility of wholeness and an attempt to grapple with the tragedy of the human condition. But while wholeness may be impossible, it is, for Aristophanes, nevertheless viewed as our original condition. Moreover, it is our glance toward this ideal past that will move us forward—that, in another of Plato's texts, will force us up the slippery path of the cave and allow us to look into Ideas that are untouched by time (Plato 1991, 514a–21d).

Throughout her work, Irigaray's main criticism of Western philosophy is that it functions as a perpetual repetition of sameness, of the predictable, of the already-said, and therefore, in a sense, already dead. It has lost its relation with desire, which, in her view, "always requires staying in connection both with becoming and the present" (Irigaray 2002, 17). This entails loss of life, of becoming, of movement in time, and of sexual difference: "With the solidification (or freezing) of space-time, the two sexes are separated into opposing binaries" (Bloodsworth-Lugo 35). A philosophy of sexual difference would have to be truthful to presence and to our own openness towards the future. "Presence" on such an account should not, however, be understood as the ever-present completeness of a metaphysics of presence. For Irigaray, presence is always incomplete and transforming, and it must be understood in terms of *co-presence*. Being is always *being-with*, which in turn means that presence is marked by difference.[4]

Only a subject-in-becoming can approach the other reciprocally, by acknowledging their own incompleteness. The round characters of the Aristophanic myth are, therefore, paralyzed by their own completeness. And hence, time freezes, becomes a time of death, or of the past, rather than a time of the living. Julia Kristeva offers an interpretation of Aristophanes's tragic myth in which she points to the fact that the original whole being is incapable of love. He "admires himself in another androgyne and sees only himself, rounded, faultless, otherless" (Kristeva 1987, 70). Interestingly, Kristeva not only points to the absence of otherness in this original schema, but she also adds that the androgyne is "*outside of time;* [. . .] he is *timeless*" (71, emphasis mine). Ignorant of difference, the androgyne is content and free from the curse of desire. This very freedom is, in Kristeva's view, what places the androgyne outside of time. There is nothing to move him. He is trapped in the dead time of sameness. Love does indeed allow for and generate renewal, but renewal only occurs when we are confronted with alterity and alteration.[5]

Irigaray urges us to return to what she calls the "time of life," understood exactly as reciprocal oscillation between two *living* and *loving* subjects. She wants to change our relation to space and time: "To go toward one another requires the elaboration of other space-times than those in which we, Westerners, are accustomed to living" (Irigaray 2002, 19). Such a relational-temporal approach, she explains, opens up the "possibility of arriving in the present, of being in the present, of being capable of co-presence" (48). Even if Aristophanes may have been aware of the impossibility of overcoming our tragic nature, the problem for Irigaray would thus be that he nevertheless upholds wholeness as an ideal to be strived for, and that difference consequently is viewed as a punishment, a deficiency, a problem to be overcome.

There is no doubt that Plato as a thinker ultimately idealizes oneness and wholeness and that he frames such wholeness in eternal atemporal terms (*eidos*). But there is nevertheless a peculiar aspect of Aristophanes's account of our originary wholeness that is worthy of our attention since it brings Plato closer to Irigaray than he might have seemed at first glance. "At first," we learn from Aristophanes, "there were three kinds of human beings, not only two as now, male and female, but also a third that was composed of the other two" (Plato 1993, 189d–e). The androgyne, "being a combination of both male and female" (189e), complicates the very notion of wholeness. Some of the spherical beings of the Aristophanic myth are marked by a kind of internal sexual difference, one that ought to interest a thinker like Irigaray.[6]

To my knowledge, Irigaray never engages at length with Aristophanes's speech, which is rather surprising given its deliberate and frequent references to sexual difference. We find the perhaps most interesting point of intersection between Plato and Irigaray if we turn to those beings of which Aristophanes himself speaks the least, namely, those "women who are split from a woman" (191e). The originary wholeness of which Aristophanes speaks here (that of a being who, after having been split, will strive for lesbian love) comes close to the account Irigaray herself gives of female subjectivity and sexuality. Throughout her work, she has emphasized the fact that female subjectivity has been conceptualized on the basis of masculine parameters: women are seen as failed men; their genitals are viewed as a male organ turned back upon itself, a nonsex. Time and again, Irigaray has suggested that we must understand women on the basis of a wholly different logic. For while man, on her account, is one, woman is two, morphologically speaking. Her genitals are formed of "two lips in continuous contact" (Irigaray 1985, 24). Within herself, she is always already two—but a specific kind of two, a two that is not divisible into one(s).

Such a sexual organ, which is never *one*, in our culture, counts as *none*. And this is how woman has become impossible to define, to name, to count. This is the mystery of the "dark continent" we call woman. In a culture "claiming to count everything, to number everything by units, to inventory everything as individualities," woman becomes the negative, the lack, "the reverse of the only visible and morphologically designatable organ"—that is, the penis (Irigaray 1985, 26). And the whole idea of unity and truth, as Irigaray writes in her poetic essay "When Our Lips Speak Together," comes from men's lack of lips, from "their forgetting of lips" (Irigaray 1985, 208). Representation cuts us up, divides us, separates us. And all we are left with are bodies that do not count, voids awaiting sustenance from the other.

However brief and incomplete this summary of Irigaray's description of female morphology may be, it should become clear that what we said earlier about the impossibility and undesirability of originary wholeness, for Irigaray, nevertheless allows for a kind of wholeness which comes very close to the one described by Aristophanes. Irigaray often speaks of the auto-affection particular to women. Woman can find pleasure in herself and her own body (understood as always already dual, the two lips chiasmically touching each other), and her emphasis on this internal affective duality of woman parallels the auto-affection experienced by the spherical women (and men) of Aristophanes's myth. That said, there nevertheless remains the issue of the irreducibility of the Irigarayan subject—the fact that woman on her account is a two that is irreducible into one(s). If Aristophanes's humans started off with "four hands and a similar number of legs" (Plato 1993,

189e) and "two sets of genitals" (190a), they now have only two hands and legs, and one set of genitals (like us), and we are told that they are careful to obey the gods so as to not be "sliced in two again" (193a), which would leave them with only one hand, one leg and half a set of genitals. These creatures most certainly can be counted—and Aristotle is careful to elaborate the numerical features of the story—whereas Irigaray defies the very basic assumption that two equals one plus one.

Understood as the striving toward (impossible) wholeness, what we have encountered so far in Plato is a protopsychoanalytic notion of desire as lack, picked up by Sigmund Freud as well as Jacques Lacan.[7] The lover seeks that which he or she does not (cannot?) have. The very structure of desire understood in terms of lack is conditioned by the idea of fulfillment, whether it can be achieved or not. In an attempt to break with a tradition that has characterized woman as a lacking being, Irigaray turns away from the language of lack, giving an account of female subjectivity in particular as a kind of wholeness that nevertheless moves toward and is moved by the (male) other. The self and the other, on her account, are not complimentary. The couple is radically asymmetrical. The point of love is thus not to fill a hole within ourselves. We are not, on her account, trying to find a long-lost other half. What is at stake, rather, is the sustainability of difference: love emerges out of the awareness that the other is and will remain a mystery to me, and the wonder that follows from encountering such an abyss.

Love—here understood as the relationship between two irreducibly different subjects (not a subject and an object)—depends on an understanding of time not as a linear-teleological trajectory (from subject to object, from past to future), but rather as a perpetual and unpredictable process of becoming that is made possible precisely through our encounter with the other. Time, for Irigaray, is thus necessarily bound up with our relation to and being with an other. The welcoming of the other, she writes in *To Be Two*, "permits respect and generation," it "encourages becoming, birth and rebirth" (Irigaray 2001, 15). But becoming is only possible if we allow the other to remain other. If we strive for fusion, we will achieve nothing but "fake offspring" in the sense of repetition: I turn the other into a mirror in which I can see my own selfsame image. Love, under such circumstances, will be futile rather than generative, and we fail to respect the uniqueness of the other.

I would like to turn now to another passage of the *Symposium*, namely, Socrates's speech, and to Irigaray's own reading of this passage, in order to flesh out what I mean by this.

Daimonic Encounters: The Intermediary Nature of Love

Socrates recounts a conversation he once had with a woman: Diotima from Mantineia, doubly other, both foreigner and woman, is introduced in her absence at this all-male event. Eros, Diotima informs the young Socrates, is neither god nor mortal. Daimonic in nature, he serves as an intermediary, and since he is "in the middle [he] fills in between the two so that the whole is bound together by [him]" (Plato 1993, 202e). Being the son of Penia (poverty) and Poros (resource), he is both "wedded to need" and "resourceful" at once (203d). Constantly on the move, characterized as a barefoot and homeless wanderer, Eros has inherited his mother's indeterminate nature. His paternal grandmother, Metis (invention), has equipped him with *techné*, "creativity," and the ability to give birth. We learn, moreover, that he sleeps in doorways and on thresholds: between inside and outside. He is neither beautiful nor ugly but, again, between the two, so as to desire and strive for the beauty that he himself lacks.

Eros, on this account, is born out of and conditioned by difference: his parents are male and female, resourceful and poor. He has no whole past to look back to or be mournful about. Does this mean that he is capable of respecting and sustaining difference? As a "seeker of wisdom," Diotima explains, Eros "is in between being wise and being ignorant" (204b), just like the philosopher, whose very existence is marked by an *aporia*. Irigaray notes that he "inherits this endless quest from his mother," that he is "a philosopher through his mother" (Irigaray 1993, 24). Etymologically, we note traces of Eros's genealogy in the *aporia* characterizing Socratic interrogation: aporetic philosophy is quite literally *nonresourceful*, echoing the paternal origin of Eros. The perplexity of the philosopher is due to the absence of Poros (or, put differently, the presence of Penia). And we notice, as we follow Diotima's speech, that what started as praise for love turns into an account of the genesis and nature of philosophy. Eros, Plato seems to suggest, is a philosopher, and philosophy is inherently erotic. Philosophy is desire, or, as we know, love of wisdom. The *Symposium*, on this account, is a text about the inaugural moment of philosophy. Why, it asks, do we begin to philosophize?

Diotima challenges the either-or dialectic that dominates our culture and laughs repeatedly at Socrates's difficulty in understanding that difference need not be oppositional—that what is lacking in beauty is not necessarily ugly, and that what is lacking in goodness is not necessarily bad. By introducing an intermediary, she offers a different logic than the one we know, a logic praised by Irigaray in her reading of this passage. In the essay "Sorcerer Love: A Reading of Plato, *Symposium*, 'Diotima's Speech,'" Irigaray notes that Diotima's dialectical method "doesn't use opposition to make the first term pass into the second in order to achieve a synthesis between the two, as Hegel does. From the outset, she establishes an *intermediary*, that will never be abandoned as a means or a path" (Irigaray 1993, 20). Everything, therefore, is "in movement, in a state of becoming" (21). Love is "never fulfilled, always becoming" (21).

This should shed light on the questions with which I opened this chapter. If love is to remain an intermediary, it cannot create fusion between a subject and an object. It must be able to cultivate two subjectivities, held together, and simultaneously kept apart, by the space-time that separates the one from the other. As Mary Bloodsworth-Lugo puts it in her reading of Irigaray: "In Diotima's speech, the role of love is not to unite men and women in a state of sameness; rather, it is to preserve and mediate their difference(s)" (Bloodsworth-Lugo 29). And as Gail Schwab notes in an article that treats ethical relations through the lens of space rather than time: "The truly ethical love relation can exist only in the 'between,' in the interval created between the one and the other. We go toward the other in response to the attraction he or she exerts upon our existence, but there is no ultimate merging or blending of the one into the other. The interval where love circulates must be maintained at the risk of negating the existence of both the one and the other" (Schwab 89).

We might want to say that to show true interest in the other is to respect that which *inter est*—that which *lies between* us and them. Such an approach would involve a "transition to a new age"—an age of sexual difference—and, again, it would require "a change in our perception and conception of *space-time* [. . .] and of the interval *between*" (Irigaray 1993, 7). Love would, in other words, have to be construed as "an intermediate terrain, a mediator, a space-time of permanent *passage*" (28), and if such a space-time is not established and maintained, there is, Irigaray claims, "no question of becoming nearer. [. . .] [P]roximity is [. . .] defined through an object and not by a movement of approximation between subjects. And this object is already in the past, not in the present or in the future" (Irigaray 2002, 26). In her own work, she has stressed the importance of such a spatiotemporal gap—and its capacity to create intimacy and proximity: "Desire demands a sense of attraction: a change in the interval, the displacement of the subject or of the object in their relations of nearness and distance" (Irigaray 1993, 8).[8]

The spatiotemporal interval of distance and proximity that unfolds between two subjects constitutes an important third term in a body of work most commonly characterized as pursuing a dialectic of two. Irigaray elaborates this further in *The Way of Love*: "It appears that the real exists as at least *three*: a real corresponding to the masculine subject, a real corresponding to the feminine subject, and a real corresponding to their *relation*. These three reals thus each correspond to a world but these three worlds are in interaction" (Irigaray 2002, 111, emphasis mine). Irigaray is careful to stress the interdependence among the three, on the one hand, yet their irreducibility to one another, on the other. Like Diotima, her dialectic is one where the third term does not merge into two that are opposite. Rather, the two are asymmetrical and irreducible—radically other to each other—and the third (that which *inter est*) is like a bridge: it provides a passage over the abyss that opens up between two subjects while at the same time keeping them apart, and, importantly, it does not itself disappear once the passage has been made. It is not like a ladder that we can get rid of once we have ascended to the next level. Throughout *The Way of Love*, Irigaray stresses that the dialectical relation she is embracing is horizontal, not vertical:

> Here again, our culture has favored verticality, the relation to the Idea allegedly at the summit of approximate reproductions, the relation to the Father, to the leader, to the celestial Wholly-Other. The relation to the other, present here and now beside or in front of me on the earth, has been little cultivated as a horizontal dimension of human becoming. Now this dimension is probably even more specific to humanity than verticality, if at least it involves the respect for the other in their irreducibility, their transcendence. (144–45)[9]

It should come as no surprise, then, that Irigaray expresses disappointment in the way Diotima's speech evolves. Having praised her attention to the intermediary nature of Eros, and—as Bloodsworth-Lugo has pointed out before me—having seen Diotima herself as representing the "(re)conception of space-time" that Irigaray calls for in her own work (Bloodsworth-Lugo 36), Irigaray is chagrined by the fact that the bridgelike nature of love comes to be replaced by a ladderlike function in the second half of Diotima's speech. Rachel Jones eloquently describes this progression: "Diotima's teaching culminates in her delineation of the so-called ladder of love: a properly educated soul will pass from love of a particular body, to a love of beauty in appearances in general, to the higher beauty of souls, and then of laws and knowledge, until finally it is drawn towards the ultimate encounter with Beauty itself" (Jones 2011, 89). Bridge is replaced by ladder; horizontal love by vertical love; and the intermediary nature of love is, as a consequence, abruptly lost.

Diotima proceeds to speak about the function of love, which she defines as "giving birth in beauty both in body and in soul" (Plato 1993, 216b). Love, when it creates offspring, is what makes us immortal: all human beings are pregnant in body and soul, and through procreation we transgress our finitude and secure a future in our children, or in the ideas that we give birth to. We recognize the emphasis on birth and procreation from the *Theatetus*, where Socrates describes his own philosophical method as a form of midwifery, giving credit to his mother, Phaenarete, who was a midwife.[10] Diotima goes on to further blur the line between bodily pregnancy and philosophical procreation, as she develops a narrative about the ascent from physical to abstract and universal beauty.

Feminist thinkers have pointed to this moment in Plato's thought as a kind of matricide, as the moment in which the male philosopher once and for all appropriates and destroys the female power of giving birth, turning it into a purely male activity inscribed in the very practice of philosophy. While Aristophanes introduced sexual difference as an integral aspect of human procreation, his speech is, simultaneously, a story of male heritage and lineage. Zeus, like the Judeo-Christian God, is the sole creator in this drama. We are told that the navel—usually the only visible reminder of our maternal origins—is a result of the skin being stretched and pulled together, "just as purses are pulled together with a drawstring" (Plato 1993, 190e). As Adriana Cavarero puts it in her reading of Aristophanes's speech: "A symbolic matricide of the first degree has already been affected here" (Cavarero 97).

Platonic thought, according to Cavarero, is "marked by a *mimetic* desire for female experience. The pregnant, birth-giving male, like the male who practices midwifery, stands as the emblematic figure of true philosophy" (92). Page duBois, similarly, argues that Plato "uses the tension between the sexes in Greek culture to assert the authority of the male at the scene of philosophy, but also, and more importantly, his own desire to appropriate the powers of the female makes that authority a very provisional one and marks the Platonic text as the threshold of a new description of sexual difference" (duBois 144). What would such a threshold signify? In what way, according to duBois, does the description of sexual difference change with Plato?

With the appropriation of the specificity of female powers, duBois argues, man becomes self-sufficient and autonomous. He no longer needs woman. Difference has been turned into hierarchal sameness. Prior to Plato, woman was other, different, unique. As a result of this appropriation, she has become same, but inferior. The female has been stripped of her metaphorical otherness (that is, her birth-giving powers) and has been turned into nothing but a defective male, defined by lack. Plato, duBois continues to argue, thus reinscribes the act of generation and reproduction and transfers it to the philosopher, whose experience in labor and birth is idealized and made to transcend that of women: "Philosophical reproduction is ascribed exclusively to men who will inseminate each other with ideas in a sexual act in which women are excluded" (152).

We find what looks like an example of this at the beginning of the *Symposium*. When Socrates first arrives at the party, after having spent some time contemplating alone on the porch, Agathon invites him to recline next to him. "Socrates," he says, "recline here beside me so that by touching you I may gain the benefit of the wisdom that came to you on the porch" (Plato 1993, 175c). Socrates sits down and replies: "I'd be happy, Agathon, if wisdom were the kind of thing that would flow from the one of us with more of it to the one with less when we touch each other, the way water flows through a piece of yarn from the fuller cup to the emptier" (175d).

This homoerotic moment embodies the critique formulated by duBois. We see, here, the articulation of a metaphoric act of procreation, in an all-male context. There is, moreover, reason to think that what Socrates here judges to be impossible is exactly what has taken place between him and Diotima. At the beginning of Socrates's recounting of their conversation, we learn that she has "instructed" him "in the activities of Love" (201d). Practically or just theoretically? We do not know. What we do know, however, is that Socrates has acquired Diotima's wisdom. David Halperin notes that Socrates "appears to have drawn off some of Diotima's wisdom, to have been filled sufficiently full of it to make him, by his own admission, an expert in erotics" (Halperin 148).

The result of this is that Diotima herself vanishes, while Socrates grows. She is absent, while he is at the center of attention at this occasion. Irigaray stresses this dynamic in her reading of the text: "Of course, once again, *she is not there. Socrates relates her words*. Perhaps he distorts them unwittingly or unknowingly" (Irigaray 1993, 27). Cavarero was not incorrect in concluding that "it is in Plato that the founding rite of matricide achieves its philosophical completion, even though not yet hardened into a systematic form" (Cavarero 9). On Irigaray's reading, Plato here offers an account that on the surface celebrates female generativity but that ultimately provides the very language and conceptual apparatus that will come to annihilate such feminine powers. And she wonders: "Is this the foundational act of meta-physics?" (Irigaray 1993, 27).

While I am sympathetic to these readings—I myself have indeed argued elsewhere that a certain kind of matricide can be located in the Platonic dialogues (Söderbäck 2016)—I think that Diotima's speech in the *Symposium* does lend itself to a different reading, worthy of our attention. To say that Plato simply appropriates female powers would be to deny his clear acknowledgment of the necessity of femininity within philosophy. Plato does, after all, not hide or silence Socrates's female teacher. Diotima is physically absent, but by no means symbolically so. The question here is if her absence is a manifestation of the appropriation of feminine powers, or (and this, I think, would be a more fruitful position to take), if it is the means by which Plato comments on the normative absence of femininity in philosophy in general.[11]

To return to Irigaray's reading of Diotima's speech, she is first and foremost concerned with the sudden loss of what she herself has praised: the intermediary and open-ended (i.e., nonlinear and nonteleological) nature of love. Echoing Plato's procreative language, she notes that "Diotima's method miscarries," that "love loses its daimonic character," and that Diotima ultimately is guilty of a "failure of love" (Irigaray 1993, 27). This is so because a split has emerged between mortality and immortality, which ultimately undermines the subversive fluidity that Diotima first formulated as her point of departure: "Something becomes frozen in space-time with the loss of a vital intermediary . . . A sort of teleological triangle is put into place instead of a perpetual journey, a perpetual transvaluation, a permanent becoming," Irigaray writes. She adds that "if procreation becomes [love's] goal, it risks losing its internal motivation, its 'inner' fecundity, its slow and constant generation, regeneration" (27). We are back again with a far too teleological-linear temporal model for love, and hence its perpetual becoming is lost, replaced by an instrumental logic of reproduction.

Love, then, is no longer an end in itself; it has been reduced to a means for an external goal (the child) with the result that a more standard Hegelian dialectic comes to govern the dynamics of love, now understood as an act of synthesis instead of the ever-oscillating movement of becoming that sustains the irreducible space between two subjects. "In the second part of her discourse, [Diotima] treated Love itself as a means. She doubled its intermediary function and subjected it to a *telos*. Her method seems less powerful here than at the beginning of her remarks, when she held love to be the mediator of a state of becoming with no objective other than becoming," Irigaray concludes (33).

For Irigaray, it is because we have lost the *in-between* that we are unable to come close to the other without appropriating him or her. Philosophy after Plato has, moreover, lost touch with the other through its priority of a language of monologue: "[S]peech speaks with itself alone"; it remains internal to the speaker and does not invite the other; it "closes up in a circle" (Irigaray 2002, 32). The time of life is lost, and all we are left with is monological discourse and an eternity already marked by death. I wonder, though, if Irigaray does not draw too hasty a conclusion here. Again, I would like to call attention to the ambiguity and tension internal to Plato's discourse (which, importantly, is *not* monologic but is presented in the form of dialogue). First of all, we must recall that the movement of ascent, for Plato, is never simply linear. We know from the cave allegory in the *Republic* that whoever is liberated from the shadowy realm of the underworld, whoever embarks on a journey of ascent, only does so in order to then turn back into the cave (voluntarily or by force). Ascent is *always* followed by descent (Plato 1991, 516e, 520c).

That said, we must note that even though the dialectical journey for Plato is one of perpetual return, that toward which we move is wholeness, whether we are in the process of ascending or descending. The *eidos* are eternal (being, not becoming), and the dialectical knower is one "who is capable of an overview" (Plato 1991, 537c). One must be capable of seeing the whole, not just the partial. If love, on Aristophanes's account, was that which aimed at binding us together and melding us into one, the role of the philosopher king, on Socrates's account in the *Republic*, is that of "binding the city together" (520a). The question is: Must we sacrifice difference to secure unity and wholeness?

Not necessarily. Ascent is followed by descent in the *Symposium*, too. Immediately after Socrates's speech, where Diotima has described the ladder of love, the feast is interrupted by the arrival of Alcibiades. Irigaray limits her reading to the discourse of Socrates and Diotima, and by ignoring the final speech of the dialogue I think she misses an important ambiguity in the Platonic account of love. Drunk and rambunctious, Alcibiades reminds us of the corporeal aspects of love, both in appearance and in speech. He enters the room accompanied by the flute girl who, at the beginning of the dialogue, had been sent away to a room in the back to ensure the exclusively male nature of the gathering. The praising of love has hitherto occurred between men alone, but, at this point in the dialogue, a woman is present (not in absentia, as was the case with Diotima, but in person). This last speech is one far removed from the abstraction of absolute, eternal beauty. Alcibiades speaks of his own personal experience of love, embodied and charged with ambivalence (he loves Socrates as much as he hates him), unfolding in its very particularity, and displaying human vulnerability. Their relation is far from pure—it is one of attraction, rejection, and jealousy. Nevertheless, the speech is constantly referred to as a discourse of truth (Plato 1993, 214e–15a).

Could it be that truth, in addition to being eternal and absolute, is the expression of singular experience, grounded in embodied vulnerability? We should keep in mind here that we no longer are dealing with a speech about Eros. The dialogue, in its very final moments, again underlines the intimate relationship between philosophy and love: Alcibiades speaks in praise of Socrates, the philosopher, and the erotic practice revealed must literally be understood as the practice of philosophy as such (not merely as a theoretical activity, but exactly as a practice that is inherently embodied and marked by and grounded in the sensual). It is worth noting that Alcibiades repeatedly refers to Socrates as being "daimonic" (219c), describing him as a Satyr and a Silenus—Greek mythological figures that are both human and nonhuman (human and goat in the first case, human and horse in the latter). Socrates is characterized as being "barefoot" (220b), as was Eros in Diotima's speech, and, at the party, they end up arguing about who should sit in the middle: Socrates, Alcibiades, or Agathon (222e–23a). We are, again, faced with love as an intermediary, always incomplete, in constant becoming.

In the final passage of the dialogue, we are told that Socrates, Aristophanes, and Agathon are the ones to last throughout the night despite excessive drinking. Aristodemus, who is the narrator of the entire dialogue, recalls that "Socrates was forcing them to accept that the same man could know how to compose both a comedy and a tragedy" (223d). Aristophanes—the comedian—has indeed offered what is arguably a tragic account of the nature and genesis of love, and Plato himself—a tragedian and philosopher—has crafted a variety of speeches in celebration of love, both tragic and comical ones, both embodied and disembodied. In relation to each other, they are contradictive, diverse, singular, and ambiguous. As such, they give us a hint of the true nature of love as being ever-changing and in-between: Eros, or love, is indeed a "great daimon" (202d), and "its fecundity is *mediumlike, daimonic*" (Irigaray 1993, 26).

Conclusion

In *I Love to You*, Irigaray brings our attention to the temporal movement of love. In saying "I love you," I make a claim that reduces my lover to an object of possession. "I love *to* you" is a gesture rather than an act of ownership and appropriation. It is a constant asymptotic "towards" that respects the irreducible space between two separate beings. The title of another of her books, *The Way of Love*, can be understood in similar terms. Love is a path, but it does not lead to an already defined end. It is the path between you and me, always there between us, assuring our connectedness but also the separation between two subjects that can never become one, nor same.

Philosophy, since Plato, has taken itself to be an erotic practice—the love of wisdom. Irigaray has repeatedly criticized this very tradition for its blindness to sexual difference. By excluding the particularities of female subjectivity, this tradition is founded on sameness and, as an extension, is incapable of articulating human relations in terms of intersubjectivity rather than subject-object-relations. My own engagement with Plato does not simply amount to the claim that "the history of metaphysics"—understood as that tradition which reduces difference to sameness, and a time of life and love to a time of progress—begins with Plato. Rather, I have tried to show how, in Plato, we find multiple voices, some that could be thought of exactly as inaugurating the abovementioned tradition, yet others that seem to articulate just the kind of relationship that I, with Irigaray, am calling for here. What I have tried to show is that the possibility of an ethical relation between two subjects depends on a reconsideration and rearticulation of the nature of love understood temporally—time here understood not as linear progress but, rather, as continuous displacement, perpetual becoming, and the co-presence that unfolds between two living and loving subjects.

Notes

1. This Platonic dialogue consists of seven speeches. A full account of Plato's views on the nature of love would demand a reading of all speeches, alongside dialogues like the *Phaedrus* and the *Republic*. I will, however, first and foremost focus on Aristophanes's and Socrates's speeches in this dialogue. My reason for turning to these two passages in particular is that they lend themselves to a discussion of the temporal aspects of love and to the role of sexual difference in the context of love. They are, moreover, arguably the most influential of Plato's discussions of

love, and Irigaray has engaged with Diotima's speech at length in an essay that I will discuss in what follows.

2. In an article entitled "Desiring Chaos: Gender, Difference, and Future Possibilities," Cris Mayo argues against the claim that Aristophanes's "account of desire is nostalgic and backward-looking," trying to make a case for futurity being the primary task of desire, its force being productive (Mayo 9). As we will see when we look at Irigaray's reading of Diotima's speech in the *Symposium*, Irigaray is highly skeptical of the characterization of love as primarily procreative since, she argues, this imposes a linear-teleological dynamic onto the sphere of love.

3. In an interview, Irigaray famously states that "between man and woman the negativity [la négativité] is, dare I say it, of an ontological, irreducible type" (Irigaray 1995, 110).

4. For an extended discussion of this claim, see Söderbäck 2013.

5. What Kristeva fails to acknowledge, however, is that the androgyne in fact *does* carry otherness within—a mode of existence that comes very close to her own account of human subjectivity as being marked by internal strangeness (Kristeva 1991). The Aristophanic creatures, I argue, may be self-sufficient and narcissistic, but they are nevertheless marked by internal strangeness, otherness, and difference—even sexual difference—as we will see in what follows.

6. The term *androgynon* is made up of the Greek words for man (*anér*) and woman (*gyné*).

7. We should also note that these creatures suffer from an acute castration complex. Just like the Freudian little boy will revere his father from fear of being castrated, humans according to Aristophanes "are afraid that if we do not maintain good order in our relations with the gods we may be sliced in two again" (Plato 1993, 193a).

8. For a thoroughgoing discussion of the role of the interval in Irigaray's work, see Hill.

9. For an extended analysis of the vertical-horizontal relation in Irigaray's work, see Schwab. Her analysis focuses primarily on issues of space rather than time, but it resonates with my analysis in that she wants to look "beyond two-dimensionality toward the fullness of space" (78), which dovetails nicely with my own attempt to move beyond a linear temporal model thought in relational terms.

10. "My art of midwifery is in general like theirs [real midwives]; the only difference is that my patients are men, not women, and my concern is not with the body but with the soul that is in travail of birth" (Plato 2003, 150b).

11. It is interesting to note that when a thinker like Hannah Arendt inscribes natality into the basic structure of human action, and when she does so without *ever* talking about it in terms of female generative powers, she is celebrated for bringing a paradigmatically feminine experience onto the philosophical scene. When Plato does something similar, he is charged with appropriating female powers rather than celebrating them. Is Plato bound to be criticized simply because he is a man?

Works Cited

Bloodsworth-Lugo, Mary K. 2007. *In-Between Bodies*. Albany: State University of New York Press.

Cavarero, Adriana. 1995. *In Spite of Plato: A Feminist Rewriting of Ancient Philosophy*. Translated by Serena Anderlini-D'Onofrio and Áine O'Healy. New York: Routledge.

duBois, Page. 1994. "The Platonic Appropriation of Reproduction." In *Feminist Interpretations of Plato*, edited by Nancy Tuana. University Park: Pennsylvania State University Press.

Halperin, David M. 1990. "Why Is Diotima a Woman?" In *One Hundred Years of Homosexuality and Other Essays on Greek Love*. New York: Routledge.

Hill, Rebecca. 2012. *The Interval: Relation and Becoming in Irigaray, Aristotle, and Bergson*. New York: Fordham University Press.

Hyland, Drew. 2004. *Questioning Platonism: Continental Interpretations of Plato*. Albany: State University of New York Press.

Irigaray, Luce. 1985. *This Sex Which Is Not One*. Translated by Catherine Porter. Ithaca: Cornell University Press.

———. 1993. *An Ethics of Sexual Difference*. Translated by Carolyn Burke and Gillian C. Gill. Ithaca: Cornell University Press.

———. 1995. " 'Je—Luce Irigaray': A Meeting with Luce Irigaray." Interview conducted by Elizabeth Hirsh and Gary A. Olson. Translated by Elizabeth Hirsh and Gaëton Brulotte. *Hypatia* 10, no. 2: 93–114.

———. 1996. *I Love to You: Sketch of a Possible Felicity in History*. Translated by Alison Martin. New York: Routledge.

———. 2001. *To Be Two*. Translated by Monique M. Rhodes and Marco F. Cocito-Monoc. New York: Routledge.

———. 2002. *The Way of Love*. Translated by Heidi Bostic and Stephen Pluháček. New York: Continuum.

Jones, Rachel. 2011. *Key Contemporary Thinkers: Irigaray*. Cambridge, UK: Polity.

Kristeva, Julia. 1987. *Tales of Love*. Translated by Leon S. Roudiez. New York: Columbia University Press.

———. 1991. *Strangers to Ourselves*. Translated by Leon S. Roudiez. New York: Columbia University Press.

Mayo, Cris Susan. 2006. "Desiring Chaos: Gender, Difference, and Future Possibilities." *Philosophical Studies in Education* 37: 9–19.

Plato. 1991. *Republic*. Translated by Allan Bloom. New York: Basic Books.

———. 1993. *Plato's Erotic Dialogues: The Symposium and The Phaedrus*. Translated by William S. Cobb. Albany: State University of New York Press.

———. 2003. *Plato's Theory of Knowledge: The Theatetus and The Sophist*. Translated by Francis M. Cornford. Mineola, NY: Dover.

Proust, Marcel. 1982. *Remembrance of Things Past*, vol. 3, *The Captive, the Fugitive, and Time Regained.* Translated by C. K. Scott Moncrieff and Terence Kilmartin. New York: Vintage Books.

Rosen, Stanley. 1968. *Plato's* Symposium. New Haven: Yale University Press.

Schwab, Gail M. 2011. "Beyond the Vertical and the Horizontal: Spirituality, Space, and Alterity in the Work of Luce Irigaray." In *Thinking with Irigaray*, edited by Mary C. Rawlinson, Sabrina L. Hom, and Serene J. Khader. Albany: State University of New York Press.

Söderbäck, Fanny. 2013. "Being in the Present: Derrida and Irigaray on the Metaphysics of Presence." *Journal of Speculative Philosophy* 27, no. 3: 253–64.

———. 2016. "In Search for the Mother through the Looking-Glass: On Time, Origins, and Beginnings in Plato and Irigaray." In *Engaging the World: Thinking after Luce Irigaray*, edited by Mary Rawlinson, 11–37. Albany: State University of New York Press.

Life-Giving Sex versus Mere Animal Existence

Irigaray's and Badiou's Paradoxically Chiasmatic Conceptions of "Woman" and Sexual Pleasure

LOUISE BURCHILL

Throughout Irigaray's corpus—from the models of female *jouissance* and morphological motifs of woman's two lips to her later paradigmatization of the desiring relation between man and woman as a new configuration of (inter)subjectivity—sex, or sexual pleasure, is conceptualized by her as a veritable event of *rebirth,* capable of bringing both partners "back to life" through replunging them "into the maternal womb and, beyond that conception, awakening [them] to another—amorous—birth" (Irigaray 2001a, 121). Such a rebirthing takes, of course, different forms for men and women; however, for this *vital* duality to be recognized within Western culture, it is requisite to dismantle the dominant (masculine) modes of thought that not only deny the existence of a sex (in all the senses of the term) nonconform to the male sexual imaginary but also obliterate the debt all living beings owe to the maternal space—literally, the life-giving sex—from which they emerge. Constitutive of our entire culture, this "oblivion of the maternal origin" (Irigaray 2004, x) has been veiled or covered over by male subjectivity's having ordered thought and modes of being-in-the-world in terms of dichotomies between sensible and intelligible, nature and spirit, body and soul, subject and object, and so on, such that the maternal world is reduced to a "natural pole" at the disposal of masculine activity. With the body thereby relegated to "pure facticity" and the sexual act to the realm of mere naturality or animal instinct, transcendence is transposed to a "higher" sphere—rather than being located, as Irigaray, on the contrary, would have it, in the already partially spiritual "here and now" of a carnal communion respecting the transcendence of the other (Irigaray 2001b, 18). A certain "prefiguration," or even "instantiation," of what a living recognition of sexual difference would entail is given, for Irigaray, by that "most divine act"—the sexual act—when the gift of "form, birth, and incarnation" is effectuated in an *exchange* recognizing the irreducible (sexuate) singularity of one and the other partner (Irigaray 1993, 51). In this case, not only can desire and love no longer be dissociated (any more than body and spirit, immanence and transcendence), but the task of cultivating desire as a between-Two, or site of mutual transcendence, is revealed as that alone "through which humanity really becomes accomplished as humanity" (Irigaray 2008, 72).

A very different conception of the sexual act and sexual difference, as well as of desire, love, and humanity, is found in the work of Alain Badiou. In principle, absolutely nothing on the level of sexed being has any pertinence for the demarcation of the categories of sexual difference as he defines these, such that the very bodies engaged in a sexual act are, in themselves, as it were, sexually insignificant and subsist simply within the brute opposition of animal sexuality. In other words, any and all sexual interaction, considered from the point of view of desire or sexual pleasure/*jouissance* alone, engages each participant solely within her or his "animal particularity" and is, thereby, strictly masturbatory: sex per se is a computation of "1 plus 1," without this yielding any "2" (Badiou 2008, 187). This incapacity to engender a between-Two follows, for Badiou, from desire's "intrinsic finitude," as determined by its being always desire of an object borne by the body—a partial object or "object *a*" in Lacan's terminology—and neither the body as such nor, much less, the other as subject. Far from bringing into play a reciprocal recognition of transcendences, desire strictly *imprisons* each of the participants in her or his particularity. That which alone introduces the dimension of sexual difference, for Badiou, is love, insofar as it places woman and man in relation to a common term or "atom of universality"—the undetermined "something" at the basis of their love—that consists, all in all, in a transmutation of the object *a*, whereby this acquires the supplementary, and "more essential," function of assuring an approach to the being of the other (Badiou and Tarby 2013, 52, 64–65). Love proposes, then, a radically new experience of the truth concerning what it is to be Two and not One, and reveals, by this very fact, that the two sexes participate in a common humanity, *universally valid* for everyone irrespective of their sex.

It is no wonder, then, that the opposition of Irigaray's and Badiou's concepts of sexual difference, love, and the sexual relationship[1] has become somewhat of a commonplace among commentators of Badiou, who discern in Irigaray's claims for a recognition of difference the perfect foil to the latter's affirmation of a "transparticular" universality. Peter Hallward, one of Badiou's most astute interlocutors, was undoubtedly the first to set down—in both the preface to his translation of Badiou's *Ethics* and the chapter of his *Badiou: A Subject to Truth* dealing with love and sexual difference—a point-by-point comparison of the "diametrically opposed" tenets of the two protagonists. Badiou is said, for example, to assign "the truth of sexual difference to an exclusively subjective realm of thought," while "Irigaray anchors it in an ultimately specified physical frame of reference, the 'body as primary home.' " Or again, Badiou would stress "the absence and impossibility of a sexual relationship," whereas "Irigaray specifies a vague notion of 'relation,' " an "essentially feminine disposition" that would constitute the " 'natural' starting point for an eventual reconciliation of the sexes, as guided by woman's primordial experience of maternity" (Hallward 2003, 189–90). The overarching opposition between Badiou and Irigaray, Hallward states, is that between philosophy and *antiphilosophy*, with Irigaray's distrust of philosophy's pretensions to truth and system leading her to affirm a kind of transcendent, ineffable meaning, lying beyond the logical structures to which cognitive propositions are confined. Badiou has himself qualified Irigaray as "the anti-philosopher par excellence," contending that she operates "a violent determination of philosophy on the basis of the category of 'woman,' "[2] such that this becomes a sort of supercognitive category in accordance with which philosophy, if it is not to be indicted as a source of illusion and will-to-mastery, must admit a feminine specificity in the realm of symbolic initiatives or truths. Such a requisite is, for Badiou (though with a certain qualification, as we shall see later), complete anathema: "woman," as an "identitarian predicate" referring to but one of the infinity of differences comprising humankind, is precisely a position that authentic thought, in its necessary universalizing scope, must cross through in its assertion of that which is the Same for everyone. In other words, given that no truth—no universal—can be premised upon the existing state of things, any position seeking to promote a particularism, such as sexuate identity, as the bearer of innovation in symbolic fields such as love, politics . . . , or philosophy, is quite simply (for the Badiou of the eighties and nineties, at least) doomed to insignificance (Badiou 2001, 25–28; 2003a, 5–15). Claims for a philosophy in the feminine, much less a feminist philosophy, are, in short, without any consequence whatsoever, as would equally be—in all logic, at least—Irigaray's contention that the cultivation of sexual difference is the only path of a true accomplishment of humanity, *qua* humanity.

This profusion of diametrical oppositions should not, however, obnubilate a cardinal point of intersection or, as it were, "fixed star" as regards the two thinkers' work—one that sets them in joint opposition to the majoritarian stance in, or of, contemporary gender studies. For both, sexual difference is a matter of an irreducible disjunction, a "constitutive Two": "there are two sexes, not one, not three, or an infinite number," in Badiou's words (2008, 226); "across the whole world, there are, there are only, men and women," in Irigaray's (1996, 47). Attempts to deconstruct the man/woman polarity in favour of a multiplicity of sexes and/or gender indistinction are, as a result, dismissed by Badiou and Irigaray alike as a form of postmodernist sophistry, fully consonant with the capitalist ideology of a generalized equivalence of values. Badiou makes this particularly clear when he denounces "the postmodernist paradigm" of a "quasi-continuous multiple of gender constructions" as doing nothing "but uphold, in the element of sex, the founding axiom of democratic materialism: there are only bodies and language, there is no truth" (Badiou 2009, 421). Irigaray, for her part, queries whether at stake in the "dream of the dissolution of material, corporal, and social identity" is nothing but money, qualifying those who seek to efface sexual difference "by resorting to monosexuality, to the unisex, or to what is called [gender] identification" as "rich" or "naïve" (Irigaray 1996, 61–62). For both, such a dream or fantasy of a proliferation of genders is illusory both in substance and intent. This "new opium of the people," as Irigaray puts it, "annihilates the other in the illusion of a reduction to identity, equality, and sameness" that ultimately leads to "a whole set of delusions" (ibid.). Echoing this insistence on a reductive sameness and monosexuality, intrinsically illusion-bound, Badiou decries the multiple gender positions promulgated by "Anglo-American gender studies" as "infinitely more coded and monotonous" than its proponents suppose. The latter's "world of sex" is, he states, "an entirely atonic world" (Badiou 2009, 421)—one in which individuals remain enclosed in their particularism or singularity, without there being the conditions, or the choice, of an experience of difference.

As framed by this shared postulate of radical duality, Badiou's and Irigaray's respective conceptions of sexual difference, while certainly divergent, prove to be more complex, more convoluted, and, in certain respects, paradoxically more complementary—in their very opposition—than commentators have hitherto countenanced. In order to elaborate this claim, we must first review the broad lines of what each of the two understands by sexual difference, beginning with the question of the relation that this would, or would not, hold to biology.

Irigaray's Analytics of Sexual Difference and the Desiring Relation Between the Sexes

Accusations of biologism have, of course, been directed at Irigaray's work from its inception, with Hallward's claim that she anchors sexual difference in "the body as primary home" situated, thereby, in a long-established current of critical commentary. Yet, while Irigaray certainly upholds sexual difference as "an immediate natural given" and "a real and irreducible component of the universal" (Irigaray 1996, 47), what this difference entails is most adamantly not for her the assertion of simple biological or natural destiny (Irigaray 2002, 128–29) but, rather, a threefold articulation of biological, morphological, and relational components. First, the relation to the mother as engenderer or the first other: given that it is not the same to be born from someone of the same sex as from someone of a sex that is different, there ensue distinct relational identities for men and women. Second, the possibility of giving life: women are able to engender like the mother, with their bodies being able to nourish others directly, while men are not. Third, the relation of corporeal morphology and the sexual act: the fact that women have an internal sexual organ and, in this sense, "make love within themselves," while men have an external sexual organ and "make love outside of themselves," entails that they relate in different ways to the other and to the self (Irigaray 2004, x; 2008, 3, 102–4, 107–8). Taken as a whole, the complex configuration of biological, morphological, and relational components that informs all these features corresponds to a radically different construction of subjectivity for the two sexes. Subjectivity being neither universal nor neutral, but *sexuately* specific, "man and woman are *culturally* different" and "do not live in the same world" (Irigaray 2002, 129; 2008, 70).

That nonrecognition of sexuate specificity and of the determining role of the maternal-feminine has yielded a "humanity" that is the reflection of male subjectivity alone—a subjectivity that, asserting itself as universal norm, sets out to create a world in its own image precisely *as a function* of its inadequate working-through of the maternal-feminine relation—is, of course, the tenet which underpins Irigaray's entire project. Constitutively founded on the exclusion or, more strictly, the *foreclusion*, of the maternal-feminine, our entire culture—philosophy and symbolic thought, along with all other forms of "existential dwelling," language per se included—has been cast in masculine terms and serves, as such, as a substitute of sorts for the relation with the mother, *qua* "first dwelling." The failure of the masculine subject to recognize the mother's singularity as the first human other, or the role his first placental dwelling plays in his affective development, condemns him, in fact, to an undifferentiated adhesion to the maternal world, from which then stems, unconsciously, his drive to supplant, appropriate, or master this world through his productions (Irigaray 2008, 101; 2010, 265–66). Man's unavowed—unconscious—nostalgia for the maternal body similarly orchestrates his desiring, affective relations, notably dooming the sexual relationship with woman to be played out on the imaginary mode of an ersatz, inversion, or apotropaic conjuration of an incestuous return to the matrix. Our tradition's dissociation of desire and love, with its attendant devalorization of the sexual act as degrading or animalistic and the projection of spiritual transcendence onto "a higher sphere," equally stems from this nonrecognition of the other. Were desire and love to be cultivated, on the contrary, as a relation between two differently sexuated identities whose distinct subjectivities or self-affections are respected, not only would man be able to "leave a horizon built without a real differing from the mother's world" but the creation of "*a shared world*" would bring about the realization of humanity as such (Irigaray 2010, 270; 2008, 75).

Insofar, then, as the desiring relation between the two sexes is—if properly cultivated—nothing less, for Irigaray, than the path to a new form of human existence, we might well return here to Hallward's claim that this possibility derives for Irigaray from the " 'natural' starting point" of an "essentially feminine disposition" towards relationality, as "guided by woman's primordial experience of maternity." Hallward's attributing to Irigaray "a vague notion of relation," variously predicated as "natural," "essential," and "primordial," amounts to an accusation of biological reductionism: woman, Hallward's Irigaray would seem to say, has an innate disposition to establishing relations with others because of the female body's capacity to give birth and/or something akin to a maternal instinct. This accords, moreover, with Hallward's immediately preceding claim that Irigaray anchors the truth of sexual difference in the body (Hallward 2003, 189).

The fundamental problem with both sets of claims—biology as the bedrock of Irigaray's concept of sexual difference as well as the natural starting point for the reconciliation she advocates between the sexes—is that they disregard the psychoanalytical underpinning of Irigaray's notion of relation. Certainly, Irigaray argues—to cite here passages Hallward might well have adduced—that "the feminine world is, *by birth*, more relational than that of the boy" (Irigaray 2010, 269, my emphasis), "the girl knows what it means to beget, it is a familiar experience for her already, through intuition or feeling" (ibid.), or, again, that "woman herself has to help man in differing his course from a maternal beginning [and] has to bring about a relational world" (Irigaray 2004, xii), but what is in question here is *not* an innate disposition: Irigaray is conceptualizing a particular modality of the primary relationship to the mother.

It is a core psychoanalytic postulate, first set out in Freud's writings on femininity and sexual difference (as well as in texts by Helene Deutsch, Melanie Klein, and other analysts) in the 1920s and 1930s, that the structural inflexions of the mother-child relationship, determinant of the construction of subjectivity, depend on whether the child is of the same sex, or not, as the mother. The first object of love for both the boy and the girl, the mother is also, for the latter, the first object of identification—a fact that helps structure, according to Irigaray, the girl's relations to others. The similarity of the girl's and mother's "bodies and psyches" would protect them "from merging into a unique entity," Irigaray argues, underlining thereby that this identification entails at the same time a necessary differentiation that ensures women's being "familiar with being two. A girl does not form a dyad with the mother but a real duality" (Irigaray 2010, 268). That said, the fact that the mother is at once identified with and introjected as the girl's first object of love does generate the danger of women's forming too great a dependence on the other within a relationship of love/desire.[3] Indeed, the risks of self-abnegation or of assimilation in the relation with the other are, for Irigaray, precisely what women need to counter through the *cultivation* of desire, with this necessitating the insertion of a limit, a negativity, or a transcendent dimension between themselves and the other. As such, while the relationship to the other is certainly, for Irigaray, a quasi-natural given of feminine subjectivity by dint of the girl's being *born* to a person of the same sex, she no less maintains that "safeguarding the *two* of the intersubjective relation" is the task, or existential trajectory, women have to actively assume if they are to secure an autonomous sexuate identity or self-affection (Irigaray 2002, 87, my emphasis).

Far from being a natural immediacy, the relation between the sexes is a matter of elaboration or of construction strictly inseparable from a process of becoming on the part of women no less than of men (Irigaray 1996, 107). Suffice it to add that the cultivation of such a relationship is in no way contingent, as Hallward would have it, on woman's purportedly "primordial experience of maternity." Irigaray consistently differentiates both reproduction and parenting from the creation of an authentic intersubjectivity between the sexes: while the latter qualifies as the "means of accomplishing human identity," reproduction is relegated—with Irigaray decisively concurring here with Badiou—to the level of instinct or "the more or less animal" (Irigaray 2002, 114–15). For there to be the Two of sexual difference, a fecundity other than that of procreation, an altogether different *poesis*, is needed: namely, an enfleshed, carnal sharing engendering a becoming-in/between-two, in excess of a so-called natural state ignoring difference and transcendence (Irigaray 1993, 5; 2002, 115).

Badiou's Axiomatics of Love and Sexual Difference

Let us turn now to Badiou's conception of sexual difference, setting out here again from the question of biology. This science is, to all intents and purposes, disqualified from furnishing a properly differentiating criterion by which sexuate positions can be distributed since, taking as its object "the simple facticity of the human animal," it fails to cross through the infinite diversity of what is given to attain the truth of that presented in an existing situation. The process of love alone furnishes a universal ground on which sexual difference can be thought, for Badiou, and it is love alone, as such, that allows the existence of two sexuated positions to be established retrospectively. Badiou's designating these positions "man" and "woman" is, accordingly, a purely nominalist gesture, independent of any empirical, social, or biological distribution; as *generic* positions defined strictly internally within the amorous process and capable of being taken up by either of the partners or by both in alternation, they "could just as well be called something else" (Badiou and Tarby 2013, 63). Badiou's statement that "love is intrinsically heterosexual" (ibid.) in no way refers, then, to empirical sex. What is paramount for him is that the Two of the lovers is not merely a numerical two but a *heterogeneous* two. The prefix *heteros* marks, in other words, the necessity that there be "something of the sexuated other" in love—an other whose sexuation is precisely assigned within the amorous process itself. Interestingly, this need to mark the *heteros* in love is, for Badiou, not only intrinsic to the amorous process per se but a defining characteristic of the *feminine* sexuated other as determined within the love relationship: "woman," in other words, is she (or he) who focuses on the existence of the Two, upholding its precedence over the One. As we shall see, this sort of internal resonance, or redoubling, between the process of love and the position woman will prove to be absolutely pivotal to Badiou's conception of sexual difference.

The question of the relation that the sexuate positions hold to biology is not, however, completely evacuated within Badiou's thinking on sexual difference, as is most notably seen in "What Is Love?" when he specifies that sexuate duality, the Two of the lovers, must be marked corporeally, with the "differential sexuate marking" of bodies furnishing the material inscription that is necessary to the process of love if it is to produce the truth of what it is to be Two and not One (Badiou 2008, 190). Biology may well, then, not furnish a criterion by which the sexuate positions can be distributed universally, but biological bodies, as distinguished by the "differential trait" that they bear, would seem to correspond overall to the nominal positions love attributes retrospectively to the individuals taken up in its process. The position "woman" would, in short, be occupied by and large by *women*, the position "man," by and large, by *men*. What this correspondence shows up, in fact, is the all-in-all resolutely dialectical manner in which love, on Badiou's understanding, subsumes and *re-marks* a given sexed or sexuate difference that would otherwise remain insignificant or nonattestable—which, in Badiou's vocabulary, is equally to say "inexistent." This is the reason Badiou stipulates that nothing on the level of sexed being has any pertinence for the definition of categories of sexual difference. Bodies outside of love are sexually neutral, as it were, completely enclosed in their singular narcissistic sphere or "brute animal sexuality."[4] "It is only in love that bodies serve to mark the Two." Love is "the place where it is set down that there are two sexuated bodies and not only one" (191).[5]

What criteria serve, then, to define sexual difference as this is attested to within the process of love? As set out in the series of axiomatic definitions Badiou furnishes in "What Is Love?," woman and man are distinguished in terms of how they *function* in love, the *knowledge* they hold in respect of love, and their relation to *humanity*, understood as the space of thought comprised by what Badiou calls the four truth procedures (art, science, politics, and love itself) but which could also be called "the Symbolic." First, "woman" is she (or he) who is concerned with ensuring that love is ongoing and re-affirmed; "man" is he (or she) who considers that, once named, love no longer needs to be proved. Second, "woman" professes the Two to endure throughout life's vicissitudes, such that what "she" knows of love is ontological in scope, being focused on the existence of the Two, or being as such; "man" focuses on the split within the Two that re-marks the void of the disjunction, such that "his" is an essentially logical knowledge, concerned with the numerical change between One and Two. Third, "woman" requires love to exist for the symbolic configuration of truth procedures to hold and to have value; "man" views each type of truth procedure to be in itself a gauge of humanity, such that each is a metaphor for the others (192–97).

Whatever the formal, axiomatic condensation of these definitions, one can hardly fail to be struck by their echoing the most common of clichés concerning the difference between the sexes—man ostensibly does nothing for and in the name of love, while woman is the being-for-love; man is silent and violent, while woman is garrulous and makes demands; the man is always viewed by the woman as someone who is going to leave or in the process of leaving (193, 195; Badiou and Tarby 2013, 62). This correspondence between his axiomatic definitions and gender stereotypes does not pose a problem for Badiou: such stereotypes are, he states, the empirical material that love works through in order to establish the truth of the sexual disjunction, and, furthermore, the "staging of sexual roles" within a dyadic gender system has the *merit* of rendering sexual disjunction visible as a "law" of the situation. Not that gender is an expression of the disjunction per se; it is but an "obscure mediation" or "mediating display" (Badiou 2008, 186). Far better, though, such a mediation than a sexual indifferentiation that, by obnubliating the disjunction, allows this to operate all the more forcefully, such that individuals are simply abandoned to a solipsistic and, all in all, purely animal, sexual regime. In this sense, gender roles' rendering sexual disjunction visible aids love to show not only that this disjunction is precisely a law of the situation but, more crucially yet, that it is nothing more than this—namely, *not* a substantial division in being itself.

Ultimately, however, Badiou's axiomatic definitions of sexual difference seem to concur with social stereotypes because the latter would themselves, in Badiou's view, concur (however "obscurely") with what has been revealed of the nature of sexual disjunction by the infinite number of amorous relationships (*qua* truth procedures) having taken place throughout history—especially as portrayed in literature (Badiou and Tarby 2013, 62). But this being the case, the intertwining of gender stereotypes and Badiou's definitions of the sexual disjunction would suggest, in the final analysis, that the "real" of sexual difference resides in (axiomatically consecrated) *sociohistorically* determined subjective positions alone. What, then, of the universality Badiou claims for the truths revealed by love—would this prove to be simply synonymous with a consistent determination, within the Western tradition, of the form taken by sexed relations in different sociohistorical configurations? And if so—regardless of whether a consistent determination of this kind does, in fact, exist in the West, much less in different cultural spheres[6]—doesn't such a claim for love's production of a universal truth pertaining to the sexes then squarely come up against the objection (as would follow from Irigaray's perspective) that all such socially consecrated sexual roles identifiable in the history of the West ultimately reflect the imaginary of one sexuate position alone: the masculine? Or, put another way, wouldn't the truth of sexual difference produced by working through the empirical material comprised of sexual clichés turn out to be, *qua* an assertion emanating from the point of view of man alone, a "truth" still firmly held within the sexual disjunction?

With these interrogations in mind, it is all the more appropriate to turn at this juncture to Badiou's "explication" with Lacanian psychoanalysis, since not only does this constitute the very core of his axiomatics of love and sexual difference, but Badiou disqualifies Lacan's "truth claims" in respect to sexual difference on the same grounds as those just put forward: namely, that these claims proceed from one sexuate position alone and, therefore, fall short of their pretention to universality. Crucially, moreover, Badiou's objections to Lacan apply—on one particular point, at least—no less to Irigaray.

Badiou's Objections to Lacan—and, by Extension, to Irigaray: Sexual Segregation and Feminine Jouissance

That there is *no* sexual relation is, in fact, the one tenet of Lacan's teaching on sexual difference with which Badiou is wholly in agreement. Even in the field of love, the sole field in which this difference can be thought, the sexual *disjunction* remains intact "because what love founds is the Two and not a relationship between the Ones in a Two" (Badiou 2008, 191). Badiou otherwise deems it a fundamental error on Lacan's part to define sexual difference in terms of the phallic function, understood as having a universal application insofar as it distributes *all* speaking beings on either side of a unary trait: having or being the phallus. Relegating this function, for his part, to the strict register of desire or jouissance alone—"jouissance, as sexual, is phallic, which is to say that it does not relate to the Other [to a sex as Other] as such" (Lacan 1998, 102)—Badiou stipulates, as already indicated, that sexual difference does not, strictly speaking, exist on this level. Women and men alike, in the pure disjunction of their respective experience, are wholly subject to the intrinsic finitude accruing to desire and its economy of the object: there is, in other words, no specifically *feminine* jouissance opening onto the infinite that women would have access to by virtue of being "not-all" under the phallic order. Indeed, for Badiou, Lacan's very claims for such a jouissance reveal his formulae of sexuation to be flawed from the start insofar as they underline that the phallic function—which does effectively hold universally, or "wholly," according to Lacan, in respect of the masculine position alone—is always already situated *within* the disjunction of the sexes and is, as such, unsuitable as a support for the universal. Only from the standpoint of the masculine position could one even conceive of an infinite, inaccessible, feminine jouissance, according to Badiou, for whom Lacan's formulae thereby uphold a "segregative thesis of sexual difference" (Badiou 2003b, 47). If the disjunction of the sexes is presumed to be such that there is no element whatsoever in common to the two, and accordingly no knowledge whatsoever on the side of one sex of the space occupied by the other, then it follows, Badiou argues, that the masculine position is fantasmatically predisposed to imagining a mysterious and potentially infinite dilation of the feminine.

While this raises the question of what mechanisms might, then, underlie (some) women's own claims of a pantheistic, infinite enjoyment, the fact remains that, for Badiou, woman's "infinitude" is both the necessary correlate of any stance maintaining a complete segregation of the sexes and sufficient proof in itself that such a stance errs in its conception of the sexual disjunction (50). For, all while agreeing with Lacan that there is no relation between the sexes, Badiou sets down that there has, nonetheless, to be at least one term with which both sexuate positions entertain a relation. This is, of course, what love brings into play since woman and man thereby share a common, if unanalyzable, element—the indefinable "something" at the basis of their love—that, by showing the positions' disjunction not to be a substantial, or ontological, one, establishes them as belonging to a single humanity.

"Love's truth" is then, for Badiou, that a common humanity is shared by the two sexes. Yet, it must be recalled that the latter relate differentially to this shared symbolic: namely, man views the symbolic sphere as a composite of the different truth procedures, with each type of truth able to stand for all the others, whereas woman privileges love as the truth procedure that would knot all the others together and without which the symbolic sphere as a whole simply does not exist. Defining woman therefore as the position that upholds love as the *guarantee* of a universality to humanity—as what ensures that this is indeed *shared*—Badiou's axiomatics of love end up assigning "the universal quantifier" to the feminine position and not, *pace* Lacan, to man (Badiou 2008, 198). Would Badiou not thereby commit the same error he detects in Lacan: namely, that of treating the problem of sexual difference from within the sexual disjunction itself? Whatever his claims that the "humanity function," assured by the common term introduced by love, is of transparticular scope and relative to men and women equally, it nevertheless remains the case that it is, indeed, *within* the terms of sexual difference as defined on the ground furnished by love that woman is marked as singularly upholding love as the guarantee of the universal whereas man, not according love such universal sway, might be said the sexuate position for which love is "not-all." A certain feminine exceptionality still haunts Badiou's revision of Lacan's formulae of sexuation: an exceptionality displaced from the field of jouissance to that of love.

Badiou and Irigaray's Chiasmatic Masculine-Feminine Take on Philosophy?

From the perspective of this broad review of Irigaray's and Badiou's respective theses on sexual difference and the sexual relation, the latter's situating a feminine singularity in relation to love rather than desire proves to be more than just a point of localized disagreement. For the critical point of divergence punctuating Badiou's and Irigaray's shared conviction of an irreducibly dyadic sexual disjunction is thereby revealed—we would contend—as far less the question of biology, *qua* an ultimate anchorage or not, than the configuration of love-passion and desire-jouissance arrayed within each of the two philosophers' thought. When viewed in this light, Badiou's and Irigaray's diametrical oppositions take on, in fact, a greater systematicity, with each of their respective positions proving not simply unacceptable in terms of the other's but always already accounted for and subject, as such, to a predetermined disqualification predicated on the series of consequences it is presumed to entail. So, for example, Irigaray's maintaining there to be an infinite feminine jouissance, as irreducible to any opposition between love and desire as it is to the "economy of the object" (Irigaray 1993, 63), condemns her conception of sexual difference, from Badiou's perspective, as flawed in the same way as Lacan's formulae of sexuation through its encompassing, thereby, the thesis of a complete segregation of the sexes. Her core tenet that "man and woman do not live in the same world" (Irigaray 2008, 70)—which, indeed, testifies to a sexed division in Being—becomes, as such, an assertion of the *impossibility* of a single, or shared, humanity, despite Irigaray's own proclamations to the contrary. However, Badiou's trenchant distinction between love and desire, with carnal exchange relegated to a resolutely animal realm of being, commits the error, from Irigaray's point of view, of "forgetting the function of sexuality as a relationship-to" (Irigaray 2001b, 22)—the fact, in other words, that desiring exchange is an "awakening to intersubjectivity," a means of acceding to the other *qua* other, of respecting her or him as an incarnate subject (25, 22).

Indeed, Badiou proves to be an exemplary representative of what Irigaray characterizes as "male philosophers' conception of carnal love." Casting the corporeal as pure facticity, the sexual act (outside of love) as at once animality and the simple quest of solipsistic pleasure through an instrumental use of another's body, Badiou's philosophy would qualify, alongside the thought of Sartre, Merleau-Ponty, and Levinas (among others), as an expression of "masculine Being and speaking" (17), in terms of which love's differentiation from desire and the silencing of feminine jouissance ensure the eschewal of the sensible masculine thought deems requisite for any access to the realm of the intelligible or "a higher sphere" of subjectivity. Sensible/intelligible, body/mind, facticity/truth, desire/love, animal/human: all these canonical dichotomies are indeed vigorously mobilized in Badiou's metaphysics, with this discursive logic testifying *in itself*, for Irigaray, to the absence of any recognition of an authentic sexual difference through its suppressing the possibility of " 'self-representation' for the feminine" (Irigaray 1985, 161).

That Irigaray counterposes "the *feminine* character" of her account of desiring relations and sexual difference (Irigaray 2001b, 17, my emphasis) to male philosophers' conception of carnal love is in conformity, of course, with her understanding of the sexes' different relationship to the symbolic. Critically, however, the "new phenomenology of the caress" she elaborates in consonance with feminine desire and intention—and which encompasses, accordingly, a greater attention to intersubjectivity than that found in the work of men—no less corresponds to that which Badiou qualifies, in his turn, as a feminine position vis-à-vis the symbolic *qua* "humanity." Irigaray's insistence on "the relationship between two" preeminently resonates, for instance, with the definition Badiou gives of "woman" as she (or he) who "focuses on the existence of the Two, or being as such," even if Badiou restricts this focus to the field of love. Yet more significantly again, her declaring that a necessary cultivation of desire(-love) between the sexes is the sole means of accomplishing humanity as such strongly accords, *mutatis mutandis*, with Badiou's definition of the feminine position as that for which the universality of truths—or the configuration of symbolic procedures within which human animals accede to their humanity—would be unassured or without value were love not to exist. This being the case, might one not then conclude that, just as Badiou proves to be an exemplary representative, from Irigaray's perspective, of a male philosopher's conception of carnal love and sexual difference, so too, *were* Badiou to accredit the notion of a specifically feminine philosophy, Irigaray's theses on sexual difference and the sexual relation would seem pretty much to fit the bill of just what such a philosophy could, or should, within a Badiouian framework, espouse?

Any such conclusion—with its claims for what we might term a "chiasmatic" masculine-feminine take on philosophy[7]—immediately, however, comes up against a major objection. Even though Badiou defines woman by the particularity of making truth, or universality, dependent upon the operation of love—seemingly marking thereby a sexuate specificity within, or with respect to, the universal that borders on a sexuation of thought itself—he firmly denies in the texts proffering this definition any possibility of truths being sexuated. Indeed, the operation of love, Badiou states, is articulated around this very paradox: namely, that the sexual disjunction is radical, yet truth is subtracted from every positional disjunction (Badiou 2008, 186)—with Badiou referring here, of course, to love's role of revealing the two sexes to share a single humanity despite their living, all in all, in "different worlds" given the radically nontransitive nature of their respective experience. As generic, (love's) truth testifies, that is, to a neutral universal, rendering absurd any such notion as a feminine philosophy (or art, science, politics, or . . . love) that would co-exist alongside its masculine counterpart. In short, in terms of Badiou's texts in the 1980s and 90s, any attempt at situating Irigaray's work as exemplary of that which, from Badiou's perspective, a female philosopher would pronounce undoubtedly constitutes a *contradictio in terminis* in more ways than one.

All that admitted though, Badiou's attributing the feminine position to be "singularly charged with the relation of love to humanity" remains, by virtue of its testifying to a sexuately differentiated relation to the universal, something of an aporia in his work—as he himself was to recognize in 2010 (Badiou and Tarby 2013, 118). Moreover, this would seem to be one of the reasons for his having, quite startlingly, announced in 2011—in a radical inflexion of his tenet of truth's "transpositionality"—the necessity of examining the way in which sexuation functions in the domains of political, scientific, artistic, and amorous truths. Now acknowledging symbolic thought to have been cast throughout our tradition in masculine terms, Badiou deems it absolutely requisite to ask today: "[W]hat do the fields of politics, art, science and love become once women fully participate [. . .] in the creative equality of symbols?" Or, conversely: "What is a woman who engages in the politics of emancipation? What is a woman artist, musician, painter, or poet? A woman excelling in mathematics or physics? A woman philosopher?" (Badiou 2011, 16). With these interrogations all finding an echo in Irigaray's work, Badiou's new recognition of a sexuation of symbolic and philosophical thought occasions his and Irigaray's diametrical oppositions on the point of love/desire to take on an intricately convoluted, differentially staggered, and, all in all, paradoxical complementarity. Whence, *from their own perspectives*, Badiou's and Irigaray's respective conceptions can indeed be seen to constitute a chiasmatic masculine-feminine take on the philosophy of sexual difference. What might, therefore, be some other possible corollaries of this chiasmic crossing-cum-divergence on the pivotal question of love and desire?

First, Badiou's identifying the feminine jouissance Irigaray upholds (and which he deems a purely masculine fantasy) as the necessary correlate of a sexuate segregation suggests a rather intriguing manner of situating Irigaray's overarching claim for a *shared* cultivation of desire/jouissance by the two sexes. To put this succinctly: Irigaray's projecting a shared desire between two, reciprocally recognized, incarnate, and differently sexuated subjects as the key to a common humanity could well be seen as of the order of a "feminine fantasy," or phantasm, that, like the masculine fantasmatic predisposition Badiou speaks of, would be consequent upon an ignorance of the space occupied by the other sex. This is to say that, in the infinity of their jouissance—for we do need to grant here Irigaray's (and innumerable others') claims in this respect—women would be fantasmatically predisposed to imagining that something of this modality in excess of the phallic economy of the object must be shared, or at least shareable, with their partner. The projection would thus be made that, were men to cultivate their desire and not simply sojourn in animal instinct (as both Irigaray and Badiou put it), then they too would go beyond an exclusively solipsistic "jouissance of the organ" to experience, if not an "infinite expansion in space"—strictly proper to feminine subjectivity for Irigaray (Irigaray 1993, 64)—something nonetheless of the order of a "joy of *being* insofar as this is traversed by the other."[8]

Second, fantasmatic or not, Irigaray's conception of desire/jouissance as the path to a shared humanity if cultivated in the respect of the auto-affective horizon of one and the other incarnate subject, could only be denounced, within a Badiouian framework, as "edenic": as promoting "an angelic jouissance" (Badiou 2002). This follows quite simply from the fact that, by claiming the two sexes capable of a reciprocal recognition of sexuate subjectivity through the cultivation of *erotic* exchange, Irigaray directly counters Badiou's core assertion that love alone furnishes the ground on which an absolute segregation of the sexes is proved untenable—or, in other words, that love is the sole field in which the two sexes share an indefinable element that assures their common humanity. From Badiou's perspective, any such claim to know something of the other sex outside of love can only emanate from a *third* position, over and beyond the sexual disjunction, such as would be the (imaginary) stance of "an angel." No such third structural position exists, however; rather that which is required for the *truth* of the sexual disjunction to be revealed is a supplementary *event*, which returns us, of course, in Badiou's case to the amorous encounter (Badiou 2008, 183–84).

What is striking, though, is that in the terms of Irigaray's conception of carnal sharing as an opening to the other *qua* other, desire in no way entails a knowledge of the other's experience—"the other who differs from me sexually is forever unknowable" (Irigaray 1993, 13)—but consists in what might be designated, if not a third structural position, a "third space-time": an intermediary *interval* in which the two sexes meet and "sometimes inhabit the same place" (17). Defying any permanent definition—for this would be to suppress it as desire—this desiring encounter, or indeed "event," is, in fact, credited by Irigaray as having something angelic about it, to the extent at least that angels are understood as figuring not a neutered, transcendent overview, but the possibility of passing from "one side to the other," such that "endlessly reopening the enclosure of the universe, of universes, identities," they would herald in this way the arrival of "a new birth, a new morning" (15–16). Accentuating, as such, the passing beyond of partitions confining each individual, each sex, to a solipsistic position allocated in terms of an economy of the object, Irigaray retorts, as it were, to those who, like Badiou, would criticize her conception of desire as edenic, that desire should no more remain calibrated in *phallic terms alone* than love should be erected as a "higher sphere" uniquely securing a shared subjectivity between-two . . . and designated as such the specific concern of women. Such a dissociation of love and eroticism is "pathological" for Irigaray, and women, she writes, "are no longer willing to be the guardians of love" as so understood (66–67). Rather than reiterating the tradition's hierarchical oppositions between desire and/or the body and a "more spiritual" love, what needs to be done is to construct a double desire between the sexes, such that these are no longer divided into positive and negative poles but find themselves taken up in a "chiasmus or double loop, in which each can go toward the other and come back to itself" (9).

Third, and finally, insofar as Badiou's axiomatics of love transmutes feminine "supplementary" jouissance into woman's upholding "love's excess over desire," we might well recall that philosophy's constitutive *foreclosure* of sexual difference—as elaborated by Irigaray, but first put forward by Lacan—can be more strictly situated as philosophy's impossibility to countenance the question of sexual jouissance, linked as this is to the unsymbolizable "Thing," or maternal body. Such a diagnosis was, again, first proposed by Lacan, and no matter how tenaciously Badiou may twist and transpose the latter's sexual formula, it is clear that from the perspective of psychoanalysis, no less than that of Irigaray's philosophy of sexual difference, he can but seem set on circumventing the "real" of the drives—which is to the say the "real" of the body. That Irigaray, on the other hand, has tirelessly undertaken to recall to philosophy (but not philosophy alone) the necessity of acknowledging the maternal body indicates, at the very least, that the recognition of a sexuately differential relation to the universal (as now hailed equally by Badiou) must, in all logic, lead not only to new forms of symbolic creation but equally to new configurations of *life-giving* desire.

Notes

1. The comparisons of Badiou's and Irigaray's notions of sexual difference that follow draw substantively on analyses I've elaborated elsewhere (Burchill 2018). The article just cited focuses, however, on Badiou's understanding of woman, truths, and philosophy, whereas my concern here is to examine the paradoxical complementarity of his and Irigaray's conceptions of woman and sexual pleasure.

2. Personal communication, December 2011.

3. One can compare here the account of female psychosexual development proposed by Julia Kristeva in the third volume of *Female Genius*. For Kristeva, the

girl's *introjection* of the mother as a source of pleasure leads to an "early psychization of the object of love," with which the ego identifies at the same time, while the girl's *projective identification* with the mother results in the "creation of a *real relationship* of dependence on that same object." The maternal other is thereby transformed into "an indispensable object, as the vital copresence of a connection to others, experienced like a *need*, always already there, [. . .] to be cultivated and maintained in external reality." This need for a psychic connection will, Kristeva underlines, persist as "an absolute necessity for female psychosexuality" (Kristeva 2004, 411–13).

4. Thanks to Eon Yorck for general guidance on the topos of animality.

5. Editor's note: The translation has been slightly modified by the author. The original translation reads as follows: "the place where it is stated that there are two sexuated bodies and not only one" (Badiou 2008, 191).

6. In *Logics of Worlds*, Badiou succinctly dismisses arguments that seek to refute love's universality by reducing the form of sexed relations to distinct cultural configurations. Ancient Greek, Roman, and medieval Japanese authors—from Sappho to Lady Murasaki—provide ample indication, he states, that "Love is an experience of truth and as such is always identifiable whatever the historical context may be" (2009, 131).

7. The "chiasmus" is a figure Irigaray employs in reference both to the double desire that needs to be established between the two sexes and the very different ordering of space and time that is proper to each of them (1993, 9, 64).

8. This definition of jouissance is gleaned from a text by Jean-Luc Nancy (1991), which attests incidentally to a male philosopher's sharing something of Irigaray's feminine phantasm (if phantasm it is).

Works Cited

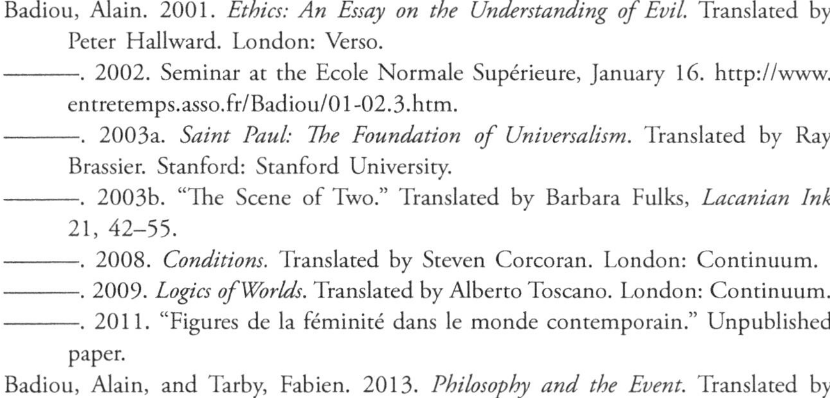

Badiou, Alain. 2001. *Ethics: An Essay on the Understanding of Evil.* Translated by Peter Hallward. London: Verso.

———. 2002. Seminar at the Ecole Normale Supérieure, January 16. http://www.entretemps.asso.fr/Badiou/01-02.3.htm.

———. 2003a. *Saint Paul: The Foundation of Universalism.* Translated by Ray Brassier. Stanford: Stanford University.

———. 2003b. "The Scene of Two." Translated by Barbara Fulks, *Lacanian Ink* 21, 42–55.

———. 2008. *Conditions.* Translated by Steven Corcoran. London: Continuum.

———. 2009. *Logics of Worlds.* Translated by Alberto Toscano. London: Continuum.

———. 2011. "Figures de la féminité dans le monde contemporain." Unpublished paper.

Badiou, Alain, and Tarby, Fabien. 2013. *Philosophy and the Event.* Translated by Louise Burchill. London: Polity.

Burchill, Louise. 2018. "Of a Universal No Longer Indifferent to Difference: Badiou (and Irigaray) on Woman, Truths and Philosophy." *Philosophy Today* 62 (Fall): 4.

Hallward, Peter. 2003. *Badiou: A Subject to Truth.* Minneapolis: University of Minnesota Press.

Irigaray, Luce. 1985. *This Sex Which Is Not One.* Translated by Catherine Porter. Ithaca: Cornell University.

———. 1993. *An Ethics of Sexual Difference.* Translated by Carolyn Burke and Gillian C. Gill. New York: Cornell University.

———. 1996. *I Love to You: Sketch of a Possible Felicity in History.* Translated by Alison Martin. New York: Routledge.

———. 2001a. "The Fecundity of the Caress: A Reading of Levinas, *Totality and Infinity*, 'Phenomenology of Eros.'" In *Feminist Interpretations of Emmanuel Levinas*, edited by Tina Chanter, 119–44. University Park: Pennsylvania State University.

———. 2001b. *To Be Two.* Translated by Monique M. Rhodes and Marco F. Cocito-Monoc. New York: Routledge.

———. 2002. *Between East and West: From Singularity to Community.* Translated by Stephen Pluháček. New York: Colombia University.

———. 2004. *Key Writings.* London: Continuum.

———. 2008. *Sharing the World.* London: Continuum.

———. 2010. "The Return." In *Rewriting Difference: Luce Irigaray and "the Greeks,"* edited by Athena Athanasiou and Elena Tzelepis. Albany: State University New York Press.

Kristeva, Julia. 2004. *Colette.* Translated by Jane Todd. New York: Columbia University.

Lacan, Jacques. 1998. *On Feminine Sexuality: The Limits of Love and Knowledge.* In *The Seminar of Jacques Lacan, Book XX, Encore.* Translated by Bruce Fink. New York: Norton.

Nancy, Jean-Luc. 1991. "Shattered Love." Translated by Lisa Garbus and Simona Sawhney. In *The Inoperative Community*, edited by Peter Connor. Minneapolis: University of Minnesota Press.

Freedom, Desire, and the Other

Reading Sartre with Irigaray

GAIL M. SCHWAB

Luce Irigaray's philosophical relationship to the thought of Jean-Paul Sartre has not been extensively analyzed in Irigaray studies,[1] perhaps because the radically independent Sartrean existentialist subject, heroically free to choose its own project and carry out its own destiny, no longer exercises the influence it once did. Later thinkers deconstructed that subject and pointed to its origin in the play of social, cultural, and historical forces beyond its control—in particular, in the differential play of linguistic structures. More broadly, throughout the late twentieth and early twenty-first centuries, Sartre has not been read extensively by feminist thinkers. Irigaray, however, has always remained a philosopher of the subject—not a philosopher of the old, supposedly neutral (actually male) singular and universal subject of Western philosophy, but a philosopher of two (future) subjects developing in the ceaseless becoming of sexual difference—and she does read Sartre. In her 2001 *To Be Two*, she looks closely at Sartre's analysis of the relations between self and other(s) as articulated in the section entitled "Concrete Relations with Others" in *Being and Nothingness* (Sartre 1966, 361–430; 1943, 413–82. Unless Sartre's 1943 text is specified, subsequent references are to the 1966 English version). She later takes up Sartre's thought again, although in a less direct and pointed way, and often through a Heideggerian lens, in *Sharing the World*. The argument that follows is an analysis—organized under the three principal rubrics of "Desire"; "Everyday Social Relations: The Other and the They"; and "Freedom"—of Irigaray's reading of Sartrean intersubjectivity, as developed principally in "Concrete Relations with Others."

Desire

Irigaray has consistently claimed, at least since the time of *I Love to You*, that one of the tasks that confronts us as we struggle to evolve as a species, and to come into our humanity, is the cultivation of desire between and among us; this theme is central to both *To Be Two* and to *Sharing the World*, and it informs her reading and critique of Sartre. According to Irigaray, we have carelessly and inappropriately tried to channel desire into two separate and equally unsuitable realms of human experience (see "Spiritual Tasks for Our Age," Irigaray 2004, 171–85). The first realm would be immediate sensation or instinct—the so-called "sex drive"—which we commoditize and sensationalize with overly glamorous and titillating and/or terrifying visual images, when we should be constructing the kinds of cultural mediations—appropriate language(s) and behaviors, representations, and institutions—that would allow us to cultivate desire, which is the aspect of our sexuality that, according to Irigaray, renders us truly human and differentiates us from animals (Irigaray 2001a, 77–94). The second realm in which we have imprisoned desire would be the Hegelian domain of genealogy, the family, and procreation, where we have attempted to hide desire from ourselves, trying more or less successfully to repress and sublimate it, tamp it down, and contain it in a supposedly "safe" place.

There is a long development on desire in "Concrete Relations with Others," which Irigaray reads in some detail in two essays in *To Be Two*—"The Wedding between the Body and Language" and "Daughter and Woman" (Irigaray 2001b, 17–29, 30–39). Sartre characterizes desire as "an attitude aiming at enchantment" (Sartre 394). He writes:

> Since I can grasp the Other[2] only in his objective facticity, the problem is to ensnare his freedom within this facticity. It is necessary that he be "caught" in it as the cream is caught up by a person skimming milk. So the Other's for-itself[3] must come to play on the surface of his body, and be extended all through his body; and by touching this body I should finally touch the Other's free subjectivity. This is the true meaning of the word *possession*. It is certain that I want to possess the other's body,

> but I want to possess it insofar as it is itself a "possessed"; that is, insofar as the Other's consciousness is identified with his body. Such is the impossible ideal of desire: to possess the Other's transcendence as pure transcendence and at the same time as *body*. (ibid.)

This analysis of desire is profoundly dualistic, and the mind/body split that underpins it is problematic for Irigaray. Subjectivity is not a nonmaterial substance hovering over, or even floating on the surface of, the body, like cream on top of milk; nor is the body a mere objective "facticity." Consciousness, or subjectivity, or freedom, cannot be possessed by somehow magically precipitating them out of the "body—'as one says of a coagulated cream or mayonnaise' " (Irigaray 2001b, 18);[4] and yet, "according to Sartre, the fulfillment of desire does not exist without such possession [. . .] The transcendence of the other is to be possessed as pure transcendence inaccessible to sensible experience, but nevertheless as body" (ibid.).

In truth, Sartre never claims that we can possess the Other. He only goes so far as to state that "it is certain that *we want to possess*" the Other, and he actually concludes that desire's quest for possession is doomed to failure, as are, generally, all the modalities of "being-for-others" that he analyzes in *Being and Nothingness*.[5] Sartre is quite clear that the possession of the other's subjectivity, and it should be added, his or her possession of mine, can only be what he calls an "impossible ideal"; the Other cannot be possessed as pure transcendence, notably because if I were to catch hold of the other's transcendence, immobilize it in his or her body, for myself, then the other would no longer be transcendence; he or she would then have become objectivity, facticity, and I would be left holding nothing that I desire—nothing at all, in fact.

> To be sure, I can grasp the Other, grab hold of him, knock him down. I can, providing I have the power, compel him to perform this or that act, to say certain words. But everything happens as if I wished to get hold of a man who runs away and leaves only his coat in my hands. It is the coat, it is the outer shell which I possess. I shall never get hold of more than a body [. . .]. I can only act upon a facticity. (Sartre 393)

Sartrean desire plays itself out in Stendhalian or Proustian terms. Its very success is its failure, as the dreamed-of possession results only in deflation—or castration, for which the empty coat is such an apt metaphor. Although Sartre has clearly understood that trying to captivate a subjectivity that would be transcendent to the facticity of the body is like trying to captivate or grasp hold of nothing at all, he is unable to go further in his analysis of what seems to him to be the ontological nature of desire itself because he lacks the theoretical tool that Irigaray will bring to bear on the problem—that is, the tool of difference, difference(s) between and among subjects. Irigaray will maintain that transcendence is not a mono-subjective phenomenon, implicating only one physical body and the "higher" consciousness that inhabits it; transcendence properly conceived is rather intersubjective and relational, implicating (at least) two different subjectivities and (at least) two different, sexuate, and potentially differently sexuate bodies. Thus, learning to cultivate desire would not entail that endlessly frustrating quest to captivate a subjectivity transcendent to the facticity of its own body, but would rather be about establishing intersubjective relations, maintaining and respecting two different freedoms and a distance between them, each transcendent to the other. " 'You who are not and will never be me or mine' are and remain you, since I cannot grasp you, understand you, possess you. You escape every ensnarement, every submission to me, if I respect you not so much because you are transcendent to your body, but because you are transcendent to me" (Irigaray 2001b, 19).

It should be noted that Irigaray does not deny the disappointing character of most desire, but rather than view desire's failure as ontological and thus inevitable, she ascribes it to the structure of contemporary social relations in Western culture, which tend toward equalization and homogenization, toward a leveling to the neutral and neuter standard, toward the effacement of differences between other and self, differences that were the initial inspiration for desire. "The falling-off of desire, its decline, comes from a loss of all singularity. [. . .] This lack of differentiation prevents the cultivation of attraction by annihilating what aroused it: the difference between two subjects. Amazingly, desire disappears if we do not take care of it" (Irigaray 2008, 74). Difference and its cultivation and maintenance become the keys to avoiding ending up holding Sartre's "empty coat."

In "Daughter and Woman," Irigaray acknowledges that Sartre does not attempt to repress desire by compartmentalizing it into the Hegelian dynamic of family relations and that he does indeed focus on the "between-two," placing "the corporeal relationship with the other in a horizontal dimension" (Irigaray 2001b, 30). However, she finds that he actually goes too far and exaggerates horizontality, neglecting the other crucial intersubjective dimension of verticality. The subject's relationships to its own and to the other gender found what Irigaray conceives as overarching generalized or universalized vertical transcendences[6]—transcendences that serve as a counterweight, balancing the overly symmetrical horizontality of desire in the face-to-face. The body that is identified with, or anchored to, the vertical transcendence of gender cannot be reduced to inert matter or to a disappointing "facticity";[7] beyond itself, it participates in relationships with its own gendered universal, as well as with the others' gendered universal. "An intention is pre-given in my body, a for-itself is inscribed in it [. . .] My body is not, therefore, a simple 'facticity;' it is a relationship-with: with me, with my gender, with the other gender" (33).

Sartre also neglects genealogical verticality, or "each subject's history and its impact upon the present encounter with the other, with others" (30). Sartrean Self and Other are depicted as too exactly equivalent one to the other; the (supposedly) two subjects in relation are really only one, because neither Self nor Other is conceived as a body "inhabited by a consciousness which begins with its first relationship with the parental other, with the mother in particular" (31). Rachel Jones has written of the philosophical subject of Western metaphysics that "his gaze is turned away from his origin in the mother [. . .], as well as away from his own body [. . .]. Acknowledging one's bodily beginnings in the mother would permit each human being a sense of their own irreducible singularity, a singularity grounded in an originary relation to an equally irreducible other" (Jones 2011, 70–71). The existentialist subject erected by Sartre, whose freedom cannot be limited by its past, springs up quite literally in a vacuum of solitude—in the very nothingness against which being itself emerges—and creates itself *ex nihilo* through its projects. It acknowledges no constitutive individual relation to any particular woman that would be its mother, and thus lacks the singularity—the difference—that grows out of the mother-child bond. Lacking in Sartre's analysis is the understanding that the body itself, dating back to the prenatal, placentally ethical relation to the mother, is an inherently relational entity, imbued with intentionality toward the other; "intention exists both on the part of the mother towards the girl or boy, and on the part of the child towards the mother. Thus, the affectionate gaze of the mother towards the body of her son and of her daughter, as well as their attention towards the mother, is forgotten in Sartre's thought" (Irigaray 2001b, 31). That intention and that attention engender singularity and difference and orient the subject toward a relation with singular and different others. Thus, we all have a relational past going all the way back to our infancy and beyond into our prenatal experience, a past that inscribes a (sexuate) relational identity in our body and our subjectivity that forms the foundation for all of our future contact and dealings with the other and with others (Irigaray 2001a, 43–49).

Irigaray has criticized our culture and our educational systems in particular for their efforts to erase this relational identity and intentionality—this potential intersubjectivity—as early on as possible in the schooling of children.[8] There on the body and in the subjectivity of girls and boys, where the potential to cultivate relation (including intra- and intersexuate relation) and desire (including intra- and intersexuate desire) had been inscribed by the originary relation to the mother, every aspect of our cultural life conspires to create *tabula rasa*, to overcome "our corporeal and affective infancy, [. . .] overturning it and substituting an abstract and solipsistic universe for it. [. . .] Each of us [becomes] a nothing of existence, an existence in which the life of the pre-given [that pre-natal and early childhood relation to the mother] has become a flight towards an impossible future" (32). And certainly Irigaray's characterization here provides a fitting description of the Sartrean existentialist subject—a "nothing of existence"—a for-itself that "is not what it is and is what it is not" (Sartre 362), whose "flight [from facticity] takes place toward an impossible future always pursued" (ibid.), for whom past relations are irrelevant in his or her permanent engagement in a project(ion) toward the future, a project(ion) which is real only insofar as it is unrealized. Irigaray would replace this "nothing of existence" with a sexuate being whose affective past creates a relational future.

Everyday Social Relations: The Other and the They

There is a brief section in "Concrete Relations with Others" where Sartre begins to ask the question of sexual difference, and where he even criticizes Heidegger for ignoring sex and rendering *Dasein* asexual.

> Existential philosophies have not believed it necessary to concern themselves with sexuality. Heidegger, in particular, does not make the slightest allusion to it in his existential analytic, with the result that his *Dasein* appears to us as asexual. [. . .] That sexual differentiation lies within the domain of facticity we accept without reservation. But does this mean that the For-itself is sexual accidentally? (Sartre 383)

What is noteworthy in this passage is the fact that Sartre makes an effort to think about sexual difference—about the maleness or the femaleness—of *Dasein* and of the for-itself, but then, "accepting without reservation" the "facticity of sexual differentiation," he never thinks through the problem of whether sexuate identity might be constitutive in the development of the for-itself. Thus, like *Dasein*, the Sartrean for-itself is a theoretically neuter, and actually masculine, entity. And the more one reads *Being and Nothingness*, the more it becomes clear that not only are there no differentiated sexes, but there is no difference at all, or any real Other or Others to be found in it; the Sartrean subject, characterized by Irigaray as "solipsistic" (Irigaray 2001b, 32) despite all of Sartre's efforts to move beyond what he calls the "reef of solipsism" (Sartre 223–52), is in relation only to itself; all "Others" are facsimiles or mirror images of this self.

As noted above, in "The Wedding between the Body and Language," Irigaray criticizes the capital "O" of Sartre's Other as "an excessively quantitative valuation" that reduces difference to hierarchical difference—that is, difference acknowledged not on its own terms but reduced to "the more or less like me"—Irigaray's other of the same. This measurement of the Other against the Self inevitably ends in conflict and can go so far as mimetic violence (Irigaray 2001b, 19). The for-itself and its so-called Others face off in an endless struggle for assertion and dominance that Sartre compares to, and acknowledges is based upon, Hegel's master and slave relation (Sartre 370). "Conflict is the original meaning of being-for-others," writes Sartre; "while I seek to enslave the Other, the Other seeks to enslave me," and "my project of recovering myself" from my alienation in the gaze of the Other is "fundamentally a project of absorbing the Other" (364). Sartre sees no way around this endlessly conflictual relation to the Other, and he is highly skeptical about the possibilities of constructing a collective subject "we" at all; he concludes that "the essence of the relations between consciousnesses is not the *Mitsein*; it is conflict" (429).[9] There is no place in Sartre's thought for that tripartite relation to the other of difference that Irigaray calls an "advent," that relation to the other that creates three "newborns"—self, other, and the relation between them—as it simultaneously maintains the integrity of both self and other, even as it regenerates and renews both their existences, while developing the relation between them as a living entity on its own, a new being, not—it should be emphasized—a child, but a space, or perhaps more properly, a dimension or a locus of energy (Irigaray 2008, 31).[10]

The Sartrean Other is capable only of partnering the Self in a dance of mirror images, and the partners can never escape from this agonizing ritual that is supposed to be their relationship. Sartre writes that "there is no dialectic for my relations to the Other, but rather a circle" (Sartre 363); that circle is the hell of the *Huis clos*, where Garcin, Inez, and Estelle are never allowed to sleep, or even blink (the dead relegated to hell are not vouchsafed eyelids), and are condemned to look at each other and be looked at, each one by the two others, as they circle round and round each other, and fight out pointless rivalries and jealousies, and form and re-form temporary and just as pointless alliances of two-against-one, over and over again for all eternity. "*L'enfer, c'est les autres.*" Consciousness, figured here as sleeplessness and "blinklessness," has become, as Irigaray writes, "a terrifying lord, a sadistic master" (Irigaray 2001b, 33), imprisoning us in not only conflictual but pathological relationships from which there is no respite or escape. Irigaray insists that the failure on the part of our cultural institutions to cultivate the differences in our relational and our sexuate identities has turned us (like Garcin, Inez, and Estelle) "each one into a zombie, into a neutral individual, into an abstract creature. The concrete encounter with the other, entering into carnal presence together with her or him, has become impossible. We are no longer two, but subjugated, both of us, to an abstract order which divides us into one + one + one" (31–32).

We see here that where a certain type of standardized, impersonal, neutral, and neutered social relation prevails, Irigaray too finds that hell is other people. She fears the 1 + 1 + 1; for her, the relation between the one and the many, the self and the anonymous They, is very much a part of this abstract and disincarnated relation between and among "zombies," or "automatons," ruled by an "imperialist despot" of a controlling consciousness. In "Daughter and Woman," Irigaray quotes a long development of Sartre's on the constitution of social relations by "manufactured objects that make me known to myself as 'they' " or them (38; Sartre 424), "that refer me to the image of my transcendence as that of any transcendence whatsoever" (Irigaray 2001b, 38; 424). This is the long passage where Sartre discusses the crowd of people changing trains at the La Motte-Picquet-Grenelle metro stop:

> To go from the subway station at Trocadéro to Sèvres-Babylone, They change at La Motte-Picquet. This change is foreseen, indicated on maps, etc.; if I change routes at La Motte-Picquet, I am the They who change. To be sure, I differentiate myself by each use of the subway [. . .] by the distant ends which I pursue. But these final ends are only the horizon of my act.

> My immediate ends are the ends of the They, and I apprehend myself as interchangeable with any one of my neighbors. (38; 424)

It can be said that there are zombieesque aspects involved in taking the metro or the subway, in moving silently through the crowd and discreetly navigating the landscape filled with others, refusing to make eye contact, blending in either by design or under the auspices of that other "imperialist despot"—habit. Such "undifferentiated" behavior may be unconscious and/or habitual; it is, however, effective. It propels one through the tunnels, up and down the staircases, through the crowds of people, and finally to one's "horizon," as Sartre calls it. Contemporary life in society, especially when it involves the use of a technology such as mass transit, does require a certain conformity to established norms, along with a certain anonymity and refusal to engage with those all around us. Our "comrades-in-transit" are They for us, just as we are no more than They to them. We are closed to intersubjectivity, at least for the length of the trip.

Sartre was, and Irigaray remains, a serious reader of Heidegger, and Heidegger's analysis of the They and its relation to *Dasein* inspires both French philosophers to consider in some detail the problem of the social They—that is, everyday social relations and the patterned behaviors, or as Irigaray might say, the "automatism," they require. In an essay entitled "Conflictual Culture and Authenticity: Deepening Heidegger's Account of the Social," Dorothy Leland looks at *Dasein*'s being-for-others and being-in-the-world. She argues that a distinction should be made between, on the one hand, "blind conformism" and, on the other hand, "conformity" (Leland 2002, 111). Leland writes:

> I come to understand the significance of chairs within my social world by learning how to sit on them and by learning that chairs are normally used for sitting. In this sense, enculturation involves conformity to norms. This conformity to norms is distinct from conformism understood as a tendency to latch onto whatever falls into the range of the familiar, the attainable, the respectable [. . . ,] closing oneself off from a deeper mode of self-understanding. (ibid.)

The type of conformism Leland is describing here, comprising a "closing-off from a deeper mode of self-understanding," might be said to correspond to Sartre's "bad faith" (Sartre 47–70); the concept as explained by Sartre is detailed and complex, but we might oversimplify and say that bad faith is fundamentally a lack of honesty on the part of the subject who refuses to acknowledge her or his actions and underlying motivations and to accept responsibility for them. Sartre's famous description of the "young woman on a date" could be an illustration of women's conformism to society's expectations about the proper behavior of a young girl with respect to sexuality (55–56). The girl knows full well—and yet pretends not to know, or perhaps more accurately, refuses to let herself know—what her date's compliments and attentiveness signify about their relationship, his sexual intentions, and her own potential sexual desires. According to Sartre, she is acting in bad faith; she avoids taking responsibility for what are, after all, sexual choices she makes in accepting her date's advances, and not the innocent and naïve lack of sexual awareness she tries to project as her date reaches for her hand. I would argue that it is this type of bad faith—an actual evasion of freedom and responsibility—that would be equivalent to "conformism."[11] Thus, Sartre, in the description of taking the metro at La Motte-Picquet-Grenelle, is actually analyzing not conformism but "conformity." Although the social "environment causes [one] to be like everyone else, to do as they do" (as Irigaray puts it in "Daughter and Woman" [Irigaray 2001b, 39]), there is no real "bad faith" or evasion of freedom and responsibility involved in changing metro trains, and although one's "immediate ends" remain those of the They, one ultimately "differentiates [oneself] from everyone else" by the "distant ends" one pursues, as Sartre writes. For Sartre, it is the distant ends—that is, one's project—that extricate one from the They and reconstitute one's subjectivity.

Irigaray, however, almost seems to find conformity too close to conformism for comfort. For her, the metro riders are automatons or zombies, and neither their "distant ends" nor the "horizon" of their intention is enough to differentiate them sufficiently from the They. She also has concerns about the type of intersubjectivity established—or in actuality, not established—through acting in concert with the They. She insists on the failure of this type of behavior to maintain an appropriate relation to the other: "I am not attentive to the other, to others, but do as they do through passivity, through egoism, I would say. I thus become an 'anybody' which only my intention toward you can help me overcome" (ibid.). To overcome the effacement of self in the They, and to reestablish proper social relations, Irigaray will require an "intention towards you"; she will require attentive and aware relationality. As Irigaray writes, "I am not reduced to an 'anybody' in the corridor of the subway station at La Motte-Picquet-Grenelle if I walk towards you. My interiority, my intention, remain my own in the crowd" (ibid.). It is only the foregrounding of the intersubjective relation that will pull her out of the crowd, give her back her unique identity, reconstitute her subjectivity as her own, and not just anybody's, as she moves through the metro with everyone else. Intersubjectivity is the only way out of the automatism, or the zombieism, of the 1+1+1.

Irigaray will further develop this radical conception of relationality and intersubjectivity in "Spiritual Tasks for Our Age," where it will no longer be about simply having "an intention towards *you*" or "walking towards *you*" (my emphasis). Intersubjectivity is to be developed far beyond relations on the one-on-one intimate level, and Irigaray calls for the cultivation and renewal of all types of social relations among differently sexuate, or indeed otherwise different, subjects. Intersubjective relations throughout all sectors of society become the foundation of a politics, and the means to the establishment, or to the renewal, of truly effective democracy. "The totality of the social fabric should consist of dual relations [between citizens] at different levels" (Irigaray 2004, 181); these dual relations must "be woven into all areas of civil order, and thus elevate it, through each and every exchange between citizens, from the natural to the spiritual, from the empirical to the transcendental" (180). The failure to cultivate these nonintimate, but rather public, professional, and political intersexuate, interethnic, interfaith, and so on, intersubjective relations between and among citizens results in the automatism or zombieism that will eventually destroy democracy since "such a society is not founded on relations among citizens, but rather on individual units subjugated to the authority of a leader, or leaders, who represent and execute the law. This opens the way for all kinds of excesses" (ibid.). Such totalitarian threats figure as a major concern in the meditation on freedom that is integral to the argument of *Sharing the World*.

Freedom

As noted previously, Irigaray's engagement with Sartre's thought is less direct in *Sharing the World* than it was in *To Be Two*. In *Sharing the World,* she is not precisely reading specific Sartrean texts the way she was in the earlier book, and she is thinking of and addressing Heidegger's thought as much as or more than Sartre's. There are, nevertheless, significant echoes of French existentialism in *Sharing the World*; it is in many ways a book about (among other things) freedom, one of the central preoccupations of *Being and Nothingness* and of Sartre's thought in its entirety. Thus, a brief (and oversimplified) look at the Sartrean conception of freedom can be illuminating if we wish to come to an understanding both of Irigaray's relationship to Sartre and of her construction of freedom in *Sharing the World*. We know that the Sartrean existentialist subject is endowed with a radical freedom; even the prisoner of war, the woman in a harem, or the slave is still free "to choose" her or his project and how she or he lives the circumstances of life (Sartre 439–40). In *Being and Nothingness*, Sartre—due to some extent to his developing leftist politics—did, however, acknowledge that even radically free beings are engaged in an historical moment and in the life embedded in it and that their freedom is thus necessarily dependent upon what he calls their "situation" (487).

Sonia Kruks has done a detailed analysis of the Sartrean concept of situation, showing how difficult it was philosophically for Sartre to curtail the freedom of the existentialist subject by integrating it into the constraints of a situation (Kruks 1990, 146–80).[12] Kruks demonstrates that, although there are certain nuances in Sartre's understanding of situation (nuances not relevant here in the context of this argument [See ibid. for extensive analysis of the problem]), it is possible to conclude that for the most part, in *Being and Nothingness*, it is the existentialist subject's project that constitutes "situation" (Kruks 66–69); that is to say that situation can impose limits on freedom only within the context of the subject's freely chosen projects. In other words, if the subject had not chosen to pursue some particular goal, no empirical reality, no given historical or social conditions or state of things could limit, or indeed further, that goal; it is the subject who sets the parameters for "situation" with his or her decisions to undertake projects and pursue goals.[13] For the radically free existentialist, the prisoner of war, the slave, and the harem girl can "choose" to live the constraints of their captivity in such a way as to affirm their freedom; I would note that Sartre provides no concrete examples explaining how the prisoner, the slave, and the harem girl might actually go about doing this.

Irigaray will take a very different view of the subject's freedom in the context of her or his historical, social, and cultural situation; it might even be said that in some ways, she lies at the opposite extreme from Sartre. One of the predominant metaphors of *Sharing the World* involves weaving(s) and interlacing(s) in which we are all caught up as in a spider's web. Although it is impossible to read *Sharing the World* and not take note once again of Irigaray's profound dismay and apprehensiveness in the face of technology, especially of computerized technology, these networks are not just the mass media and the internet. Her networks are conceived as much more extensive than our dependence upon computing and telecommunications; I have elsewhere compared Irigaray's networks to the Lacanian symbolic order—that preexisting set of laws and conditions we are born into and are forced to negotiate our way through linguistically, socially, psychologically, and emotionally (Schwab 2011b, 3–4). I would broaden that concept here to note that, within Irigaray's networks, the nonhuman worlds of human-made objects and of nature are as important as the human:

> To come into the world means to enter into an interlacing of relations between living beings, things, human subjects, and [. . .] objects of the environment fabricated by humans. [. . .] One who is born enters [a] world that predetermines their point of view, their choices, their present intentions or their future plans—inside a horizon that they believe they give in complete freedom to their world. [. . .] And what they imagine to be their freedom is already conditioned by the relational weaving from which they thought it was distinguished. (Irigaray 2008, 64–65)

Irigaray here underlines one of her principal differences from Sartre, as she insists on the subject's "subjection" to and misrecognition and misunderstanding of the power of networks—networks that prevent human beings from, as Irigaray writes, "perceiving the real by themselves and from making up their own mind and acting altogether freely" (64). She compares this authority, or this social determinism, of the network to totalitarianism (65), further claiming that what institutional, governmental, or systemic totalitarianisms actually do is articulate on the political and national, or even international level, the preexisting suppression of difference(s), and the preexisting uniformities, conformities, and conformisms accepted and practiced by all of those caught up in the network—that is, by all members of a society, or even by all participants in a more generalized supernational cultural tradition like contemporary Western culture. Irigaray insists that totalitarianisms are not only imposed from above by autocratic leaders and police and military apparatuses; they are also created and reinforced from below by citizens engaged in the relentless leveling of differences and the establishment of the authority of the neutral and the universal, and, as we have seen, disengaged from appropriate intersubjective social relations. Furthermore, such totalitarianisms are ironically lived and understood as "freedom" by those caught up inside them. We might take as an example of this misapprehension of freedom the encouraged, if not enforced, consumerism of Western culture, where the proliferation of products and objects for sale is represented by manufacturers, advertisers and marketers, economists, and politicians as "freedom of choice," when these products and objects end up being no more than an obligation to spend, waste, discard, and respend on whatever new and "necessary" product comes along next, in the process, destroying the environment and ensuring that all of us remain on the treadmill powered by the engine of Western economic "growth."[14]

How then is it even possible to speak of freedom in the context of totalitarian conditions of which we are not aware and which we even blindly interpret as "freedom?" For Irigaray, the only possible answer lies, just as it did in the case of the zombies and automatons in the La Motte-Picquet-Grenelle metro stop—in intersubjectivity, in actually "sharing the world" with the other and with others. We have noted above the struggle for assertion and dominance that Self-Other relations imply in the Sartrean system; it is worth repeating the Sartrean formula here: "[T]he essence of the relations between consciousnesses is not the *Mitsein*; it is conflict" (Sartre 429). Obviously, the exercise of freedom comes under this general rule governing the Self-Other relation. As the subject carries out her or his projects, he or she comes up against the freedom of the Other, who is in the process of carrying out her or his own quite possibly contradictory or conflicting projects, or as Sartre writes, "My freedom [. . .] finds its limits [. . .] in the existence of the other's freedom" (525). Irigaray will not deny that the other poses a certain limit to my freedom. She is quite clear that "the other stops my projection towards the infinite. The other intervenes in my project [. . .]. The other arrests my impetus towards a future [. . .] by setting against it the limit imposed by another transcendence, that of the other" (Irigaray 2008, 85). Irigaray appears to be deliberately using existentialist language here, emphasizing "transcendence" and that projection into the future that is so central to Sartrean freedom. However, she goes on to establish a major difference between her own concept of freedom and that of the existentialist. For her, the individual subject's project is itself limited and represents a circumscription around freedom, because it originated in and remains part of the network in which the subject is and has always been caught up. The project may seem to be infinitely open, unique, and highly original, but that is only another illusion created by the network, which determined the project's nature and its goals and, in some ways, made it inevitable that it should take the form that it takes. For Irigaray, however, the possibility exists for a project to shake itself loose from the network; it can be "liberated" through intersubjectivity and the subject's engaged relation with (the) other(s).

Irigaray will claim that even as the other's freedom limits my freedom to expand my project, it is also the other of difference who creates a new and unforeseen space into which my freedom and my project open up. This is not a space that I had been planning on, where I had already projected myself with my goals and ends, but a totally new space, one that I had never foreseen and would not have been able to foresee since it existed only outside the network in which I have always been and continue to be caught up.

> What was imagined as freedom by philosophy is thus to be rethought . . . [. . .] The Western philosopher considers that the relation to the world is determined by a single center or source, a single opening to the world. Now the freedom of the other represents another opening, another project or center with respect to the world (76). [Engaging with it], I will have gained a new freedom. (89)

In creating "another opening," "another center" from which the perspective on the world is fundamentally different from our own, our relation to the other—not to the anonymous they or Them, but to another, or others, whose difference we recognize and acknowledge—allows us to catch a glimpse of another world. This is a totally different world from our own, originating as it does in a different network; part of the tragic paradox of *Sharing the World* is that we are forever alienated from that other world the other sees and in which the other dwells. We can never go there. There is no question of our integrating into that world, nor of the other integrating into ours. If we are to share, we must create that consummately Irigarayan place or space—a "threshold" or an "interval"—an opening that would allow us both egress from our own world and entrance into another—totally new and previously unimagined and unimaginable—where we can go together. Temporarily. There is no question of staying there. If we should try to do that, we would end up imprisoned in another network; we can only go there together with the other, and then come back, forever changed ourselves, liberated, to further change our own already changed worlds. Without the other, I would remain unknowingly and unquestioningly inside the weaving and interlacing of the network holding me in place. In Irigarayan thought, the other *is* my hope of freedom—the very possibility of my freedom.

Notes

1. See Phyllis Kaminski's "Daughters, Difference, and Irigaray's Economy of Desire" in this volume, for an exception to this rule.

2. Sartre frequently capitalizes the word "other." Irigaray, who finds Sartre's capital letter "excessively quantitative" (19), also uses the capital at times. In this chapter, I will use the capital letter in the Sartrean context and the lowercase letter in the Irigarayan context.

3. Technical definitions for the expressions "for-itself" (*le pour-soi*), "in-itself" (*l'en-soi*), and "facticity" (*la facticité*) are provided in the glossary included at the end of the Hazel Barnes English translation of *Being and Nothingness* (Sartre 629–30). I would grossly oversimplify and describe the for-itself as conscious existence, intentional existence, subjectivity; the for-itself contrasts with the in-itself—that is, nonconscious being, the being of phenomena, as Barnes explains, or objectivity. "Facticity" might be equated with "thingness"; it corresponds to the in-itself and objectivity (see Sartre 73–102).

4. It should be noted that, although Irigaray is supposedly providing a (rare for her) direct citation in quotation marks, Sartre actually only compares the body's ensnared transcendence to "cream"; no mention is made of "mayonnaise"—either in Hazel Barnes's English translation or in his original French (Sartre 1943, 444).

5. That is (along with desire), love, masochism, indifference, hate, and sadism (Sartre 361–412).

6. See Irigaray 2001a, 43–49, for a detailed elaboration of relational identity.

7. For a detailed discussion of the vertical/horizontal theme in Irigaray and particularly of the vertical transcendence of gender, see Schwab 2011a, 77–97; Deutscher 1994, 102–4; and Deutscher 2002, 95–98.

8. See Schwab 2016 for a discussion of the educational system and pedagogy.

9. Sartre's Other (so-called) is truly Irigaray's "other of the same," and nowhere is the sameness of the Other more obvious than in his language itself. It is full of what I might call Sartre's "mirror-image style." A couple of examples: "While I seek to enslave the Other, the Other seeks to enslave me." "The Other is on principle inapprehensible; he flees me when I seek him and possesses me when I flee him" (Sartre 408). "One must either transcend the Other or allow oneself to be transcended by him" (429).

10. See Hill 2012 for a detailed discussion of the interval.

11. We might regret that Irigaray has never chosen to comment on Sartre's description of the "bad faith" of the young woman on a date, Perhaps she would have underlined the male's equivalent conformism and lack of forthrightness as regards his own sexual intentions in this situation.

12. Kruks shows how Sartre failed to work out the complexities of "freedom in situation in *Being and Nothingness* and was ultimately forced to take the problem up again in the *Critique of Dialectical Reason* (1976)," where she finds that he succeeded, even though no one was really paying much attention anymore (Kruks, chapter 5, 146–80).

13. Sartre gives the example of the mountain climber (Sartre 487–89), which Kruks discusses as well (Kruks 66–67). Until the climber actually decides to tackle a particular ascent, the mountain cannot be an impediment to his or her freedom; it is only a neutral fact. Sartre calls it a "brute existent," an in-itself with no intrinsic meaning. It is only the climber's freely undertaken decision to climb that renders the mountain either "possible" or "impossible" to climb; it is only the freedom of the climber that gives the mountain meaning and thus creates the mountain climber's situation.

14. See Cheryl Lynch-Lawler's "The Re-Enchanted Garden" and Rebecca Hill's "Between Her and Her" in this volume.

Works Cited

Deutscher, Penelope. 1994. " 'The Only Diabolical Thing about Women': Luce Irigaray on Divinity." *Hypatia* 9, no. 4 (Fall): 88–111.

———. 2002. *A Politics of Impossible Difference: The Later Work of Luce Irigaray.* Ithaca, New York: Cornell University Press.

Hill, Rebecca. 2012. *The Interval: Relation and Becoming in Irigaray, Aristotle, and Bergson.* New York: Fordham University Press.

Irigaray, Luce. 2001a. *Le Partage de la parole.* Oxford: Legenda.

———. 2001b. *To Be Two.* Translated by Monique M. Rhodes and Marco F. Cocito-Monoc. New York: Routledge.

———, ed. 2004. *Key Writings.* Luce Irigaray. Continuum: London and New York.

———. 2008. *Sharing the World.* Continuum: London and New York.

Jones, Rachel. 2011. *Irigaray: Towards a Sexuate Philosophy.* Cambridge, UK: Polity.

Kruks, Sonia. 1990. *Situation and Human Existence: Freedom, Subjectivity, and Society.* London: Unwin Hyman.

Leland, Dorothy. 2002. "Conflictual Culture and Authenticity: Deepening Heidegger's Account of the Social." In *Feminist Interpretations of Martin Heidegger*, edited by Nancy J. Holland and Patricia Huntington, 109–27. University Park: Pennsylvania State University Press.

Sartre, Jean-Paul. 1943. *L'Etre et le néant: Essai d'ontologie phénoménologique.* Paris: Gallimard.

———. 1947. *Huis clos*, suivi de *Les Mouches.* Paris: Gallimard.

———. 1966. *Being and Nothingness: An Essay on Phenomenological Ontology.* Translated by Hazel Barnes. New York: Philosophical Library.

Schwab, Gail. 2011a. "Beyond the Vertical and the Horizontal: Spirituality, Space, and Alterity in the Work of Luce Irigaray" In *Thinking with Irigaray*, edited by Mary C. Rawlinson, Sabrina L. Hom, and Serene J. Khader. Albany: State University of New York Press.

———. 2011b. Book Review of Luce Irigaray's *Sharing the World, Teaching, Conversations*. *Metaphilosophy* 42, no. 3 (April).

———. 2016. "Creating Inter-Sexuate Inter-Subjectivity in the Classroom? Luce Irigaray's Linguistic Research in Its Latest Iteration." In *Engaging the World: Thinking after Irigaray*, edited by Mary C. Rawlinson. Albany: State University of New York Press.

Daughters, Difference, and Irigaray's Economy of Desire

PHYLLIS H. KAMINSKI

> The transition to a new age comes at the same time as a change in the economy of desire.
>
> —Irigaray 1993a, 8

In the present age, violent conflict is decimating populations, and transnational capitalism is the world's fastest-growing religion, "binding all corners of the globe more and more tightly into a world view and set of values" (Balakrishnan 45). The global market feeds on desire and sells satisfaction at ever-higher prices. Faced with deadly and death-dealing global conflicts, Luce Irigaray continues to look to an impossible future, imagining an economy founded on loving exchange rather than on relations of power and domination. The question of the recognition of difference presents itself in all its facets (philosophical, mystical, psychological, cultural, legal, linguistic, and religious) throughout the Irigarayan corpus, and, in her project, desire and difference, cultivated in terms of the asceticism of the negative and the positive sharing of dynamic eros, remain necessary conditions of possibility for a new economy of relations. While Irigaray's commitment to transformation of consciousness through spiritual practice speaks of the urgent need for both personal and collective efforts to address injustice and dehumanization in cultures and their institutional structures, her writing on the sharing of breath and on creating cultured relations between human subjects who can recognize difference inspires hope that we can transform inherited structures and existing patterns.

It is in this light that I claim that the position of the daughter in the Irigarayan corpus provides a way out of the economy of the same and into an economy of difference. While, on one level, Irigaray intends the term "daughter" to designate individual bodied persons in all their concreteness, her understanding is never simply biological. "Daughterness" is also a structural concept, one that brings self-awareness and self-understanding, through patterns of familial, social, and economic exchange, always in relation to the existing order and its expressions of desire. Changing that order involves a spiritual becoming wherein adult daughters realize autonomy and relatedness with (m)others like themselves, and, recognized as desiring subjects in their own right, no longer serve as objects of exchange among men. Thus, the place of the daughter throughout her individual life cycle is a touchstone to the kind of transformed relations (both interpersonal and social) that Irigaray envisions and hopes to enflesh.

Reading Irigaray's insistence on the possibility of sexual difference in the present economy as "anticipatory," Penelope Deutscher asks: "What would it mean to support a multicultural politics that affirmed the specific needs and rights of cultures to whose articulation girls and women of different generations actively contributed?" (Deutscher 4–5). I ask a related question: "What would it take to realize a world where the lives of girls and women of different generations and diverse commitments were valued in themselves?" In order to advance answers to those questions, I will articulate my understanding of the pivotal position of the adult daughter in the transformation of consciousness required for realization of a new economy of relations. That transformation, with its necessary Irigarayan double dialectic of words and bodies, unfolds the many-layered and interconnected meanings of desire.

To ground my argument, I draw primarily on three key texts, "Any Theory of the Subject," from *Speculum*; "Daughter and Woman," from *To Be Two*; and "Spiritual Tasks for Our Age," from *Key Writings*. I have chosen these texts since they articulate the daughter's exile from her own desire(s), her becoming a subject, and her sharing with others in ways that illumine the limitations and possibilities of Irigaray's spiritual conception of difference and the mystery of human being and becoming.

"Any Theory of the 'Subject' ": Daughters and Desire in the Present Economy

Desire grounds the Irigarayan project at every level. In rethinking models of desire in masculine and feminine subjects, Irigaray seeks to create a space for bodily desire that is transcendent and does not objectify the one desired. Thus, she looks not only to sexual attraction for another but also to the original relation with the first other, the mother, as key to the cultivation of intersubjective desire. Reading and responding to the multileveled meanings of desire throughout her work requires that we reconceive what is natural and cultural, corporeal and spiritual. In so doing, we come to see how the daughter (as child and as adult) figures in the unmasking and the construction that distinguish Irigaray's exploration of sexual difference, of the spiritual development of human subjects, and of sociopolitical structures that recognize difference(s).

Rather than develop in detail how Irigaray exposes masculine construction and manipulation of desire in relation to the Western psychoanalytical and philosophical tradition, I begin with "Any Theory of the Subject." Located in the central section of *Speculum* (1985a), this text unfolds the dark spaces where "woman" lies hidden and begins moving the reader's consciousness from Freud's "blind spot" to Plato's "hystera." Here Irigaray's own two lips theorize subjectivity. She speaks the individual and social parameters of masculine ideas of female sexuality, woman's subjectivity, and the implications of the present economy for daughters. If, for Freud, as she has shown, the little girl does not exist except as "a little man" (Irigaray 1985a, 26) who "functions as a *hole*" (71), for Irigaray, the nonexistent girl-child supports the phallic economy; her existence as a desiring subject also holds the key to its deconstruction. Having used her specular lens to open spaces hitherto closed, Irigaray turns dominant cultural syntax upside down and inside out as she seeks to imagine an economy of relations that recognizes an "other" who is irreducibly different. The linguistically silenced, invisible, mute feminine subject completely exiled from her desires must find a way in and beyond a "hom(m)osexual" economy that denies the specificity of her desires and renders her unable to speak her pain or her pleasure. The daughter who dares to say "I am not the hole" threatens the subject who desires to be "the whole."

Undervalued worldwide culturally, socially, and economically for themselves, female children are most vulnerable to oppressive patriarchal systems.

If they survive early childhood, daughters are more likely to die before age four, and they are more apt than sons to receive poor healthcare, inadequate nourishment, and limited education (Kurz and Prather 1995). In the present global economy, girls, still largely nonexistent as subjects in the Irigarayan sense, remain valuable commodities prized for their functionality and their service to masculine desires. They are, in Irigaray's words, "the loose coin, the currency of exchange" (Irigaray 2000, 19). Young virgins are prized as disease-free objects of pleasure in sex trafficking and as paragons of purity in traditional religious communities. Girls and women also provide much of the work force in most of the world, functioning to satisfy the desires of others, but exiled from any desires of their own.

Irigaray's concave lens exposes the (non)position of the flesh-and-blood daughter-women I have just described; "subjectivity denied to woman: indisputably this provides the financial backing for every irreducible constitution as an object: of representation, of discourse, of desire" (Irigaray 1985a, 133). Silenced in the symbolic system "she" supports, "she" remains a mute mirror for masculine desires. She is neither seen, nor can she see herself as belonging to herself/being for herself. Daughterly desires "underwent abortion" in girlhood, and they "continue to be aborted" throughout the lives of women (Irigaray 2000, 26) in our technological, globalized economy.

The daughter's inability to reflect desires of her own is further complicated by the fact that the "I/she" struggles to become self-conscious in conflicted, unsymbolized, and largely unconscious relations to the all-powerful, yet castrated mother. In her analysis of the plight of flesh-and-blood daughters in relation to their mothers in *This Sex*, Irigaray diagnoses the multiplicity of women's roles related primarily to male desires as symptomatic of the cultural pathology infecting and affecting all women:

> There is no possibility whatever, within the current logic of sociocultural operations, for a daughter to situate herself with respect to her mother: because, strictly speaking, they make neither one, nor two, neither has a name, meaning, sex of her own, neither can be "identified" with respect to the other . . . How can the relationship between these two women be articulated? Here, for example, is one place where the need for another "syntax," another "grammar," of culture is crucial. (Irigaray 1985b, 143)

It is that need for a different syntax and grammar of culture that continues to preoccupy Irigaray. In dominant social, religious, and economic cultures, "the daughter" has little or no place to become an adult "I/she."

We know that advertising uses sexual cues to sell almost any product; as David McCarthy comments, however, we are less aware that "our sexual desires are structured and constrained by the systems of exchange where they appear" (McCarthy 88). This market economy values the daughter only insofar as she serves the desires of others as slave, sex object, wife, or mother. If *his* desire expresses an insatiable need to fill a lack, to contain and possess that which he desires, the daughter learns to read herself in terms of her desirability, one whose value derives from service to others. *She* has no consciousness of herself as a subject with specific desires of her own:

> She is the reserve of "sensuality" for the elevation of intelligence, she is the matter used for the imprint of forms, gage of possible regression into naïve perception, the representative representing negativity (death), dark continent of dreams and fantasies, and also eardrum faithfully duplicating the music, though not all of it, so that the series of displacements may continue, for the "subject." (Irigaray 1985a, 141)

Irigaray's words stretch in every direction. The English translation of "Any Theory" evokes the image of the feminine subject as the Pythia perched precariously over the Delphic cave, miming "induced desires and suggestions foreign to her still hazy consciousness" (ibid.). The French adverb *pithiaquement* suggests a psychosomatic condition which can be both caused and cured by persuasion and suggestion. *Doublure aliénant* (175) in translation becomes "delirious double" (141), but *doublure* also suggests "a lining," that which gives shape and structure to a garment but remains unseen. Irigaray both struggles and plays to articulate the power of current "erections" of the masculine subject in her efforts to express the material function of the invisible feminine subject in a masculine economy. Any attempt of the daughter-m(other)-woman to speak (I/she or you/her) disrupts this economy and often evokes violent reactions.

Ultimately, women are trapped in the never-ending game of illusory or distorted reflections in phallic technological exchanges in a world increasingly fractured by ethnic conflicts, tribal vendettas, and wars. The "father," desiring reproduction of the status quo, imposes order—no matter how repressive. Those who desire a different world—one in which all life can flourish—shake the very foundation of the "palace of mirrors" (137) "he" has erected. As noted above, current statistics verify that daughters are the biggest losers wherever these games are played. That is why, I suggest, Irigaray has consistently maintained that the position of daughters is crucial to the transformation of socioeconomic and cultural relations (Irigaray 2000, 21). Women may currently be losing "the game" in global systems of domination, but Irigaray's words give hope. "He" is "out of breath" (Irigaray 1985a, 139). "She" asks "How find a voice, make a choice strong enough, subtle enough to cut through those layers of ornamental style, that decorative sepulcher, where even her breath is lost?" (143). These Irigarayan questions and the irruption of creative energy speak a world of difference that is not and cannot be contained by violent relations of dominance and power, insatiable production and consumption. The energy of "her" being may be repressed in every way—through linguistic, psychosocial, religious, or political structures. "He" may intensify efforts to contain her as hysteric, mad; he may redouble efforts to represent her desire in his terms; he may proclaim new orthodoxy and social structures designed to keep her in her place. Nevertheless, the energy of sexual difference as Irigaray conceives it abounds and can transform "his" definitions of desire (142). Her specular theory and spiritual practices would cultivate desire and recognize it: "Elsewhere. Burning still" (146).

To Be Two: "Daughter and Woman"

To Be Two holds onto Irigaray's urgent questions as she moves into the space opened in *Speculum*. "Daughter and Woman" (2001) continues her dialogue with the philosophers (this time, Sartre), as she examines how to move beyond the economy of the same and "to think an identity which is different from the one we know, an identity in which the relationship with the other is inscribed in the pre-given of my body" (34). While Irigaray appreciates Sartre's attempts to situate bodied relations in a horizontal dimension in terms of a present encounter with the other, she faults his neglect, not just of each subject's history, but even of their having been born (30). According to Irigaray, Sartre negates the first carnal relationship with the mother. He abstracts. For him, we exist in concrete, corporeal relations, but there is a disincarnate, split quality to his "consciousness-gaze" and "body facticity." Everyone's beginning encounter with an "other" occurs with the body of the mother. "In fact," Irigaray writes, "intention exists both on the part of the mother towards the girl or boy, and on the part of the child toward the mother. The affectionate gaze of the mother towards the body of her son or her daughter, as well as their attention towards the mother, is forgotten in Sartre's thought" (31).

Since that original encounter with the (m)other differs for a boy or a girl, Sartre's neglect of that first bodied relation serves neither men nor women in their development of consciousness. It does a particular disservice to the daughter in that, as Irigaray has shown, daughters know their bodies first in contiguous relationship with their mothers. The relations and intentions inscribed within woman's body orient her to the mother as one who is like her but also other. The dominant economy depends on severing the daughter's ties with the mother and ruling women's desires through the law of the father. In that economy, not only have daughters been denied desires of their own, but their very right "to be" is often precarious. Even cultures that value mothers do not necessarily welcome the arrival of female children. Neera Sohoni notes:

> Ironically, for all its indispensable social value, the reproductive capacity of the female does little to enhance a girl's status or worth either in the family or the society. If anything, it only places further constraints on her in terms of food taboos and other more repressive practices such as foot-binding, purdah (enforced seclusion), early marriage, and genital mutilation, all of which are aimed at controlling her mobility and sexuality. (Sohoni 1995)

In contrast to those who construe sex and gender as fixing a relation between the sexes in terms of heterosexual complementarity, Irigaray offers a dialectical/dialogical theory of sexual difference that relates sexuate bodied reality always already in relation to an other (of the same or different sex). The challenge of being born woman *and* becoming woman is generational and incarnational. Irigaray takes both of these into account in her construction of a female subjectivity that recognizes sexual difference. Her theory of subjectivity "implies a negative, a not being the other, a not being the whole, and a particular way of being: tied to the body and in relationship with the other, including therein the return to the self" (Irigaray 2001, 34). However, an economy that is truly intersubjective can develop and thrive only when daughters in all their difference(s) have the right to their own lives. They are neither nobodies nor interchangeable "any bodies" of existence (39). They must have an interiority of their own from within which they will recognize desires proper to their unique being and becoming. They will then be able to discover the tangibility of their transcendence animated by their own intentions and not determined by the world surrounding them.

If desire in the hom(m)osexual economy arises from unconscious longing for the origin of life, for the return to the maternal body "coded as a matter of rights, property, and possession, [or] repressed as scandalous" (Bergoffen 153), changing that economy involves changing that "code." "Daughter and Woman" articulates Irigaray's commitment to the "two" necessary for relationships that fulfill our humanity. It also grounds desire in the maternal body that does not reduce women to humanity's "reproducer." As Debra Bergoffen suggests, "Irigaray is not critical of the desire to return to the origin" (154). Rather, she exposes the sexuate nature of the mother-child relation, and she grounds her understanding of sexual difference in that bodied desire. Bergoffen's keen analysis of Irigaray's couples—the placental mother-child couple; the daughter-mother couple; and the man-woman couple—points to the cultural and religious limits affecting daughters (both children and adults) in the present economy and opens a space for the emergence of sexual difference as a political force. In Irigaray's new relational economy, women discover space to express *their* desire. Bergoffen writes:

> The strategy of working through the myths of woman as mother (the patriarchal reproductive vessel) and daughter (the one who hates her mother and envies her father and brothers) [. . .] teaches us how to understand what *Speculum* means when it speaks of the ways in which patriarchy systematically erases the gap between men's and women's desire and eliminates any desires originating in the daughter. It also shows us that discourse of the gap is vulnerable to appropriation by patriarchal discourses of difference unless it is supplemented by and understood through the discourse of the between. (156)

When Irigaray hints that women "can perhaps better conceive the two of subjectivity, of gender, and not only the one" (Irigaray 2001, 34), she draws on all three couples that she has explored to create an alternative to human being and becoming in the present economy. The "daughter and woman" is capable of a bodied consciousness that redefines desire in all its materiality and its transcendence. She is an adult subject-agent when, in Irigaray's terms, she can say to the (m)other, "You are the one who helps me to remain in myself, to stay in myself, to contain or keep me in myself, to remain present, presence: the possibility of being in myself, of attempting to cultivate the in-stasy and not only the ex-stasy" (37). In the space created within themselves and between themselves and an other, daughter-women can begin to build an economy which recognizes that "consciousness, truth, and ideality are two" (36).

There remains much to unravel in Irigaray's paradigmatic—and problematic—heterosexual couple, but those of us who work in patriarchal religious settings find hope in her insistence on subjectivity for the daughter-woman, in her reinterpretation of the fecundity of sexual love, and in her continued work on the cultivation of desire. The economy of the same still dominates, as evidenced by increasingly violent struggles within Christian religious groups over civil unions or marriage for same sex couples, abortion, the death penalty, the ordination of women and openly gay men or women, and even liturgical language. All of these concern in one way or another the desires of those who continue to assert the power of heteronormativity over sexual difference. Irigarayan wonder (adapted from Descartes' passions) opens different possibilities for sexual, spiritual, and ethical relations between two individuals and within and beyond religious groupings. As Debra Bergoffen summarizes: "the question of sexual difference concerns the difference between legitimating a paradigm of sociality that welcomes the singularity of difference and enforcing a paradigm that recognizes individuals only insofar as they instantiate the universal of their patriarchal sexed identities" (Bergoffen 162). Irigaray imagines an intersubjective economy where masculine and feminine subjects do not desire possessions; rather, they desire their own being and becoming as connected to and fostering the being and becoming of the other(s).

As Irigaray thinks the future, love in all its bodied expressions is radically transformed. Relationships with God, others, and the world will not be prescribed from the outset, but they will unfold in the dynamics of human consciousness and relations between and among individuals and culture. When the daughter-woman discovers her place, in relationship with her m(other), she knows, from within her body, the divine, "present as the mystery that animates the copula, the *is* and the *being* of sexual difference" (Irigaray 1993a, 19). In the space-time of her interiority, "desire is no longer a yearning for the unattainable, or the need to fulfill conventional romantic scripts. Aligned with wonder, desire, operating in a mediatory mode, permits the inception of a love that is divine" (Joy, O'Grady, and Poxon, 60). Constructing a new economy of relations calls for cultivating that desire in ways that "simultaneously represent an event that allows for the constitution of an interiority and a task to be performed" (Irigaray 2001, 38). The spiritual dimensions of that task are becoming ever more integral to an Irigarayan construction of difference.

"Spiritual Tasks for Our Age"

Luce Irigaray has long been convinced that any change in the economy of relations involves rethinking religion. For her, that rethinking involves the unbreakable connection between the personal and the social in spiritual becoming. Irigaray pointed to this specifically in "Women, the Sacred, and Money" when she affirmed that changes in the economy of consciousness involve transformation of our understanding of nature and culture in their relation to sacrifice, power, and love (Irigaray 1993b, 75–88). In "Spiritual Tasks for Our Age" (2004), a more recent dialogue with French Canadian feminists, Irigaray suggested five spiritual tasks involved in the transformative process: (1) rethinking God as energy; (2) reconceiving moral and ethical normative models; (3) gaining access to a new form of transcendence within relations between and among individuals that recognize difference; (4) the creation of sexed relations in the public sphere that are not reduced to natural intimacy but instead are expanded to recognize difference in collective relations and are woven into all areas of civil order; and (5) a mystical respect for the mystery of otherness (171–85). I will focus on the movement of sexed relations from the intimate to the collective and on the establishment of a pragmatic political mysticism that resists traditional definitions, as flesh-and-blood adult daughters labor to change themselves and political, legal, linguistic, and religious structures.

Irigaray claims that relations between the sexes "must be woven into all areas of civil order, and thus elevate it, through each and every exchange between citizens, from the natural to the spiritual, from the empirical to the transcendental" (180). If older forms of "natural" sexual difference nourished desire, new understandings "compel us to transformations of desire, of thinking, to civil forms of meeting and cohesion of which we have hardly an idea" (Irigaray 2002, 145). Thus, when Irigaray encourages women to be faithful to their gender, "gender represents a destination to the other more than it represents a biological destiny" (Irigaray 2001, 33). The daughter discovers her subjectivity in the space within herself and in the interval between herself and an other. In thinking women's spirituality through the daughter, the greatest challenge lies in moving relations with the other from the intimate to the collective. The daughters with whom I work hunger to claim their agency as women and to move beyond private solutions as they struggle to integrate gender studies perspectives on difference and desire with the inherited notions of spirituality, romance, religion, and success still shaping their lives. The pervasiveness of the problem on college campuses has been documented in works such as Courtney Martin's *Perfect Girls, Starving Daughters* (2007) and Donna Freitas's *Sex and the Soul* (2008). In diverse ways, daughters of all ages who undertake transformative practice seek not only their own intimate "between" but also a social space.

Our religious tradition has expended extraordinary amounts of energy (human and fiscal resources) in order to maintain the economy of the same; it has made and continues to make efforts to shore up traditional understandings of family, love, gendered identity within common humanity, and a religious faith that seeks justice and stands in solidarity with the poor, but it has failed to recognize difference. Given the power of this economy, it might be that Irigaray's turn to mysticism and "a negative pathway, a nocturnal approach" is, perhaps, the only path open to daughters who seek to realize their desires and to cultivate social relations that are creative of a life-giving future (Irigaray 2004, 183). It is a path that both beckons and disorients us, as individuals and as members of various social groupings. Both in her critique of Western culture and in her commitment to Eastern spiritual practices, Irigaray has demonstrated that we become spiritual through concrete bodied relations and through broadening the questions that arise from our desires: "Whom do I love? And who am I to love? Who am *I*? Who are *you*?" (1996, 139). In *I Love to You*, Irigaray, tapping the roots of her Catholic cultural formation, spoke of the cultivation of carnal love as "the transubstantiation of the self and his or her lover into a spiritual body" (139). In *To Be Two*, she refers to the incarnational mystery of human being and becoming. Every sexuate body, animated by intentions toward the other (and not simply determined by the surrounding world), expresses something of what the twentieth-century theologian Karl Rahner calls "holy mystery" (Rahner 53). The incomprehensible mystery we call God has entered human history, so that to love another as other is to share in the mystery of incarnate love—a love that is both divine and human (119). Irigaray's thought takes this Rahnerian perspective forward to uncharted paths. Sexuate becoming involves journeying within ourselves and, in relation, "welcoming mystery and difference, thus modifying our energy, but not forcing it into compartments or into sharply defined and paralyzing forms" (Irigaray 2004, 182).

The risk of paralysis is strong. Daughters desirous of spiritual becoming at this moment in history face what Constance FitzGerald describes as "impasse and dark night" (FitzGerald 1996). FitzGerald integrates John of the Cross's classic "dark night of the soul," with contemporary experience of "the dark night of the world," where violence, suffering, and the experience of personal, social, and potentially global disintegration threaten us on all sides. FitzGerald probes the depths of the impasse and suggests, in ways that resonate with Irigaray, that

> impasse can be the condition for creative growth and transformation [. . .]: if the limitations of one's humanity and human condition are squarely faced and the sorrow of finitude allowed to invade the human spirit with real, existential powerlessness; if the ego [. . .] is willing to admit the mystery of its own being and surrender itself to this mystery; if the path into the unknown, into the uncontrolled and unpredictable margins of life, is freely taken when the path of deadly clarity fades. (413–14)

Both FitzGerald and Irigaray recognize the ambiguous position of daughters in the darkness of the present image-oriented information economy. Both claim that women have a special role to play on this path if a new order, a new economy of relations, is to emerge. Irigaray's commitment to practices that augment breath (within oneself and shared with an other) can encourage women in all their difference(s) to develop their own ways of cultivating and educating the senses that function in the dark: "touch and being touched, especially at a distance; and listening while remaining attentive to a silence where the other as such, as a mystery, can be revealed, and can happen the unexpected event of an encounter with him, or her" (Irigaray 2004, 183).

In their respective settings, Irigaray and FitzGerald know how vital it is to conserve energy in the darkness of today's world. Contemplative practices do not validate things as they are; nor do they keep women passively exiled from their own desires. Rather, FitzGerald asserts that dark contemplation fosters new relations with God, with the self, and with others, "a new and integrating spirituality capable of creating a new politics and generating new social structures" (FitzGerald 432). Irigaray links the transcendence of desire with a new stage in the constitution of consciousness: "Awareness of what we are and of the task incumbent upon us as human beings [. . .] can awaken or reawaken our consciences, not to the established order, but to an order yet to be invented and respected by us, in relation to ourselves, to the other and to others, and to the world" (Irigaray 2004, 184). The escalation of violence and the plight of daughters around the globe speak of the urgent need not to abandon or dissipate the energy of our deep desire for life in the present economy. Instead, we need to cultivate a different way of being and becoming in the world.

In calling recognition of sexuate subjectivity "a *new task for our culture, notably in the articulation between nature and transcendence*" (178), Irigaray is well aware that she is challenging all of us who dialogue with her work to share the labor of exploring and expanding each of those terms. I hope to have unfolded ways in which "daughterness" figures in Irigaray's multiple approaches to genealogical relations, to sexuate subjectivity, and to incarnate spiritual desire. Daughters already know the multiplicity of relations that stifle them. Women (all of whom are daughters) who come to recognize each other as other—both like and unlike, desired and desiring—become subjects who are poised, in Irigaray's words, "to free and cultivate energy, a relational human energy still and always to be discovered and elaborated—in oneself, for oneself, for and with the other" (Irigaray 2008, 72). Contemplative practice not only changes their worlds but will also sustain their labor to negotiate social relations that transcend binaries and recognize and respect difference(s). The question of when we will we share a world where the lives of girls and women are valued in themselves and where they recognize and realize their desires remains hidden. Do we have enough breath and free-flowing energy among us, with all our difference(s), to remain on the transformative path that can create such a world?

Works Cited

Balakrishnan, Radhika. 2001. "Capitalism and Sexuality." In *Good Sex: Feminist Perspectives from the World's Religions,* edited by Patricia Beattie Jung, Mary E. Hunt, and Radhika Balakrishnan. New Brunswick, NJ: Rutgers University Press.

Bergoffen, Debra. 2007. "Irigaray's Couples." In *Returning to Irigaray: Feminist Philosophy, Politics, and the Question of Unity,* edited by Maria C. Cimitile and Elaine P. Miller, 151–72. Albany: State University of New York Press.

Deutscher, Penelope. 2002. *A Politics of Impossible Difference: The Later Work of Luce Irigaray.* Ithaca: Cornell University Press.

FitzGerald, Constance. 1996. "Impasse and Dark Night." In *Women's Spirituality: Resources for Christian Development,* edited by Joann Wolski Conn, 410–35. New York: Paulist.

Freitas, Donna. 2008. *Sex and the Soul: Juggling Sexuality, Spirituality, Romance, and Religion on America's College Campuses.* New York: Oxford University Press.

Irigaray, Luce. 1985a. *Speculum of the Other Woman.* Translated by Gillian C. Gill. Ithaca, NY: Cornell University Press. *Speculum de l'autre femme.* Paris: Editions de Minuit, 1974.

———. 1985b. *This Sex Which Is Not One*. Translated by Catherine Porter. Ithaca, NY: Cornell University Press. *Ce Sexe qui n'en est pas un*. Paris: Editions de Minuit, 1977.

———. 1993a. *An Ethics of Sexual Difference*. Translated by Carolyn Burke and Gillian C. Gill. Ithaca, NY: Cornell University Press. *Ethique de la difference sexuelle*. Paris: Editions de Minuit, 1984.

———. 1993b. *Sexes and Genealogies*. Translated by Gillian C. Gill. New York: Columbia University Press. *Sexes et parentés*. Paris: Editions de Minuit, 1987.

———. 1996. *I Love to You: Sketch of a Possible Felicity in History*. Translated by Karin Montin. New York: Routledge. *J'aime à toi*. Paris: Bernard Grasset, 1992.

———, ed. 2000. *Why Different? A Culture of Two Subjects* (with Sylvère Lotringer). Translated by Camille Collins, Peter Carravetta, Ben Meyers, Heidi Bostic, and Stephen Pluhácek. New York: Semiotext(e).

———. 2001 *To Be Two*. Translated from the Italian by Monique Rhodes and Marco F. Cocito-Monoc. New York: Routledge. *Essere Due*. Torino: Bollati Boringheri, 1994.

———. 2002. *Between East and West: From Singularity to Community*. Translated by Stephen Pluháček. New York: Columbia University Press. *Entre orient et occident: De la singularité à la communauté*. Paris: Bernard Grasset, 1999.

———. 2004. "Spiritual Tasks for Our Age," translated by Gail Schwab. In *Key Writings*, edited by Luce Irigaray, 171–85. New York: Continuum. "Tâches spirituelles pour notre temps," *Religiologiques* 21: 17–34.

———. 2008. *Sharing the World*. New York: Continuum.

Joy, Morny, Kathleen O'Grady, and Judith L. Poxon, eds. 2002. *French Feminists on Religion: A Reader*. New York: Routledge.

Kurz, Kathleen M., and Cynthia J. Prather. 1995. *Improving the Quality of Life of Girls*. New York: UNICEF.

Martin, Courtney. 2007. *Perfect Girls, Starving Daughters: The Frightening New Normalcy of Hating Your Body*. New York: Free.

McCarthy, David Matzko. 2007. "Fecundity: Sex and Social Reproduction." In *Queer Theology*, 86–95. Oxford: Blackwell.

Rahner, Karl. 1966. "The Concept of Mystery in Catholic Theology" and "On the Theology of the Incarnation." In *Theological Investigations*, vol. 4. Translated by Kevin Smyth, 36–73, 105–20. Baltimore: Helicon.

Sohoni, Neera. 1995. "The Invisible Girl." In *Choices: A Publication of the United Nations Development Programme*. http://www.guidetoaction.org/magazine/july96/invisgrl.html.

PART III

REVITALIZING HISTORY, PHILOSOPHY, PEDAGOGY, AND THE ARTS

The Age of the Spirit

Irigaray, Apocalypse, and the Trinitarian View of History

EMILY A. HOLMES

In a review essay of various introductions to and collections of feminist theology, thealogian Carol P. Christ asks whose history it is that we are writing in published collections on women and religion (Christ 2004). Because feminist texts are subject to institutional constraints, and because the discursive positions of their authors are shaped by situations of power and politics that these authors did not create, their writings must be evaluated with the same hermeneutics of suspicion applied to male-authored religious texts. Christ worries that feminists contribute to the suppression of their own history by consciously or unconsciously repressing elements of the past that are uncomfortable for those who have found a modicum of access to privilege in seminaries and universities: the contributions of women of color and lesbians, for instance, or the influence of feminists from non-Christian religions, including goddess thealogies, on the origins and development of Christian feminist theology. How we tell our history matters; it matters politically and ethically, and it matters theologically if we wish to avoid acts of matricide in suppressing the contributions of other women. Moreover, how we position ourselves, our current work, and our future in relation to the history of women and religion matters. The way we narrate history, the way we conceive what history is and what it is for, can support or it can inhibit feminist values of experience, embodiment, equality, and respect for difference.

In what follows, I examine two iterations of a similar conception of history, one by the contemporary French feminist philosopher Luce Irigaray, and the other by the twelfth-century Calabrian abbot Joachim of Fiore and his followers. Each of these conceptions of history is rooted in a reading of Revelation—that is, the book that concludes the Christian Testament and whose Greek name, Apocalypse, has given rise to a whole genre of religious writings and movements.[1] Revelation narrates the culmination of history in the triumph of good over evil and the return of Jesus the Christ. Irigaray and Joachim, perhaps surprisingly, share a trinitarian view of history occurring in three distinct, if overlapping, stages: the ages of the Father, the Son, and the Spirit. In her writings, Luce Irigaray echoes her medieval predecessor Joachim of Fiore, as well as the enthusiastic application of his thought by a thirteenth-century woman-centered heretical sect known as the Guglielmiti. When Irigaray invokes the language of three eras of history, it carries the history of its meaning(s) with it.[2] For this reason, the echoes of Joachim's medieval interpretation of Revelation are of interest to contemporary feminists as we consider how to construct and narrate our own history.

Luce Irigaray is hardly an apocalyptic thinker, but several commentators have emphasized the future orientation of her work (Whitford 1991; Irigaray 1995). She argues for the recognition of sexual difference, of at least two ontologically distinct but equal subjects, in an era that is both yet to come and, in some sense, already here, at least provisionally in her own writings. In Christian theological terms, this aspect of her thought can more precisely be described as *eschatological*—that is, concerned with the future end or goal (*telos*) of human history and its culmination in the *eschaton* (last things). Like other eschatologies, hers is concerned with the effect of a future vision on the life of the present and our interpretation of the past. This future orientation corresponds with Irigaray's larger conception of history, or History, as she often writes, with deliberately Hegelian and Marxist metaphysical echoes (Irigaray 1996). History, for Irigaray, is neither the past series of events nor our narration of them, but a much larger and inherently meaningful process in which we take part, consciously or not, as it unfolds through our actions, gestures, and words.

Irigaray divides Western history into three eras identified with the Christian Trinity of Father, Son, and Spirit, as she indicates early in her *Ethics of Sexual Difference*. In a section titled "Parousia," a word that indicates the second coming of Jesus on the last day, she writes:

> The third era of the West might, at last, be the era of the *couple*: of the spirit and the bride? After the coming of the Father that is inscribed in the Old Testament, after the coming of the Son in the New Testament, we would see the beginning of the era of the spirit and the bride. With father and son summoned for the coming of this third age in the parousia. The father comes and disappears; the son comes and disappears; the incarnation of the spirit has never taken place except, prophetically, at Pentecost. The spirit appears as the third term. The term of alliance, of mediation? (Irigaray 1993a, 148)

Irigaray's reference to the era of "the spirit and the bride" in this passage invokes the very end of the book of Revelation and, thus, an explicitly apocalyptic framework for her conception of history. The final chapters of Revelation include a vision of the creation of "a new heaven and a new earth" after the ultimate triumph of good over evil. The narrator of the book is granted a vision of a city, "the new Jerusalem," which descends from heaven, "prepared as a bride adorned for her husband," also described as "the bride, the wife of the Lamb" (Rev. 21:1–2, 9 New Revised Standard Version [NRSV]). At the end of time, the visionary writes, the Spirit and the bride—that is, the holy city—are prepared for Jesus's return:

> See, I am coming soon; my reward is with me, to repay according to everyone's work. I am the Alpha and the Omega, the first and the last, the beginning and the end. [. . .] The Spirit and the bride say, "Come." And let everyone who hears say, "Come." And let everyone who is thirsty come. Let anyone who wishes take the water of life as a gift. [. . .] The one who testifies to these things says, "Surely I am coming soon." Amen. Come, Lord Jesus! (Rev. 22:12–13, 17, 20 NRSV)

Irigaray draws on this extraordinarily complex textual imagery in her invocation of the Parousia, the spirit, and the bride. She does not, to be sure, interpret the passage as a description of the afterlife or as the wedding of the patriarchal Christian church with the second coming of Jesus as bride-groom, two traditional Christian interpretations. Nor does she follow contemporary biblical scholars who see in the city a metaphor for the idealized Christian community, its survival and ultimate triumph over the violence of the Roman Empire as experienced by persecuted first-century Christians

(Wainwright 1993; Minear 1966). Rather, in the rich metaphorical language of Revelation, Irigaray discovers a wedding of "the feminine" (as symbolized by the bride—that is, the city) with the divine (indicated by the figure of Jesus/the Lamb). For her, the concluding chapters of Revelation describe, and perhaps foretell, a new era of sexual difference: the era of the couple, joined together in a joyous and eschatological wedding.[3] A wedding of the *couple* is only possible in an age in which *women* can also see themselves as divine, which is how Irigaray interprets the image of the bride—a figure of the divine feminine (Newman 1995).

In her more recent writings, Irigaray again takes up the image of a new stage in human history (Irigaray 2002, 98, 100ff, 115). In "The Age of the Breath," she describes at length the third age:

> In my opinion, the third age, the age of the Spirit, rather corresponds to the age of cultivation, by man and woman, of the divine breath they received as human beings. [. . .] The third age corresponds, in fact, to the one which unites the earliest time and the most future time, that is, the beginning of natural life and the accomplishment of spiritual life. In other words: the age which reunites the breath of the woman-mother with the divine redemption of humanity. (Irigaray 2004, 168)

Irigaray expands upon the notion of a third age of history in this essay by interpreting the age of the spirit etymologically as the age of the breath. Reading this passage in light of the earlier one from *Ethics*, the third age appears as the era of the couple, in which pairs such as nature/culture, flesh/spirit, and woman/man are connected by means of a third term, such as breathing, that mediates between the two. Irigaray's early work demonstrates in detail how these pairs function in Western discourse as hierarchically ordered binary opposites in which the inferior pole, identified as feminine and maternal (nature, matter, flesh), is erased or violently suppressed (Irigaray 1985). In her later work, the breath or embodied spirit emerges as the sensible transcendental that mediates between the two that had previously been hierarchically opposed.[4] Mediation by a third forms a new relationship between the two as a *couple* through recognition of sexual difference—that is, of the "twoness" of being human—and offers a passageway between nature/culture, flesh/spirit, and human/divine by means of the breath. The "third age" thus refers at once to the era of the couple, the era of the "third" that mediates between the two, and the era of the spirit/breath that functions as that "third."

Irigaray frequently describes Western history in trinitarian terms. But why speak of a "third age" that is yet to come? Why three stages of history at all? Surely history can be described and categorized in any number of ways. Gerda Lerner, for example, uses two primary, overlapping rubrics in her historical analysis: the creation of patriarchy and the rise of feminist consciousness (Lerner 1986; 1993). For Irigaray, the three eras of history correspond to the manifestations of the three persons of the Christian God, culminating in the third age, which is the age of the spirit, the breath, and the couple. She writes in the essay "Divine Women": "It is true that Christianity tells us that God is in three persons, three manifestations, and the third stage of the manifestation occurs as a wedding between the spirit and the bride. Is this supposed to inaugurate the divine for, in, with women?" (Irigaray 1993b, 62). This invocation of three historical eras that correspond to the Christian Trinity of Father, Son, and Holy Spirit leads the reader back to the great medieval apocalyptic thinker Joachim of Fiore.

Joachim of Fiore's Spiritual Men

Born around 1135 in Calabria, Joachim experienced a spiritual conversion after a pilgrimage to the Holy Land and tried living as a hermit and as an ordained preacher before finding his calling as a monk (McGinn 1985, 18–30). He quickly became abbot of his monastery, which he affiliated with the Cistercians, eventually leaving to found his own monastic order at San Giovanni, high in the mountains of southern Italy. Struggling with his interpretation of Revelation, Joachim received two visions, one on Easter and one on Pentecost. These visions opened the meaning of the book to him and revealed the concordance, or harmony, between the Old and New Testaments of the Christian Bible, which for him was the key to all human history, past, present, and future (21–22). Near the end of the twelfth century, he was compelled to speak out and share his insights, because, as he put it, "the preestablished time has come" (190). Joachim soon developed a reputation as a prophet who could interpret the Bible to discern the outcome of contemporary and future events. He subsequently met with several popes and secular rulers who sought his advice, including Richard the Lionheart, who visited on his way to the Third Crusade.

Like all literate medieval Christians, Joachim read the Bible intertextually, as a rich tapestry of layered literal, typological, allegorical, and anagogical meaning that could only be discerned through long and careful study (124). Based on his insight into Revelation and his identification of the harmony between the Testaments, Joachim discerned three overlapping ages of human history. He identified these ages with the three persons of the Trinity and with the divisions of the Bible. "There is one Father," he writes in his *Book of Concordance*, "to whom the Old Testament especially pertains, one Son of God to whom the New pertains especially, one Holy Spirit who proceeds from them both and to whom pertains especially that mystical understanding which, as has been said, proceeds from the two Testaments" (translated in McGinn 1979b, 120). Two testaments correspond to two persons, Father and Son, while the Holy Spirit is identified with the *spiritualis intellectus*, the spiritual understanding of the harmony between the two testaments and its significance for history (102–3).

The two testaments and three persons of the Trinity indicate three periods of time that Joachim says we ought better to call *status*, or states.[5] The three *status* of Father/Old Testament, Son/New Testament, and Spirit/spiritual understanding correspond further to three orders of the people of God: "The first of these orders is composed of those who are married, the second is composed of the clergy, the third of monks" (translated in McGinn 1979b, 124–25). The married order bears the image of the Father because marriage begets children; the clerical order bears the image of the Son or Word of God that they preach; and the monastic order lives according to the spirit rather than the flesh and so bears the image of the Holy Spirit (129–30). Joachim's dense and complex writings are accompanied by diagrams and figures that demonstrate the overlapping and organic relationships among the three ages. He repeatedly describes the three *status* in organic terms of growth, fruit-bearing, and harvest, introducing for the first time a sense of history as progressive, as the gradual unfolding of an eternal divine plan (McGinn 1985, 123, 190–91). In Joachim's view, Christ remains the center point of salvation-history and is not superseded by later religious developments. However, the people of God are made increasingly spiritual by the special work of the third person of the Trinity, the Holy Spirit.

Calculating forty-two generations for each status and thirty years per generation, Joachim found himself at the transition to the third age, which, after a time of crisis and tribulation, would issue in a millennial reign of peace before the end of time.[6] The events described symbolically in the book of Revelation would soon be enacted in history. According to Joachim, this new era would be led by *viri spirituales*, spiritual men of a higher order of monastics who were granted the spiritual understanding of the Bible (16, 112–13). The utter absence of women is notable in all three orders: they can be neither married fathers, nor clerical sons, nor monastic spiritual men.[7] Because there are two testaments, Joachim writes, "we acknowledge two times and two peoples—the time of the fathers and that of the sons, the Jewish people and the Gentile people from whom proceeds the one church of spiritual men."[8] A similar, noncontroversial point is also made by Luce Irigaray, among many other feminists: Judeo-Christian history is patriarchal. But what comes after the time of the fathers and that of the sons?

The Spirit Incarnate in the Body of a Woman

In the century after Joachim's death, many people felt that the age of the Spirit he had prophesied was at hand. New mendicant orders, the Dominicans and the Franciscans, seemed to fulfill his prophecies of a new age of spiritual men. From his writings, it is clear that Joachim did not envision any change in the social or religious position of women in the coming time of the spirit; it is doubtful he considered the status of women at all as he identified the three ages so closely with masculine social and religious roles. But a group that gathered around a holy woman in Milan was inspired by Joachim's trinitarian theology of history to take his ideas in a surprisingly bold direction.

This sect, known to scholars as the Guglielmiti, revered a woman, Guglielma, as the incarnation of the Holy Spirit and the inaugurator of the third age.[9] Reconstructed from the records of their trial for heresy, the story of the Guglielmiti is as follows: Sometime in the 1260s, the Bohemian princess Blažena Vilemína arrived in Milan. Under the Italianized name of Guglielma (Willemina), she took up a life of charity, and her piety, good works, and charisma quickly attracted admirers. She was buried at the Cistercian monastery of Chiaravalle after her death in 1281, and a cult grew up around the tomb of the holy woman. The orthodox veneration of the saint served as a cover for nearly twenty years for Guglielma's more radical followers, who believed that the holy woman was not merely pious and charitable, but was in fact the Holy Spirit—that is, she was God, incarnate in the body of a woman. This group had two leaders: a man, Andrea Saramita, who likely introduced the Joachite interpretation of the third age; and a woman, Sister Maifreda, a nun of the Humiliati order who regularly celebrated mass with the host blessed on Guglielma's tomb and distributed to her followers.[10] On Pentecost in the Jubilee year of 1300, Guglielma's bodily resurrection was eagerly anticipated. Her followers believed her return would initiate the third age by formally and publicly appointing Sister Maifreda as pope, electing women cardinals and converting pagans, Muslims, and Jews. The Guglielmiti purchased elaborate robes for Guglielma's return and wrote new gospels and hymns to celebrate the coming age.[11] Inquisitors became suspicious, however, when Guglielma's disciples prepared to celebrate Easter mass on her grave in anticipation of her resurrection. In addition to condemning Sister Maifreda, Andrea Saramita, and others as relapsed heretics, inquisitors had Guglielma's remains exhumed and burned along with her followers.[12]

In many ways, the religious beliefs of the Guglielmiti follow a certain logic; they were responding to the absence of the feminine in the all-male Christian deity, and they worried about the consequences of that absence for salvation (Wessley 1978, 300). If the second person of the Trinity was incarnate in the body of a man, and thereby accomplished the salvation of some, they argued, shouldn't the third person of the Trinity be incarnate in the body of a woman, in order to complete the salvation of all? Without a divine feminine incarnate in a woman's body, women were left outside the salvation of the church (Newman 1995, 194). The incarnation of the Spirit in Guglielma thus remedied a perceived limited atonement by Christ, that is, the idea that Christ had become incarnate, died, and resurrected only for the salvation of some people, but not all. By supplementing—that is, both completing and superseding—the work of Jesus, Guglielma would initiate an era of universal salvation and inaugurate the third age, to supersede the previous two eras of Father and Son. The Guglielmiti found intellectual support for this interpretation in the writings of Joachim of Fiore, although he certainly never predicted that the Holy Spirit would become incarnate in the body of a woman nor that the pope of the third age would be female.[13] The "feminist" element, if one can anachronistically call it that, seems to be all the Guglielmiti's own.

Incarnation in History

Two elements stand out in the beliefs of the Guglielmiti that anticipate and resonate with the writings of Luce Irigaray: a feminine incarnation of the divine and a trinitarian conception of history.[14] The Guglielmiti venerated a female body as the divine incarnate. The radical claims regarding the divinity of Guglielma's body fall at one end of a continuum of medieval women's spirituality. Caroline Walker Bynum has shown how medieval women's bodies at times became the privileged site for miracles, attesting to God's presence in the world through their extreme feats of suffering in imitation of Christ and their food miracles, such as their own inability to eat or their miraculous feeding of others. Medieval women's piety took this particular somatic shape, she argues, because of women's bodily identification with Christ, who, by becoming wounded flesh that is broken and eaten, was understood to have identified in a special way with women (Bynum 1987 and 1991; Reineke 1990). Jesus's own flesh was often described in feminine terms: Jesus bled, he gave birth to the church, he nourished the faithful in the Eucharist, and his human body had no other earthly source than his mother Mary (Bynum 1984). Because Jesus's human body was so frequently understood as analogous to a woman's body, his incarnation, passion, and the Eucharist became the focus of medieval women's piety, and their bodies became the locus where God was manifest through extraordinary and miraculous phenomena. Veneration of Guglielma as the female incarnation of the divine lies at the extreme of this continuum of medieval women's spirituality. Given the ways in which female flesh has often been degraded in the hierarchical dualisms operative in Christian theology, to divinize female flesh as the incarnate Spirit reverses the traditional discourse on the theological role of women's bodies. One might say it redeems them.

Irigaray evokes this moment in women's history in "La Mystérique," her essay on medieval women's mysticism at the heart of *Speculum of the Other Woman*, but her most explicit call for women's incarnation of the divine occurs in the essay "Divine Women."[15] Being able to envision God as feminine or women as divine, Irigaray argues, following Feuerbach, is a necessary dimension of the third age of history. The era of the couple—that is, the era of the breath and the spirit—cannot take place unless women can also be seen as embodying divinity. Although Guglielma and her medieval contemporaries embraced the divine potential of female bodies, Irigaray rejects the idea of a metaphysically real God who intervenes in human history from above, which they would have taken for granted. She also rejects the idea of waiting passively for a God who is yet to come in favor of an incarnation of God here and now:

> We still have to await the god, remain ready and open to prepare a way for his coming. And, with him, for ourselves, to prepare, not an implacable decline, but a new birth, *a new era in history.* [. . .] This creation would be our opportunity [. . .], by

> means of the opening of a sensible transcendental that comes into being through us, of which we would be the mediators and bridges. Not only in mourning for the dead God of Nietzsche, not waiting passively for the god to come, but by creating him among us, within us, as resurrection and transfiguration of blood, of flesh, through a language and an ethics that is ours. (Irigaray 1993a,129)[16]

The second coming of Christ, in her view, is the incarnation of the divine here and now, potentially in each person. "Becoming divine" takes place directly in the body through spiritual practices such as yogic breathing, song, or prayer, that link nature with spirit. Conscious breathing is thus the task of the third age, the new era of history in which women and men cultivate and exchange the breath they received from the mother, linking breath to divinity. While Irigaray leaves undetermined what becoming divine looks like in practice, this call for a diverse, sexuate, and breath-filled incarnation of the divine in multiple bodies is theologically suggestive. Whether or not Irigaray is intentionally alluding to her medieval precedent in the Guglielmiti, her call for a feminine incarnation of the divine in the third age of history echoes their beliefs in the female embodiment of Spirit.

The beliefs of the Guglielmiti also indicate the diverse uses to which a Joachite conception of history can be put. Irigaray's invocation of three historical ages culminating in a new era of the spirit, breath, and the couple echoes Joachim's trinitarian and apocalyptic theology of history. Her description of the conditions necessary for the recognition of sexual difference indicates a new way of life, just as Joachim hoped for a new, peaceful era of "spiritual men" and ecclesiastical renewal, and just as the Guglielmiti hoped for women's equal leadership in the church and universal salvation. The sexed couple functions for Irigaray as the spiritual men do for Joachim: both signs and initiators of the third age. Calls for an imminent transition in history, using the language and imagery of the apocalypse, can still authorize radical social movements, just as they did in the time of Joachim and the Guglielmiti.

Whose History?

The trinitarian conception of history as developed by Joachim and echoed by Irigaray is deeply problematic, however, as we consider the uses to which history is put. An understanding of history in three ages implies Christian triumphalism and supersession of Judaism. The Guglielmiti sought the ultimate triumph of Christianity over both pagans and Muslims. This apparent triumphalism is especially worrisome as some see Joachim's third age as the inspiration for Hitler's Third Reich (McGinn 1985, 2). A view of history as inexorably leading to a new, spiritual era can authorize movements for violence, scapegoating, and cultural and religious genocide as easily as it can inspire movements for justice and equality.

The apocalyptic language Irigaray uses to introduce her understanding of the third age is also problematic in relation to its biblical and historical context. Irigaray evokes the image of the spirit and the bride as a wedded couple. A careful reading of Revelation, however, indicates that no wedding takes place between the spirit and the bride. Rather, the anticipated wedding is between the holy city, New Jerusalem, which is described as a bride, and the wounded lamb, an image of Jesus. This discrepancy may be a simple misreading of the text, but the gendered imagery of the passage is also troubling. While cities are frequently personified as feminine in ancient texts (the same book of Revelation includes the iconic "Babylon"), this holy city of the New Jerusalem is remarkable in that it is composed of 144,000 male virgins, identified as "those who have not defiled themselves with women" (Huber 2008, 3–28). These male virgins that compose the city as the bride of the lamb can be understood either as a rejection of the Roman discourse of masculinity by the nascent Christian community or as the complete and ultimate eradication of women, as male virgins take over the female role of bride and marry a male Christ (Pippin 1992; 1999, 122–25). On either interpretation, the gender dynamics of the passage are much more complex than Irigaray indicates in her deployment of apocalyptic language and, in the original historical context (the first century Roman empire) at least, cannot be taken as warrant either for an era of sexual difference or for the incarnation of the divine in women.

What, then, does Irigaray gain by using the difficult language of apocalypse and the trinitarian interpretation of history? Irigaray's relationship to the texts and figures of the Western philosophical and religious tradition is complicated, and this relationship is precisely what is at stake in her philosophy of difference. She frequently takes images and ideas out of their original context to reinterpret them in light of her own philosophical interests. Although her method is at times properly deconstructive, it more often operates through what we might call poetic license, metonymy, or free association. This hermeneutical approach is at play in Irigaray's references to the third age of the spirit. Taking the idea of three ages of history, which she may have inherited from Joachim, a path of association develops: from the idea of the culmination of history one is led to the book of Revelation, where a wedding takes place—a representation, for her, of a couple and of sexual difference. The wedding joins a bride to Christ—an image of the feminine joined with divinity. Irigaray's evocation of the third age of the spirit is thus a compression of the trinitarian conception of history with the wedding at the conclusion of Revelation, in which the feminine is wedded to the divine and the couple together figures an era of sexual difference. Following the chain of association further, the concept of "spirit" leads etymologically to "breath"—and thus an indication of a new era focused on the cultivation of breathing. Breathing connects the body with the divine, the flesh with spirit, and the couple, male and female. The breath or the spirit functions as the "third term" that mediates between the two. And the idea of a "third" leads back to a conception of history in trinitarian terms, culminating in the "third" age.

Although this chain of associations may not be textually or historically accurate with respect to Revelation or to Joachim's writings, it is a fertile connection of ideas. In each case, "the symbol gives rise to thought," in Paul Ricoeur's phrase (1967), through a productive process of interpretation. The imagery of Revelation gives Irigaray a couple in which women can see themselves as also divine, and the trinitarian conception of history invites the idea of a coming era of flourishing, even divinity, for women and men. This new era, however, is not inevitably determined by an all-powerful God who acts in history; nor does it unfold organically according to divine providence. The meaning of history is created through human political, philosophical, and religious intervention, rather than through divine intervention. Human beings, men and women, are responsible for bearing the divine in their own bodies, breath, and words and thereby inaugurating a new stage in human history through the transformation of the present.

The trinitarian conception of history is one way of situating the emergence of feminism in relation to the overwhelmingly patriarchal span of recorded human history, the time of fathers and sons. Joachim's conception of history was once taken as authorization for a new moment, however brief, of gender equality, leadership of women, and sexuate incarnation by the Guglielmiti. Perhaps Irigaray's prophetic hope is that her deployment of the same language will have similar effects. Her optimistic vision is both future oriented, toward a new era of sexual difference that is yet to come, and a realized eschatology: the third age is already here, in our bodies, in our breath (Irigaray 1993b, 62, 71).

Irigaray's use of apocalyptic and eschatological language is imaginative, just as her description of history on the cusp of the third age is powerful. As a way of understanding the past and our relationship to it, however, the trinitarian schema risks obscuring the complexity of history—and of women's religious history in particular. Because this view of history relegates the Jewish and Christian past entirely to patriarchy, it prevents us from appreciating the multifaceted ways in which women have negotiated their religious lives and even found transformation and empowerment within their religions. The reality of women's religious history is extraordinarily complex; there is no clear "female train of thought" coming down through the ages. Lineages of ideas and practices are hard to trace because women's religious lives are so often invisible to textual traditions. This history does not unfold in a preordained, arboreal fashion of the sort pictured by Joachim; it takes place underground, through rhizomatic connections (Deleuze and Guattari 1987, 5–25). At times, women such as Guglielma have been seen as the incarnate divine, while others have imaged God in female form, but these ideas are interwoven with acts of misogyny and suppression. It would be a mistake to take a trinitarian view of history as a literal or metaphysical description of the past or present. At best, we can read Irigaray's apocalyptic language just as we must read the language of Revelation: as metaphorical, sometimes obscure, but frequently fertile images that give rise to hope in the present in light of the future.

Notes

Earlier versions of this chapter were presented at the Third Annual Conference of the Luce Irigaray Circle and at the annual conference of the Southeastern Commission for the Study of Religion. I wish to thank the audiences at these sessions; my respondent, Gertrude Postl, for her thoughtful comments; and Lynn Huber for commenting on an earlier version of this essay.

1. For an alternative feminist theological approach to the language and imagery of apocalypse, based in process philosophy, see Keller 2005 and 1996.

2. Irigaray's use of Joachim's language is of hermeneutical interest, regardless of its source. When asked about possible Joachite influence on her thought, she responded, "If I think of an idea, it is mine, even if someone else has also said it." Interview with author, June 23, 2006.

3. For a critical overview of the problem of heterosexism in Irigaray's references to "the couple," see Joy 2006, 97–101. Feminist theorists who extend Irigaray's sexual difference to other forms of difference, including sexuality and race, include Pheng Cheah and Elizabeth Grosz 1998, 19–42, and Ellen T. Armour 1999.

4. See Holmes and Škof 2013.

5. Joachim's exegesis is complex, calculating time according to the number of generations in a particular *tempus* or *status*. See his *Book of Concordance*, book 2, part 1, ch. 4 (translated in McGinn 1979b, 124).

6. Joachim of Fiore, *Book of Concordance*, book 2, part 1, ch. 10 (translated in McGinn 1979b, 133).

7. Tina Pippin argues that the misogynistic author of Revelation ultimately bars women from the kingdom of God; Joachim's silence on women in the three ages of history can be understood, on this reading, as simply repeating a prior biblical erasure (Pippin 1999).

8. Joachim of Fiore, *Expositio in Apocalypsim* (quoted in McGinn 1985, 171).

9. Almost all information on the Guglielmiti comes from the inquisitorial records of their trial, in Tocco, ed. 1899, 309–42, 351–84, 407–32, 437–69. I have also relied on the work of Wessley 1978, 289–303; Newman 1995, 182–223; and Muraro 1985. For the complete story of Guglielma, including the fifteenth-century revival of her orthodox cult, see Newman 2005.

10. For subtle differences in the theologies of Maifreda and Saramita, see Muraro 1985, 132–34, and Newman 1995, 186–95, 212–13. See also Muraro 1996, 63–76.

11. None of these, unfortunately, survives. Although they were presented at the trial, it is presumed that they were burned along with the bodies of the heretics (Tocco, ed. 1899, 331, 333, 374).

12. They had already been interrogated and had abjured in 1284 (see Newman 1995, 194, and Wessley 1978, 302).

13. See McGinn 1979a, 126–41, 146–48; see also Reeves 1969, 16–27, 401–15, and Reeves 1976, 50.

14. Although Irigaray nowhere mentions the Guglielmiti by name, the inclusion of Muraro's essay "Avant et après" in her collection *Le Souffle des Femmes* indicates familiarity with them.

15. See also "The Crucified One," in Irigaray 1991, and "The Redemption of Women," in Irigaray 2004.

16. Editor's note. Emily A. Holmes has modified the translation as follows: Irigaray's emphasis has been removed from "sensible transcendental" and from "we would be," and Holmes has added emphasis to "a new era in history." She has also changed "by conjuring him up among us" to "by creating him among us."

Works Cited

Armour, Ellen T. 1999. *Deconstruction, Feminist Theology, and the Problem of Difference: Subverting the Race/Gender Divide*. Chicago: University of Chicago Press.

Bynum, Carolyn Walker. 1984. *Jesus as Mother: Studies in the Spirituality of the High Middle Ages*. Berkeley: University of California Press.

———. 1987. *Holy Feast and Holy Fast: The Religious Significance of Food to Medieval Women*. Berkeley: University of California Press.

———. 1991. *Fragmentation and Redemption: Essays on Gender and the Human Body in Medieval Religion*. New York: Zone Books.

Cheah, Pheng, and Elizabeth Grosz. 1998. "The Future of Sexual Difference: An Interview with Judith Butler and Drucilla Cornell." *Diacritics* 28, no. 1: 19–42.

Christ, Carol P. 2004. "Whose History Are We Writing? Reading Feminist Texts with a Hermeneutic of Suspicion." *Journal of Feminist Studies in Religion* 20, no. 2: 59–82.

Deleuze, Gilles, and Félix Guattari. 1987. *A Thousand Plateaus: Capitalism and Schizophrenia*. Translated by Brian Massumi. Minneapolis: University of Minnesota Press.

Holmes, Emily A., and Lenart Škof, eds. 2013. *Breathing with Luce Irigaray*. London: Bloomsbury.

Huber, Lynn. 2008. "Sexually Explicit? Re-reading Revelation's 144,000 Virgins as a Response to Roman Discourses." *Journal of Men, Masculinities, and Spirituality* 2, no. 1: 3–28.

Irigaray, Luce. 1985. *Speculum of the Other Woman*. Translated by Gillian C. Gill. Ithaca: Cornell University Press.

———. 1991. *Marine Lover of Friedrich Nietzsche*. Translated by Gillian C. Gill. New York: Columbia University Press.

———.1993a. *An Ethics of Sexual Difference*. Translated by Carolyn Burke and Gillian C. Gill. Ithaca: Cornell University Press.

———. 1993b. "Divine Women." In *Sexes and Genealogies*. Translated by Gillian C. Gill. New York: Columbia University Press.

———. 1995. "Je—Luce Irigaray." Interview with Elizabeth Hirsh and Gary A. Olson. *Hypatia* 10, no. 2: 93–114.

———. 1996. *I Love to You: Sketch of a Possible Felicity in History*. Translated by Alison Martin. New York: Routledge.

———. 2002. *Between East and West: From Singularity to Community*. Translated by Stephen Pluháček. New York: Columbia University Press.

———. 2004. "The Age of the Breath" and "The Redemption of Women." In *Key Writings*. London: Continuum, 168–69, 150–64.

Joachim of Fiore. 1979. *Book of Concordance*. In *Apocalyptic Spirituality*. Translated by E. Randolph Daniel, and edited by Bernard McGinn. New York: Paulist.

Joy, Morny. 2006. *Divine Love: Luce Irigaray, Women, Gender, and Religion*. New York: Manchester University Press.

Keller, Catherine. 1996. *Apocalypse Now and Then: A Feminist Guide to the End of the World*. Minneapolis: Fortress.

———. 2005. *God and Power: Counter-Apocalyptic Journeys*. Minneapolis: Fortress.

Lerner, Gerda. 1986. *The Creation of Patriarchy*. New York: Oxford University Press.

———. 1993. *The Creation of Feminist Consciousness: From the Middle Ages to Eighteen-seventy*. New York: Oxford University Press.

McGinn, Bernard. 1979a. *Visions of the End: Apocalyptic Traditions in the Middle Ages*. New York: Columbia University Press.

———, ed. 1979b. *Apocalyptic Spirituality*. New York: Paulist.

———. 1985. *The Calabrian Abbot: Joachim of Fiore in the History of Western Thought*. New York: Macmillan.

Minear, P. S. 1966. "Ontology and Ecclesiology in the Apocalypse." *New Testament Studies* 13: 89–105.

Muraro, Luisa. 1985. *Guglielma e Maifreda: Storia di un'eresia femminista*. Milano: La Tartaruga.

———. 1996. "Avant et après dans la vie d'une femme, dans l'histoire des femmes." In *Le Souffle des Femmes*, edited by Luce Irigaray, 63–76. Paris: ACGF.

Newman, Barbara. 1995. *From Virile Woman to WomanChrist: Studies in Medieval Religion and Literature*. Philadelphia: University of Pennsylvania Press.

———. 2005. "The Heretic Saint: Guglielma of Bohemia, Milan, and Brunate." *Church History* 74, no. 1: 1–38.

Pippin, Tina. 1992. *Death and Desire: The Rhetoric of Gender in the Apocalypse of John*. Louisville, KY: Westminster/John Knox Press.

———. 1999. *Apocalyptic Bodies: The Biblical End of the World in Text and Image*. London: Routledge.

Reeves, Marjorie. 1969. *The Influence of Prophecy in the Later Middle Ages: A Study in Joachimism*. Oxford: Oxford University Press.

———. 1976. *Joachim of Fiore and the Prophetic Future*. New York: Harper & Row.

Reineke, Martha J. 1990. "'This Is My Body': Reflections on Abjection, Anorexia, and Medieval Women Mystics." *JAAR* 58, no. 2 (Summer): 245–65.

Ricoeur, Paul. 1967. *The Symbolism of Evil*. Translated by Emerson Buchanan. New York: Harper and Row.

Tocco, Felice, ed. 1899. "Il Processo dei Guglielmiti." *Rendiconti della Reale Accademia dei Lincei: Classe di Scienze Morali, Storiche e Filologiche*. Ser. 5, vol. 8 (Rome): 309–42, 351–84, 407–32, 437–69.

Wainwright, A. W. 1993. *Mysterious Apocalypse: Interpreting the Book of Revelation*. Nashville: Abingdon.

Wessley, Stephen. 1978. "The Thirteenth-Century Guglielmites: Salvation through Women." In *Medieval Women*, edited by Derek Baker, 289–303. Oxford: Blackwell.

Whitford, Margaret. 1991. *Luce Irigaray: Philosophy in the Feminine*. New York: Routledge.

Tragedy

An Irigarayan Approach

ALISON STONE

In this essay, I suggest that Irigaray's writings about ancient Greek tragedy allow us to reconsider a political problem with the idea of the tragic. This problem arises in connection with the view that human suffering is tragic if it is inescapably necessary and is recognized and positively accepted *as* necessary. For feminists, however, much suffering that has traditionally been seen as inescapably necessary is actually a contingent result of oppressive power relations. This might suggest that feminists should avoid the category of the tragic on the grounds that it has reactionary implications, falsely passing off contingent social relations as existential inevitabilities.[1] In contrast, I suggest that Irigaray's work gives us a way to retrieve the category of the tragic from this political concern by distinguishing between two forms of the tragic: historical and existential. I explore this distinction with reference to Irigaray's view of mother-daughter relationships because these are central to her reading of the Greek tragedies. She interprets the tragedies as showing that their female characters suffer because of their damaged relationships to their mothers and so, ultimately, because of the patriarchal order which has inflicted this damage. The tragedies show us that this suffering is necessary not in the nature of existence but only given this particular, patriarchal form of sociopolitical order, an order that is itself historically arising, contingent, and changeable. As such, the tragedies can motivate us to change this order.[2]

The Politics of the Tragic

Let me begin by exploring the political problem that is arguably bound up with the category of the tragic. Tragic theory starts with Aristotle's definition of a tragedy as a *mimesis* (imitation or representation) of an action involving a "change of fortune" from good to bad (whether actual or narrowly averted), which arouses our pity and fear and thereby "effect[s] the *katharsis* of such emotions" (Aristotle 37). Tragedy arouses the audience's mental distress (on the protagonists' behalf), a distress that is peculiarly satisfying or valuable because it results in emotional clarification. This is because the tragedy shows us the causal necessity with which the reversal of fortune ensues from the initial situation in which the characters are placed (Rorty 3–6). The plot (*muthos*) highlights the narrative shape of the events represented, so we see how the misfortune flows from its antecedent conditions. In turn, the tragedy indirectly shows us the general necessity of misfortune in human life due to the mutability of circumstances, against which we can never immunize ourselves because our control over the course of our lives is incomplete (see Jones 48). For Aristotle, then, the misfortune depicted in the plot is tragic because it occurs necessarily and because the plot shows us that this misfortune is inevitable, thereby bringing us emotional clarification, including reconciliation to this necessity.

This broad view of the tragic persists in much subsequent tragic theory, even that of Nietzsche, although his account of tragedy in *The Birth of Tragedy* of 1872 is deeply anti-Aristotelian in its emphasis on the fundamentally nonrational, primal, chaotic—Dionysian—sources of the tragic. For Nietzsche, tragedies, by showing us the destruction of their heroes or heroines, show us the painful Dionysian truth about the world. This truth is that suffering is inescapable, because joy and suffering are inextricably connected within life's web of creation and destruction. This truth is terrifying, but tragedies strengthen us to confront and embrace it. Nietzsche takes the view that suffering counts as tragic when it is necessary and when we view it *as* a necessity that we are to embrace.

Both Aristotle's and Nietzsche's views are politically problematic. They both suggest—for Aristotle because circumstances are mutable, for Nietzsche because of what he elsewhere formulates as the "law of life" (Nietzsche 1994, 126)—that misfortune and suffering are inescapably necessary in human life.[3] But, if so, then it seems that political efforts to bring about far-reaching structural improvements to the quality of our lives, including through pursuit of gender justice, seem to be misguided—a conclusion that Nietzsche draws in *The Birth of Tragedy*:

> Dionysiac man might be said to resemble Hamlet: both have looked deeply into the true nature of things, they have *understood* and are now loath to act. They realize that no action of theirs can work any change in the eternal condition of things, and they regard the imputation as ludicrous or debasing that they should set right the time which is out of joint. (Nietzsche 1956, 51)

The tragic view is not that we cannot make any improvements at all to the quality of our lives. The tragic concern rather is that if we try to make far-reaching, radical, systematic improvements, then this bespeaks a superficial, optimistic viewpoint that shrinks from life's true horrors. For on the tragic view, misfortune and suffering are inescapable facts of human existence, so our real task is to fortify ourselves to embrace these facts, not hide from them in comforting but ultimately futile projects of social amelioration. What we might describe, then, as the tragic critique of progressive politics has two main dimensions: first, that suffering cannot be eradicated from human life in any event, and, second, that the effort to eradicate it reflects a cowardly flight from the inescapable reality of suffering. From this standpoint, piecemeal social improvements are acceptable since they do not reflect the same kind of deluded optimism. But radical social change, of the kind championed by most feminists, is problematic.

Reacting against this kind of conservative deployment of the idea of the tragic, some socialist and feminist literary theorists, such as Jonathan Dollimore (2004) and Catherine Belsey (1985), have concluded that the idea of the tragic naturalizes inequalities—or "mystifies suffering" in Dollimore's words (2004, 190), portraying human unhappiness not as the result of changeable social structures but as eternally ordained and immutable. Therefore, these theorists have tended to avoid the category of the tragic, reinterpreting many tragedies as concerned with political conflicts rather than existential necessities. For instance, Jonathan Dollimore reinterprets Shakespeare's *King Lear* as being about mundane conflicts around the transmission of property and authority. Nevertheless, when we suffer on behalf of fictional characters in tragedies, we do come to some kind of appreciation of the inevitability of suffering in human life. There is, thus, surely value in the category of the tragic; Aristotle and Nietzsche are broadly right that it is in this area that the particular value and importance of tragedy lies.

Freud and the Tragic Effect

In light of these general problems regarding the tragic, I want to return to Irigaray's readings of the Greek tragedies. The *Antigone* of Sophocles is her main preoccupation, but she also engages closely with other tragedies, in particular Aeschylus's *Oresteia*.[4] She also engages with modern readings of these tragedies, most obviously Hegel's and Lacan's readings of *Antigone*, but plausibly also Freud's theory of tragedy (although in this last case Irigaray does not say so explicitly).[5] By looking at how her readings of *Antigone* and the *Oresteia* relate to Freud's theory of tragedy, we can clarify how Irigaray reads the tragedies as being about mother-daughter and not only Oedipal father-son relationships. In turn, this can shed new light on the political problems surrounding the tragic.

Did Freud have a "theory" of tragedy? Certainly, Greek tragedy was important for his thinking. It gave him the story of Oedipus, and it enabled him to conceive of psychoanalysis, initially, as the "cathartic" method of discharging pent-up emotions by speaking them. Freud's thematic discussions of tragedy, though, are few. His most important is of *Oedipus Rex* in the *Interpretation of Dreams* of 1900. Freud opposes the then-popular view that *Oedipus Rex* works its "tragic effect" on us because it dramatizes the inescapability of fate. Rather, Freud says, "If King Oedipus moves modern humanity no less than he did the contemporary Greek one, the explanation . . . is to be looked for in the particular nature of the material" (Freud 1991, 262) with which the tragedy deals. It deals with a man killing his father and marrying his mother, thereby fulfilling our universal unconscious wishes to do these things, wishes that we all felt as children but have since repressed. *Oedipus Rex* compensates us for having had to repress these wishes by showing us in its hero a fantasy version of ourselves who fulfills those wishes after all. The effect of tragedy thus relies on our identifying with the hero, who embodies the unconscious fantasies of author and audience.

On learning what he has done, Oedipus is horrified and blinds himself. Likewise, Freud says, we "shrink back from [Oedipus] with the whole force of the repression by which those wishes have since [childhood] been held down within us" (ibid.). As adults who have internalized the law against gratifying these wishes, we are anxious about the punishment that we know must befall Oedipus. Our anxiety is dissolved when Oedipus suffers punishment. *Oedipus Rex* shows us our unconscious desires gratified *and* satisfies our prohibitive superegos by showing us the ensuing punishment that Oedipus undergoes. Tragedies thus provide a safely contained gratification for the wishes that no civilized order can accommodate, but that cannot be extirpated and must find some level of release. As such, tragedies act as a kind of safety valve helping to uphold the civilizational status quo. Freud's overall understanding of the psychical "economics" of how *Oedipus Rex* moves us may be reconstructed as follows. Seeing our unconscious desires gratified temporarily gives us pleasurable relief from the effort of repressing them. But we now succumb to anxiety about the punishment that we anticipate—and anticipate realistically, knowing as we do that such wishes must be repressed.[6] When the hero is seen actually to undergo a reversal of fortune that constitutes an effective form of punishment, this dissolves our anxiety, and an overall decrease in psychical expenditure results. And, for Freud, any such reduction in mental excitation is pleasurable. So, he concludes, "the prime factor is undoubtedly the process of *getting rid* of one's own emotions [. . . and] the consequent enjoyment corresponds [. . .] to the relief produced by a thorough discharge" (Freud 1985a, 121).

With this account of how tragedy moves us, Freud transforms Aristotle's conception of *catharsis*, medicalizing it. While Freud agrees with Aristotle that tragedies give satisfaction because they are cathartic, Freud gives that claim the new sense that tragedies effect an artificially controlled release and dissolution of mental excitation. Freud thereby seems to have dropped Aristotle's idea that tragedies bring us clarity concerning the necessity of suffering. But perhaps, after all, Freud retains that idea. For the tragic sequence of events in *Oedipus Rex* shows us not only that Oedipus must be punished, but also, indirectly, that insofar as we, the audience, unconsciously wish to commit incest and parricide, we all must suffer the prohibition of these wishes. Hence tragedies disclose to us that repression is necessary to human life; total liberation of our violent and sexual urges is not an option.

I have been discussing Freud's account of *Oedipus Rex* as if it were also an account of tragedy per se.[7] After all, Freud claims that *Oedipus Rex* has its "universal power to move us" in a tragic way only because the work deals with wishes both universally felt and universally prohibited. If *Oedipus Rex* only has its tragic effect because of its subject matter, then, by implication, all tragedies worthy of the name must likewise deal with the Oedipus complex, recounting the ordeals of the Oedipal son. The further a tragedy departs from that subject-matter, the less tragically effective—the less a genuine tragedy—it will be. What, then, of a tragic hero such as Orestes, the protagonist of the *Oresteia*, who kills his mother, Clytemnestra, to avenge his father, Agamemnon, whom Clytemnestra had murdered in revenge for his sacrifice of their daughter, Iphigeneia? Orestes, too, can be seen to be in the throes of the Oedipus complex once we factor in Freud's later idea that the "positive," parricidal Oedipus complex is always accompanied by a "recessed" negative Oedipus complex in which the son loves his father and rivalrously identifies with his mother, whom he wishes to supplant, murderously so. The Oedipus complex includes many permutations of feeling and can thus allow for Orestes killing Clytemnestra out of love for his murdered father.

Even so, is the Oedipus complex really the subject matter of *all* genuine tragedies? Surprising as this might seem, perhaps it is if, as Freud holds, the Oedipus complex embraces all conflicts of men with authority figures or with powers, such as fate, that can be seen as representing a controlling authority. Moreover, for Freud, the modern tragedies written in (what he sees as) more civilized, more repressed societies generally portray the Oedipus complex only in disguise. Thus, for Freud, Hamlet's desire for his mother and hostility to his father never come out but instead inhibit him from killing Claudius, with whom he unconsciously identifies. Tragedies can deal with the Oedipus complex obliquely as well as openly.

What, though, can Freud make of female tragic characters such as Antigone, Medea, or Clytemnestra? The issue is not marginal: of thirty-two surviving tragedies, only one has no female character (Wohl 2005, 146). When Freud wrote *The Interpretation of Dreams*, he assumed that girls undergo an Oedipus complex inversely symmetrical to that of boys, so women unconsciously love their fathers and hate their mothers. The paradigmatic tragic woman would then be a woman who is Oedipally devoted to her father—such as Electra, who joins Orestes in the wish to kill Clytemnestra and avenge Agamemnon, urging Orestes to carry out matricide. Another such paradigm might be Iphigeneia, who so loves and worships Agamemnon that she willingly allows him to sacrifice her, according to Euripides in *Iphigeneia in Aulis* (Euripides 2013). Apparently, then, the approach to tragedy that Freud developed with reference to male heroes can simply be extended to the female heroines and characters of many classical tragedies. On this extension, the tragic female heroine wishes to replace her mother (to kill her mother, or to take her mother's place as supreme love object for the father), and the heroine undergoes punishment as a result (unlike Orestes, Electra drops out of the story of the *Oresteia* after the murder of Clytemnestra and therefore is never acquitted of the crime as Orestes is, so she is never set free from her matricidal wishes; for her part, Iphigeneia is sacrificed).[8] Thus, the tragedies may be thought to dramatize the truth that civilization commands and requires us to repress our incestuous and murderous wishes, this time those that women direct towards their fathers and mothers respectively. However, Irigaray questions the validity of this simple extension of the Oedipal paradigm to tragic women, as we can now explore.

The Antigone Complex

When discussing the Greek tragedies, Irigaray reworks Freud's ideas about tragedy in several ways.[9] She traces the implications for tragedy of Freud's later recognition that male and female courses of psychical development are *a*symmetrical and that the dominant factor in the female psyche is the phase of *pre*-Oedipal attachment to the mother. This leads Irigaray to generate a new view of the psychodynamic dimension of tragic heroines, a view in which Antigone is paradigmatic. Freud gradually realized that girls and boys do not develop symmetrically. He expressed this realization in "Some Psychical Consequences of the Anatomical Distinction between the Sexes" (see Freud 1977a). *Both* girls and boys first love their mothers, Freud recognizes here. This is presumably due to the social convention for women and mothers to be the primary caregivers, although Freud does not spell this out. Whereas the boy, Freud tells us, abandons his love for his mother at around five years old under the threat of castration, the girl of a similar age rejects her mother on "discovering" that she and her mother have already been castrated. In this light, the girl retrospectively blames her mother for all the other disappointments she has undergone—weaning, toilet-training, the arrival of siblings, and so on. Now hating her mother, the girl breaks from her, by extension becoming contemptuous of other women too. At least if the girl follows the path of "normal femininity," she now takes her father as her new love. From now on, the girl's position is Oedipal: loving her father, hating her mother. More precisely, the girl renounces her mother in two stages, according to Freud. The first stage—of reaction to the supposed discovery of castration—occurs when the girl is around five years old. She then enters the "latency period," from age six onward, when issues of sexual identity become dormant, but in puberty and adolescence sexual issues resurface, and, with them, the girl enters her second, renewed stage of hating her mother in favor of her father.

However, in two very late essays, Freud suggests that girls do not completely abandon their early love for their mothers after all. These essays are "Female Sexuality" (1931) and "Femininity," a chapter of his 1933 *New Introductory Lectures on Psychoanalysis* (see Freud 1977b, 1973a). Here he recognizes that girls merely repress but do not renounce their maternal attachment. Girls' earlier bonds to their mothers persist in repressed form *in* their attachments to their fathers; by endlessly restaging the latter in all their later love relationships women restage the former too. A woman's bond with her mother always remains—"surprisingly," to Freud—the overwhelmingly important bond of her life. Freud does not explore what these realizations about female development imply for his earlier account of tragedy. But if women's overwhelming love is and remains love for their mothers, then, perhaps, the paradigmatic tragic woman is not Electra, fixated on her father, but rather someone attached to her mother. This, Irigaray suggests in *Speculum*, is Antigone.

Prima facie, though, it is her dead *brother,* Polyneices, to whom Antigone is devoted and whom she insists on burying. However, Antigone declares that she is devoted to Polyneices *because* he is of the "same womb" as she is. When Creon asks her whether she is not ashamed to depart from public opinion, she retorts that she feels "no shame for revering those of the same womb" (Sophocles 2003, 75, line 562). As Tina Chanter remarks, here Antigone "makes kinship a function of the female procreative power: she defines kinship in terms of the womb (*splanchna*)" (Chanter 1995, 292, n. 55). Antigone is attached to Polyneices *because* she is attached to this "same womb," namely, her mother, Jocasta. In her care for her same-womb-brother's corpse, Antigone remains loyal to her mother and to the laws regarding burial and blood loyalty which Jocasta has transmitted to her from preceding generations of mothers. These laws, transmitted along the female line, are symbolized as the preserve of female divinities: Hestia, the hearth goddess; the Erinnyes, the goddesses who seek to avenge maternal blood in the *Oresteia.* Antigone, then, seeks to preserve her bond with her mother and with her real and symbolic foremothers, and she opposes the political order personified by Creon which commands her to abandon this bond. By adhering to her bond with her mother, Antigone perhaps fulfills a typical mother-centered female fantasy just as Oedipus fulfills the typical male fantasy. Yet, rather than being exemplary in her love of her mother, Antigone appears exceptional. The female characters in Greek tragedies are more often fixated on male figures, as are Iphigeneia and Electra; or Alcestis, who is willing to die in place of her husband; or Medea, whose passionate love for her husband, Jason, turns into equally impassioned hatred when he drops her for a new wife; or Phaedra, afflicted by desire for her stepson in the *Hippolytus* (the last three characters are in Euripides 1955).

However, mother-daughter relationships can be manifestly absent and yet latently present. If, as Freud maintained, women's bonds with their mothers undergo a particularly deep repression underneath women's love for their fathers, then, being so deeply repressed, the mother-daughter bond cannot easily be depicted directly; the hostility of the female superego to its rehabilitation will be especially easily aroused. To depict the bond, a more oblique approach is required. If we follow Freud's account of typical femininity, this will presumably involve depicting the daughter's love for her mother at work in what is less repressed—her attachment to her father or other male figures. How, then, do we know that what is being depicted is the daughter's bond to her *mother* at all? The case of Antigone is instructive because she tells us that she loves Polyneices because she loves her mother through him. Moreover, Antigone *shows* us this love for the mother as well as stating it. There is something notoriously inexplicable about her professed preference for Polyneices over any husband or child (Sophocles 2003, 95, line 968), which scandalized nineteenth-century classicists because they found it incestuous. The love seems inexplicable because it is disproportionate to the merits of Polyneices in his life and has no prospect of reciprocation. Antigone's love is *excessive* in relation to its manifest object. Irigaray's suggestion is that this excess shows where Antigone's love for Jocasta is fueling her passion; the excess shows us that her love aims through its manifest object at another object, the mother.

Indeed, in this respect, Antigone follows a pattern that we find in many other Greek heroines: excessive love for men who neither deserve nor reciprocate it. The husband for whom Alcestis dies is cowardly enough to accept her sacrifice; Jason abandons Medea in the interest of prudence after she has given up everything—her birth family and native land—for him; Iphigeneia is willing to die for the father who is ultimately prepared to sacrifice her in hope of winning the Trojan war; Phaedra desires a highly chaste stepson who finds the idea of their liaison repugnant. If Antigone is, as Irigaray seems to suggest, the paradigmatic heroine, then we are being invited in all these cases to read the excess of these women's passions as the trace of their repressed love for their mothers. Unable to find outlet or expression, this love can only manifest itself in women's inordinate attachment to male figures.[10]

An exception to this pattern might be found in the myth of Persephone and Demeter, which predates the Greek tragedies: the oldest surviving version of the story is the Homeric Hymn to Demeter, which dates from around 650–550 BCE. When Persephone (at first called simply Korê, "girl") is abducted from her mother Demeter by Hades with Zeus's consent, Korê longs to return to her mother, and Demeter uses her powers over the harvest to inflict famine on humanity and so persuade the male gods to relinquish Persephone—although only during spring and summer of each year, due to Hades's trickery with the pomegranate seed(s). From Irigaray's perspective, this myth testifies to an earlier historical period when mother-daughter bonds had not yet been destroyed and when mothers retained considerable cultural, religious, and social power. Yet here too the mother-daughter bond is under threat from the male gods, who are cementing their alliances by treating Korê as a mere object of exchange, who must be torn from her mother so that she can serve in such exchanges. The patriarchal setting depicted in the tragedies—in which mother-daughter bonds are already damaged—was thus already coming into being when the Demeter-Persephone myth took shape (Schwab 2010, 85).

The Greek tragedies seem, from their later vantage point, to bear out the pattern Freud detected whereby women endlessly replay their early bond with their mothers, seeking to recreate its intensity in inappropriate places. Since women's wish to relive their early love for the mother is unconscious, hidden beneath manifest hostility to the mother, fathers and father-substitutes become the ideal recipients of women's love (enabling women to combine unconscious love for the mother with conscious mother rejection). But none of these men will ever reciprocate women's passion, because men's loyalty to the polis will always come first. This loyalty to the polis arises because men must abandon their mothers and identify with their fathers and the paternal law, whereas women have no equivalent motivation to abandon their relationships to their fathers and other men. In sum, the tragedies provide a dramatization of how the psychical and social orders lock together to ensure misfortune for women, who are forced to turn towards male figures who will rarely if ever reciprocate the women's devotion, all as the effect of the repressed mother-daughter bond.

Starting from Freud's account of female development, Irigaray positions Antigone as the paradigmatic tragic heroine, not only in loving her mother but also in channeling this through love for a man, her brother. Irigaray has reworked Freud's focus on the tragic hero's Oedipal wishes into a focus on the tragic heroine's love for her mother—a love that is asymmetrical to the hero's love for his mother because it is pre-Oedipal and more deeply repressed. Yet the repressed nature of this love means that Antigone is manifestly focused on male figures, both Polyneices and her father Oedipus, for whom she cares in *Oedipus at Colonus*, after he has blinded himself. In this respect, as Gail Schwab remarks, Antigone is "the daughter of her father far more than that of her mother" (2010, 84). From Irigaray's perspective, as I am interpreting it, however, Antigone's very fidelity to male figures is the index of the attachment to her mother that she cannot openly experience and live out.[11]

Radical Tragedy

The second way in which Irigaray reworks Freud's theory of tragedy rests on her criticisms of Freud's view that patriarchy is an invariant necessity of civilization, as he maintains in *Totem and Taboo* (Freud 1985b).[12] These criticisms lead Irigaray to reread the Greek tragedies—especially *Antigone*, but also the *Oresteia*—as showing that patriarchy is not natural but politically imposed. In this way, tragedy becomes construed as a radical, socially critical art form. For Freud, as we have seen, works can affect us tragically only if they show unconscious wishes punished as well as gratified. From a purely Freudian perspective, then, female tragic characters would have to be punished for their unconscious love for their mothers even though this love has manifested itself only obliquely. Punishment must ensue because it is an anatomical-cum-civilizational necessity that the little girl's love for her mother should be, and remain, repressed. Irigaray's criticisms of Freud's account of female castration complicate this picture. Irigaray broadly accepts Freud's description that the girl does in fact reject her mother, but she denies that this happens because the girl "discovers" their shared lack of a penis. It happens because the girl internalizes the message of the patriarchal symbolic order that she is "castrated." Merely man's "other," she is not a sexuate being in her own right but one whose clitoris is a mutilated, castrated, version of the penis, indexing her whole status as one who is merely an inferior version of the man. The girl blames her inferior status on her mother because she learns from the surrounding culture that her mother, too, is "castrated"—a defective, second-rate being—from whose defects those of the girl must derive. The breaking of the mother-daughter bond is not the inevitable result of anatomical facts, but the effect of a patriarchal symbolic order, an order premised on symbolic matricide: the symbolic murder, or denial, of the "woman-mother," the mother who is a subject of a specifically female kind (see Irigaray 1993, 7–21).

Antigone is punished for her fidelity to the maternal womb and to maternal laws by Creon. Since Creon is—as Irigaray takes from Hegel—the agent of the polis and of civil law, *Antigone* can be read as showing that the prohibition on and repression of the mother-daughter bond is *socio-politically* enforced, not naturally determined (see Hegel 1977). *Antigone* shows us that this prohibition is a foundation stone of the patriarchal social order that has installed itself by political means—as we see when Creon uses the state to enforce this order. The same truth, that patriarchy is a historical artefact, can be discerned from the *Oresteia*. Orestes kills Clytemnestra to avenge his father, Agamemnon; that Clytemnestra had murdered him to avenge their daughter, Iphigeneia—that is, in defense of mother-daughter bonds—is never considered as a mitigating or justifying factor. And, eventually, Orestes is acquitted of the crime of matricide by an Athenian jury, an acquittal that Aeschylus portrays as foundational to a civilized order that accords the polis and its obligations rightful priority over the bonds of maternal blood. The Erinnyes, the female divinities who had sought to punish Orestes for committing matricide, are placated and incorporated into the Athenian state under the tutelage of Athena, the goddess who professes that she is "always for the male / with all [her] heart, and strongly on [her] father's side" (Aeschylus 1953, 161, lines 737–38). So, the repression of mother-daughter bonds is, explicitly, the result of a legal and political decision.

Whether or not the tragedians intended to support patriarchy, the key point is that their works show patriarchy installing itself and thus show patriarchy to be a historically instituted order—not an invariant necessity of either anatomy or language but a contingent order, enthroned by political means at a certain period, and so capable of being *de*throned. Thus, the tragedies can be read, against the grain, as showing the historical specificity of the paternal order that they help to transmit, enabling criticism of this order even as they transmit it. Consider the *Oresteia*. It is clearly concerned with the conflict of two orders, the paternal and the maternal. The events that unfold suggest that the paternal order requires the breaking of the mother-daughter bond. The military needs of Agamemnon require that Iphigeneia should be torn away from her distraught mother, Clytemnestra, and Clytemnestra's apportioned punishment is death when her fidelity to Iphigeneia leads her to avenge her daughter by murdering Agamemnon. The appointed position of the daughter within the rising paternal order is that of Electra, who hates her mother and identifies with her brother, Orestes.

And the whole chain of events results in the consecration of the patriarchal, "civilized" order. Even though Aeschylus apparently endorses this consecration—as marking a progression toward greater civilization—he also shows this consecration to be a historical result that is, by implication, contingent. His narrative shows us that human life could be lived, and used to be lived, differently, and that that difference involved bonds of attachment between mothers and daughters.

For Irigaray, tragedy need not be conservative. Tragedies can expose that the prohibitions under which we labor when we are tragically affected are politically imposed—imposed by the patriarchal order that has made itself law. Tragedies can show us that the prohibition on women's love for their mothers is not an invariant necessity of civilization but is only necessary for a certain form of civilization. However, now we return to the political problem with the tragic. If, with Irigaray, we read the tragedies as showing us that their female characters suffer because of a historically contingent patriarchal order, then perhaps these female characters are not really *tragic*. After all, their predicaments turn out to reflect mundane matters of politics and oppression, not deep existential truths about the necessity of suffering in human life, or, as for Freud, such truths as the necessity of sexual repression, or of the division between unconscious wishes and the conscious, rational order. Perhaps, then, Irigaray has moved away from the category of the tragic towards reading the ancient tragedies as concerned with particular historical and political conflicts.

By reading Irigaray differently, however, we can retain more notion of the tragic. The tragedies, when read as narrating the rise of patriarchy, *do* show us that the suffering of women such as Antigone, Clytemnestra, and Iphigeneia is necessary. The tragedies show this suffering to be not ontologically necessary but *historically* necessary—that is, necessary to a certain, historically arisen, form of social order: the paternal, matricidal order. As I defined the tragic earlier, the suffering of the female characters would be tragic if it was narrated by the tragedies *as* necessary in a way encouraging some appreciation of that necessity on our (the audience's) part. On Irigaray's reading, these narratives of suffering indeed bring emotional clarification that a certain sociosymbolic order, not the eternal order of things, imposes suffering on women—but does so nonaccidentally, as a structural dimension of that order qua patriarchal. This clarification is positive not because it fosters reconciliation to the inevitable, but rather because it fosters in us the recognition that things could be different and that we should seek social change. This recognition of the need for change corresponds to the fact that the Greek tragedies impart insight into suffering that is *historically*, not existentially, necessary. The suffering remains tragic because it is not merely contingent. It is necessary within a certain social order, and the tragedies expose that to be the case. This insight, however, encourages us to change the kind of order that makes this suffering necessary.

The Tragic: Between Metaphysics and History

So far, what seems to emerge from Irigaray's readings of the tragedies is that the fictional lives of their female characters are tragic because they are narrated in a way that brings into view the necessity by which these lives go badly. She suggests that the suffering of the tragic female characters obeys a logic that we can also discern in women's real-life experiences. In the case of fictional characters such as Electra and Antigone, the events of their lives are placed within the tragedies in a narrative structure such that they follow one another necessarily, exposing the historical necessity of what happens. Irigaray provides women with a particular theoretical framework in which to recognize and articulate the narrative shape that (from Irigaray's perspective) women's lives already have in reality. It is a framework that highlights the sufferings that women undergo because of their damaged relationships to their mothers. In the perspective Irigaray provides, these sufferings are necessary given the symbolic order under which women live. Women's real lives, then, already have an incipient narrative shape whereby accession to a culture that construes women merely as "castrated," or as man's Other, necessarily induces a damaging repression of early mother-daughter bonds. Irigaray's theory and the Greek tragedies make us explicitly aware of that narrative shape of women's lives under patriarchy, but they do not impart to women's lives a shape that those lives did not already have; they merely articulate the real, implicit narrative shape of those lives. If it has been a central motif of tragic theory that suffering is tragic when it is necessary and is viewed and accepted as necessary, then there are different kinds of tragic suffering: different in what kind of necessity they have and what kind of acceptance befits them. Suffering that stems from our finitude is existentially necessary and merits an attitude of affirmation, or at least reconciliation. On the other hand, suffering that is rooted in particular social systems is historically necessary. The fitting attitude toward this kind of suffering is appreciation that it is necessary only given a certain social-symbolic order and that this order can and should be changed.

Notes

1. For discussion of such problems, particularly as they arise out of Marxist literary theory, see also Felski 2004 and Sands 2004.

2. Irigaray's readings of the Greek tragedies have recently received extensive consideration in *Rewriting Difference*, Tzelepis and Athanasiou eds. (2010).

3. In full: "All great things collapse by themselves, by an act of self-cancellation: this is what the law of life wills" (Nietzsche 1994, 126). As Werner Hamacher remarks, then, this law is equally the law of death—the law that no life is possible without death (Hamacher 127).

4. Irigaray has discussed Antigone many times, in shifting ways (see Muraro 1994). Among these discussions, Irigaray suggests in *Speculum* that Antigone acts—defying Creon by burying her dead brother Polyneices—out of fidelity to her mother and maternal line, Polyneices being of the "same womb" as Antigone, as we will see below. Subsequently, Irigaray becomes more critical of Antigone, notably suggesting in *Sexes and Genealogies* that Antigone is serving the state by trying to compensate for the crimes of her warring brothers (see Mader 97). As for the *Oresteia*, Irigaray discusses it in her essay "Body against Body: In Relation to the Mother" (*Le corps-à-corps avec la mère)*, originally delivered as a talk in 1980 and included in *Sexes and Genealogies*. She interprets the *Oresteia* as showing that a symbolic matricide is at the root of Western civilization.

5. There is already extensive literature on Irigaray's engagements with Hegel and Lacan on Antigone. See, *inter alia*, Battersby 1998, Chanter 1995, Hutchings 2003, and Leonard 2005. How Irigaray's interpretation of the tragedies relates to Freud's, though, has not been previously considered.

6. Here I am interpreting Freud's earlier view of tragedy in light of his later theory of anxiety, articulated most fully only in 1933. On this theory, anxiety is first and foremost the affect in which we register real dangers, notably including the danger of castration with which we are threatened during the Oedipus phase (Freud 1973b). Although Freud understood anxiety differently at the time of *The Interpretation of Dreams*, it is his later theory of anxiety that best allows us to make sense of his approach to tragedy in that book.

7. Although he does not explicitly put it forward in those terms in *The Interpretation of Dreams*, in the 1905–6 essay "Psychopathic Characters on the Stage," Freud extends his account of *Oedipus Rex* into a general sketch of how dramas and tragedies affect us (see Freud 1985a, 119–28).

8. Irigaray remarks that "Electra, the daughter, will remain mad. The matricidal son, on the other hand, must be saved from madness so that he can found the patriarchal order" (Irigaray 1993, 12). As Christina Wieland adds, unlike Orestes, Electra "is not accused, not persecuted, not tried, and not exonerated; she is simply overlooked as irrelevant or unimportant" in the later parts of the *Oresteia* (Wieland 2002, 42). Regarding Iphigeneia, ancient sources conflict; in

some she is not killed but only transported to the island of Tauris, with an animal sacrificed in her place.

9. Sjöholm (2004) uses the phrase "the Antigone complex" as a way of characterizing modern European culture's preoccupation with a kind of exorbitant female desire. I am using the phrase to mark out a cluster of female pre-Oedipal fantasies about the mother which constitutes a counterpart to Freud's Oedipus complex.

10. There are clues in tragic and other literature about the force of women's repressed love for their mothers. For example, the passion for her stepson which afflicts Phaedra, although sent by Aphrodite to punish him for his chastity, can also be seen as reflecting Phaedra's descent from her mother, Pasiphae, whose lustful copulation with a bull had spawned the Minotaur. Phaedra ultimately succumbs to her uncontrollable passion as her mother did to her lust for the bull, so Phaedra's passion embodies her inescapable bond with her mother. See Reckford 1974.

11. In *Speculum*, Irigaray also suggests that, being repressed, this love for Jocasta regresses into the form of an immediate identification that compels Antigone to reenact Jocasta's fate. Just as Jocasta killed herself, so Antigone kills herself after Creon has walled her into the cave to die (Irigaray 1985, 219).

12. The meaning of the word "patriarchy" is of course contested. I use it to mean a fraternal social order operating under the aegis of a symbolic father.

Works Cited

Aeschylus. 1953. *Oresteia*. Translated by Richmond Lattimore. Chicago: University of Chicago Press.

Aristotle. 1987. *Poetics*. Translated by Malcolm Heath. Harmondsworth: Penguin.

Battersby, Christine. 1998. *The Phenomenal Woman*. Cambridge, UK: Polity.

Belsey, Catherine. 1985. *The Subject of Tragedy*. London: Routledge.

Chanter, Tina. 1995. *Ethics of Eros: Irigaray's Rewriting of the Philosophers*. New York: Routledge.

Dollimore, Jonathan. 2004. *Radical Tragedy: Religion, Ideology, and Power in the Drama of Shakespeare and His Contemporaries*. Third edition. Basingstoke: Macmillan.

Eagleton, Terry. 2003. *Sweet Violence: The Idea of the Tragic*. Oxford: Blackwell.

Euripides. 1955. *Euripides I*, edited by David Grene and Richmond Lattimore. Chicago: University of Chicago Press.

———. 2013. *Euripides V*, edited by Mark Griffith, Glenn W. Most, David Grene, and Richmond Lattimore. Chicago: University of Chicago Press.

Felski, Rita, ed. 2004. "Rethinking Tragedy." *New Literary History* 35, no. 1.

Freud, Sigmund. 1973a (1933). "Femininity." In *New Introductory Lectures on Psychoanalysis*. Translated by James Strachey. Harmondsworth: Penguin.

Freud, Sigmund. 1973b (1933). "Anxiety and Instinctual Life." In *New Introductory Lectures on Psychoanalysis*. Translated by James Strachey. Harmondsworth: Penguin.

———. 1977a (1925). "Some Psychical Consequences of the Anatomical Distinction between the Sexes." In *On Sexuality*, edited by Angela Richards. Harmondsworth: Penguin.

———. 1977b (1931). "Female Sexuality." In *On Sexuality*, edited by Angela Richards. Harmondsworth: Penguin.

———. 1985a. *Art and Literature*, edited by Albert Dickson. Harmondsworth: Penguin.

———. 1985b (1913). "Totem and Taboo." In *The Origins of Religion*, edited by Albert Dickson. Harmondsworth: Penguin.

———. 1991 (1900). *The Interpretation of Dreams*, edited by Angela Richards. Harmondsworth: Penguin.

Hamacher, Werner. 1999. *Premises: Essays on Philosophy and Literature from Kant to Celan*. Stanford, CA: Stanford University Press.

Hegel, G. W. F. 1977 [1807]. *Phenomenology of Spirit*. Translated by A. V. Miller. Oxford: Clarendon.

Hutchings, Kimberly. 2003. *Hegel and Feminist Philosophy*. Cambridge, UK: Polity.

Irigaray, Luce. 1985 (1974). *Speculum of the Other Woman*. Translated by Gillian C. Gill. New York: Columbia University Press.

———. 1993 (1987). *Sexes and Genealogies*. Translated by Gillian C. Gill. New York: Columbia University Press.

Jones, John. 1962. *On Aristotle and Greek Tragedy*. London: Chatto & Windus.

Lacan, Jacques. 1992. *The Ethics of Psychoanalysis 1959–1960*, edited by Jacques-Alain Miller. New York: Routledge.

Leonard, Miriam. 2005. *Athens in Paris: Ancient Greece and the Political in Post-War French Thought*. Oxford: Oxford University Press.

Mader, Mary Beth. 2010. "Antigone and the Ethics of Kinship." In *Rewriting Difference: Luce Irigaray and "The Greeks,"* edited by Tzelepis and Athanasiou, 93–104. Albany: State University of New York Press.

Muraro, Luisa. 1994. "Female Genealogies." In *Engaging with Irigaray: Feminist Philosophy and Modern European Thought*, edited by Carolyn Burke, Naomi Schor, and Margaret Whitford, 317–34. New York: Columbia University Press.

Nietzsche, Friedrich. 1956 (1872). *The Birth of Tragedy*, published with *The Genealogy of Morals*. Translated by Francis Golffing. New York: Doubleday.

———. 1994 (1887). *On the Genealogy of Morality*. Translated by Carol Diethe. Cambridge: Cambridge University Press.

Reckford, Kenneth J. 1974. "Phaedra and Pasiphae: The Pull Backward." In *Transactions of the American Philological Association* 104: 307–28.

Rorty, Amélie Oksenberg. 1992. "The Psychology of Aristotelian Tragedy." In *Essays on Aristotle's Poetics*, edited by Amélie Oksenberg Rorty. Princeton, NJ: Princeton University Press.

Sands, Kathleen M. 2004. "Tragedy, Theology and Feminism in the Time after Time." *New Literary History* 35, no. 1: 41–61.

Schwab, Gail. 2010. "Mothers, Sisters, and Daughters." In *Rewriting Difference: Luce Irigaray and "The Greeks,"* edited by Tzelepis and Athanasiou, 79–92.

Sjöholm, Cecilia. 2004. *The Antigone Complex*. Stanford, CA: Stanford University Press.

Sophocles. 2003. *Antigone*. Translated by Reginald Gibbons and Charles Segal. Oxford: Oxford University Press.

Tzelepis, Elena, and Athena Athanasiou, eds. 2010. *Rewriting Difference: Luce Irigaray and "The Greeks."* Albany: State University of New York Press.

Wieland, Christina. 2002. *The Undead Mother: Psychoanalytic Explorations of Masculinity, Femininity and Matricide*. London: Karnac.

Wohl, Victoria. 2005. "Tragedy and Feminism." In *A Companion to Tragedy*, edited by Rebecca Bushnell. Oxford: Blackwell.

The Ethics of Elemental Passions in Eugène Guillevic and Luce Irigaray

EVA MARIA KORSISAARI

Your lips.[1]

The one,
The other.
*
Think
That there are moments

When for you
I am

Lighter than air.

—Eugène Guillevic 1981

For Eugène Alphonse Marie Guillevic, who characterized himself as a "prehistoric man," living "more in the elements than in society" (Guillevic 1999, 34), all things are continuously in touch with other things, and the task of poetry is to describe and participate in these contacts. Naming opens up the possibility of connecting with the things themselves; it does not, however, signify a move into the realm of ideas, since, for Guillevic, the concrete is the most real. As he explains: "I participate. My sensitivity takes part. There is an earthy, mythical side there. My poetry shows solidarity. It is with . . ." (34). The verses above can be found near the beginning of the *Magnificat* cycle from his collection *Trouées. Poèmes 1973–1980* (1981). The form of the collection resembles the form of many of his other collections, most of which consist of short poems, all illuminating the theme of the collection from different perspectives. One valid key to this collection and also to Guillevic's whole oeuvre could be a question found in the "Montées" ("Ascents") section of *Trouées*: "How not to abandon each other,/How not to cling to each other?" (Guillevic 1981, 97). I suggest that in *Trouées*, Guillevic seeks answers to this question—he searches for ways to relate to the world and to the other that would avoid both abandonment of and control over the other.

I shall concentrate here on the *Magnificat* cycle. The word is church Latin and a title for the hymn of praise to Mary found in the gospel of Luke, which has become an essential part of Catholic liturgy (Luke 1:46–55). Guillevic's *Magnificat* is also a hymn of praise, although very different from the hymn to Mary. The fifty-one poems in the *Magnificat* are very short, consisting of only a few fragmented verses. Blanks create pauses and breathing spaces, so that they resemble excerpts from a dialogue. The speaker depicts and describes, asks and appeals, and directs the words to another. Though only one person speaks, the other is close, present. Though only one voice is heard, pauses encourage the other to speak too. To whom does the speaker speak? Perhaps to a woman? The speaker does refer to this other using the word "femme" (woman) in one of the poems in the end of the cycle (124). And the speaker? The sex of the speaker is not revealed; however, the speaker does refer to entering into the other (115, 116, 119, 120). . . Perhaps a man?

The lovers are close to each other throughout the whole cycle. In them and between them a whole universe is created, a universe consisting of earth, water, fire, and air—a world whose elements are the horizon, humus, bacteria, seas, surges, tides, landslips, coves, lava, wellsprings, the Gulf Stream, oceans, molecules, petals, volcanos, salt, iodine, magma, caverns, continents, space, islands, algae, rocks, sun, winds, rivers, streams, crops, and plants.

Besides a place and places, time and times are also created between the lovers. The speaker tells about moments "Before the time of speech" (113) and mentions "prehistory" (118). The speaker believes that "Eternity//Is an open space" (119), and that "Thus, the present,/The past, the future//Can weave/The same time" (120). The lovers seem to understand time not as related to their deaths, as a descending line, but in relation to the world and its elements, eternal and changing, in whose eternity and changeability they also take part. *Magnificat* takes the reader directly to the heart of the places and times it depicts. However, the words of its speaker do not form a narrative or attempt to give a general view, a full portrait of either of the lovers, a full portrait of their universe. Depicting carnal love, Guillevic mobilizes the vocabulary of the elements. The speaker describes the experiences of the lovers by comparing their modes of being and moving to the movement of earth, water, fire, and air. The liquids of their bodies move "Like lava" (114) and "Like the Gulf Stream" (115). Their lips pressed together resemble "The fever of rocks," (123) and their breathing "Is that of the tides" (123). By representing the lovers as akin to the elements, the speaker of the *Magnificat* implies, first, that they are not unconnected to the world, but are parts of the universe and at the same time touched and affected by it.

The mode of being of the elements is characterized not by permanency and stability but rather by movement and changeability. The speaker in *Magnificat* also implies that, in sensuous proximity, the lovers are not manifested to each other in a clear-cut, but rather in an obscure, fashion. "More or less" (121), the speaker claims, and even the world does not appear as well-defined but as blurred. By representing the lovers as akin to the elements, the speaker suggests, second, that the lovers are not solid or stable, but, like earth, water, fire, and air, susceptible to metamorphoses. In a world where everything is forever changing, where stones grind into sand, water freezes into ice, fire and air transform into smoke, air and water vaporize into fog, a penis can grow and harden, labia moisten and swell, bodies become sweaty, nipples become erect, sight become fuzzy, and pain become pleasure . . . In these transformations it is not a question of one mode of being substituting for another—there is instead a continuum, and changes follow each other endlessly, just as ice can melt into water or vaporize into clouds.

There is also a third parallel between the experiences of the lovers and the being and motion of the elements. Just as I am invigorated and revitalized when resting on a smooth rock, listening to the sea's waves, warmed by the sun, and cooled by the breeze, I am also invigorated and revitalized when another's body burrows into my flesh, another's saliva moistens my lips, another's caresses affect me, and another's breath mixes with mine. Representing the lovers as resembling the elements, the speaker in *Magnificat* indicates, third, that lovers' encounters in the sensual, sensuous realm can fortify and strengthen them—that their carnal intimacy affords a living space and a resting place for them. "My continent.//My ocean/Of continents," says the speaker (119), and: "In you//The world condenses/

Without contracting" (112).

Like Guillevic, Luce Irigaray has depicted carnal love with the help of the vocabulary of the elements. Earth, water, fire, and air appear especially in her works of the early 1980s. In *Marine Lover of Friedrich Nietzsche* (1991a), Irigaray suggests that Nietzsche forgets to think about water, and, in *The Forgetting of Air in Martin Heidegger* (1999), that Heidegger forgets to think about air; they both founded their philosophical systems on rock-solid ground, which they are likewise unwilling to recognize as matter. In *Elemental Passions* (1992), Irigaray's aim is to discuss love between two and nuptials between microcosm, macrocosm, and the gods. The narrator of the book is in quest of herself: she wonders who she is as a woman in love, who her beloved is, and how they could encounter each other, address each other, touch each other, love each other. Between nature and culture, night and day, sun and moon, vegetable and mineral, empirical and transcendental, she questions the binary hierarchies set up between these dimensions of the universe and succumbs to the elemental passions.

Irigaray brings erotic love and the elements together for many of the same reasons as Guillevic. First, she wants to remind the reader that earth, water, fire, and air still constitute our world and continuously touch our bodies. She explains in "Divine Women" that when composing *Marine Lover*, *The Forgetting of Air*, and *Elemental Passions*, she wanted to study our relations to the natural phenomena that constitute the origin of our bodies, of our lives, and of our environment, as well as the flesh of our passions. Poetry recalls the elements, but our so-called human sciences do not, Irigaray regrets. She writes: "We still pass our daily lives in a universe that is composed and is known to be composed of four elements: air, water, fire, and earth. We are made up of these elements and we live in them. They determine, more or less freely, our attractions, our affects, our passions, our limits, our aspirations" (Irigaray 1993b, 57). Second, with the help of the elements, Irigaray, like Guillevic, wants to portray humans as intertwined with the world and as inclined to transmutations, and at the same time to call into question the idea that reality consists of sharp-edged subjects, solid objects, and discrete, sustainable forms—she wants to concentrate on lived experiences instead of abstractions. As the narrator in *Elemental Passions* says: "My life is all suppleness, tenderness, mobile, uncertain, fluid" (Irigaray 1992, 23).

And, finally, like Guillevic, Irigaray wishes to make manifest that just like coming into contact with the elements, touching the other and being touched by the other can also revive us. In the last chapter of *An Ethics of*

Sexual Difference, entitled "The Fecundity of the Caress," she writes from a woman's perspective about the intersubjective, intercorporeal sphere created by the lovers' communion in pleasure. She affirms that this is a vital condition to all of us:

> Before orality comes to be, touch is already in existence. No nourishment can compensate for the grace or work of touching. Touch makes it possible to wait, to gather strength, so that the other will return to caress and reshape, from within and from without, a flesh that is given back to itself in the gesture of love. [. . .] To realize a birth that is still in the future. Plunging me back into the maternal womb and beyond that conception, awakening me to another birth—as a loving woman. (Irigaray 1993a, 187)

By bringing together love and earth, water, fire, and air, both Guillevic's *Magnificat* and Irigaray's *Elemental Passions* describe a love relationship where the lovers, in ways characteristic of the elements, intertwine with each other and are affected by each other without identifying or merging with each other. In such a loving demarcation of boundaries, the lovers are not wholly distinct or divorced from each other, but are parts of and parties to each other's emotional and physical experiences. That you are feeling pleasure is one part of my pleasure. And that I am feeling pleasure is one part of your pleasure. I am not you, but I am me-loving-you, me-touching-you, me-loved-by-you, me-touched-by-you. Or, conversely, as Irigaray's narrator in *Elemental Passions* remarks: "My death is inside your own. We shall die together if you do not let me go outside your sameness" (Irigaray 1992, 14).

The entwining, intertwining of the lovers is, of course, most concrete when they make love. Their boundaries become penetrable, permeable, and their bodies become responsive, hospitable. Face to face, skin to skin, they do not merge with each other; enfolding each other, within each other, they do not melt into one, though their bodily fluids may mix. Thanks to their intimacy, a common sphere is created, a fermentation, which makes it possible for them to play, rebel, transform, forget, grow, remember, enjoy. In *Magnificat*, the speaker says: "You let me/Enter into you.//You let me stay/Long enough to nourish life" (Guillevic 1981, 116). And in *Elemental Passions*, the narrator explains:

> If, in affecting you, I affect myself, the body-instrument opposition

> no longer holds. For the instrument which I am in order to affect you is itself affected as a body, just as your body, which I affect, is an instrument which affects me. [. . .] I participate in your affections just as you take pleasure in mine. That does not mean they are indifferent. But I take pleasure and you take pleasure in these differences, in this difference, as in an over-abundance of riches. Experiencing you, experiencing me, espousing you, espousing me, we are more than one. And two. (58)

For many years, Irigaray's writings were interpreted from the psychoanalytic perspective in Anglo-American commentaries.[2] However, some recent research on her thought has taken seriously the connections her philosophy has to the phenomenological tradition.[3] Irigaray herself has also made these connections apparent by addressing phenomenologists; she has both criticized their theories and developed their thoughts. As already mentioned, in *The Forgetting of Air,* she is in dialogue with Martin Heidegger. In *Ethics of Sexual Difference* (1993a), she addresses, among others, Maurice Merleau-Ponty and Emmanuel Levinas; in *I Love to You: Sketch of a Possible Felicity in History* (1996a), she mentions Edmund Husserl; in *To Be Two* (2000), she debates with Merleau-Ponty, Levinas, and Sartre. She also says in a 1996 interview that a certain recourse, or return, to the phenomenological method seems necessary to her in order that some natural, corporeal, sensible realities enter into the universe of the rational; and, thus, she undertakes an outline of a phenomenology of the caress between lovers. (Irigaray 1996b, 351, 356). Although in *Elemental Passions* Irigaray does not mention any phenomenologist by name, I argue that she discusses the phenomenological tradition, and especially Merleau-Ponty's phenomenology of the body and Levinas's ethics. *Elemental Passions* formulates a philosophy of intersubjectivity and intercorporeality, and its main aims are to illuminate how we relate to the world and to the other in an affective way and to develop a new understanding of the relation between self and other in erotic encounters.

Describing the affective basis of our being is also Merleau-Ponty's task in his *Phenomenology of Perception* (1962). He shows how we approach the world primarily by moving, feeling, and perceiving, rather than by knowing, believing, or assuming. Thus, the toucher and the touched do not divide into a subject of the act and the object of the act but intertwine with each other. Merleau-Ponty describes this intertwining by comparing it to our erotic experiences. He claims that if we try to see how a thing or a being begins to exist for us through desire or love, we shall better understand how things and beings can exist for us in general (Merleau-Ponty 1962, 154). In *Time and the Other* (1987), Levinas, for his part, tries to rethink the relationship with the other as neither a fusion nor a conflict of wills. He claims that, in the relationship with the other through Eros, the feminine other is not experienced as a similar being or a contrary will, but as an absolute other, forever mysterious and unreachable to man. For Levinas, the pathos of love consists in an insurmountable duality of beings (Levinas 1987, 84–90).

Despite their shared themes, Irigaray does not simply agree with the theories of embodiment and interpersonal relations elaborated by the existentialist-phenomenological tradition of philosophy. She also argues that they do not recognize and value the specificity of the feminine mode of experience. Though Merleau-Ponty claims that the body connects us to the world and to others, Irigaray argues that, in his depictions of the intertwinings of the subject and the world, a hierarchy is still involved. For example, in *The Visible and the Invisible* (1987), Merleau-Ponty characterizes the one who touches and the one who is touched by comparing them to the two lips, which for him, however, retain the polarity of subject and object (Merleau-Ponty 1987, 130–55). According to Irigaray, the male philosopher cannot take into account the other, woman, differing from him sexually, or, for example, the ways woman's lips or hands press against each other without the polarity of the subject and the object, the active and the passive (Irigaray 1993a, 151–84). And though Levinas claims in *Time and the Other* that in love the feminine is experienced as essentially other (Levinas 1987, 84–90), Irigaray argues that for him love is autistic, egological, and solitary, as the distance is always maintained from the other in the experience of love (Irigaray 1991b, 109–18; 1993a, 185–217). In addition, in *Totality and Infinity: An Essay on Exteriority*, Levinas values the erotic relationship mainly for purposes of reproduction, and he finally states that paternity is the most important relationship because only in paternity can man become other to himself and have victory over death (Levinas 1969, 267–80; Irigaray 1993a, 185–217).

In my view, both Irigaray in *Elemental Passions*, quite intentionally, and Guillevic in *Magnificat*, possibly unintentionally, take Merleau-Ponty's philosophy further—they endeavor to describe the primordial dimensions of subjectivity and intersubjectivity, that affective and sensible level where our relations with the world or others are not analyzable in instrumental or practical terms. And likewise, they take Levinas's philosophy further—they endeavor to describe an eroticism where the lovers would recognize each other as different and, concurrently, engender pleasure both in them and between them, in that loss of boundaries that takes place for both when they cross the skin and enter into the mucous membranes of the body. Irigaray and Guillevic both introduce—Irigaray philosophically, and poetically, and Guillevic poetically, and philosophically—the touch of the caress.

While elaborating a phenomenology of the caress, Irigaray advocates that a caressing subject is able to do something that a subject approaching the other in the utilitarian or the objectifying mode cannot: give space to the other and to the other's becoming without imposing his or her own needs and goals onto the other. The caressing touch does not grasp the other; neither does it reject the other. Instead, it searches, proposes and waits, wonders and rouses, salutes and shelters. By approaching the other through caresses, the lover lets the other be, and at the same time encourages the other to become. By encouraging the other to become, the lover helps the other to reincarnate, and at the same time gains a chance to reincarnate as well. In the words of Irigaray's narrator in *Elemental Passions*: "And I was changed into a cloud. Not in ecstasy nor dissipated into the air, but a body animated throughout. Living and aroused in each part of my flesh. And I no longer knew death, but resided in a lightness where everything embraced everything else. I had not lost my edges. [. . .] I was created by you, still faithful to what I was" (Irigaray 1992, 99–100). In *Magnificat*, amorousness, in its lack of orientation and target, in its generosity and compassion, offers the lovers an opportunity for idling and lingering, for metamorphoses and rebirths. "We have all the time in the world/To be just the two of us//Caressing our borders" (Guillevic 1981, 25). Thanks to a cherishing, caressing touch, the lover approaches the beloved both actively and passively, both with devotion and ardor, neither grasping nor rejecting.

In addition to caressing, Guillevic also depicts other gestures that cultivate the ethics of erotic encounters so vital for Irigaray. Like Irigaray, who understands a man and a woman not as complementary to each other, contradictory to each other, or as versions of the same, but as two irreducible subjects, Guillevic represents lovers as respecting their differences: the lovers in *Magnificat* remain two. This being-two is demonstrated, first, in the speaker's style of addressing the other. The speaker does not keep up a self-sufficient monologue but directs the words to the other. The fragmented style suggests that the speaker is not all there is, and the interrogative mode assures that the other is valued. "In you, I am/Mandated—//To what?" the lover asks (113). "Stay. Stay," the lover urges (124).

This being-two is recognized in the carnal intimacy shared by the lovers. They both have their own borders, their own places, and although it is possible to cross these borders, and although it is possible to welcome the other inside, this crossing and welcoming is only temporary. At least for Guillevic's speaker, who seems to be able to penetrate deep into the other, the temporary nature of the visits is difficult to accept. "I fall/Outside of you,//Out of the empire/Where your portal lies," the speaker says (115), and "What is to be done/As this body feels exiled" (116). Even so, the lover does not bitterly reject the other, nor does the lover cling nostalgically to the other. The feeling of exile passes as well, and the drawing-away enables a coming-closer again.

In addition, the lovers in *Magnificat* remain two because they comprehend each other as changeable and apprehend love as motion. Thanks to the metamorphoses experienced in the affective dimensions of subjectivity and intersubjectivity, the beloved does not appear to them as one and the same, but as other, always different and forever foreign. The lovers do not dream about becoming one. Instead, they may both be transformed into something wondrous. The speaker fantasizes: "There are no birds/More sparrowhawks than we" (120). And thanks to the intertwinings experienced in the sensible dimensions of subjectivity and intersubjectivity, the relationship with the other does not appear to them as a harbor or a monument but as dynamic and magnetizing. The lover claims: "Respite/Was not for us.//Movement/Is our repose." (119). The narrator in *Elemental Passions* shares this experience: "Movement is my habitat. My only rest is motion" (25).

In *Magnificat*, Guillevic writes about carnal love in a poetical style. The lover speaks taciturnly, fragmentarily, even mysteriously, referring trustfully to a "we." The addressed other is at all times close by. In *Elemental Passions*, Irigaray writes about carnal love in a lyrical prose. The lover speaks wonderingly, passionately, even confrontationally, yearning for an amorous dialogue on love with the beloved. However, the addressed other is sometimes afar, aloof. Even though their genres, styles, and emphasis are different, I propose that Guillevic and Irigaray share a cause in *Magnificat* and *Elemental Passions*: there is an ethics in sensibility, and the caressing touch makes ethics possible even in the most elemental of erotic encounters.

Notes

I warmly thank Sara Heinämaa, Kuisma Korhonen, Virpi Lehtinen and Kirsi Saarikangas for their insightful questions and enlightening comments.

1. All translations from Guillevic's *Trouées. Poèmes 1973–1980* are my own. The asterisk (*) indicates a shift to a different poem.

2. See Moi 1985; Grosz 1989; Whitford 1991. With regard to *Elemental Passions*, see Canters and Jantzen 2005.

3. See Chanter 1995; Vasseleu 1998; Heinämaa 2007, 243–65; Lehtinen 2014. With regard to *Elemental Passions*, see Sjöholm 2000.

Works Cited

Canters, Hanneke, and Grace M. Jantzen. 2005. *Forever Fluid: A Reading of Luce Irigaray's* Elemental Passions. Manchester: Manchester University Press.

Chanter, Tina. 1995. *Ethics of Eros: Irigaray's Rewriting of the Philosophers.* New York: Routledge.

Grosz, Elizabeth. 1989. *Sexual Subversions: Three French Feminists.* St. Leonards: Allen and Unwin.

Guillevic, Eugène. 1981. *Trouées. Poèmes 1973–1980.* Paris: Gallimard.

———. 1999. *Living in Poetry: Interviews with Guillevic.* Translated by Maureen Smith. Dublin: Dedalus. *Vivre en poésie. Entretien avec Lucie Albertini et Alain Vircondelet.* Paris: Stock, 1980.

Heinämaa, Sara. 2007. "On Luce Irigaray's Phenomenology of Intersubjectivity: Between the Feminine Body and Its Other." In *Returning to Irigaray: Feminist Philosophy, Politics, and the Question of Unity*, edited by Maria C. Cimitile and Elaine P. Miller, 243–65. Albany: State University of New York Press.

Irigaray, Luce. 1991a. *Marine Lover of Friedrich Nietzsche.* Translated by Gillian C. Gill. New York: Columbia University Press. *Amante marine de Friedrich Nietzsche.* Paris: Éditions de Minuit, 1980.

———. 1991b. "Questions to Emmanuel Levinas: On the Divinity of Love." Translated by Margaret Whitford. In *Re-reading Levinas*, edited by Robert Bernasconi and Simon Critchley, 109–18. Bloomington: Indiana University Press.

———. 1992. *Elemental Passions.* Translated by Joanne Collie and Judith Still. London: Routledge. *Passions élémentaires.* Paris: Éditions de Minuit, 1982.

———. 1993a. *An Ethics of Sexual Difference.* Translated by Carolyn Burke and Gillian C. Gill. Ithaca, NY: Cornell University Press. *Éthique de la différence sexuelle.* Paris: Éditions de Minuit, 1984.

———. 1993b. *Sexes and Genealogies.* Translated by Gillian C. Gill. New York: Columbia University Press. *Sexes et parentés.* Paris: Éditions de Minuit, 1987.

———. 1996a. *I Love to You: Sketch of a Possible Felicity in History.* Translated by Alison Martin. New York: Routledge. *J'aime à toi. Esquisse d'une félicité dans l'histoire.* Paris: Grasset, 1992.

———. 1996b. "Thinking Life as Relation: An Interview with Luce Irigaray." Interviewers: Stephen Pluháček and Heidi Bostic. *Man and World: An International Philosophical Review* 29, no. 4 (October): 343–60.

———. 1999. *The Forgetting of Air in Martin Heidegger*. Translated by Mary Beth Mader. Austin, TX: University of Texas Press. *L'Oubli de l'air chez Martin Heidegger*. Paris: Éditions de Minuit, 1983.

———. 2000. *To Be Two*. Translated by Monique M. Rhodes and Marco F. Cocito-Monoc. New York: Routledge. *Essere Due*. Torino: Bollati Boringhieri, 1994.

Lehtinen, Virpi. 2014. *Luce Irigaray's Phenomenology of Feminine Being*. Albany: State University of New York Press.

Levinas, Emmanuel. 1969. *Totality and Infinity: An Essay on Exteriority*. Translated by Alphonso Lingis. The Hague: Martinus Nijhoff and Duquesne University Press. *Totalité et infini: Essai sur l'extériorité*. Paris: Kluwer Academic, 1961.

———. 1987. *Time and the Other*. Translated by Richard A. Cohen. Pittsburgh: Duquesne University Press. *Le temps et l'autre*. In *Le choix, le monde, l'existence*. Grenoble and Paris: B. Arthaud, 1947, 125–96.

Merleau-Ponty, Maurice. 1962. *Phenomenology of Perception*. Translated by Colin Smith. London: Routledge & Kegan Paul. *Phénoménologie de la perception*. Paris: Gallimard, 1945.

———. 1987. *The Invisible and the Invisible*. Translated by Alphonso Lingis. Evanston: Northwestern University Press. *Le visible et l'invisible*. Paris: Gallimard, 1964.

Moi, Toril. 1985. *Sexual/Textual Politics: Feminist Literary Theory*. London: Methuen.

Sjöholm, Cecilia. 2000. "Crossing Lovers: Luce Irigaray's *Elemental Passions*." *Hypatia* 15, no. 3 (Summer): 92–112.

Vasseleu, Cathryn. 1998. *Textures of Light: Vision and Touch in Irigaray, Levinas and Merleau-Ponty*. London: Routledge.

Whitford, Margaret. 1991. *Luce Irigaray: Philosophy in the Feminine*. London: Routledge.

Deconstruction, Defiguration, Disconcertion

On Reading *Speculum de l'autre femme* with Derrida and Lacan

ANNE VAN LEEUWEN

Introduction

In an interview conducted a year after the publication of *Speculum*, Irigaray was asked to reflect on the structure of this text and to explain her decision to begin with a critique of Freud. Her response was the following:

> Strictly speaking, *Speculum* has no beginning or end. The architectonics of the text, or texts, confounds the linearity of an outline, the teleology of discourse, within which there is no possible place for the "feminine," except the traditional place of the repressed, the censured. Furthermore, by "beginning" with Freud and "ending" with Plato we are already going at history "backwards." But it is a reversal "within" which the question woman still cannot be articulated, so this reversal alone does not suffice. [. . .] For what is important is to *disconcert* the staging of representation according to exclusively "masculine" parameters, that is, according to a phallocratic order. (Irigaray 1985b, 68, my emphasis)

By articulating the central gesture of *Speculum* in these terms, Irigaray highlights the proximity of this text to early work of both Lacan and Derrida. According to Irigaray, *Speculum disconcerts* the phallocentrism of representation, an operation she distinguishes from a simple reversal of this "masculine" order. With a minimal shift, Irigaray's characterization of *Speculum* could equally describe the early work of Lacan and Derrida. While Lacan *defigures* the phallocentrism of representation,[1] Derrida *deconstructs* this order, and in neither case do these gestures constitute a simple inversion. Irigaray thus situates *Speculum* in line with these projects without simply allying it with either.

The task of this chapter is to elucidate this proximity and distance. On the one hand, the proximity of these three thinkers is clear; indeed, at a certain level of analysis, their projects are indistinguishable. In different ways, each identifies the order of representation as the legacy of Platonism, and each of these projects takes up the Nietzschean task of reversing this order. Moreover, for each of these thinkers, this reversal is crystallized in the notion of originary difference. On the other hand, their projects differ with respect to the way that each articulates the temporal and modal index of this origin. For Derrida, originary difference refers to primordial repetition. As such, it belongs to the order of *possibility*—this difference is the condition of possibility of the order of identity that it founds. For Lacan, originary difference refers to the signifier. As such, it belongs to the conjectural order of the *future anterior*—a difference will have always been misrepresented as identity. For Irigaray, originary difference refers to sexual difference. As such, this difference belongs to the order of possibility and conjecture, at once constitutive and inconclusively futural, and, in both senses, troubling the order that it founds and in which it will have always been effaced.

Derrida's Deconstruction of Husserlian Phenomenology

Speech and Phenomena (1973) functions at once as a close reading of Husserl's discussion of the sign (*Zeichen*) in the first volume of his *Logical Investigations* (2001) and as a critical engagement with Husserlian phenomenology more broadly. For Derrida, Husserl's discussion of the sign brings into focus a tension that subtends the project of phenomenology as a whole (Lawlor 2002, 170). On the one hand, phenomenology is a philosophy of perception and intuition in which the immediacy and undivided unity of self-presence functions as its foundational principle (i.e., presence is the standard of evidence and the ground of apodicticity). On the other hand, phenomenology is a philosophy of temporality in which alterity is inscribed in the self-identity of the present.[2] According to Derrida, this tension is crystallized in Husserl's discussion of the sign. Husserl aligns the sign with representation as *Vorstellung* (re-*presentation*) thereby identifying the expressive dimension of the sign (*Ausdrücke*) with the immediate self-presence of meaning that, according to him, belongs to representations of perception and intuition; at the same time, Husserl also identifies *Vergegenwärtigung* (*re*-presentation) or the structure of iterability as the condition of presence (meaning) as such. The sign is thus at once identified with the punctual, undivided unity of representation as *Vorstellung* and with iterability or representation as *Vergegenwärtigung* as the condition of possibility of presence.[3]

According to Husserl, the sign is conventionally understood as a composite of two parts, the sensible body of the sign (i.e., "the articulate sound-complex [or] the written sign") and its meaning or sense (Husserl 2001, 188). Here, Husserl defines the sign in terms of two functions of representation, "expression" (*Ausdruck*) and "indication" (*Anzeichen*). While expression refers to the presence of ideality to consciousness (i.e., re-*presentation* as *Vorstellung*), indication refers to the formal possibility of *re*-presentation independently of any and every actual presentation (i.e., representation as *Vergegenwärtigung*).[4] Expression, for Husserl, refers to the sense-filled or sense-informed complex of word and meaning in which the indicative elements intimate meaning. In turn, indication refers to the sensible mark (the sound pattern or scrawl) that intimates a meaning (communicating, informing, or manifesting this meaning) but is not identical with this meaning.[5]

According to Husserl, the distinction between expression and indication is asymmetrical. Indication is constituted through its conjunction with expression—expression confers a significative function on otherwise mute marks or sounds. Expression thus constitutes the threshold between grapheme or phoneme as indicative components of meaningful signs and inarticulate marks or sounds that intimate nothing. In contrast, disjoined from indication, expression retains its significative status. That is, according to Husserl, expression coincides with mental acts that are the locus of meaning, acts that are "immediately present to the subject in the present moment" (Derrida 1973, 48). Indication is not needed to manifest the existence of these acts (of meaning), "for the acts in question are themselves experienced by us at the very moment (*im selben Augenblick*)" (58). Indication would thus be gratuitous in the face of "the non-alterity [or] non-difference in the identity of presence as self-presence" (58). Husserl's distinction between expression and indication thus functions to align the sign with representation as *Vorstellung* (re-*presentation*) and reduce *Vergegenwärtigung* (*re*-presentation—repetition or reproduction of presentation).

In *Speech and Phenomena*, Derrida *reverses* the asymmetry of this distinction and thereby *reinscribes* the notion of the sign.[6] *Vergegenwärtigung* refers to the infinite and indefinite possibility of *re*-presentation that is irreducible to any and every re-*presentation* of the object to consciousness. What this means, according to Derrida, is that the condition of presence (the presentation of meaning to consciousness) is the nonpresence of any and every ideal object or meaning before consciousness; in other words, the infinite and indefinite possibility of *re*-presentation (*Vergegenwärtigung*) implies, paradoxically, the necessary possible absence of any re-*presentation* (epresentation as *Vorstellung*) (see Lawlor 2002, 172). In this sense, Derrida argues that representation as *Vorstellung* (the *proximity and presence of meaning before consciousness*) depends on representation as *Vergegenwärtigung* (repetition or reproduction of representation). With this reversal, however, the idea of the sign is radically reinscribed: rather than essentially secondary and derivative, *Vergegenwärtigung* is constitutive. Re-*presentation*, the self-presence of meaning in the undivided unity of the temporal present, is conditioned by *re*-presentation—iterability or repetition (see Derrida 1973, 60). This reversal, however, "radically destroys any possibility of simple self-identity" (66). According to Derrida, *Vergegenwärtigung* is thus the condition of possibility and impossibility of *Vorstellung* and *re*-presesentation the ungrounding ground of re-*presentation*.

Deconstruction can be understood on the basis of this twofold gesture. Having affirmed *Vergegenwärtigung* as the ground of *Vorstellung*, repetition supplants the self-identity of presence as originary and original. Primordial repetition, however, neither precedes nor functions as the *a priori* condition for the order of representation; rather, it is positioned dialectically with respect to this order.[7] In this sense, primordial repetition refers to a constitutive condition that is not a transcendental one. As Derrida puts it: "ideality, which is but another name for the permanence of the same and the possibility of its repetition, does not exist in the world, *and* it does not come from another world; it depends entirely on the *possibility* of acts of repetition. *It is constituted by this possibility*" (52, my emphasis).[8] What deconstruction retrieves from phenomenology, understood as transcendental philosophy, then, is the modality of *possibility*. Primordial repetition is therefore a condition, not in the sense of referring to an *a priori* foundation but rather in the modality of possibility—both as that which enables or *makes-possible* and as that which does not belong to the order that it founds (i.e., "this world" as the world of presence) and thus marks the impossibility of simple identity of presence. Primordial repetition thus refers to original and originary difference precisely in this twofold sense of possibility and impossibility.

Lacan's Deformation of Freudian Psychoanalysis

Lacan's return to Freud is facilitated by and mediated through his engagement with structuralist linguistics. Famously, Lacan interprets Freud's account of the unconscious in terms of a structuralist theory of signification. What Lacan takes up from structuralism is an account of difference as the "principle" of "signification."[9] By positing difference as constitutive, structuralism marks the emergence of a conception of language understood not as representation but as a system of differential articulation. Lacan thus adopts Saussure's account of difference as constitutive while reinscribing the meaning of the sign. His transformation is twofold: he inverts the asymmetry that is implicit in Saussure's functional definition of the sign and reformulates the relationship between signified and signifier. According to Lacan, the signifier "materializes and realizes the operation of difference"; in this sense, it names not only one of two parallel differential series but also the mechanism of differential articulation as such (Weber 1991, 31). According to Lacan, the primacy of the signifier is thus synonymous with the primacy of difference as the "principle" of signification.[10] This primacy, however, only refers to the movement of differential articulation, a movement that constitutes identity. In this sense, "the signifier names the process through which identity is produced in the first place" (64). As such, the signifier is not a substantive but an activity and movement, the trajectory of which is identity, or as Lacan puts it, its "falling out" into the signified.

Lacan's account of the relation between signified and signifier is elaborated in his famous discussion of the mirror stage. The mirror stage describes the constitution of identity as a process that "misrepresents difference in the image of identity" (106). Within this account, Lacan argues that identity is specular—it is constituted through the mediation of the Other. The specular Other, however, is not a mimetic representation; instead, it is a simulacrum, a copy with no original. Identification, however, requires that the anticipatory projection be disavowed and that the image conform to an antecedent identity (ibid.). The simulacrum is thus dissimulated as a copy. In virtue of this dissimulation, the alterity of the specular Other will have always been reduced to the identity of self-presence and the debt of identity to this specular Other disavowed. In this sense, Lacan argues that the order of representation institutes the modal and temporal structure of the future anterior, constituting an identity that *will have always been* present (6–7).

Lacan's defiguration of the phallocentrism of Freudian psychoanalysis can be understood in these terms.[11] In his return to Freud, Lacan retrieves the theory of phallic primacy along with the theory of castration. For Freud, at least on the face of it, these theories suggest that sexual difference can be represented in terms of the identity of the phallus. This is clear in Freud's account of phallic primacy in his 1923 Essay on "The Infantile Genital Organization of the Libido" (1923). Here, he argues that phallic primacy implies that "for both sexes, only one genital, namely the male one, comes into account. What is present, therefore, is not a primacy of the genitals, but a primacy of the phallus" (Weber 1991, 142). Castration, in these terms, would refer to the vicissitudes of psychosexual development on the basis of the real or threatened deprivation of this organ. Lacan's return to Freud and his retrieval of the phallocentrism of psychoanalysis de-forms (*ent-stellen*) the theory of phallic primacy.[12] Indeed, contra Freud, Lacan shows that the phallus does not belong to the order of presence (neither *Vorhandenheit* nor *Vorstellung*) but rather marks the misrepresentation of difference as identity (Lacan 2006, 579). The phallus of Freud's account of phallic primacy belongs to the order of the imaginary and is correlated with demand. As such, the phallus functions as simulacrum; its identity is constituted on the basis of narcissistic projection (the universal ascription of a penis); demand constitutes this primacy rather than being confirmed by it and finds confirmation only through the dissimulation of this constitutive projection and disavowal of this retroactive logic. Like the accomplishment of identity in the mirror stage, then, the phallus marks the structure of representation as one that misrepresents difference as identity (Weber 1991, 145).[13] For Lacan, the phallus thus represents sexual difference not in terms of its identity (i.e., in terms of the logic of phallic and castrated, and thus in terms of presence and absence); it represents sexual difference as "a difference that is impossible to apprehend in terms of presence and absence" (ibid.). Lacan thus defigures (*ent-stellen*) the phallocentrism of Freudian psychoanalysis by dis-locating or dis-placing the phallus from the purview of representation (*Vor-stellung*).

Disconcertion of Sexual Difference

Like Lacan, Irigaray's return to Freud returns to his account of phallic primacy. According to Irigaray, the primacy of the phallus implies that there is a singular origin and essence of genital sexuality (i.e., that there is only one sex/organ)[14] and that the vicissitudes of "masculine" and "feminine" psychosexual development can be represented in terms of this singular origin. Very simply, according to Irigaray's interpretation, phallic primacy implies that sexual difference can be represented in terms of the identity of phallus. Yet insofar as sexuality is represented with respect to this identity, difference can be accounted for only in terms of resemblance or analogy to this identity.[15] This is precisely what Irigaray demonstrates in the first section of *Speculum*. According to Freud, while "masculine" sexuality is represented in terms of the identity of the phallus, "feminine" sexuality can be represented by way of resemblance and analogy (e.g., the clitoris is like a penis, the little girl's stimulation of her clitoris is like the little boy's stimulation of his penis, and in this sense, the little girl is like a little boy). Moreover, when Freud points to a breakdown of resemblance (e.g., in the case of castration anxiety), the aim and object choice of "feminine" sexuality are still articulated by analogy with the aim and object of "masculine" sexuality. To the extent that "feminine" sexuality cannot be represented in terms of resemblance or analogy with phallic identity, it can be represented only as a determinate negation (i.e., in privative terms with respect to the identity of the phallus).[16] In this sense, any representation of "feminine" sexuality is thus inscribed within the purview of the identity of the phallus.[17]

Irigaray does not claim, however, that the inadequacy of this representation could be remedied or that the logic of representation could be expunged of patriarchal vestiges. Indeed, in the context of criticizing this foreclosure of the "representation" and "symbolization" of the "feminine," she insists that "none of these words [is] adequate, as all are borrowed from a discourse that aids and abets that prohibition" (Irigaray 1985b, 83). Instead, Irigaray unsettles the primacy of phallic identity as the matrix of sexual difference, showing that what the phallus represents, "*but only by effacing it*, is the differential relation of the sexes" (Weber 1991, 145). Phallic primacy, then, does not imply that sexual difference can be represented in terms of the identity of the phallus; instead, it implies that sexual difference will have always been misrepresented as identity (Irigaray 1985b, 26).[18] "Masculine" and "feminine" sexuality (mis)represent a differential relation that cannot be accounted for in terms of the logic of presence and absence.

In the final chapter of *Speculum*, Irigaray argues that this position is anticipated and prefigured in Plato's allegory of the cave. In this allegory, the cave represents the origin of being and truth (the good). Yet, as Irigaray shows, to represent this origin is to submit the condition of being and truth to the order that it founds: the origin of visibility and presence is represented in terms of visibility and presence. This origin is thereby represented in terms of its concomitant division or bifurcation of the sensible. As she points out, it is the transition from the interiority of the cave to the light of day and the return to darkness that differentiates the sensible from the intelligible. In other words, it is only in virtue of emerging from and returning to the cave that the truth of this order will have always been impoverished with respect to the truth of the light of day. Differentiation articulates and thereby constitutes the distinction between the sensible and the intelligible in which this differentiation will be effaced (represented as a division between extant orders). Through this representation, difference is hypostatized as an axis of symmetry, a bar or a divided line that demarcates the sensible and the intelligible or the empirical and the transcendental.

In its representation, this originary difference is elided. This allegory asserts that constitutive conditions of representation can in fact be brought into view. The origin is thereby annexed within the order of representation, inscribed in the "self-realization of an identity that has always already been virtually present to itself" (Weber 1991, 6–7). Possibility inscribed in the order of the actual and the originary difference of this constitutive condition is thus effaced. To the extent that representation can reflect and symbolize its own origin and foundation, nothing is other to this order and simple self-presence expunged of alterity. On this basis, originary difference will always have been inscribed within the division of the bifurcation of the sensible and its logic of presence and absence. The "sensible," or the "empirical," is represented only in terms of resemblance or analogy with the identity of "ideal" or "transcendental," or in terms of the determinate negation of this identity. Originary difference is thereby reduced to terms of resemblance, analogy, or negation and thus becomes derivative of identity.

On this basis, the significance of Irigaray's attempt to "disconcert" the phallocentrism of representation comes into view. To disconcert phallocentrism is to trouble the staging of representation in terms of the identity of the phallus. It is, first of all, to show that the origin of representation is other to the order of representation as presence, and thereby to trouble the possibility of simple self-presence. This originary difference does not exist in another world (as transcendental) but in the mode of possibility. The phallocentrism of representation is thus troubled by a condition of possibility that it cannot represent and thereby reduce to the terms of identity. Second, to disconcert phallocentrism is to show that the origin of representation will have always been misrepresented in terms of the identity of this order. Yet this misrepresentation is conjectural; it belongs to a time that has never fully taken place. Originary difference, for Irigaray, thus refers at once to a possibility and to an inconclusive futurity, to difference that concomitantly constitutes and troubles the order of representation.

Conclusion

I have tried to elucidate a difference in the otherwise "nearly complete affinity" between the early work of Derrida, Lacan, and Irigaray. I have tried to show that the minimal distance between these projects can be elucidated on the basis of their respective accounts of originary difference. For Derrida, originary difference refers to primordial repetition. This difference belongs to the order of possibility—it is both archaic and inapparent, engendering the order of representation (identity as self-presence). For Lacan, originary difference refers to the signifier. This origin will have always been misrepresented vis-à-vis identity of the order of representation that it founds. For Lacan, both identity and originary difference exist in the modality of inconclusive futurity. For Irigaray, originary difference refers to sexual difference. What she shows is that this origin refers to a differential relation that is condition of both possibility and impossibility of identity. Originary difference is effaced in its representation in the terms of the identity of the phallus. Sexual difference thus refers to the fecundity of the condition of possibility that troubles the order that it constitutes in the same gesture and to the inconclusive futurity of an origin in which it will have been forgotten and effaced.

Notes

1. This is the term that Samuel Weber invokes and makes thematic in *Return to Freud: Jacques Lacan's Dislocation of Psychoanalysis* (1991). Weber points out that defiguration is a translation of *Ent-stellung*, which could also be translated as deformation, distortion, dislocation, or displacement. According to Weber, Lacan's interpretation dislocates (*ent-stellen*) Freud's phallocentrism by displacing it from the order of representation (*Vorstellung*).

2. "[A]lterity is in fact the condition for presence, presentation, and thus for *Vorstellung* in general" (Derrida 1973, 65).

3. See Lawlor 2002, 173.

4. Derrida emphasizes that indication refers to a mode of representation that coincides with *nonpresence* insofar as iterability refers to the infinite and indefinite possibility of repetition. See Derrida 1973, 50.

5. Indeed, according to Husserl, "expressions function meaningfully even in isolated mental life, where they no longer serve to indicate anything" (Husserl 2001, 183).

6. Rodolphe Gasché's *Inventions of Difference.*

7. See Derrida 1973, 68–69.

8. For Derrida, this is also why meaning is infinitely and indefinitely deferred: as ideal and thus formal, meaning belongs to the order of the possible rather than actual, the order of repetition rather than identity. And in this sense, it is also the condition of impossibility of that which founds.

9. As Weber points out, Lacan's proximity to and anticipation of Derrida are clear (see Weber 1991, 27).

10. "In Saussure, however, the primary distinction is neither that of representation and referent, nor that of signifier and signified. Rather, it is that of difference as the principle upon which the function of the signifier as well as that of the signified is 'founded' " (Weber 1991, 27).

11. What Lacan introduces is thus a nonsynthetic dialectical relationship of *Ent-stellung* and *Vor-stellung.* Here, once again, we are struck by the parallel with Derrida, his account of the non-synthetic "dialectical" relation of *Vergegenwärtigung* and *Vorstellung* (see Derrida 1973, 69).

12. Defigure not in the sense of transforming or making appear differently but of subtracting from the order of appearance and presence as such—to remove from the order of representation. In turn, then, this means to displace and dislocate from the field of presence—not to transpose to another world as a different field of presence, a transcendental one, but to displace to another modality of this world than the actual, the apparent, and the present.

13. Or, as Lacan puts it, "it is the signifier that is destined to designate meaning effects as a whole, insofar as the signifier conditions them by its presence as signifier" (Lacan 2006, 579).

14. As Irigaray puts it, "as far as the differentiation into two sexes is concerned, we can know something certain about only one of the terms of the difference [. . . ,] and this one term will be constituted as 'origin,' as that by whose differentiation the other may be engendered and brought to light" (Irigaray 1985a, 21).

15. As Irigaray puts it, "the girl, let us repeat, has no right to play in any manner whatever with any representation of her beginning, no specific mimicry of origin is available to her: she must inscribe herself in the masculine, phallic way of

relating to origin, that involves repetition, representation, reproduction" (Irigaray 1985a, 78).

16. "Envy, jealousy, greed are all correlated to lack, default, absence. All these terms describe female sexuality as merely the *other side* or even the *wrong side* of a male sexualism" (Irigaray 1985a, 51).

17. "A man minus the possibility of (re)presenting oneself as man = normal woman" (Irigaray 1985a, 26).

18. I am indebted to Mladen Dolar's formulation in "One Divides into Two."

Works Cited

Derrida, Jacques. 1973. *Speech and Phenomena: And Other Essays on Husserl's Theory of Signs.* Translated by David B. Allison and Leonard Lawlor. Evanston: Northwestern University Press.

Dolar, Mladen. n.d. "One Divides into Two." Unpublished manuscript.

Gasché, Rodolphe. 1994. *Inventions of Difference: On Jacques Derrida.* Cambridge: Harvard University Press.

Husserl, Edmund. 2001. *Logical Investigations*, edited by Dermot Moran. Translated by J. N. Findlay. Vol. 2. New York; London: Routledge.

Irigaray, Luce. 1985a. *Speculum of the Other Woman.* Translated by Gillian Gill. Ithaca: Cornell University Press.

———. 1985b. *This Sex Which Is Not One.* Translated by Catherine Porter. Ithaca: Cornell University Press.

Lacan, Jacques. 2006. *Ecrits.* Translated by Bruce Fink. New York: Norton.

Lawlor, Leonard. 2002. *Derrida and Husserl: The Basic Problem of Phenomenology.* Bloomington: Indiana University Press.

———. 2003. *Thinking Through French Philosophy: The Being of the Question.* Bloomington: Indiana University Press.

Weber, Samuel. 1991. *Return to Freud: Jacques Lacan's Dislocation of Psychoanalysis.* Translated by Michael Levine. Cambridge: Cambridge University Press.

Dewey and Irigaray on Education and Democracy

The Classroom, the Ineffable, and Recognition

TOMOKA TORAIWA

Luce Irigaray distinguishes two ways of conceiving democracy. According to the first, "democracy can be understood as the reduction of all people to individuals sharing a common undifferentiated (co)existence and discourse" (Irigaray 2008a, 70). This has been the way democracy has been understood and practiced throughout Western history, and it has led to extraordinary violence and oppression. According to the second, which for Irigaray fulfills the true promise of democracy, "democracy can be understood as an opportunity for each one to live one's own singularity" (ibid.). Democracy means establishing a constant relation "between two," between the one and the other, with neither one merging into the other. If we fail to recognize this, democracy becomes "an anonymous community of people in which we lose our subjectivity, our desire, our happiness" (ibid.). In this sense, democracy for Irigaray is a practice and a way of being in which the subjectivity and uniqueness of the two is preserved. In this paper, I explore Irigaray's conception of democracy, discuss its relevance to the field of education and the ways in which it can translate into a pedagogical practice, and attempt to identify the unique contributions of her approach, in particular in relation to John Dewey's efforts to develop a pedagogy in line with his own understanding of democracy.[1]

Dewey, one of the primary figures of philosophical pragmatism, is arguably the most influential American philosopher of education of the first half of the twentieth century, as well as a philosopher of democracy. His understanding of democracy and the terms of his philosophy, although very different from Irigaray's, resonate with her approach. For him, as for Irigaray, democracy is "a mode of associated living, of conjoint communicated experience" (Dewey 1916/1980, 93). He envisions a democratic community in which individuality is realized through "face-to-face relationships" (Dewey 1927/1984, 371). For him, as for Irigaray, democracy starts "between two." And like Irigaray, he views human being as intrinsically embedded in a relationality that is not hierarchical but, to use Irigaray's term, horizontal, grounded in horizontal relationships in difference. Comparing horizontal and vertical relationships, Irigaray writes:

> There is a difference in subjective economy between the hierarchical transmission of an already established discourse and language, order and law, and the exchange of a meaning between us here and now. The first model of transmission or instruction is more parental, more genealogical, more hierarchical; the second more horizontal and intersubjective. The first model risks enslavement to the past, the second opens up a present in order to construct a future. (Irigaray 1996, 45–46)

For Irigaray, as well as for Dewey, interaction in horizontal relationality enables the one and the other to grow continuously, without a fixed end.

Education is a central element in the philosophy of both Irigaray and Dewey. Indeed, both Irigaray and Dewey suggest that the realization of a horizontal type of relationality hinges on education. For Irigaray, teaching has traditionally been an act of transmitting the logic of the one based on the same. With this in mind, she examines children's writing and drawings and tries to imagine a different pedagogy that would open a space for otherness, so that the other will not merge into the one, and so that a relationship between two will develop. Dewey, for his part, tackles the dichotomy between traditional education and child-centered education, arguing that neither guides students to become individuals able to participate fully in a democratic society. For him, an educational environment conducive to democracy involves a practice of interaction between student and teacher wherein the student's power to grow and develop leads him or her through a constant reconstruction of experience under the appropriate guidance of the teacher.

However, the attempt to develop a pedagogy able to realize this type of democracy raises a difficult question: How would it be possible to cultivate a pedagogical practice that would result in horizontal relationships in difference, given that the educational relationship is inevitably vertical and largely one-sided? In the educational relationship, one person precedes the other; the teacher is expected to be a repository of established meanings and to transmit them to the student. Teachers are expected to guide students. How is it possible to prevent that guidance from becoming a tool for shaping students' subjectivities? Even if vertical relationships are a condition for cultivating horizontal relationships in the classroom, even if their ultimate aim is to develop horizontal relationships, do they not frequently become oppressive? The vertical relationship can become "restrictive and enslaving," determining a fixed end for students and imposing an absolute truth on the other, an outcome contrary to the ideal of democracy in both Irigaray and Dewey. This is the starting point of Irigaray's reflections on education and a paradox fully acknowledged by Dewey. He is well aware of the impossibility, if not the absurdity, of a child-centered education in which the child is left free to express him- or herself without any guidance from teachers. For Dewey, however, tradition is an important factor for personal growth in power and freedom only insofar as it serves to release the powers of learning, to spark the student's own desires and imagination (Dewey 1926/1984, 57).

Dewey's Democracy and Education

The formulation of an idea of democracy as something that is "more than a form of government" (Dewey 1916/1980, 93) occupies a central place in Dewey's philosophy. As noted above, for him, democracy is "primarily a mode of associated living, of conjoint communicated experience" (ibid.). It consists in "[a] society of free individuals in which all, in doing each his own work, contribute to the liberation and enrichment of the lives of others," and it "is the only environment for the normal growth to full stature" (Dewey 1934/1986, 202–03). Moreover, for Dewey, democracy necessarily involves a form of relationality in which everyone is able to realize his or her own potentialities. He writes: "A being connected with other beings cannot perform his own activities without taking the activities of others into account. For they are the indispensable conditions of the realization of his tendencies" (Dewey 1916/1980, 16). As a person participates in a life with others and interacts with others, he or she also contributes to those others' lives. As he or she maximizes the potentialities of his or her own life, so do the others, and they participate in a constant recreation of self and other. For Dewey, an individual is embedded in a type of relationship that requires each person to take into consideration the existence of others, the perspectives of others, a life with others. In this sense, Dewey's idea of democracy involves a conception of social relations that calls for the horizontal type of relationality that is at the heart of Irigaray's own understanding. It calls for horizontal relationality since it does not assume a fixed end that should be attained by all people regardless of differences, nor a fixed law according to which they are hierarchically categorized. For Dewey, horizontal relationships are, in fact, the ideal type of relationships in a democracy. A person grows and becomes in relation to someone or something other, and this becoming and growing is always happening so long as the individual is in a relation with an other in which neither one imposes his or her subjectivity on the other.

For Dewey, school is supposed to be one of the privileged sites where students learn how to be and how to grow in relationships with other people—under appropriate guidance. School for Dewey is a miniature society that provides students with an environment in which they interact with a variety of others and come into contact with a variety of differences: "It is the office of the school environment to balance the various elements in the social environment, and to see to it that each individual gets an opportunity to escape from the limitations of the social group in which he was born, and to come into living contact with a broader environment" (Dewey 1916/1980, 24–25). But this is possible only through the intention of educators. There is always a danger, then, that this "intention" of educators can become coercive and oppressive. For Dewey, in a sense, an educational environment always involves a vertical relationality, since it is teachers who organize the environment and arrange it according to their, as well as their society's, intention. Fully aware of this, Dewey warns that education can easily turn into a site in which teachers dictate to students, becoming the voice "of a *finished* classic tradition." If a teacher dictates, "his students are disciples rather than learners. Tradition is no longer tradition but a fixed and absolute convention" (Dewey 1926/1984, 58). In that case, the teacher suppresses "the emotional and intellectual integrity [of students . . .]; their freedom is repressed, and the growth of their own personalities stunted" (ibid.).

Dewey also warns that giving students complete freedom can be as restrictive as the verticality and authority coming from above. Without proper guidance, he suggests, students' reactions are likely to be "casual, sporadic" (Dewey 1926/1984, 59), and they may confuse what is merely a stage in their learning with something fixed and absolute. In that case, students would be unable to develop a practice that allows them to interact with others in difference, and growth becomes impossible. If teaching, then, involves what seems to be an almost inevitably vertical relationship, a guidance from above, and if, at the same time, leaving students without such guidance is not the solution, how is it possible to teach and cultivate a practice that develops horizontal relationships in difference?

The Ineffable: A Potential Space for Mediating the Vertical and the Horizontal

Dewey's approach to answering this question is promising; its potential lies in what he sees as the ineffable aspect of all reflective thinking, of the process of thinking and engaging with an otherness that lies beyond one's knowledge and intelligence—beyond the terms of one's reflectivity.[2] In order to understand the concept of the ineffable in Dewey's philosophy, it is helpful to discuss "experience" briefly. Dewey's philosophy of experience grounds itself in the fecundity of nature because for Dewey "knowing" starts from "primary experience." According to Dewey, experience "recognizes in its primary integrity no division between act and material, subject and object, but contains them both in an unanalyzed totality" (Dewey 1925/1981, 18). In primary experience, things exist in their immediacy without being discriminated or classified; things are enjoyed in their totality. In this kind of primary experience, the ineffable reveals its existence:

> [I]n every event there is something obdurate, self-sufficient, wholly immediate, neither a relation nor an element in a relational whole, but terminal and exclusive [. . . ,] irreducible, infinitely plural, undefinable and indescribable qualities which a thing must *have* in order to be, and in order to be capable of becoming the subject of relations and a theme of discourse.

> Immediacy of existence is ineffable. But there is nothing mystical about such ineffability; it expresses the fact that of direct existence it is futile to say anything to one's self and impossible to say anything to another. [. . .] Things in their immediacy are unknown and unknowable, not because they are remote or behind some impenetrable veil of sensation or ideas, but because knowledge has no concern with them. (74, italics in the original)

Indeed, for Dewey, the ineffable is something that cannot be known by knowledge or intelligence. Existing reality is always beyond the range of languages and ideas. It can be experienced only as it is. This ineffable points at the limit of the self and of the discourses the self possesses, and it reveals the space(s) one does not occupy, where one meets the otherness of the other.[3] Awareness of the ineffable opens a space in which one does not absorb the otherness of the other. It makes present a space for "uncertainty, indeterminacy, or contingency," introduced by the touch of the ineffable in the other (Dewey 1940/1986, 111). This allows for a becoming of both the self and the other in unpredictable ways, free from the predetermination of regulations and law. It provides room for something genuinely new and novel to arrive for the two. The ineffable is thus essential for a horizontal relationality in difference to unfold. It contains the potential for "genuine transformations" (109).

In the places in which Dewey elaborates on the process of reflectivity, however, the potential of the ineffable evaporates. In his discussions of reflectivity, indeed, otherness becomes irretrievably assimilated in the confines of the existing, thinking self. For Dewey, thinking is the activity by which one makes connections between things that had no previous connection to one another. It involves "the intentional endeavor to discover *specific* connections between something which we do and the consequences which result, so that the two become continuous" (Dewey 1916/1980, 152, italics in the original). This need for continuity in thinking implies that when faced with the unfamiliar, the contrary, or the incompatible—that is, when facing the ineffable—the thinker uses information stored from past experience with which he or she tries to take account of the current situation. This, according to Dewey, leads to a constant process of expansion and reorganization of the experience of the self, broadening the self's perspective and incorporating the unfamiliar. Thus, the quality of experience changes and becomes "reflective *par excellence*" (ibid., italics in the original). Yet this also suggests that the ineffable is translated and thus reduced to the existing terms of the thinker, rendered safe and familiar. Through the process of thinking, things beyond the self are perceived intelligently and become visible and located in the already established tableau of classification and discrimination. Thus, otherness is redrawn in the image of the self, and this is true for the student as well as the teacher. What Dewey fails to see is that something has to be present, has to be brought into the process of reflectivity that will prevent the absorption of the other. This is where I suggest that Irigaray's concept of space and the need to safeguard the space between the one and the other in ethical relation can clarify what Dewey has termed "the ineffable" and can help provide an answer to Dewey's dilemma, by allowing us to think carefully about how to cultivate a practice able to develop horizontal social relations in a setting—education—that is, by its very nature, vertical.

Irigaray's Critique of Education

In a way, Irigaray's entire vision of education can be seen as an attempt to address the absence of horizontal relations in the classroom. Irigaray argues that "the moralistic discourse about a citizenship respectful towards otherness has been an abstract, and, one might say, an ideological teaching that has not opened up practical ways of meeting and coexisting in difference, especially with those closest to us" (Irigaray 2008a, 140). Moreover, these educational discourses are blind to the fact that they are themselves grounded on an ethics of sameness—as is the case for the type of reflective thinking that Dewey posits—and as a consequence, their practice leads to a subjectivity that makes no real room for the other. The other ends up adsorbed into the self. Regardless of how well intentioned and progressive it may seem, education fails to include the real otherness of the other and fails to create a space in which both the self and the other may grow on their own terms. "Subject-object relations, competitive relations with a peer, or peers, within a one-many configuration, and hierarchical relations define the dominant model" (Irigaray 2008d, 210). In the current educational culture, there is no room for students to "speak freely, notably about things that teachers do not want to listen to" (203). It is a culture that alienates the child's subjectivity from the classroom. What is at work is a vertical relationship between the teacher and the student that controls what can and what cannot be uttered and thus prepares students to become "good citizens." What is missing here is an ethical gesture, an active moral agency, that safeguards a space of intersubjectivity, not just in the relations between students but also in the teacher-student relationship—a relationship that is necessarily a vertical, authoritative one.

Irigaray's argument on civic education is in fact echoed, albeit in very different terms, in Sarah Hoagland's critique of paternalism and her concerns with ethics (Hoagland 1988). It is useful to review briefly Hoagland's ideas and apply them to the field of education; for her, paternalism teaches children a type of moral agency that is restrictive and disempowering, hides otherness, leads to a complete absence of sensitivity to the other, and therefore leaves no room for a continuous process of becoming. Hoagland writes:

> I have been arguing that paternalism does not serve us; it leads us to pursue power as control, and as a result we undermine our own and each other's moral agency. [. . .] Paternalistic thinking, the belief that it is appropriate to act for (not with) someone, keeps us believing that we can do things without knowing others or understanding their perceptions and world-view in relation to our own (often called "objectivity" in science); it encourages atomistic individualism. (139)

This is indeed the result of an entire moral education, of the ways in which children are taught to make moral decisions. In situations that require students to choose and act in the face of the unfamiliar and different, they react according to paternalistic principles and force those principles on others—their ethical gestures recreating the conditions that prevent the expression of their own, as well as others', subjectivities. There is no room to imagine the otherness of the other, let alone a chance to generate new terms that are neither the one's nor the other's but that speak to both, the one and the other.

Irigaray's Ethical Gesture of Recognition: A Space to Safeguard the Ineffable

Irigaray's ethical gesture of recognition may be a key to safeguard space between the one and the other in an educational environment, although I suggest that it is the awareness of Dewey's ineffable that makes the conditions for recognition possible to begin with, for it is the ineffable that defines precisely the site in which recognition has to be effected in the classroom. According to Irigaray, "horizontal relations in difference" allow the one and the other to maintain their own subjectivities and "to become" with faithfulness to their own natures, while enabling a dialogue between the two subjectivities (Irigaray 2008d, 217). For that to happen, an active gesture of recognition is required:

> I recognize you signifies that you are, that you exist, that you become. With this recognition, I mark you, I mark myself with incompleteness, with the negative. Neither you nor I are the whole nor the same, the principle of totalization. And our difference cannot be reduced to *one* hierarchy, *one* genealogy, *one* history. (Irigaray 1996, 105, italics in the original)

Recognition involves becoming aware of the limitations of one's self and of the impossibility of reducing the other to the one. Recognition never assumes the wholeness of the one or of the other, never allows for the projection of the one onto the other; on the contrary, recognition agrees "to be questioned by a different meaning, by a world whose sense remains invisible to us but which we agree to welcome, by which we agree to be questioned and touched when listening to it" (Irigaray 2008b, 232). It is "a way of opening ourselves to the other and of welcoming this other, its truth, and its world as different" (ibid.). Recognition supposes a respect for invisibility. Everything is not necessarily visible from our own perspectives, for if we assume that everything can be seen and perceived, there will be no room left for acknowledging difference, for developing a horizontal relation in difference. This ethical gesture involves, then, an acceptance of the invisibility that exists between the one and the other. As Irigaray writes: "It would [. . .] be useful to become aware of the plurality of our perceptions and of the part of invisibility that we must respect in our relations with all living beings, especially, although not only, with human beings" (Irigaray 2008a, 148).

In contrast to Irigaray's insistence on invisibility and on the moral awareness required to maintain it, Dewey does not assume any experience of invisibility in perception; in spite of his ideas on the ineffable, he grounds perception in that which is made visible. For Dewey, education is the "reconstruction or reorganization of experience which adds to the meaning of experience, and which increases ability to direct the course of subsequent experience" (Dewey 1916/1980, 82). He writes that "the *measure of the value* of experience lies in the perception of relationships or continuities to which it leads up. It includes cognition in the degree in which it is cumulative or amounts to something, or has meaning" (147, italics in the original). Insofar as the quality of life is changed, the experience becomes educative. That is, when life leads "to an enrichment of its own perceptible meaning" (82), the activity that it is engaged in can be considered educative. For Dewey, perception inevitably involves judging and thinking and naming in order for the things perceived to have meaning.

A relationality grounded in a recognition of the two changes the culture of the classroom because recognition presupposes that the existence of the other is necessary in order for me to be the one I am and to become who I will be.[4] "To become," for Irigaray, means to manifest one's own self in line with one's own nature, while recognition makes room for the other to manifest his or her own self in line with his or her own nature in its otherness. The one and the other are transcendent to each other; however, without the existence of the other, it is impossible to manifest one's own nature or to become. In effect, Irigaray's argument on recognition suggests that the existence of the other is necessary in order for the self to become one as one, to grow. In the classroom, recognition not only prevents students from dominating one another, but just as importantly, it also prevents the teacher from dominating students, because recognition preserves something new that has not yet been manifested within them. This something new, the otherness of the other, is not absorbed by the teacher since the teacher remains within his or her limits, aware of what is beyond his or her own sense of self in the becoming of his or her students.

Hanna Arendt (1968/1993) presents a strong argument for the need for such an ethical gesture on the part of the teacher. Indeed, Arendt tries to reconcile the dichotomy of verticality and horizontality by giving more attention to the teacher's role in educational settings. According to her, the school is a place where the traditional, represented by the teacher, and the new and novel, represented by the child, meet one another. For Arendt, it is the teacher's responsibility to preserve the tradition, as well as to assure the renewal of the world through the becoming of the child. Drawing on Arendt, M. Gordon claims that educators must exercise an authority that assumes responsibility both for the world and for those who are being educated. This authority that assumes responsibility is necessary in order to protect the educated from harm and to preserve the possibility of renewal. For Gordon, educators mediate between the world (the tradition) and those who are being educated. He states, "[I]t is precisely the authority relation and its corresponding conservative attitude that make room for renewal and innovation" (Gordon 1999, 171). The verticality of the teacher-student relation is thus fully acknowledged. Indeed, according to Gordon, Arendt claims that the past and the relation of authority are essential in order to help children realize their potential for creating something new. However, Arendt further suggests that this needs to be accompanied by an ethical gesture, and she is aware of the potential role of the ineffable in realizing what we have seen is the horizontality necessary for democracy. Thus, while acknowledging the authoritative role of teachers, she is also conscious that the novelty that students bring in cannot yet be named and that the safeguarding of that novelty is key to the preservation of the otherness of the other. Yet what we are still missing is a clear suggestion of what that responsibility involves and how it can take form in actual educational practice. The dilemma remains, although it can now be phrased in somewhat different terms: How can the space opened by the ineffable be preserved in education? How can we safeguard a space that is neither the one's nor the other's and in which the seed of horizontal relationality in difference can be sown?

Irigaray and Cultivating the Opening to the Other in the Classroom

Irigaray gives few suggestions about how to develop a method to nurture and cultivate the ethical gesture of recognition. She explains what is wrong with traditional and with civic education; although she advances a persuasive theory of what needs to be done, she provides no concrete method to make changes in the classroom, in particular insofar as the relations between teachers and students are concerned. Her few concrete suggestions address the opening and cultivation of a space of intersubjectivity between students, particularly as it concerns sexuate education. In an article entitled "Creating Inter-Sexuate Inter-Subjectivity in the Classroom?: Luce Irigaray's Linguistic Research in Its Latest Iteration," Gail Schwab describes one example of sexuate classroom practice and pedagogy (Schwab 2016). She argues that Irigaray's linguistic exercises, conducted to reveal and explore sexuate differences in language usage between boys and girls, may have significant pedagogical value (ibid.). In the deployment of these exercises in the classroom, students are given cue words, such as "I . . . you," "I . . . she," "I . . . he," "with," "together," and asked to make sentences using these cues (Irigaray 2008d, 206). Teacher and students then analyze the results together and discuss reasons for the perceived linguistic differences. Schwab, following Irigaray, has found that this type of activity can open a space for an ethical and communicative step in which the class engages in conversation "to change not just language but inter-sexuate relations" (Schwab 2016, 148). Furthermore, Irigaray claims that, after asking students to think of an activity that would please both boys and girls and encouraging students to communicate with respect for their differences, she witnessed "some very dynamic and interesting exchanges" (Irigaray 2004, 83). The pedagogical value of these linguistic exercises in cultivating "inter-sexuate inter-subjectivity," and in opening a space in which difference is recognized, is potentially powerful.

However, what remains unclear is how it is to be conducted or structured in order to become effective. We get a glimpse of their pedagogical value, but we do not see how Irigaray generates an environment in which these exchanges among students become possible. The exchanges are not random. They do not occur in a space free of verticality. They happen under the careful direction and guidance of a teacher who has some control over the classroom environment. In this sense, we see only the effects and not the process of the teacher ensuring a space not only between boys and girls but also between the teacher herself and the students—a space in which the teacher would put her authority on hold, to use Arendt's wording, and avoid projecting her self onto the students while the students engage in the exercise. Ultimately, Irigaray will never suggest a method; nor, according to her own theory, should she suggest one. From the moment that a standard or a definitive way to create horizontal relations in difference is set, it becomes paternalistic and thereby denies the very idea of horizontal relations in difference. However, it is still possible to suggest that it is the teacher's role to guide students and enable them to cultivate the ethical gesture of recognition, to help students attain their particular self in its singularity, and to lead them to find their own words and means to express this self, without assimilating or projecting themselves onto the other. In the educational relationship, the teacher is the one who must lead by making the first gesture of recognition. According to Irigaray, the task of teaching is "guiding, [. . .] helping the other to discover one's own path, to enter the space and time of his or her proper life and to accomplish it as a human being" (Irigaray 2008b, 234). In such a case, the otherness of the other is respected, and the student, in turn, learns the gesture of recognition.

It is not an easy task. Irigaray is mindful of our tendency to possess the other, to absorb the other, and to project our discourse onto the other. And she acknowledges that it is the attempt to prevent this tendency, made more pronounced by the verticality of the teacher-student relationship, that is at the core of the gesture of recognition:

> Respect for the other as standing beyond the limits of one's own world—that is, for the other as transcendent to me and to my horizon—disciplines the immediacy of the need to go beyond our limits. This need, originally natural and vital, can develop as an instinct for possession, for appropriation or domination to the detriment of the other, or it can be cultivated as a specifically human way to enter into relation with the different other, whose irreducibility is recognized. Taking into consideration this horizontal and qualitative transcendence trains our sensibility, provides limits that permit it to be cultivated and attain a transcendental character. (Irigaray 2008c, 134–35)

We are inclined to see ourselves in the other; therefore, we inevitably develop a vertical relationship with the other. Yet Irigaray believes that through the gesture of recognition this inclination can be "re-directed" (in Dewey's sense) towards horizontality. And, as I have already suggested, it is indeed at this juncture that Dewey's ineffable becomes of use. For if the otherness of the other is invisible to us, if we have no intellectual perception of this otherness, we nonetheless have a sense—perhaps a poetic sense—of it in the form of the ineffable that we experience but that remains beyond comprehension. By letting recognition circulate and simultaneously seizing the experience of the ineffable, both to respect the otherness of the other and to cultivate our respective yet different subjectivities, we may be able to go beyond the dilemma of vertical and horizontal in education.

As Irigaray expresses it in the quote above, the other establishes limits and, in this sense, brings into view the horizon beyond which lies the transcendence of the other. In an article entitled "Beyond the Vertical and the Horizontal," Schwab discusses Irigaray's use of the term "mystery" (Schwab 2011). Mystery is the nature of what is beyond the horizon delimited by the other. Mystery as a human phenomenon is that which "provides the ground for the paths we must walk in our intellectual and emotional approach to the other and creates the space for the recognition of the limit of our understanding of her or his being. [. . .] In acknowledging mystery, we acknowledge the limits of our capabilities even as we strive to maximize them in our living relation to the other" (93). This Irigarayan mystery resonates with Dewey's ineffable; it is what must be cultivated. The ethical gesture of recognition, I suggest, is necessary to be true to this mystery beyond the horizon, the mystery of the ineffable, as it helps generate the horizontal relationality in difference. In the gesture of recognition, a teacher becomes a locus of the educative environment in and through which each student will learn how to be true to the sense of the ineffable in the other and how to become while being true to the ineffable in her- or himself.

There is no possible prescription for practicing the ethical gesture of recognition. It has to be tailored for the particular sensibility of each student-teacher relationship. A whole relationship is thus nurtured through the ethical gesture of recognition, one able to create a "culture that could meet the aspirations and necessities of our times, [. . .] considering difference itself as the source of their relationship and their becoming" (Irigaray 2008d, 218). Through such an education, one can envision democracy since, from it, "a society would be formed starting each time from two, whose relations result in a lively interweaving" (205). This is the starting point from which a true dialogue unfolds, a dialogue that allows each subjectivity to develop in its own way and from which a democracy develops in which each singularity is able to flourish without doing violence to self or other.

Notes

I would like to express my gratitude to Gail M. Schwab for allowing me to read her 2016 article before its publication and for giving me permission to cite it. Also, she gave me some significant feedback in editing this essay to polish the argument.

1. There are several articles that discuss Irigaray's philosophy of education. See Peers 2005, 2011; Galea 2010; Rasheed 2007; Schwab 2011, 2016. To my knowledge, no one has attempted to engage Irigaray's ethical gesture of recognition to think about educational practice.

2. Some scholars have criticized Dewey's take on the ineffable. See Gale 2006, Garrett 1973. Others see the importance of the ineffable in Dewey's philosophy of experience. See Pappas 2008, McClelland 2008.

3. See Hildebrand 2011 for a discussion of the paradoxical nature of the ineffable in Dewey's philosophy of experience. What I am suggesting is that recognizing the ineffable is one way to approach the other whose language is totally different from ours. We then know that our method is fallible and that "there is no certainty that it can resolve all disagreements or prevent all complaints over 'oppression,'" but we remain "reverent of the perspectives of others and the need to keep creating democracy as we all try to get along" (603).

4. See Irigaray 1996, 112. Drawing from Irigaray's philosophy, Chris Peers (2011) points out that the "formalized reciprocity" of gender neutrality in pedagogy, accompanied by the establishment of authority, "renders the classroom whole, and affords sameness to teacher and learner" (770). This formalized reciprocity eventually fashions the classroom as a site where there is a constant prevention of differentia-

tion of being. As I have stressed in this chapter, what I am trying to argue is that it is the ineffable that makes the conditions for the ethical gesture of recognition possible and this, in turn, enables the differentiation of beings.

Works Cited

Arendt, Hannah. 1968/1993. *Between Past and Future: Eight Exercises in Political Thought.* New York: Penguin Books.

Dewey, John. 1916/1980. *The Middle Works, 1899–1924*, vol. 9, *1916: Democracy and Education*, edited by J. A. Boydston. Carbondale: Southern Illinois University Press.

———. 1925/1981. *The Later Works, 1925–1953*, vol. 1, *1925: Experience and Nature*, J. A. Boydston, ed. Carbondale: South Illinois University Press.

———. 1926/1984. "Individuality and Experience." In *The Later Works, 1925–1953*, vol. 2, *1925–1927: Essays, Reviews, Miscellany, and the Public and Its Problems*, edited by J. A. Boydston, 55–61. Carbondale: Southern Illinois University Press–.

———. 1927/1984. "The Public and its Problems." In *The Later Works, 1925–1953*, vol. 2, *1925–1927: Essays, Reviews, Miscellany, and The Public and Its Problems*, edited by J. A. Boydston, 235–372. Carbondale: Southern Illinois University Press.

———. 1934/1986. "The Need for a Philosophy of Education." In *The Later Works, 1925–1953*, vol. 9, *1933–1934: Essays, Reviews, Miscellany, and A Common Faith*, edited by J. A. Boydston, 194–209. Carbondale: Southern Illinois University Press.

———. 1940/1986. "Time and Individuality." In *The Later Works, 1925–1953*, vol. 14, *1939–1941: Essays, Reviews, Miscellany, and A Common Faith*, edited by J. A. Boydston, 98–114. Carbondale: Southern Illinois University Press.

Gale, Richard M. 2006. "The Problem of Ineffability in Dewey's Theory of Inquiry." *Southern Journal of Philosophy* 44, no. 1: 75–90.

Galea, Simone. 2010. "Reflecting Reflective Practice." *Educational Philosophy and Theory* 44, no. 3: 245–58.

Garrett, Roland. 1973. "Dewey's Struggle with the Ineffable." *Transactions of the Charles S. Peirce Society* 9, no. 2: 95–104.

Gordon, Mordechai. 1999. "Hannah Arendt on Authority: Conservatism in Education Reconsidered." *Educational Theory* 49, no. 2: 161–80.

Hildebrand, David L. 2011. "Pragmatic Democracy: Inquiry, Objectivity, and Experience." *Metaphilosophy* 42, no. 5: 589–604.

Hoagland, Sarah L. 1988. *Lesbian Ethics: Toward New Value.* Palo Alto, CA: Institute of Lesbian Studies.

Irigaray, Luce. 1996. *I Love to You: Sketch for a Felicity within History.* Translated by Alison Martin. New York: Routledge.

———. 2004. "Towards a Sharing of Speech." Translated by Gail M. Schwab. In *Luce Irigaray: Key Writings*, edited by Luce Irigaray, 77–94. London and New York: Continuum.

———. 2008a. *Conversations.* London and New York: Continuum.

———. 2008b. "Listening, Thinking, Teaching." In *Luce Irigaray: Teaching*, edited by Luce Irigaray with M. Green, 231–40. London and New York: Continuum.

———. 2008c. *Sharing the World.* London and New York: Continuum.

———. 2008d. "Teaching How to Meet in Difference." In *Luce Irigaray: Teaching*, edited by Luce Irigaray with M. Green, 203–18. London and New York: Continuum.

McClelland, Ken. 2008. "John Dewey and Richard Rorty: Qualitative Starting Points." *Transactions of the Charles S. Peirce Society* 44, no. 3: 412–45.

Pappas, Gregory F. 2008. *John Dewey's Ethics: Democracy as Experience.* Bloomington: Indiana University Press.

Peers, Chris. 2005. "The 'First' Educator?: Rethinking the 'Teacher' through Luce Irigaray's Philosophy of Sexual Difference." *The Australian Educational Researcher* 32, no. 1: 83–100.

———. 2011. "Freud, Plato and Irigaray: A Morpho-logic of Teaching and Learning." *Educational Philosophy and Theory* 44, no. 7: 760–74.

Rasheed, Shaireen. 2007. "Sexualized Spaces in Public Places: Irigaray, Levinas, and an Ethics of the Erotic." *Educational Theory* 57, no. 3: 339–50.

Schwab, Gail M. 2011. "Beyond the Vertical and the Horizontal: Spirituality, Space, and Alterity in the Work of Luce Irigaray." In *Thinking with Irigaray*, edited by Mary C. Rawlinson, S. L. Hom, and S. J. Khader. Albany: State University of New York Press, 77–97.

———. 2016. "Creating Inter-sexuate Inter-subjectivity in the Classroom? Luce Irigaray's Linguistic Research in its Latest Iteration." In *Engaging the World: Thinking after Irigaray*, edited by Mary C. Rawlinson. Albany: State University of New York Press.

Discursive Desire and the Student Imaginary

KAREN SCHILER

> In some cases, student responses to oppositional political discourse can be quite extreme. They perceive such discourse not as a teacher's honest expression of identity but as an act of political terrorism. [. . . T]hey are assassinated, as subjects, by a discourse that purports to be educational. What is at stake for them in such discourse is simply survival.
>
> —Marshall Alcorn 1995, 337

In his survey for *College Composition and Communication*, entitled "Composition at the Turn of the Twenty-First Century," rhetoric and composition scholar Richard Fulkerson points to the presence of the critical/cultural analysis approach to composition instruction in academic journals (659) and spends much of his time discussing how that approach—that comes to us from cultural studies—is arguably the most dominant among composition pedagogies—and not without its problems. Within the critical/cultural analysis paradigm, often tellingly referred to as a "liberatory project," it is generally held that composition courses ought to teach first-year students how to critically evaluate and compose texts that will help them participate in the conversations of the academy and, eventually, in society at large.

In this chapter, I outline the main features of the critical/cultural analysis approach for such high-stakes writing instruction, primarily through the influential work of compositionists James Berlin and Lester Faigley, paying particular attention to how this approach has traditionally conceptualized student subjectivity. I then discuss how compositionist Marshall Alcorn has used the psychoanalytic theory of Jacques Lacan to offer a corrective complication of student subjectivity in *Changing the Subject in English Class: Discourse and the Constructions of Desire* (2002). In response, I propose that Luce Irigaray offers a more fitting perspective on subjectivity, and her perspective raises interesting questions regarding the liberatory project itself. Furthermore, while Alcorn takes time to examine libidinal language operating through the student, his critique could be enriched by time spent reflecting on how libidinal language operates through the teacher; Irigaray makes space for such reflection. If we compare Irigaray's discussion of female desire with the imagined perspective of student desire, we can see that by leaving room for a "student imaginary" we are led to question the entire project of liberation itself. I maintain that Irigaray's work on subjectivities allows us to question—with sympathy and a healthy skepticism—the intentions of the critical/cultural analysis approach to writing instruction, as well as envision what might be gained by doing things differently. Irigaray's work might suggest that we shift our disciplinary discussions of composition pedagogy from the perspective of "us" training "them," to one of inviting Other (student) voices. Irigaray's imaginary can greatly enrich our pedagogical awareness of how desire and agency circulate in both student and teacher, shifting our pedagogical project from one of liberation to one of transformation.

In describing the disciplinary development of the critical/cultural analysis approach, Fulkerson refers to a larger "social turn" within the field of composition, a turn that many fields in the humanities have certainly experienced to varying degrees. For Fulkerson, the genealogical sources of the social turn's influence on composition are postmodernism, feminism, and British cultural studies. While acknowledging that these sources are hardly uniform in goal or methodology, he believes that the critical/cultural analysis composition pedagogies they have inspired "can all be seen as similar 'emancipatory movements in composition.' " Fulkerson goes on to emphasize that these pedagogies focus on educating students on how to read and resist social texts that reinforce the subordination of certain groups. Ultimately, Fulkerson argues, this results in a shift from an emphasis on improved writing to an emphasis on "liberation" instead (Fulkerson 660).

Within the broader Western history of composition's rhetorical inheritance, we note that the art of rhetoric arose as a way to move citizens from philosophy to consensual political action. In "Poststructuralism, Cultural Studies, and the Composition Classroom: Postmodern Theory in Practice,"

Berlin asserts that Socrates, Plato, and Aristotle all taught "the counterpart of freshman composition" (Berlin 1992, 24). Thus, the project of liberation can be viewed as a contemporary, activist extension of writing instruction's democratic potential. The goal here "is to empower or liberate students by giving them new insights into the injustices of American and transnational capitalism, politics, and complicit mass media" (Fulkerson 661). Hence, we see the reason for the name "liberatory project" within disciplinary discussions of composition pedagogy. In sum, those engaged in a liberatory project usually view rhetoric as social-epistemic; they believe that languages reflect our socially constructed knowledge(s) and that the instructor's charge is to liberate students from oppressive and inherited ideologies.

Liberating the Student-as-Subject

Many would argue, Fulkerson included, that the most well-known figure responsible for popularizing a liberatory approach is compositionist James Berlin, who defined the goal of composition studies in "Composition and Cultural Studies" as follows: "Our larger purpose is to encourage our students to resist and negotiate [. . .] hegemonic discourses" (Berlin 1991, 50). In "Rhetoric and Ideology in the Writing Class," Berlin writes that "for social-epistemic rhetoric, the subject is itself a social construct that emerges through the linguistically-circumscribed interaction of the individual, the community, and the material world" (Berlin 1988, 489). Here, we do well to take note: the subject's construction occurs socially, but the stuff of the structure itself is ideology: "Ideology addresses or interpellates human beings. It provides the language to define the subject, other subjects, the material and social, and the relation of all of these to each other" (Berlin 1992, 23). For Berlin, "teaching is never innocent. Every pedagogy is imbricated in ideology, in a set of tacit assumptions about what is real, what is good, what is possible, and how power ought to be distributed" (Berlin 1988, 492). Ultimately, Berlin goes on to argue that expectation, emotion, and desire are all shaped by ideology; ideology also "naturalizes certain authority regimes . . . and renders alternatives unthinkable" (Berlin 1992, 18), which suggests that our ability to teach students a critical engagement with ideology is nothing short of a social commitment.

An alternative view on how the subject is structured is provided in the almost as influential, albeit more ambivalent, work of compositionist Lester Faigley in *Fragments of Rationality* (1992); Faigley describes how composition (and early process theory and pedagogy) sprang up "against a backdrop of numerous calls for social groups and individuals to look within themselves for their own identities"—that is to say that the changes of the 1960s prompted many idealistically to place their hope in civic participation and the liberal individual, who would surely do good if only given a voice and tools for empowerment. Alas, citing novelist Don DeLillo's insistence that the assassination of John F. Kennedy brought on a growing unease among these same idealists, Faigley points to the concurrent "growing awareness of randomness, ambiguity, and chaos" as having shaped the zeitgeist of our present day (Faigley 1992, 3), and he argues that many of us point to this as "postmodernism."

In a reflection of the larger culture, where "counterculture art, music, and dress of the 1960s were soon coopted and commodified" (225), Faigley argues that composition found itself domesticated by the basic concept that writing is a process. Instead of showing students model texts and expecting them to magically imitate them, the thinking was that we ought to point out the often uncomfortable process of writing, in no small part to highlight the initial reading, brainstorming, drafting, and revision involved. Disagreements notwithstanding, the idea of process grew in disciplinary popularity. Faigley's pointed use of the word "domestication" underscores the problematic establishment of process theory as "Home" within composition. Faigley suggests that the problem with process theory in particular, which posits that writing is a process that can be broken down and taught, is its reliance on "a fiction of textual coherence. The student writer's skill in representing his or her life experience as complete and noncontradictory is taken as confirmation that the rational subjectivity of the author is identical with the autonomous individual" (ibid.). In other words, Faigley worries that process theory encourages a domesticating view of the activity of writing itself: we validate the status quo, and we validate ourselves as individuals by presenting our experiences rationally and coherently. Faigley's concerns about the process approach and the fiction of the coherent subject within discussions of writing instruction can be read as a reflection of Jean-François Lyotard's postmodernist "incredulity toward metanarratives" (Lyotard 1984, 3). An additional problem with process theory as composition's "Home" was that the process itself became codified into a one-way circuitry of steps that suggest a one-size-fits-all notion of process, which could result in exactly the kind of identity-flattening student experience that most good teachers would wish to avoid.

As we move on to a critique of the liberatory project in earnest, I want to suggest that the two reconceptualizations of the subject offered by Berlin and Faigley are missing something that psychoanalysis in general, and Irigaray in particular, can provide. For Berlin, the major structuring force of the subject is ideology. While this does much to underscore the importance of the liberatory project's goal of coding and decoding, it also holds to a coherent discourse as structuring the subject first and foremost. For Faigley, the structuring force is a subject-preceding situatedness among competing discourses. While this is more nuanced, he still refers to discourse as primary in power, which leaves us to wonder: What impact, if any, can an agent's desire have on identity and relations? Is there knowledge or experience a subject can have that is able to exist prelanguage, or prediscourse? In short, is there something more to say about the interior of the subject before we insist that it is constructed by that which we, the composition and rhetoric instructors, are fortunate enough to already be experts in?

The Other Subject in the Classroom

In *Changing the Subject in the English Class: Discourse and the Constructions of Desire*, compositionist Marshall Alcorn uses psychoanalysis, specifically the work of Jacques Lacan and Slavoj Žižek, to make a case for social constructionism that still provides vocabulary for complexifying the individual. Alcorn reminds us that the subject contains more complex mechanisms; one can be both socially constructed and moved by what seem like autonomous choices: "Drive is an important but elusive concept for a psychoanalytic social theory because it designates a structure that acts like instinct but is determined by speech demands . . . But though drive is experienced as a natural response of the body, it is, in fact, a social construction. It is constructed by social interaction, by Lacan's laws of the signifier" (Alcorn 2002, 98). If we view a college student's contribution to a discussion as powered by drive, we begin to recognize that it acts like something natural (instinct), and, thus, the student is probably not accustomed to questioning it. Yet, it does not appear unless in response to discourse, which may be a part of a larger ideology (speech demands). Here Alcorn gives compositionists room to insist that much of a subject's identity is socially constructed. He also acknowledges just how difficult it is for subjects to change their behavior via rational recognition and desire: to expect a student to encounter a challenge to her previously held beliefs, revise her earlier sense of self, and proceed with confidence suddenly seems a bit tenuous, if not unrealistic.

To be clear, Alcorn is explicitly sympathetic to the liberatory project itself: "My goal is not to attack cultural studies but to freshen and deepen its grasp of human subjectivity, to argue for a more flexible and complex perspective that will allow cultural studies to engage students more effectively" (2). In fact, Alcorn devotes a good portion of his book to exploring why a liberatory project is worthwhile, and, consequently, how disappointing it can be when classroom dynamics suggest that the liberation may not have gone as productively as the instructor had hoped. Composition instructors

> see their teaching in political terms; they want to change the world, and this means that they want to change the subjectivity of their students. In doing cultural studies, many teachers want to make their students more politically responsible; more in dialogue with the great social movements that dominate our time. Thus, the subjectivity of the student becomes a subject that the method of cultural studies works on as it responds to the subject matter of a text. (Ibid.)

Teachers with political goals can have a simple view of subjectivity that, given their training in a critical/cultural analysis approach to writing instruction, may account for the entanglement of social forces but does not include a nuanced understanding of psychoanalytic layers. Drawing from Sigmund Freud's work on hysteria and mourning, as well as Lacan's work on the relationship of language to identity and the unconscious, Alcorn provides more.

In "Mourning and Melancholia," Freud defines mourning as the "reaction to the loss of a loved person, or to the loss of some abstraction which has taken the place of one, such as one's country, liberty, an ideal, and so on" (Freud 1916, 243). Alcorn points out that mourning is a type of libidinal attachment that is particularly powerful and cannot simply be abandoned even if we rationally know we must give it up. This would explain why some students, when confronted with knowledge that challenges previously held beliefs, still go through a "painful and protracted mode of reflection. [. . . I]t is a complicated labor we perform on the many and varied imagery of that to which we are attached" (Alcorn 27). It may seem alarming to bring in so emotionally charged a description of students in the composition classroom, but it also suggests that such emotional behavior is natural, as Freud insists: "It is also well worth notice that, although mourning involves grave departures from the normal attitude to life, it never occurs to us to regard it as a pathological condition. [. . .] We rely on its being overcome after a certain lapse of time" (Freud 243–44). Alcorn contends that "because ideology operates at the level of personal emotional experience" (Alcorn 29), we need to explore how to teach students to reason through conflicting libidinal attachments in order to achieve political goals.

Alcorn writes: "Berlin valued the right political ideas over expressive writing. I argue that political ideas will never be right until there is attention to and freedom in self-expression" (3). We see that Alcorn highlights the subject's interiority, stressing its social importance by insisting that "freedom is not, as most liberals assume, a simple, spontaneous act. It is, instead, a difficult discipline that requires the kind of struggle that all writers engage in as they struggle to find their own conflicting thoughts and take responsibility for those thoughts on paper" (ibid.). This would suggest that if composition instructors attempt cultural criticism for the sake of liberation, they should not expect a spontaneous ideological blossoming of the student but rather prepare for a struggle.

In fact, Alcorn identifies this sort of "liberal naïveté" as a disciplinary shortcoming: "[C]ultural studies often assumes that if we teach politically correct knowledge, we can generate politically correct practice and make political decisions to help those who suffer" (5). Yet, by prioritizing self-expression and observing the amount of discipline involved, we see that generating correct practice is not so easily achieved. Alcorn argues that "the teaching of such knowledge is not enough . . . In order to use knowledge for social progress, desire must be mobilized" (ibid.). Here the introduction of desire truly takes on epistemic and social importance. "Desire itself must be altered if knowledge is to be effective in solving social problems. Thus, I advocate a form of teaching that is responsible not simply to knowledge but also to desire" (ibid.). Alcorn assumes that, with a sufficient understanding of the mechanism of desire, it is possible for a teacher to engage more humanely in liberatory instruction. Yes, a student will experience a consequent mourning as she begins to recognize her own ideologies as flawed and comes to understand her desires as having been partly responsible for an inability to see these flaws. However, the informed teacher can address this mourning, identify and redirect the responsible desire, and, eventually, through reading and writing, reshape the student's drive. If we were to take a step back and view both teacher and student in this hypothetical classroom, we might envision it as a site of circulating desire: the teacher's caring, corrective desire to liberate the student from flawed ideology effectively leads the student to reshape her desire in a way that leads to certain social progress. This vision, however, encompasses certain problems.

Female Desire and Student Imaginaries

I appreciate Alcorn's work to complexify student subjects and, consequently, elaborate on the social epistemic potential of recognizing student desire in the classroom. Nevertheless, I have reservations that a possible outcome of accepting these revelations is that knowing how to critically read and write ideology isn't actually enough to change conditions for the better and that we must further commit to teaching our students what to desire. Apparently, we must help them not only read to uncover ideology, but interpret it in the proper way, and then help them learn how they ought to feel about it. While Alcorn states, "I do not advocate that classrooms become sites for therapy" (ibid.), I would argue that such a relationship between teacher and student is perhaps more fraught with troubling doctor-client authority than can be simply acknowledged and then wished away.

Elsewhere, Alcorn observes that "reducing unconscious conflict, as analytic practice dramatically demonstrates, is not a simple matter accomplished efficiently and effectively by rational and informative speech. Saying to a person, 'Look at these conflicting codes; you have unconscious conflict here,' does not make that person recognize and resolve such conflict" (22). Here we might use Irigaray's work in *This Sex Which Is Not One* to consider the problem of conflict:

> Must this multiplicity of female desire and female language be understood as shards, scattered remnants of a violated sexuality? A sexuality denied? The question has no simple answer. The rejection, the exclusion of a female imaginary certainly puts woman in the position of experiencing herself only fragmentarily, in the little-structured margins of a dominant ideology, as waste, or excess, what is left of a mirror invested by the (masculine) "subject" to reflect himself, to copy himself. (Irigaray 1985, 30)

In applying these ideas to the teacher-student relationship, must we classify student multiplicities of desire, or libidinal language, as shards? Must we ask them to deny those shards which we view as primitive, or undeveloped? If we do assume this to be our responsibility, what are the chances that we misidentify such alternate libidinal identities? Are we forcing our students into a space where the dominant ideology, albeit a socially progressive one, allows them to experience their other selves only as waste? This is a dangerous game, especially when we are admittedly working with emotionally charged thinking and intense identification.

The idea that composition must handle conflict is not one I object to; however, deciding which social commitments my students ought to care about and which they ought to leave behind, sometimes even at the cost of substantial mourning, is an idea that troubles me. Irigaray notes that the aforementioned male subject role leaves woman to recover her desire "only in secret, in hiding, with anxiety and guilt" (ibid.). A further potential consequence is that it is only a matter of time before the subject resents the ideology that inspires such anxiety and resents having to recover the self in secret. Irigaray might suggest that this is the result of a limited conception of desire, that most of us "have not begun to envision the cultivation of energy which could result from relating to each other with respect for difference(s)" (Irigaray 2008, 205). If my students are expending most of the emotional energy in my classroom constantly questioning their ideologies, reflecting through mourning, and retraining their desire, then perhaps I ought to expand my vision of how much energy I need to commit to respecting their difference(s). Irigaray elaborates in "Teaching How to Meet in Difference" that from such a perspective, "the regulation of energy would come from us, from the development of our desire, and would not be imposed on us by norms external to us" (ibid.). To allow for this development, I, as the teacher, must allow for a student imaginary.

Earlier, I discussed the tenet of the liberatory project which holds that "freedom and rationality are developmental tasks that must be taught and learned" (Alcorn 28). This would seem to justify the composition teacher's role as liberator: if the teacher doesn't instruct the student in the ways of freedom, how will it be learned? Yet Alcorn's words only a few pages later prompt us to wonder whether the move toward liberation and toward conditions that struggle to minimize social suffering can, in fact, be gained through suffering: "If ideologies are bad, they are bad not because some authority says so, but because they make us, or people we care for, suffer . . . [Yet some subjects] would often rather suffer from a bad ideology than suffer from changing their ideology. Ideology can be the bad mother who is better than no mother" (30). What is revealing about this quote is what it suggests about the potentially harmful ideological project of liberation to begin with. In the classroom, the power relationship between the teacher and student can result in the student suffering from the teacher's ideology, especially if the teacher is operating under the libidinal urge to make the classroom ideologically cohesive. Even as students sacrifice their own home discourse out of a desire to cohere with the ideology presented by the teacher, this change is perhaps not justified by the student's own embodied experience. If we compare the student role with that of the female, we might reimagine this continuing work as its own type of fantasy, with troubling conclusions: "Woman, in this sexual imaginary, is only a more or less obliging prop for the enactment of man's fantasies. That she may find pleasure there in that role, by proxy, is possible, even certain. But such pleasure is above all a masochistic prostitution of her body to a desire that is not her own, and it leaves her in a familiar state of dependency upon man" (Irigaray 1985, 25). At worst, students are props for the teacher's fantasy of liberation. At best, students' new libidinal attachments suggest either a dependency on the teacher or a resentment of her or him.

To return to the mother analogy, the liberatory project is perhaps quick to assume that the instructor-mother is better than the student's previous mother; thus, we as teachers rely on the student to adopt us into the vacuum of the ideological mother we have demolished. Again, are freedom and rationality developmental tasks best taught by a teacher who imposes libidinal cohesion upon students? Irigaray might respond by questioning the roles of those involved in such constant work. When it comes to the teacher-student/doctor-patient relationship, we ought to ask whether there is any potential damage from the work being done. Irigaray might point out that after such treatment:

> She will not say what she herself wants; moreover, she does not know, or no longer knows, what she wants. As Freud admits, the beginnings of the sexual life of a girl child are so "obscure," so "faded with time," that one would have to dig down very deep indeed to discover beneath the traces of this civilization, of this history, the vestiges of a more archaic civilization that might give some clue to woman's sexuality. (Ibid.)

The real question becomes whether what we perceive to be a symbolic flexibility that allows for the developmental accomplishment of tasks such as freedom is in fact an imposition of a new set of desires, one that will cause previously known libidinal language to fade. "That extremely ancient civilization would undoubtedly have a different alphabet, a different language," and surely freedom is something that can exist in other languages (ibid.). All languages have a rich degree of complexity, and it does not follow that the developmental task of freedom as it exists in the language of the academy (albeit the postmodern composition instructor's academic language) is necessarily the only language in which freedom exists.

Furthermore, we need to recognize that composition's social agenda has another serious problem; as Irigaray writes: "To date no political theory or political practice has resolved, or sufficiently taken into consideration, this historical problem. [. . . W]omen do not constitute, strictly speaking, a class, and their dispersion among several classes makes their political struggle complex, their demands sometimes contradictory" (32). Here, the parallel between woman and student may be a stretch, insofar as Irigaray speaks of a female struggle that has elements of class consciousness. Students do not all identify with each other in a way that is linked to something as fundamental as gender. Yet, they too are dispersed across complex groups, all in at one end of the power balance within the university classroom. Whether or not they are conscious of themselves as the audience of those demonstrating their academic knowledge power, students are frequently in such a position, and due to a larger social constraint (getting the good grade to get the job to make money, etc.), students will submit "to a culture that oppresses them, uses them, makes of them a medium of exchange, with very little profit to them" (32).

Perhaps the most direct objection we can make against Alcorn is supplied by Irigaray's explicit critique of psychoanalysis in "Psychoanalytic Theory: Another Look" (34–67), which concludes with the charge that psychoanalysis has established a certain destiny for the female and that the "historical determinants of this destiny need to be investigated" (32). Using the female perspective to question the role of the teacher as authority, "we might suspect the phallus of being the contemporary figure of a god jealous of his prerogatives" (ibid.): the teacher cannot allow discourses within the student that have not been sanctioned by her or his own postmodern knowledge. "We might suspect it [this postmodern knowledge] of claiming, on this basis, to be the ultimate meaning of all discourse, the standard of truth and propriety, in particular as regards sex, the signifier, and/or the ultimate signified of all desire, in addition to continuing, as emblem and agent of the patriarchal system, to shore up the name of the father (Father)" (66). Recall Faigley's concern that a process pedagogy resulted in patterns of writing and consequently thinking that reinforced a fiction of coherence. Alcorn's psychoanalytic response may provide us with a more nuanced understanding of subjectivity, but it does not sufficiently question whether a professor should really be trying to shape a student's subjectivity in the first place. Irigaray points out how that assumption is latent within a patriarchal psychoanalytic framework.

On a practical level, perhaps teachers should view the classroom not as a site for liberating students, but as a series of opportunities for multidirectional transformation. As teachers, we must check our expectations of student "liberation"; we must be willing to encounter student language that has been socialized to imitate but that will occasionally speak of desires that we haven't imagined. Our pedagogical theorizing and scholarship, therefore, should reflect a willingness to make space for what we may not already know. As Irigaray insists at the outset of "Teaching How to Meet in Difference," the teaching she advocates "allows the girls and boys to speak, and particularly to say things that they usually keep to themselves or whisper to each other. Of course, the matter is not to deprive them of their secrets but to invite them to speak freely, notably about things that teachers do not want to listen to" (Irigaray 2008, 203).

When I assign an essay asking students to argue for their vision of the way the world should be, I need to remember that their answer will be caught up, not only in their desire to see the world change, but also in their desire to exist in our classroom and my desire to know that they are thinking carefully and lovingly about what change is. I want to listen attentively, making space for any secrets they may want to share. If we seek to achieve the kind of reflection that postmodernity has suggested our subjectivity requires, if we want to investigate our own libidinal urges, we as composition instructors need to be vigilant not to place ourselves in the authorial role of arbiter of discourse and desire. We must leave room for student configurations of desire that are beyond our imaginings and be hesitant about imagining ourselves as liberators lest we predetermine our students' discursive destinies.

Works Cited

Alcorn, Marshall. 1995. "Changing the Subject of Postmodernist Theory: Discourse, Ideology, and Therapy in the Classroom." *Rhetoric Review* 13, no. 2: 331–49.

———. 2002. *Changing the Subject in English Class: Discourse and the Constructions of Desire.* Carbondale: Southern Illinois University Press.

Berlin, James. 1988. "Rhetoric and Ideology in the Writing Class." *College English* 50, no. 5: 477–94.

———. 1991. "Composition and Cultural Studies." In *Composition and Resistance*, edited by C. Mark Hurlbert and Michael Blitz, 47–56. Portsmouth, NH: Boynston/Cook.

———. 1992. "Poststructuralism, Cultural Studies, and the Composition Classroom: Postmodern Theory in Practice." *Rhetoric Review* 11, no. 1: 16–33.

Bruffee, Kenneth. 1984. "Collaborative Learning and the 'Conversation of Mankind.'" *College English* 46, no. 7: 635–52.

Faigley, Lester. 1992. *Fragments of Rationality*. Pittsburgh: University of Pittsburgh Press.

Flower, Jennifer, and John Hayes. 1981. "A Cognitive Process Theory of Writing." *College Composition and Communication* 32, no. 4: 365–87.

Freud, Sigmund. 1916. "Mourning and Melancholia." In *The Standard Edition of the Complete Psychological Works of Sigmund Freud*. Translated by James Strachey, 237–58. London: Hogarth.

Fulkerson, Richard. 2005. "Composition at the Turn of the Twenty-First Century." *College Composition and Communication* 56, no. 4: 654–87.

Irigaray, Luce. 1985. *This Sex Which Is Not One*. Translated by Catherine Porter. Ithaca, NY: Cornell University Press.

———. 2008. "Teaching How to Meet in Difference." In *Luce Irigaray: Teaching*, 203–18. London: Continuum International.

Lyotard, Jean-Francois. 1984. *The Postmodern Condition: A Report on Knowledge*. Translated by Geoff Bennington and Brian Massumi. Minneapolis: University of Minnesota Press.

Building Sexuate Architectures of Sustainability

PEG RAWES

Sexuate Difference and Sustainable Architectural Design

In her preface to *Key Writings* (2004), Irigaray writes that sexuate difference "first articulates nature and culture." Drawing out the ontological significance of the relationships among sex, nature, and culture, she argues that "without working through this relation from the very beginning, we cannot succeed in entering *into relation* with all kinds of other" (my emphasis) (Irigaray 2004, xiv). Alison Stone has usefully described this approach in Irigaray's later work as a "realist essentialism,"[1] in which male and female sex differences are real, naturally existing expressions—independent of an individual's and a society's cultural expressions of sexual difference (Stone 18–19). My discussion here follows Stone's definition in its focus on the complementary significance of the natural and the cultural formation of sexed subjectivities and on the ways in which relationships are formed among women, men, and their respective environments—in particular, the built environment. Sexuate difference embodies our relationship with the built, architectural, and spatiotemporal constitution of the world. In addition, it constitutes our relationships with the natural environment and its resources and phenomena, and it defines the relationship between women and men, as well as their relationships with themselves.

Rather than emphasize architecture's status as a profession that prioritizes unethical and unsustainable architectural design that contributes to global property speculation and economic markets, this discussion focuses on sustainable architectural design, which is composed of *relational* practices between sexuate individuals and cultures, and through which ethical homes, workplaces, villages, towns, and cities can be generated. More specifically, sustainable architectural design is especially significant when it enables *sexuate* relations, spatiotemporal inhabitations, and the well-being of communities whose diverse needs are not met by the majority markets. These ethical forms of design are distinct from technocratic sustainable architectural design, which operates in the global capitalist building industries that dominate the most competitive commercial sectors of the built environment (and produce large-scale, low-quality but high-profit urban regeneration or housing schemes). In these market-led contexts, sustainable green or eco design is therefore also often seen as an extension of their logic of technical efficiency or design improvement; these negative attitudes were also reflected in the decade after the Bruntland Report[2] when the profession's evaluation of sustainability tended to prioritize quantitative "energy efficiency" over the significance of a building's qualitative "ecology" of social and cultural relations. Now, however, awards, such as the American Institute of Architects' annual Top-Ten Green Project Winners, acknowledge both the quantitative improvement to the environment by carbon remediation or free technologies *and the qualitative and social benefits* to the individuals and communities who use the building (American Institute of Architects 2014).

However, strong vested interests in large-scale, commercial, and advanced technological approaches, especially in the growing South East Asian and Middle Eastern markets, are still very active (see, for example, the UAE's investment in low-carbon technologies for its "eco-city," Masdar City).[3] Since the turn of the century, the commercial architectural design profession has consolidated its technological approaches to sustainable development. However, since it is an industry that is also constituted by global capitalism, frequently, when sustainable design improvements are made to the built environment (e.g., the much-celebrated return to the urban park in the global north, such as the High Line in New York), the tension between meeting the vocal interests of the corporate and large-scale social versus the "minor" interests of the local communities still means that sustainable design does not necessarily prioritize the specific needs of those who do not see themselves as the economic beneficiaries or the "majority."

It is therefore important to remind the architectural profession that sexed conceptualizations of sustainability operate with reference to the critical and ontological thinking about environmental and human relations that women's environmental activism and feminist theorization have examined since the 1960s, including Irigaray's critiques of the cultural, political, and ethical formation of women's sexuality and power. Important cultural understandings of sustainable ecological thinking by other feminist philosophers, such as Lorraine Code, are also pertinent here; Code draws attention to the ethical responsibility required to protect existing, and create future, sustainable *relations* in our social, natural, cultural, and built environments:

> Ecological thinking is not simply thinking about ecology or about the environment: it generates revisioned modes of engagement with knowledge, subjectivity, politics, ethics, science, citizenship, and agency, which pervade and reconfigure theory and practice alike. [. . .] *Ecological thinking is about imagining, crafting, articulating, endeavoring to enact principles of ideal cohabitation* (my emphasis). (Code 24)

Unlike the highly technocratic definitions of sustainability that I mentioned earlier, Code's elegant ecological thinking helps to show how feminist conceptualizations of ecological and sustainable relationships address the current overriding focus on large-scale governmental and private industrial investment in market-driven ecotechnologies and sciences (e.g., the still-problematic manufacture of biofuels). Instead, feminist environmental and ecological philosophy recuperate overlooked historical, political, and ethical responses back into contemporary approaches to sustainability—responses that are beneficial not only to the architectural design professions' ethics, but also to the well-being of society as a whole, and the protection of natural environments. Informed by these approaches, architectural sustainability may then manifest the complex interrelationship between culture and nature on the local spatiotemporal scale of everyday domestic and community inhabitations, as well as on global (or planet-aware) scales of environmental relations and communities.

Before examining specific architectural forms of sexuate sustainable design in more detail, I first want to address some of the issues surrounding Irigaray's view of architecture, in order to highlight its value, but also to acknowledge that her writings do not, in themselves, present as rich an understanding of sustainable practices in architectural design as those developed by feminist architects, architectural historians, and theorists. In part, these issues appear to arise because she has not drawn from work already achieved in the discipline which has retrieved and promoted sexed modes of design. This problem is most evident in the essay "How Can We Live Together in a Lasting Way?" (Irigaray 2004, 123–33), in which Irigaray proposes designing the domestic space of the home into two separate spaces of inhabitation: one for the man and the family, and another for the woman and mother. For me, the essay raises questions about Irigaray's understanding of design; I agree that she is correct to question how architectural design creates positive and negative sexuate spatiotemporal relations for women and mothers in the home and to ask how these operate culturally and symbolically, yet I find her proposition of dividing the home into two separate spaces a troubling continuation of a binary spatiotemporal logic. Irigaray's position highlights the gap between her approach and the positive creative work by feminist architectural practitioners over the past forty years to resist reducing architectural practice and experience into simple binary divisions (see, for example, Coleman, Friedman, Hayden, Heynen, Kanes Weisman, and Rendell).[4] By omitting these sustained feminist debates inside the architectural design profession and in its academic communities, Irigaray's argument comes unfortunately close to reinforcing problematic spatial hierarchies and homogeneity that many female *and* male poststructuralist practitioners, theorists, and historians have worked hard to challenge. Irigaray's cultural analysis of geometric subject-object relations remains tied to a still-reductive conceptualization of geometry—a *formal disembodied* procedure generating self-same morphologies, which has been critiqued as universal, modernist, and patriarchal in architecture. Rather than generating new or repressed heterogeneous, spatiotemporal material relations that are present in the "minor" geometries of Spinoza, Bergson, or Nietzsche, Irigaray's binary linguistic "architecture" of girls and boys emphasizes her distance from more subtle arguments about the spatiotemporal forces and relations that operate in critical forms of architectural design (Irigaray 2004, 127–29).[5]

Consequently, because of this proximity to historically reductive binary spatiotemporal architectural thinking, the potential relevance of Irigaray's ontological arguments for sexuate sustainable life and architectural practice remains limited for many *women and men* in the profession who work against dominant forms of deterministic spatiotemporal conceptualizations. However, more positive expressions of sustainable sexuate relations between men and women are evident in her other texts. Examples are her exploration of the social and political architecture of her friendship and work with Renzo Imbeni in *I Love to You: Sketch of a Possible Felicity in History* (1996) and her engagement with Heidegger's and Hölderlin's discussions of dwelling in

The Way of Love, where she develops a poetic psychophysical architectural metaphor of ontological dwelling—a sustainable sexuate *architectural ontology*—in the final essay, "Rebuilding the World" (Irigaray 2002, 137–66).

> Thus, to dwell is, according to Hölderlin, for example, a fundamental trait of the human condition. [. . .] To construct only in order to construct nevertheless does not suffice for dwelling. A cultivation of the living must accompany a building of that which does not grow by itself. For a human, the two do not seem separable. To cultivate human life in its engendering and its growth requires the elaboration of material and spiritual frameworks and constructions. These should not be opposed to the becoming of life, as they have too often been, but provide it with the help indispensable for its blossoming. (144)

This sexuate poetics reflects, much more closely, design practices that develop sexed and poetic, physical and psychological forms of architecture.[6] Irigaray's "Being-Two in Architectural Perspective" also shows a more positive way of thinking about how architecture can generate diverse sexuate modes of dwelling, connecting a poetics of "building" to the design processes and materials involved in architecture: "Building a home must entail a concern for raw or transformed material through projects, technique, and technology. But could an architect build houses for others if he, or she, is not capable of building their self?" (Irigaray 2008, 59). Irigaray's discussions about sustainability and architecture are therefore helpful for showing how the discipline has the capacity to be a creative and critical site of sexuate thinking.

Her critique of negative spatial relations is also still important given the extent of the rise in social inequity and homogeneity to which global capitalist architecture has contributed (perhaps most strongly represented by the ubiquitous spread of the poorly designed developer-led commercial glass and steel tower block). Irigaray's criticism of these toxic expressions of asexuate culture and environmentally negligent forms of unsustainable urban growth is in sympathy with Marxist architectural and urban criticism, which has sought to expose and resist the damaging short-term expansionist aims of global developers and speculative investors.[7] Unsurprisingly, these unsustainable forms of architecture and urbanism often rely upon equally unsustainably commodified technological industries and process, yet they may also use the rhetoric of social sustainability in their claims for positive regeneration but, in fact, seek primarily to maximize their profits and stay competitive in the global market. Writing on sustainable architecture back in the early 2000s, architect Jason McLennan observed how architectural firms may claim that they employ sustainable design in their practices, but this does not amount to a committed and enduring adherence to the principal that sustainable design should "maximize the quality of the built environment, while minimizing or eliminating negative impact to the natural environment" (McLennan 4).

Positive sustainable approaches to reducing carbon emissions in the production and inhabitation of the built environment include locally sourced renewable energy (e.g., thermal, wind, or solar power); materials and labor from local suppliers, or the manufacture of resources close to the building and design site (e.g., recycling local materials, or reducing carbon footprints through the supply of local timber); and using low-energy technologies for reducing the impact of carbon emissions in housing and work buildings (e.g., passive ventilation systems for heating, or the collection and reuse of rain water). However, in the most aggressive developer-led sections of the industry, the continued use of unsustainable manufacturing processes and markets means that, overall, the impact of sustainable design technologies on the production of the built environment remains fundamentally restricted.

Over the past ten years, these imbalances have risen substantially: for example, the increasingly dysfunctional UK housing crisis has exposed the extent to which the built environment is used as a short-term speculative market not just by private investors, but also by governments, at the expense of real social well-being (Rawes 2017). Recent fiscal measures (taxes and financial products, such as buy-to-let mortgages) in the United Kingdom have categorically weighted the benefits in the interest of the large housing developer, private landlord, and speculative investor in short-term profits. In contrast, lack of housing security has become the norm for many across UK society, not just for the most economically in need, but also for the previously secure middle classes (e.g. families who rent, young professionals, the elderly). There is also a chronic shortage in new homes being built, and, most recently, the government withdrew its commitment to zero-carbon standards on new homes.[8]

Yet sexuate definitions of architectural design do also exist in the discipline. Practiced by women and men, these approaches are evidence of the complex qualitative *and* sexuate nurturing of environmental and cultural sustainability for communities in the global north and south. In the last section of this chapter, I will present two examples of architectural design practice showing how Irigaray's theories of sexuate life and contemporary architectural practices are reflected in, and can enable, real sexuate sustainability, where relations between women, men, and their environment are nurtured by design that is sympathetic to Irigaray's advocacy of building sustainable sexuate life.

A Critique of Technology

While approaches to sustainable architecture have become more widespread over the past twenty years, the commercial profession still resists acknowledging its imbrication with technocratic scales of industrial interest and continues to overlook the value of environmental debates and critiques (including feminist criticisms) which are skeptical about over-reliance upon technological solutions for the long-term survival of the planet's ecology and resources. In this context, Irigaray's 1986 essay on nuclear power remains an interesting example of a sexed environmental critique that has a renewed pertinence today, given our focus on efficient post-oil, low-carbon resources and technologies. Written almost thirty years ago in response to the Chernobyl accident, *Thinking the Difference* (1994) is one of Irigaray's strongest critiques of advanced positivist science and technology. Drawing partly from her own sexuate political collaboration with the Italian Communist Party (PCI) in Bologna, she explores the relationship between sustainable and unsustainable forms of energy in "A Chance to Live," the first essay of the book. She examines how cultures of destructive technology, as manifested in the Chernobyl nuclear disaster, fundamentally alter the natural cycles of energy distribution in the environment and how they "neutralize" the value of sexuate difference for understanding environmental relations (Irigaray 1994, 7–8).[9]

Revisiting her earlier critiques of energy in Freud's theorization of desire in *Speculum* (1985) and *An Ethics of Sexual Difference* (1993), Irigaray argues that Freud's conceptualization of sexual drives operates from a "repetitive, explosive, non-evolutive" economy of energy that negates the reality that female sexuality expresses a "dissipative" form of energy (Irigaray 1994, 20). Although her earlier essay, "The Mechanics of Fluids," engages with the radical physicist Ilya Prigogine's theory of "dissipatory" structures (Irigaray 1985, 124), here her critique of energy is developed through an interrogation of sexed energetic drives in psychoanalysis. She questions Freud's sublimation of the senses to economies of singularity and equivalence that deny the distinctions among skin, solid, or fluid matter, to highlight how women's bodies and sexual energy involve distinctly *other* modes of psychic and material power that are not directed towards singular outcomes: "[W] omen do not have the same relationship to entropy, to homeostasis, to release. Their internal regulation is much stronger, and it maintains them in a constant, irreversible process of growth. This is not necessarily negative; it is not necessarily a process of degeneration or accumulation" (Irigaray 1994, 25). Thus, for Irigaray, a sexuate form of energy is not dependent upon repetitive cycles of saturation and expenditure. It is composed of constantly changing, durational, and incremental relations and thresholds that are distinct forms from the traditional physical, thermodynamic model of energy production.[10] Her examination of the correlation between sustainability and women's low-impact energy and psychophysical nature versus a male psychophysical tendency toward unsustainable relations highlights how sustainable relations between human culture and the environment are also dependent upon energetic durations, not guaranteed by the highly unstable principles of energy consumption and expenditure that underpin advanced technologies such as nuclear power. Her critique questions the belief that sustainable energetic relations can be defined only through technoscientific disciplines. But her argument also reflects the deep-seated contemporary anxiety about the dangers of investing in high-risk nuclear energy versus the benefits of low-energy provision and incremental approaches to designing the built environment that low-risk sustainable design makes possible. Here, then, Irigaray's poetic, sustainable sexuate human relations and energies also connect with women and men in the built environment professions who are critical of the global reliance upon unstable energy sources.

When taken on its own, however, Irigaray's focus on the destructive impulse of modern technology raises difficult questions for the profession—in particular, her rejection of physical models of thermodynamics. This issue is especially problematic for discussions of sustainability because understanding thermodynamic principles of energy conservation is still necessary to environmental criticism, education, and activism. For the time being, science still has a role to play in contributing towards *changing* our behaviors in energy use and consumption, and towards *developing* new ethical ecotechnologies (e.g., for improving renewable energy-source capture technologies, such as wave and solar power or thermal heat-pumps). So, although Irigaray is tolerant of some modern building technologies, it remains questionable whether she fully accepts the viability of ethically produced advanced ecotechnologies for addressing the environmental impact of the built environment.

Overall, Irigaray's sustained opposition to science and technology suggests that she would be unlikely to modify her position so far as to consider ways in which advanced ecotechnologies could contribute towards enabling sexuate architectural sustainability. However, if we are to realize genuine sustainable change, it is unwise to completely discount the possible benefits of ethical forms of ecotechnology from our approaches to sustainable design. In addition, architectural design is a discipline within the building industry that trains many women (50 percent of British and US architecture students are women); this means that educators and architects have a responsibility to create sexuate futures for female architectural students and to enable women in the profession to build ethical, poetic, and technologically sustainable designs. This is all the more important since surveys also show that the number of women who are in the profession in the United Kingdom is still below 30 percent.[11] Nevertheless, Irigaray's technological skepticism reminds us that the development of any technology can only generate enduring sexuate sustainable relations through a commitment to sexuate cultures.

Sexuate Architectures of Sustainability

Sustainable architectural design theory and practice are also fruitful for extending Irigaray's philosophy of sustainability when it promotes the importance of ontological thinking for developing enduring modes of sustainable design. American architect Jason McLennan and British product designer Stuart Walker are examples of designers who have addressed sustainability in relation to ontological considerations. Each is skeptical of the uncritical reliance upon myths of progressive technological development in modern Western culture; each engages with ecological thinking developed by the modern environmental movement, and each endorses critiques of disembodied technologies. Both designers also consider the value of enduring cross-cultural traditions in sustainability—for example, in their rejection of unnecessary consumption and in their reminders that sustainability principles are often integral to much vernacular and regionally specific architecture that uses local climatic and environmental factors as design constituents (e.g., rammed earth, adobe, or stone dwellings designed to absorb and conserve solar energy in climates with extreme temperature fluctuations).

Stuart Walker's theory of sustainable design highlights the ethical and environmental costs if we do not change our behaviors and relationships with material culture and the natural environment. He refers to traditional transcultural knowledges that preview our now-acute awareness that we are likely to be "the cause of our own destruction" (Walker 17). He observes that sustainability discourses from the 1960s and early 1970s social activism and protest movements (including feminism and environmentalism) are akin to powerful political myths that capture both, on the one hand, "the fragility of the planet and, on the other hand, social inequalities and human rights" issues of justice (21). Sustainable design therefore offers us the potential to express embodied and poetic ways of being that oppose the desire for, and the consequent dependence upon, conspicuous consumption, disembodied scientific invention, and technological commodification. Jason McLennan's *Philosophy of Sustainable Design: The Future of Architecture* charts the evolution of a sustainable design philosophy, which,

> unlike some philosophies, does not have one author, nor a divine source, and is continuing to develop and evolve. [. . .] It recognizes that we are on a path towards a sustainable future, and that as much as some of us would like it to be different, we cannot instantly get there because of perceived barriers that may as well be real, and also because of some very significant economic, political, religious, and technological barriers. (McLennan 37)

He identifies six key principles that have been developed by sustainability designers and environmentalist activists since the 1960s: these include "respect for" (1) natural systems, (2) "human vitality," (3) ecosystems, (4) "cycles of life," (5) energy and natural resources, and (6) holistic processes (38). In addition, McLennan promotes the value of older cross-cultural technologies that disrupt our reliance upon high energy consumption and production cycles (for example, the use of straw bales or rammed earth as building materials), thereby suggesting ways in which low-energy sustainable modes of designing and building may also be commensurate alternatives for Irigaray's critique of high-risk modern technologies.

For these designers, sustainable thinking is therefore realized in the physical manufacture of the artifact; in the cultural, political, and economic relations that construct the design; in its patterns of use and occupation; and in its duration within the society and environment in which it exists. Sustainable design is an ontological matter, not just a technocratic response to environmental crises in the modern world. However, Walker and McLennan remain silent about the sexuate nature of sustainable design. But, as we shall see, these ontologies do exist in, for example, an architectural practice that has worked with communities in Paris, Dakar, Senegal, and a University in Hale County, Alabama. Each demonstrates ways in which poetic sustainable architectural design is produced, reflecting Walker and McLennan's design ethics and Irigaray's sustainable sexuate ontology.

Over the past fifteen years, architect Doina Petrescu's collaborative practice, Atelier d'Architecture Autogérée (AAA, or Studio for Self-Managed Architecture), has brought together architects, artists, urban planners, landscape designers, sociologists, students, and residents from local communities to develop "architecture [that] is at the same time political and poetic, as it aims above all to 'create relationships between worlds' " (Petrescu 60). These architectural projects in France, Germany, Belgium, and the United Kingdom have taken everyday activities—gardening, cooking, conversation—as social architectures, which can then be used by local residents for transforming local urban spaces into shared self-managed architectures of participation. The Parisian La Chappelle "ECObox" projects of 2001 and 2006 developed locally run and locally sourced recycled gardens in which locals curated activities that expressed the "biodiversity" of the local population (www.urbantactics.org). In 2004, in collaboration with women from REFDAF (*Réseau des femmes pour un développement durable en Afrique* [Women's Network for Sustainable Development in Africa]) and students from the University of Sheffield, United Kingdom, where she teaches, Petrescu developed a self-build workshop for Senegalese women. Local Dakar women were introduced to building methods that they could use to build a City of Women (*Cité des femmes*) in Keur Massar, Dakar (Réseau 2009), and to build prototype walls from local recycled materials, such as sand bags and tires.

Most recently, since 2008, AAA has collaborated with the local authority and communities in the northern-Parisian suburb of Colombes to develop a large environmental infrastructure, titled "R-Urban." This network of "resilient" social, economic, and technological ecologies or infrastructures has resulted in the design of an urban microfarm and market, Agrocité (figure 1, pg. 310), an eco community center that uses low-carbon technologies to provide self-run community support services, including workshops (such as the recycling workshop seen in figure 2, pg. 310), and advisory groups for the local population: architectural ecologies that are not defined by short-term economic gain but that respond to the community's needs and invest in environmental design processes that are managed by the community itself.[12]

Figure 1. Agrocité, R-Urban, 2015: © AAA.

Figure 2. Recyclab, R-Urban, 2015: © AAA.

Since its inauguration by architect Sam Mockbee in the 1990s, and now recently under the leadership of Andrew Freear, Auburn University School of Architecture's Rural Studio at Newburn, Hale County, Alabama, provides an architectural education that prioritizes the physical and social fabrication of low-energy building techniques for local low-income communities in Alabama (Freear, Berthel, and Dean 2014; www.ruralstudio.org/). Students learn through working together in teams designing and building homes and projects for specific members of the community. Their training involves them on-site in live projects managing the design and fabrication processes in consultation with clients, so that low-cost but innovative buildings use locally sourced and recycled materials, including straw bales, license plates, tires, carpets, or local cedar and round woods. Over the past twenty years, and through their "20K-House Program" (Freear, Berthel, and Dean 24), low-income families have been given the opportunity to live in bespoke homes that meet their specific needs rather than the debt-laden option of being housed in unsustainable trailer homes that, because of the region's high humidity, can have life spans of as little as fifteen years, which often means that families are paying for the trailers long after they have begun to deteriorate beyond adequate repair.[13]

Christine's house, in the town of Mason's Bend, was built over a period of two years by two final-year students during 2004 and 2005 (figure 3 below).

Figure 3. Christine's House 2005, View of Exterior with Wind Tower: © Tim Hursley and Rural Studio.

With its walls constructed from "bricks" made of newspaper and local earth, it modifies rammed-earth adobe building techniques and, although needing modification to achieve efficient heating, its tower is designed using passive cooling systems derived from sub-Saharan and Middle Eastern regions (Freear, Berthel, and Dean 76). Figure 4 (below) shows the "clubhouse" for girls and boys in the town of Akron, Alabama, in 2007. Owned by the city, the club was designed to provide educational studios and a covered basketball court. Students raised funds and developed activity programs for the club. The cover for the court was built using a "lamella" construction technique, which was also used in India in the modern cardboard tube architecture of Japanese architect Shigeru Ban and used historically by Palladio (Freear, Berthel, and Dean 120).

Although not run on the principle of sexuate sustainability, this community-based educational program nevertheless provides a unique and important example of sustainable educational and community design in an economically deprived region of the United States. Both female and male students work in teams to design and build the houses, and social connections are established between the architectural community and local

Figure 4. Akron Boys and Girls Club 2007, Interior Shot with Children Playing Basketball: © Tim Hursley and Rural Studio.

residents in the region. This real-time, practice-based architectural education is also in dramatic contrast to traditional architectural studio-based academic environments, which can often be far removed from the actual communities and environments where buildings exist in the world.

These examples of critical and ecologically responsible architectural practices contribute to an evolving sustainable design ontology. Constituted by complex and dynamic relations among human, material, structural, spatiotemporal, cultural, political, and economic factors, AAA and Rural Studio show how architecture is always created within specific globally and locally aware environmental and cultural relations. Critical and ecological forms of architectural design can create spaces for sexuate living, and their material, aesthetic, and psychic expressions of sustainability offer important insights about how Irigaray's ontology of sexuate sustainability can be enriched within interdisciplinary contexts. Sustainable architectural design is therefore the creation of positive enduring modes of living between women and men, of inventing or repurposing techniques that develop ethical physical relationships among human dwellings, the protection of the environment, and natural resources.

Notes

The author and editor thank Bloomsbury Publishing Plc. for permission to reprint a short extract from an earlier publication of Peg Rawes, "Biopolitical Ecological Poetics," chapter 1 of *Poetic Biopolitics: Practices of Relation in Architecture and the Arts*, edited by Peg Rawes, Timothy Mathews and Stephen Loo. London: I.B. Tauris, an imprint of Bloomsbury Publishing Plc., 2016.

1. Stone writes: "Realist essentialism, then, can [. . .] be expressed as the view that natural differences exist, prior to our cultural activities" (see Stone 18–19).

2. The 1987 UN-commissioned Bruntland report defined sustainable development as that which "meets the needs of the present without compromising the ability of future generations to meet their own needs." Its concept of "needs" connects humanitarian issues of poverty with "limitations imposed by the state of technology and social organization" with regard to "the environment's ability to meet present and future needs" (Bruntland 1987; see also Adams 2006.) During the 1990s, the commercial sector tended to address these issues with reference to positivist technological rhetoric. In the past fifteen years, however, charities and practices that do not use such technocratic approaches have also developed, including Architecture for Humanity (US) (although recently closed and criticized for its use of volun-

teers), Lacaton and Vassal (France), Estudio Teddy Cruz (USA), and the architects mentioned in this chapter. McDonough and Braungart (2002) have also made the case for creative large-scale and low-energy approaches to technology and recycling.

3. Master planned by Foster and Partners, Masdar City has claimed to be one of the first entirely low-carbon, car-free cities, powered entirely by renewable energies, including solar power (BBC News 2015).

4. For further feminist critiques of architectural history, theory, and design, see Coleman, et al. 1996; Hayden 2002; Friedman 1988; Heynen, et al. 2005; Kanes Weisman, et al. 1996; and Rendell 2000 and 2010.

5. For further discussions of "embodied geometry" in Western philosophy, see Rawes 2008. See Rawes 2007 for discussions of more productive spatiotemporal analyses and figures in Irigaray's work, especially in *Speculum of the Other Woman, Marine Lover of Fredrich Nietzsche,* and *This Sex Which Is Not One.*

6. For further discussion of sexed poetics in architectural design, see, for example, Rendell 2006, Rawes 2013, and Rawes et al. 2015b.

7. Marxist critiques of the links between architecture and capitalism include Harvey 2006 and Jameson 1991.

8. The UK government's commitment to sustainability remains in place insofar as one of its new ecotowns, Bicester, northwest of London, has gone on-site (see Eco-Bicester 2014). However, this is seen as a project that is strongly driven by short-term interests in construction industry jobs and a political response to the chronic shortage of new-built housing in the United Kingdom.

9. Stone discusses Irigaray's analysis of the relationship between male sexuality and destructive tendencies: "Irigaray's analysis of male sexuality implies that it generates practices and technologies which operate detrimentally to other elements of male embodiment. It appears that, for Irigaray, male corporeality turns against itself, some of this corporeality perpetrating violence against others" (Stone 136–37).

10. Paradoxically, although utterly opposed to Irigaray's critique of nuclear power and energy, James Lovelock's discussion of the "conservation" of thermodynamic energy in renewable energy resources like wind and solar power has striking parallels to Irigaray's emphasis on a dissipative distribution of energy; for example, he discusses how heat is conserved, not lost, in the absorption of solar energy by ice and water (Lovelock 80–81).

11. Numbers of women in the United Kingdom in the profession have increased in recent years (Mark 2015); however, there are still many examples of seriously poor equal rights employment practices (Chevin 2013).

12. Despite the success of this project and its benefit to its local communities, local authority withdrew support from the AAA project in favor of developing a parking garage. The practice generated an international petition to oppose the decision.

13. This information came from a lecture given by Andrew Freear, director, Rural Studio, at the Bartlett School of Architecture UCL, London, December 14, 2005.

Works Cited

Adams, William M. 2006. *The Future of Sustainability: Re-thinking Environment and Development in the Twenty-First Century*. Report of the World Conservation Union (IUCN). http://cmsdata.iucn.org/downloads/iucn_future_of_sustanability.pdf.

The American Institute of Architects (AIA). 2014. "AIA Committee on the Environment Top Ten Projects," http://www.aiatopten.org/taxonomy/term/9.

Atelier d'Architecture Autogérée (AAA). http://www.urbantactics.org/projects/projects.html (accessed August 3, 2015); http://r-urban.net/blog/projects/ (accessed August 3, 2015).

BBC News. April 3, 2015. "Working Lives UAE: Business Leader." http://www.bbc.co.uk/news/world-middle-east-31986648. Site no longer active.

Bruntland Report. 1987. *Our Common Future, Report of the World Commission on Environment and Development, World Commission on Environment and Development.*

Chevin, Denise. December 2, 2013. "Female Architects Face the Mother of All Inequality Problems." In *Building Design*, http://www.bdonline.co.uk/female-architects-face-the-mother-of-all-inequality-problems/5064239.article.

Code, Lorraine. 2006. *Ecological Thinking: The Politics of Epistemic Location*. Oxford: Oxford University Press.

Coleman, Debra, Elizabeth Danze, and Carole Henderson. 1996. *Architecture and Feminism*. New York: Princeton Architectural Press.

Eco-Bicester. 2014. "What Is an Eco-Town?" http://www.ecobicester.org.uk/cms/content/what-eco-town#.VcDjCzBViko.

Freear, Andrew, Ethel Berthel, and Andrea Oppenheimer Dean. 2014. *Rural Studio at Twenty: Designing and Building in Hale County, Alabama*. New York: Princeton Architectural Press.

Friedman, Alice T. 1988. *Women and the Making of the Modern House: A Social and Architectural History*. New York: Abrams.

Harvey, David. 1996. *Spaces of Global Capitalism*. London: Verso.

Hayden, Dolores. 2002. *Redesigning the American Dream: The Future of Housing, Work, and Family Life*, New York: London: W. W. Norton.

Heynen, Hilde, and Gülsüm Baydar, eds. 2005. *Negotiating Domesticity: Spatial Productions of Gender in Modern Architecture*, London: New York: Routledge.

Irigaray, Luce. 1985. *This Sex Which Is Not One*. Translated by Catherine Porter with Carolyn Burke. Ithaca: NY: Cornell University Press, 1977.

———. 1994. *Thinking the Difference: For a Peaceful Revolution*. Translated by Karin Montin. London, New York: Continuum-Routledge, 1989.

———. 2002. *The Way of Love*. Translated by Heidi Bostic and Stephen Pluháček. London, New York: Continuum.

———. 2008. *Conversations*. London, New York: Continuum.

Jameson, Fredric. 1991. *Postmodernism, or, the Cultural Logic of Late Capitalism*. London: Verso.

Kanes Weisman, Leslie, Diana Agrest, and Patricia Conway. 1996. *The Sex of Architecture*. New York: Harry N. Abrams.

Lovelock, James. 2009. *The Vanishing Face of Gaia: A Final Warning*. London, New York: Allen Lane.

Mark, Laura. June 4, 2015. "Number of Women Architects on the Rise in AJ120 firms," *The Architects' Journal*. http://www.architectsjournal.co.uk/home/events/number-of-female-architects-on-the-rise-in-aj120-firms/8684222.article.

McDonough, William, and Braungart, Michael. 2002. *Cradle to Cradle. Remaking the Way We Make Things*. New York: North Point.

McLennan, Jason. 2004. *The Philosophy of Sustainable Design: The Future of Architecture*. Kansas City: Ecotone.

Petrescu, Doina. "How to Make a Community as well as the Space for It." *Re-public: Re-imagining Democracy*, http://www.re-public.gr/en/?p=60 (accessed July 14, 2009).

Rawes, Peg. 2007. *Irigaray for Architects*. New York, London: Routledge.

———. 2008. *Space, Geometry and Aesthetics: Through Kant and towards Deleuze*. Basingstoke: Palgrave Macmillan.

———, ed. 2013. *Relational Architectural Ecologies: Architecture, Nature and Subjectivity*. New York, London: Routledge.

———, Tim Mathews, and Stephen Loo, eds. 2016. *Poetic Biopolitics: Relational Practices in Architecture and the Arts*. London: IB Tauris.

———. 2017. "Housing Biopolitics and Care." In *Critical and Clinical Cartographies: Architecture, Robotics, Medicine, Philosophy*, edited by Andrej Radman and Heidi Sohn. Edinburgh: Edinburgh University Press.

Réseau des femmes pour le développement durable en Afrique (REFDAF). 2004. http://www.refdaf.org/-L-atelier-de-construction-.html.

Rendell, Jane, Barbara Penner, and Iain Borden. 2000. *Gender Space Architecture: An Interdisciplinary Introduction*. London, New York: Routledge.

———. 2006. *Art and Architecture: A Place Between*. London: I. B. Taurus.

———. 2010. *Site-Writing: The Architecture of Art Criticism*. London, New York: Routledge, 2010.

Rural Studio. http://www.ruralstudio.org/.

Stone, Alison. 2006. *Luce Irigaray and the Philosophy of Sexual Difference*, Cambridge: New York: Cambridge University Press.

Walker, Stuart. 2006. *Sustainable by Design: Explorations in Theory and Practice*. London: Earthscan.

Habitats for Desire

Sculptural Gestures toward Sexuate Living

BRITT-MARIE SCHILLER

> Art has not only [. . .] to express or to give an image of reality, but to create another reality, by transforming the real.
>
> —Luce Irigaray 2004, 98

Architecture can be said to be an extension of the body. Although Louise Bourgeois is not an architect, she invokes the language of architecturality in her art (Bal 2001), and a sense of habitat renders her drawings and sculptures architectural. Mimicking the domestication of the female body, Bourgeois's drawing *Femme-maison* helps us to explore answers to Luce Irigaray's question "How can we live together without eradicating oneself or the other?" (Irigaray 2004, 124).

The drawing *Femme-maison* (1946–1947) shows a hybrid of architecture and the human body (Morris 13), sexed female. Like some overwhelmed and engulfed caryatid, a woman is subsumed under the house that encloses her as she holds it up. The building is diminutive, like a doll's house, and the woman's body accommodates the structure that both shelters and imprisons her. It is a house that functions to make her forget or lose her own identity (Irigaray 2004, 124). A tiny arm is raised in a gesture of "help!" or "hello!," and a bigger arm dangles from the other side, which, combined with "the simple graphic style, the scale of this figure, and the incongruous juxtaposition of the two hands, a little one and a big one, suggests a mother-daughter relationship" (Nixon 67). She who inhabits this house is infantilized, her thinking domesticated, her voice mute. This housewife's upper lips are sealed, so she cannot articulate her world, her experience, or her desire; she seems a displacement of the little mermaid whose (genital) lips are sealed shut (Tseelon 1995). This living arrangement appears to eradicate her. In this house, living together might be seen as "assimilated to a fusion," as Irigaray puts it, "a confusion of people imagined as intimacy or proximity" (Irigaray 2004, 131). Although this is not necessarily indicated by an external façade, Irigaray claims that those who design standard housing are "primarily concerned with subsistence: shelter, recuperation through eating and sleeping, provision of basic hygiene" (123). In such a typical house, there is no space for flourishing or becoming, only for sustenance and needs. If space is a metaphor for desire (Kristeva 252), that space is collapsed here; this is not a habitat for desire, but rather a dwelling that suffocates vitality.

In order to think about a living arrangement where it might be possible to live together and keep desire alive, a cohabitation that might safeguard sexual difference, I draw on two sculptures that I find evocative in imagining and articulating how to cultivate sexuate living—living with respect for sexual difference. Richard Serra's *Joe* (1999) and Louise Bourgeois's *Spider* (1997) embody, respectively, male and female sexual specificity, while also suggesting spaces for sexuate living. In the argument that follows, I label a framework rooted in the morphology of the female body a "labial framework," and I offer an alternative to a phallic framework that I call "permeable phallicism" (see below and also Schiller 2012). Louise Bourgeois's *Spider* is a gesture toward a female space of sexual difference, a labial territory protected by a spider, and Richard Serra's *Joe* can be seen as an artistic gesture toward a male internal space grounded in a framework/an imaginary of permeable phallicism (Schiller 2010). In answer to Irigaray's question, "Is not art a means of creating reality and not only of reproducing it?" (Irigaray 2004, 97), I suggest that these two sculptures, Bourgeois's cell and Serra's torqued spiral, are expressive of what *might be* rather than merely reproducing what *is.* Through their architectural scale, both sculptures evoke habitats and illustrate Irigaray's ideal of sexuate living without eradicating the self or allowing it to be eradicated.

Becoming a Subject of Her Own Desire

Simone de Beauvoir famously wrote: "One is not born, but rather becomes, a woman" (Beauvoir 249). In a somewhat similar vein, Freud declared the interest of psychoanalysis to be *not* to describe what a woman is, but rather how a child develops into a woman (Freud 1933, 116). He takes his model for gender differences from his perception of biology: male sex cells are actively mobile and search out the female ovum, which is immobile and passively waiting (114). Guided by what Irigaray calls sexual *indifference* (Irigaray 1985b, 76), he proclaims that "the little girl is a little man" (Freud 1933, 118), with aggressive impulses, which, Freud says, "leave nothing to be desired in the way of abundance and violence" (ibid.). Anatomy is, for Freud, destiny, and the destiny of "normal femininity" is the recognition of being deprived of a penis—castrated. This recognition leads to a repudiation of the mother, who not only gave birth to a penisless creature, but who is, herself, without a penis. This lack results, according to Freud, in her being "debased in value for girls, boys, and men" (127). Since both sexes are here organized around phallicism, sexual difference collapses into one conceptual framework, one imaginary—the phallic. Within this framework, femaleness is characterized either as non-phallic or as inadequately phallic. *Femme-maison* captures this woman, already eradicated, without her own desire or subjectivity, living subsumed under her habitat.

Irigaray has claimed that playing with mimesis challenges a subordinate position as it begins to undermine it by repeating the ideas elaborated or manifested through a male imaginary, "so as to make 'visible' by a playful repetition, what was supposed to remain invisible" (Irigaray 1985a, 76). In assuming the feminine role deliberately, mimicry "converts a form of subordination into an affirmation, and thus begins to thwart it" (ibid.). In *Femme-maison*, Bourgeois repeats the living arrangement wherein a woman is domesticated and eradicated, so as to make visible her subordination and thereby challenge it. The houses in the *Femme-maison* series are square, nearly hostile (Bal 2001), with the female body semitransfigured into a habitat of which someone else is master. *Femme-maison*, a woman-house. Without the possessive particle "*de*," as in *femme de foyer* (housewife), or more literally in this context, *femme de maison*, the passive construction changes into active, the object to subject, thus converting a form of subordination into affirmation. As Irigaray puts it, "To play with mimesis is thus, for a woman, to try to recover the place of her exploitation by discourse, without allowing herself to be simply reduced to it" (Irigaray 1985a, 76). It is a way of drawing attention to, and making visible, the phallic imaginary.

Irigaray provocatively writes, "By our lips we are women!" (209–10). The lips of the mouth and the lips of the genitals make for a felicitous doubling of sexuality and speech for representing female desire and subjectivity. Since lips are rooted in the morphology of the female body—that is, in the experiences of female anatomy, not the anatomy "itself"—I propose that a *labial framework* offers a powerful representation of female desire and subjectivity. Lips are inherently double, irreducible to one or to the penis; thus, a labial representation is irreducible to a phallic imaginary (Schiller 2012). Lips capture an openness, a horizontality, a threshold between the inner and the outer, and a passage for speaking. Irigaray focuses on the transition, the interval, as a space occupied by desire. Lips do not assimilate, reduce, or swallow up unless they are reduced to a means of consumption or utility. Lips offer a shape of welcome, but do not assimilate. They are gathered, without suture, and remain half open. The doubling of lips suggests a plurality in the speaking subject, a heterogeneity that forms a whole without being "congealed in reproductions" (Irigaray 1985a, 216). Several ways of speaking resound between our lips. A labial framework offers a powerful female imaginary for representing a female subjectivity (Schiller 2012), and a shape of welcome to sexuate living.

According to Freud, the first erotic stirrings are labial. In noting the pleasure and satisfaction a child finds "by sucking rhythmically at some part of the skin or mucous membrane," he locates the origin of a psychosexual drive in the lips (Freud 1905, 181). Freud continues in what I consider a labial mode: "It was the child's first and most vital activity, his sucking at his mother's breasts, or at substitutes for it, that must have familiarized him with this pleasure. The child's lips, in our view, behave like an erotogenic zone, and no doubt stimulation by the warm flow of milk is the cause of the pleasurable sensation" (181). If he is correct, it might be that an amplification of pleasure in the swelling, moistening folds of the genital labia unfolds a sexual pleasure that continues in a girl's experience, while the first labial erotic stirrings diminish in a boy's. Within the traditional, phallic representation of desire, the sexual drive aims to release its tension and return to a state of equilibrium. This phallic framework has captured the essence of the boy's experience, while it has made the girl's experience appear diffuse and unorganized. Within a theoretical framework that offers a different mode of representation, female sexuality can be articulated as a matrix of erotic sensations that circulate in the body in waves of swelling wet mucous engorgements (Schiller 2012). As Simone de Beauvoir notes, the male organ is "simple and neat as a finger," while the female is "concealed, mucous, and humid" (Beauvoir 1970, 362). She adds, "Man gets 'stiff,' but woman gets 'wet' " (369).

Thinking in terms of permeability and fluidity, Irigaray conceptualizes the lips as a "threshold that gives access to the *mucous*" (Irigaray

1993, 18). A threshold is a limit between inside and outside, a *limen* (fr. Latin). Liminality, in turn, is a space between precedent and possibility (Turner 1974), between the familiar and the unknown, wherein paradigms can be reimagined and rethought. Akin to a transitional space, a liminal space invites thinking *about* the imaginary rather than being thought *by* it. As a transitional space, an interval, a half-open space, the threshold of the lips is stranger to dichotomy and opposition (Irigaray 1993, 18). The threshold is the point of access to the mucous and affirms otherness while protecting it (Irigaray 1996). The mucous lends itself to representations of the unthought and the nontheorized (Whitford 1991), and Irigaray claims that "no thinking about sexual difference that would not be traditionally hierarchical is possible without thinking through the mucous" (Irigaray 1993, 110). Mucous has no permanence, no fixed form, but it always leaves a trace. It is *incontournable* (Irigaray 1985b), neither simply solid, nor simply fluid. It is interior, experienced from within, as cells are. Although Louise Bourgeois's *Spider* does not obviously evoke a mucous space, it is a cell, and the spider surrounding the cell creates an interval, a fluid threshold.

From 1986 to 1998, Bourgeois made a series of roomlike sculptures she called *Cells*, many constructed of materials from demolished houses. While the *Femme-maison* series portrays the exterior of buildings, the *Cells* exhibit mostly interior scenes evoking the interiority of cells, inside the body, inside prisons, inside monasteries. Bourgeois's series of *Cells*, connected by architecturality, can be read as gestures toward different organizations of space. In particular, *Spider* makes a sculptural-architectural gesture toward a female sexuate space, an autonomous territory protected by the spider. Cells, like lips and apartments, are contiguous and make us conscious of limits. In an interview, Bourgeois says that cells can be communist cells, prison cells, and "especially the cells of our blood . . . little entities that are next to each other and are different from each other" (in Morris, 71). A cell is akin to a closet, the closet that as a queer space is both a prison and a safe space. Elizabeth Grosz suggests that gay communities have extended the closet to enclose spaces for the generation of subcultures, for the embodiment of a heterocentric community, spaces defined by sexual pleasure (Grosz, 9). Could one think of extending the cell as a space of sexual difference for the generation of a labial culture and sexuate living?

Spider is a round cage made of woven steel, measuring 4.5 meters in diameter and 5 meters in height. The giant spider surrounding the cell confounds inside and outside, as a porch or a portico does. While the legs, because of their scale, stand like seven columns around the cell and cover the roof, the spider is at the same time inside the cell. A sac of eggs, part of the spider's body, is suspended from the middle of the ceiling, open to let the eggs drop into the space of the cell, which is clearly sexed female. The sac is made of the same woven steel as the cell, which makes it both a part of the spider's body and an outside container. If you enter this work of art, walking between the giant legs that guard the cell, you find yourself inside the spider's body and outside the cage. The tension is increased by the half-open door making a welcoming gesture—as do lips—although you are not allowed to enter. You are at once invited in and refused entry, a quasiparticipant (Potts 2008). The spider and the cell cannot be separated in this rejection of dichotomies. Body and habitat perform a work of art that gestures toward an architecture sexed female.

While you are bodily engaged as viewer/participant, and refused entry, you are also invited to wonder. There are mysteries to explore in this house, which is not a home. The objects do not fill daily needs, nor do they fill the space. Placed on or leaning against the walls, the objects contribute to opening up space, as if to suggest a different mode of habitation, one of desire. The chair is empty, the door left ajar, and a key dangles inside, out of reach. The walls are porous, the whole structure permeable, more holes than material. You become a voyeur, a specular invader of this space (264). As if to underscore this, two hollowed-out marrowbones, suggestive of a pair of binoculars, are stuck into the wired mesh. You look at remnants and fragments—an old discarded perfume bottle, three glass jars placed upside down, a pocket watch, a tiny locket, some medals, a number of tapestry fragments. Fragments are the elements that a restorer works with, that the archeologist seeks and tries to make sense of, as does the dreamer (Bal 78). The fragments in the cell, however, resist restoration or unification into some whole.

Cellular architecture embodies tensions—of confinement and refuge, of separation and solitude, of health and disease. Cells exist next to, yet apart from one another. Irigaray suggests that in sexuate living, the activity of residing is done in apart-ments, separate spaces structured by sexuate specificity (Irigaray 2004, 126). In these spaces, vitality and desire can be awakened by differences, open for becoming and not merely for needs and sustenance (130), thus rehabilitating what Irigaray calls a female "homelessness," the lack of an adequate language to "house" women (Irigaray 1993, 126–28). *Spider* gestures toward a cellular architecture that can be imagined as labially organized. The porous walls of the cell here resonate with the tentative and open nature of articulating a female subjectivity within a labial framework, as well as a rejection of splitting and dichotomizing (Schiller

2012). "We must center the house starting from the desire of each one and the relationship between them. This requires at least a double centering: the dwelling of her and the dwelling of him" (Irigaray 2004, 100). Living together has all too often been a fusion, a confusion, imagined as intimacy (131). The cell makes a gesture toward a female space for residing, rehabilitating female homelessness.

The spider cannot be separated from the cell. It surrounds the cell, is the cell. The spider's legs create and protect a space, like a porch that wraps around a house, neither interior nor exterior, like a threshold, a porous welcoming space. The porch is inside the columns of the spider's legs yet outside the cell. It seems to serve the double function of providing a space for cultivating dialogues as well as a space that protects the internal cell, safeguarding the difference between two subjects and preventing their collapse into one subject and one object. The columned porch is like the intermediate terrain that Irigaray refers to as a "mediator of becoming" (1993, 33), an interval where connection and love can circulate without merger or assimilation. This "in-between" is created and cultivated between the one and the other and provides a space for recognition of the limit of our understanding of the other's being (Schwab 2011). It maintains a sense of mystery or wonder in relation to the other. The interval and its mediating images, such as lips, threshold, and mucous, serve as elements that contribute to repairing a neglected imaginary, the previously unsymbolized aspects of feminine existence (Schwab 1994, 369). The lack of definite boundaries leads to a dwelling that can house female subjectivity as well as contribute to "a mutual crossing of boundaries which is creative, and yet where identity is not swallowed up" (Whitford 167). Within a psychoanalytic register, Jessica Benjamin refers to this as the psychoanalytic third, a mental space that cultivates intersubjectivity, a creative tension between separate yet connected beings (Benjamin 1998). As a space that cultivates dialogues between the two sexes, or any couple, a porch is in between public and private domains. The inhabitant welcomes an other onto a porch, or into a courtyard, and the other recognizes being in a nonpublic space that is also a nonprivate space, a kind of reception area that makes a gesture toward receptivity to the other.

Spiders

As guardian and protector, the spider might also be seen as a holding environment, a container, a safe space (Winnicott 1971). Reminiscent of the children's book *Charlotte's Web* (White 1952), it might stir up memories, moods, and mystery in each viewer's internal life. The scale evokes characters in animal fables and undercuts the illusion of representationalism; the enormity of the piece makes the viewer feel like a child. Like *Femme-maison* and *Spider,* Bourgeois's *Maman* (1999), an enormous spider, made of bronze and steel, over thirty feet tall, also embodies play with mimesis. The scale invokes monumentality, which is typically aimed at humbling and seducing people into submission and obedience to power and domination. But by representing a small and ungrandiose creature on such an excessive scale, Bourgeois both plays with and counters monumentality (Bal 2001); employing mimicry, "it converts a form of subordination into an affirmation and thus begins to thwart it" (Irigaray 1985a, 76). *Maman* simultaneously evokes and rejects monumentality in its playful mimetic gesture. While the imposing size of the legs makes them function as columns, they also suggest lightness as they taper to fine points barely touching the floor, like a dancer who seems to defy gravity (Bal 2001). However, the spectator might be caught in a web of fears, for spiders are also predators patiently waiting for their prey to be caught on sticky threads. Bourgeois's spider is a maternal spider, and she has named the giant sculpture, now exhibited in Bilbao, Spain, *Maman.* She has specifically associated the spider with her own mother, describing both woman and arachnid as "deliberate, clever, patient, soothing, [and] reasonable" (Bourgeois 170). We should note, however, that mothers, no less than spiders, can be menacing creatures.

Bourgeois's spiders embody a dialectic between sculpture and architecture and also between reparative tenderness and aggressive attack (Potts 262). The tension between the predatory animal and the reparative, comforting mother lands us in Kleinian territory. The good mother, the good breast, is loved and the object of gratitude; the bad mother, the bad breast, is hated, spat out, an object of envy (Klein 1975). For Melanie Klein, aggression is an innate, primary drive, which affects development. Splitting-off—that is, recognizing and at the same time refusing to recognize—and denying and disowning aggression and hatred can lead to destructive violence, fragmentation, and/or dissociation. This stalls the integration of love and hate and forecloses recognition and acceptance of ambivalence.

I suggest that *Maman* engages with and questions the cultural fantasy of the all-giving, benevolent mother (Harris 1998). This traditional ideology has contributed to women's discomfort with aggression. The mother/daughter relation is one of both love and hate, tenderness and aggression; however, hate and aggression are often split off, denied, and repressed. The fear of acknowledging hate might originate in the very realistic fear of the aggression and destructive violence actually inflicted on women and in the desire to find in the mother/daughter bond a haven from this reality. It might also be a fear that aggression and its manifestations in competition and ambition are seen as masculine desires, forbidden and dangerous to femininity and leading to a loss of goodness. Competition between women might threaten an idealized relation. Such fears can lead to women habitually undermining or destroying their own prospects and opportunities, as well as inhibiting creativity and foreclosing sexuate living, extended to the difference within difference, the differences among and within women (Schor 62).

Many women make the distinction between assertiveness, as a positive and healthy energy, and aggression, as a negatively charged and dangerous affect (Harris 1998). I follow Adrienne Harris's model of aggression as neutral, spanning a continuum of manifestations from motility, activity, assertion, and competitiveness, to envy, anger, destructiveness, hatred, and rage (36). According to this model, aggression is not a defensive, secondary reaction to impingements, injury, or neglect, but a primary drive. Let us consider the story of Arachne, the mythic first weaver (Ovid 1986), who was not afraid of aggression, competition, or ambition. Her tapestries were wondrous, and Athena, the divine weaver, was enraged that Arachne would not acknowledge her talent as a gift from the goddess. Athena would not let this self-sufficiency and refusal of humility go unchallenged. She set up her loom and, unafraid of divine envy, so did Arachne, her heart set on victory. When Athena looked at her competitor's weaving and found no fault, she repeatedly struck the girl on the forehead. Unable to endure such divine rage and envy, Arachne sought to hang herself. Feeling pity and saying, "Live but hang, you wicked girl," Athena changed the girl into a spider, who, "as a spider still/Weaving her web, pursues her former skill" (125). The successful result of ambition in the finished work was a threat that Athena could not tolerate. She punished Arachne with sadistic retaliation, as do many parents who are unable to contain a child's aggression. Arachne's ambition, competitiveness, and lack of humility unleashed such rage in Athena that the girl could not survive it.

The aggression and energy of an active child can be appreciated and safely limited or rejected as exhausting, excessive, and punished as unacceptable, especially in girls. Our culture has traditionally shown more tolerance for boys' aggression. Girls' intense feelings and passions are often met with judgmental fears and crushed because the mother experiences her own feelings of aggression as dangerous and destructive. If a mother is able non-judgmentally to accept being experienced as a spider, both protecting *and* threatening, her daughter might not be caught in a web of repressed fears and threatening fantasies. This assumes that the mother is comfortable with her own aggression and ambivalence, her love and hate for her child. Her conscious acknowledgment of this is likely to liberate her daughter from destructive fantasies and lead instead to the development of a more integrated psychic structure. "Hatred unknown or disavowed is what does so much damage" (Harris 1998, 37–38). *Spider* and *Maman* make gestures toward "re-weaving the maternal web" (Kristeva 249) in such a way that aggression does not go underground to be destructively acted out. Consciously acknowledged aggression can strengthen the mother-daughter relationship and enable the two to live together in a more lasting way. The freedom to articulate and acknowledge aggression, instead of repressing and denying it, will in turn make the daughter less likely to accept subordination and domestication in a habitat of which someone else is master.

A Framework of Permeable Phallicism: Stepping Back from Mastery and Domination

Masculinity has been founded on "femiphobia," a defensive counteridentification with the mother, borne by unconscious hatred of the part of the self that is experienced as feminine (Diamond 2006; see also Schiller 2010). To be normatively masculine is, according to Michael Diamond, to be stoic, to minimize feelings of hurt and loss, to remove oneself emotionally from pain, to become indifferent. Being told that boys don't cry, a boy rejects his mother as comforter and begins to gather that he is to suffer alone, that he is to need no one. Disidentifying from maternal and nurturing characteristics, the boy begins to perform a culturally sanctioned masculinity by overinvesting in the phallus as a compensation for loss, and (later) by experiencing genitality as penetration in the service of mastery and potency. Being what Butler calls melancholically gendered (Butler 1997), this man numbs himself to pain and to loss. He becomes impenetrable. His masculinity is built on a repudiation of femininity, a vigilance against gender wounding, against the shame and humiliation of being seen as feminine. His autonomy is defensive, built on a suppression of dependency needs. This conception of masculinity begins to leave him in exile with what Dianne Elise refers to as a "citadel complex" (Elise 518). Phallicism becomes a fortress of emotional self-sufficiency and impenetrability, wherein masculinity is sequestered, emotionally and psychically inaccessible. How can we envision masculinity without these rigid structures of phallic monism? Are there ways of constructing masculinity other than on the psychic shoals of loss, repudiation, disidentification, and unconscious hatred of femininity?

The classical construction of masculinity as emotionally self-sufficient, dominant, and invulnerably enclosed within a citadel complex does not lend itself to interactions on a horizontal axis of nondefensive openness. In an effort to step back from the vertical axis of power and domination, the male subject needs to give up (the fantasy of) being an omnipotent subject—one who attempts to suppress heterogeneity both among subjects and within subjects (intersubjectively and intrapsychically)—and to give up being a narcissistic subject—one who is unable to experience the other as a separate subject (Layton 1998). For this, we need gestures toward maleness as limited and incomplete, which means being able to let the other be and being able to let the other come to encounter him, without discounting the other's subjectivity and without reducing it to his own world. An incomplete and limited attitude respects the insurmountable limits of each subjectivity and recognizes that the other is not at the disposal of the one (Schiller 2011).

In order to come to see himself as limited, and the other as irreducibly different, the male subject needs to work through his omnipotent fantasies. To distinguish between the other as a fantasy, assimilated through identification or repudiation, and the other as a separate subject, the other must be conceived and experienced as an external being. The recognition of the other as irreducibly different and beyond the control of the one maintains a tension between separateness and connection. This can lead to a desire for the other, not as an object reflecting the male subject, a projection of his disowned and split-off parts (Benjamin 2000, 301), but as a subject. In order to break out of "the narcissistic circuit of the subject," as Butler puts it (Butler 2000, 278), one must realize that it never was about owning the other. The psychic issue for the male subject is to be willing to be a receptacle for his own repudiated parts (the maternal nurturing and vulnerable parts) and not use the other to hold them. Only through a capacity for containing and owning his split-off parts, and by seeing himself as incomplete and limited, can the male subject recognize and respect the other as an irreducibly different subject.

Richard Serra's enormous torqued spirals and ellipses invite entry and enfold and embody the spectator/participant. They suggest a conception of masculinity as a permeable phallicism (Schiller 2010). In terms of sexuality, perhaps phallic penetration might be experienced as being enfolded, and associations of penetrating with possessing, conquering, and mastering can fall away as the viewer lets him- or herself be folded into the curved, leaning forms of Serra's sculptures. Using *Joe* as a compass in the terrains of uncoded and nonnormative masculinities, I envision "torqueing" the normative, conventional concept, and gesture toward a masculinity anchored in an imaginary of permeable phallicism.

Joe (named for Joseph Pulitzer) is a sculpture at the Pulitzer Foundation for the Arts in St. Louis, a torqued spiral with leaning diagonals and accelerating curves. It is a massive sculpture with a man's name, almost an everyman's name, and made by a man. Richard Serra created *Joe* from five contiguous steel plates that have rusted to a sensuous golden brown. They are connected as a continuous skin that is twelve feet high, forty-five feet across, two inches thick, and "wrapped into an ever-tighter configuration towards the center" (Curtis 32). The huge dynamic force of *Joe* is conditioned by a circle on the bottom and a smaller circle on top, which gives you a sense of its surfaces either falling away from you or reaching up over you. As you approach *Joe* at the end of an open-air courtyard, an opening at a tilting angle invites you to enter its inner space.

The skin is our largest organ, and it is the first organ through which meanings are exchanged (Anzieu 1989). It is a surface of inscription, providing an imaginary space for inscribing a permeable masculinity (Schiller 2012). The skin is intermediary and transitional. It faces inward and outward. It is a mode of connecting with others and also a mode of shielding the self, even to the extreme of fortressing (Harris 2005). Serra's torqued skin, like ours, separates and unifies; it is intermediate, transitional, and permeable. Holding polarities in tension without collapsing, the circular, winding skin towers above the spectator, impenetrable like the walls of a citadel, at the same time as it opens up an invitation to get inside. It yields entry. Both impermeable and permeable, at once solid and fragile like our own skin, this sculptural skin evokes heavy industrial factories (Schjeldahl 2007) at the same time as it is exposed as a porous membrane, a roughly textured rusty skin. There is a prohibition on touching, as there are multiple prohibitions on touching human skins. The museum stations guards by this skin, signaling the fear of damage and mutilation. Skins that need such protection are considered fragile, vulnerable to epidermic marks of disruption.

Can a male/phallic psyche be penetrated as this torqued circle is, penetrated as a way of being experienced and discovered? To be permeable is to acknowledge a longing to be penetrated, a desire for active receptivity and surrender and also a desire to penetrate the other, not in the sense of possessing or mastering, but rather coming to know, discovering the other (Ghent 1990; see also Schiller 2011.) This is letting go; it is letting the other in, taking in the other's point of view, while letting the other be and remain other (Benjamin 2004). Phallicism as horizontally open and permeable, rather than vertically oriented, in the sense of being hierarchically dominating and assimilating, suggests an acceptance of being limited and incomplete—that is to say, not mistaking being a part for the (narcissistic) whole. An incomplete male subject welcomes the other, not trying to assimilate or master the other, but rather making an effort to cultivate an interval that safeguards alterity. In order to "incomplete" himself, the masculine subject sees himself not as one half, not as complementary to the other, nor as an opposite, but as different. He recognizes that the other is not at his disposal (Irigaray 2002). A limited and incomplete phallic subject is, however, not all receptivity. As permeable, he holds the wish to be penetrated in tension with the wish to penetrate. Beyond normative phallicism, the wish to penetrate can be experienced as motivated by wonder, by a passion to approach, to contemplate, by a desire to know deeply, while safeguarding an interval between self and other (Irigaray 1993). A permeable psyche opens masculinity to a sense of interiority and vulnerability, to a capacity for surrendering, for letting go, not *to* the other, but *with* the other. The inner opening, like a courtyard, can be experienced only by entering *Joe*, thus making a gesture toward an interiority that opens up a space for receptive surrender and a welcoming of the other into a habitat of desire.

Sexuate Living

Bourgeois's *Spider* is a gesture toward a female sexuate space, a labial territory protected by a spider, neither interior nor exterior, a porous space, an open threshold for welcoming the other, without being eradicated or assimilated. This resonates with Irigaray's claim that the female needs to become a subject of her own desire. Serra's *Joe* is an artistic gesture toward a masculinity grounded in a permeable phallicism. The torqued spiral winds inward toward an opening, like a courtyard, also a porous space in the sense of being neither completely interior nor completely exterior, a place for welcoming others, a gesture toward the male subject's task of stepping back from domination and from reducing the other's subjectivity to his own world. This resonates with a psychic space, an architecture of interiority that opens up a receptive space for both surrender and desire to come to know the other.

A cell and a torqued spiral constitute two sexually specific ways of gesturing toward sexuate living. Through their architectural scale both Bourgeois's *Spider* and Serra's *Joe* suggest habitats that articulate artistic answers to Irigaray's question as to how we can live together without eradicating self or other. They gesture toward habitats for cultivating desire.

Works Cited

Anzieu, Didier. 1989. *The Skin Ego.* Translated by C. Turner. New Haven: Yale University Press.

Bal, Mieke. 2001. *Louise Bourgeois'* Spider*: The Architecture of Art-Writing.* Chicago: University of Chicago Press.

Beauvoir, Simone de. 1970. *The Second Sex.* Translated by H. M. Parshley. NewYork: Bantam Books.

Benjamin, Jessica. 1998. *Shadow of the Other: Intersubjectivity and Gender in Psychoanalysis.* New York: Routledge.

———. 2000. "Response to Commentaries by Mitchell and by Butler." *Studies in Gender and Sexuality* 1, no. 3: 291–308.

———. 2004. "Beyond Doer and Done To: An Intersubjective View of Thirdness." *Psychoanalytic Quarterly* 73, no 1: 5–46.

Bourgeois, Louise. 2008. "Ode à ma Mère." In *Louise Bourgeois,* edited by Frances Morris. New York: Guggenheim Museum.

Butler, Judith. 1997. *The Psychic Life of Power: Theories in Subjection.* Stanford: Stanford University Press.

———. 2000. "Longing for Recognition: Commentary on the Work of Jessica Benjamin. *Studies in Gender and Sexuality* 1, no. 3: 271–90.

Curtis, William. 2001. "Spaces Between." In *Abstractions in Space: Tadao Ando, Ellsworth Kelly, Richard Serra,* edited by L. Stein. St. Louis: The Pulitzer Foundation for the Arts.

Diamond, Michael. 2006. "Masculinity Unraveled: The Roots of Male Gender Identity and the Shifting of Male Ego Ideals throughout Life." *Journal of the American Psychoanalytic Association* 54, no. 4: 1099–1130.

Elise, Dianne. 2001. "Unlawful Entry: Male Fears of Psychic Penetration." *Psychoanalytic Dialogues* 11, no. 4: 499–531.

Freud, Sigmund. 1905. "Three Essays on the Theory of Sexuality." In *The Standard Edition of the Complete Psychological Works of Sigmund Freud,* vol. 7, edited by James Strachey, 123–243. London: Hogarth.

———. 1933. *New Introductory Lectures on Sexuality: Lecture XXXIII: Femininity.* In *The Standard Edition of the Complete Psychological Works of Sigmund Freud,* vol. 22, edited by James Strachey, 112–35. London: Hogarth.

Ghent, Emmanuel. 1990. "Masochism, Submission, Surrender." *Contemporary Psychoanalysis* 26: 108–36.

Grosz, Elizabeth. 2001. *Architecture from the Outside: Essays on Virtual and Real Space.* Cambridge: MIT Press.

Harris, Adrienne. 1998. "Aggression: Pleasures and Dangers." *Psychoanalytic Inquiry* 18: 31–44.

———. 2005. *Gender as Soft Assembly.* Hillsdale: Analytic.

Irigaray, Luce. 1985a. *This Sex Which Is Not One.* Translated by C. Porter. Ithaca: Cornell University Press.

———. 1985b. *Speculum of the Other Woman.* Translated by G. Gill. Ithaca: Cornell University Press.

———. 1993. *An Ethics of Sexual Difference.* Translated by C. Burke and G. Gill. Ithaca: Cornell University Press.

———. 1996. *I Love to You: Sketch for a Felicity within History.* Translated by A. Martin. New York: Routledge.

———. 2002. *The Way of Love.* Translated by H. Bostic and S. Pluháček. London: Continuum.

———. 2004. *Luce Irigaray: Key Writings.* London: Continuum.

Klein, Melanie. 1975. *Envy and Gratitude.* New York: Delacorte.

Kristeva, Julia. 2008. "Runaway Girl/Louise Bourgeois: From Little Pea to Runaway Girl." In *Louise Bourgeois,* edited by Morris, 246–52.

Layton, Lynne. 1998. *Who's That Girl? Who's That Boy? Clinical Practice Meets Postmodern Gender Theory.* Northvale, NJ: Jason Aronson.

Morris, Frances. 2008. "I Do, I Undo, I Redo." In *Louise Bourgeois,* edited by Morris, 11–17.

———, ed. 2008. *Louise Bourgeois.* New York: Guggenheim Museum.

Nixon, Mignon. 2005. *Fantastic Reality: Louise Bourgeois and a Story of Modern Art.* Cambridge: MIT Press.

Ovid. 1986. *Metamorphoses.* Translated by A. Melville. Oxford: Oxford University Press.

Potts, Alex. 2008. "Hybrid Sculpture." In *Louise Bourgeois,* edited by Morris, 258–65.

Schiller, Britt-Marie. 2010. "Permeable Masculinities: Gender Reverie in Richard Serra's Torqued Sculptures." *Studies in Gender and Sexuality* 11, no. 1: 35–46.

———. 2011."The Incomplete Masculine: Engendering the Masculine of Sexual Difference." In *Thinking with Irigaray,* edited by Mary C. Rawlinson, Sabrina L. Hom, and Serene J. Khader, 131–51. Albany: State University of New York Press.

———. 2012. "Representing Female Sexual Desire within a Labial Framework of Sexuality." *Journal of the American Psychoanalytic Association* 60, no. 6: 1161–97.

Schjeldahl, Peter. 2007. "Industrial Strength: A Richard Serra Retrospective." In *The New Yorker:* June 11, 18.

Schor, Naomi. 1994. "This Essentialism Which Is Not One: Coming to Grips with Irigaray." In *Engaging with Irigaray: Feminist Philosophy and Modern European Thought*, edited by Carolyn Burke, Naomi Schor, and Margaret Whitford, 57–78. New York: Columbia University Press.

Schwab, Gail. 1994. "Mother's Body, Father's Tongue: Mediation and the Symbolic Order." In *Engaging with Irigaray*, edited by Carolyn Burke, Naomi Schor, and Margaret Whitford, 351–78.

———. 2011. "Beyond the Vertical and the Horizontal: Spirituality, Space, and Alterity in the Work of Luce Irigaray." In *Thinking with Irigaray*, edited by Mary C. Rawlinson, Sabrina L. Hom, and Serene J. Khader, 77–97.

Tseelon, Efrat. 1995. "The Little Mermaid: An Icon of Woman's Condition in Patriarchy, and the Human Condition of Castration." *International Journal of Psychoanalysis* 76: 1017–30.

Turner, Victor. 1974. *Dramas, Fields, and Metaphors: Symbolic Action in Human Society*. Ithaca: Cornell University Press.

White, E. B. 1952. *Charlotte's Web*. New York: Harper & Brothers.

Whitford, Margaret. 1991. *Luce Irigaray: Philosophy in the Feminine*. London: Routledge.

Winnicott, Donald. 1971. *Playing and Reality*. London: Tavistock.

The Feminist Distance

Space in Luce Irigaray and Jane Campion's *The Piano*

CAROLINE GODART

Cinema reinvents life by deploying bodies through very particular spatial and temporal arrangements; thinking life through film thus allows for both the aesthetic and the philosophical explorations of time and space. This essay will focus on the latter. Feminist film critics approaching the question of space have mainly concentrated on the gendered signification of travel and movement, or of certain locations, such as the city or the home. But what would it mean to define spatiality itself in feminist terms? And how could it be made relevant to an exploration of sexual difference in cinema? Luce Irigaray suggests intriguingly in the opening pages of *Ethics of Sexual Difference* that we will only move beyond phallocentrism once women have developed a space and time of their own (7), and she elaborates a compelling theory of spatiality in "Place, Interval" (Irigaray 1993, 34–58). Grounded in a close analysis of Jane Campion's 1993 movie *The Piano*, this chapter considers the numerous points of convergence between the philosopher and the director, arguing that they both develop a twofold understanding of space as either the condition of woman's self-affirmation or the medium of her disappearance.

In the context of cinema studies, Irigaray's name tends to be associated with scholarship from the 1980s and the 1990s. Yet, besides my own,[1] two books were published in the past ten years, one by Caroline Bainbridge

(2008) and another by Lucy Bolton (2011), offering approaches to film that are entirely grounded in her philosophy.[2] Surprisingly, Bainbridge and Bolton are the first to produce book-length, fully fledged Irigarayan cinematics; even at the height of psychoanalytical feminist film criticism, few arguments were entirely based in her work, although she was often briefly referenced. It is above all in literary studies that Irigaray's influence was felt at the time, as her disruptions of phallocentric language lend themselves ideally to the study of literary texts. Conversely, her distrust of visuality (at least as it functions in phallocentrism) may have made film scholars reluctant to resort systematically to her work. Further, because her books were at their most popular when the critical influence of psychoanalysis was at its strongest, she is often overly associated with the latter, even though the scope of her work encompasses most of the major figures of the Western philosophical tradition. In this essay, I concentrate on her discussion of Aristotle in *Ethics of Sexual Difference* (1993, 34–58), where she reworks his concept of the interval to develop her own theory of space and time.

If Irigaray deserves renewed critical attention, Campion's movie does too. *The Piano* holds a particular place in the history of cinema, as perhaps the most influential film made by a woman; not even Kathryn Bigelow's 2008 *The Hurt Locker* can rival its combination of high profits and critical acclaim.[3] The movie was a blockbuster,[4] and Campion went on to win many awards; most notably, she was the first (and so far the *only*) woman to win the Golden Palm at the Cannes Film Festival, establishing her as the leading female director of her time.[5] Furthermore, *The Piano* was the subject of considerable academic scrutiny, which, given the film's release in the early 1990s, relied mostly on psychoanalytical and generic perspectives; yet this dense, complex movie invites a much wider array of interpretations.

The film tells the story of Ada McGrath (Holly Hunter), a nineteenth-century mute Scotswoman pianist who is forced into marriage to a landowner in New Zealand named Alistair Stewart (Sam Neill). She is shipped to the island with her young daughter, Flora (Anna Paquin), who speaks sign language and serves as her interpreter. Ada further expresses herself through her piano, with which she entertains a fervent relation. She manages to resist her husband's advances but soon finds herself faced with an almost impossible bargain; George Baines (Harvey Keitel), another white man on the island (albeit one who is close to the local Maori population and speaks their language), has bought the piano from Stewart, and he offers to give it back to her in exchange for escalating sexual demands. Ada accepts very reluctantly and soon finds herself lying naked in Baines's bed:

a few keys for a few favors. Her initial displeasure and fear are obvious to the viewer, but Baines remains impervious, until he unexpectedly declares his love for her. In a surprising turn, Ada falls in love with him, and the two start an intense affair. She also seeks to infuse this blossoming sensuality into her marriage: on two consecutive nights, she wakes Stewart up with caresses that she does not allow him to reciprocate. He cannot bear being objectified and is noticeably uncomfortable, but he develops an amorous passion for her. When Flora lets him know about her mother's liaison with Baines, he is devoured by jealousy and brutally chops off one of Ada's fingers. He then realizes that he cannot force upon her the kind of intimacy that he craves and tells Baines to take her away. As Baines and Ada are sailing forth to a new life, Ada demands that her piano be thrown overboard, and she lets herself be carried down with it. Once she is under water, a force that she herself describes as her "will" chooses to survive and manages to get her back to the surface. She is then seen having started her new life with Baines and Flora in a pretty white house in Nelson, New Zealand. In an interesting turn, *The Piano* has yet another ending; in the very last shot, Ada sees herself, as she sometimes does at night, dead, under the sea, tied to her piano.

Toward Ada: Camera Work and Characterization

Throughout the film, an insurmountable distance separates Ada from those who share her life (with the exception, to a certain degree, of her daughter) and from the spectator. She is detached because of her muteness and lack of facial expressions and also because of a natural elegance that lends her an almost other-worldly quality. She is one of the most fluid characters ever seen on the screen; her every move, from the torsion of her hand when she caresses her daughter's head to her flight in the woods when Stewart tries to rape her, is marked by the same ethereal grace and poise. The camera itself, when it comes near her, often engages in "lushly graceful movements . . . swirling around her, creating complex arabesques" (Polan 2001, 29). Her grace both seduces us and keeps us at bay.

The film's last two scenes aptly illustrate the spatial arrangement that underlies Ada's characterization. After she has survived drowning, we see her leading an idyllic existence in Nelson with Flora and Baines. They live in what seems to be a welcoming, bright white house; Baines has fashioned a metal finger for Ada, so she can continue to play the piano, and she is learning to speak (she had suddenly stopped as a young child). In an overflow of delightfulness, Flora is even seen doing cartwheels in the garden, in a white dress, in slow motion. In a voice-over, we hear Ada say that she is ashamed of her difficulty to speak, but this does not prevent Baines from being lovingly devoted to her. She practices speaking with a black scarf on her head, which he tenderly removes, and he kisses her with passion. Her adoring gaze tells the measure of her love for him. Nothing, it seems, could trouble such a blissful tableau. But, in the next sequence, the brightness of marital life in Nelson is replaced by the dark, cloudy sea. The piano is there, at the bottom of the ocean, covered in algae, and Ada, tied to it with a cord, floats above her instrument. The voice says, "At night, I think of my piano in its ocean grave, and sometimes of myself, floating above it. Down there, everything is so still and silent that it lulls me to sleep. It is a strange lullaby and so it is. It is mine." She then recites the following lines from Thomas Hood's poem "Silence": "There is a silence where hath been no sound/There is a silence, where no sound may be/In the cold grave, under the deep, deep sea." The camera moves back from a close-up of the piano to the point where Ada has become a distant dark spot in the gloomy, turbid waters.

The great complexity of this vision contrasts with the simplicity of the scene in Nelson. Ada is learning to speak and, thus, abandoning what seems to have been her willful ostracism from the community and the clearest sign of her staunch attachment to her own autonomy. She may have been sold into marriage by her father and sent to the other end of the world to live with a man she has never met, but she has kept herself shielded by deliberately refusing to engage in spoken language. Therefore, that Ada would learn to speak in the penultimate scene raises the question of her autonomy in her new life with Baines. Yet the underwater sequence shows that, even in Nelson, a part of her has remained inalienable. Ada has not become completely absorbed into the norms of Victorian femininity, but she keeps that other self in the deep, where she can visit it at will. The final image itself is highly ambivalent, very far from a celebratory embrace of feminine triumph: the old piano is attached to both death (the coffin, the ocean grave) and sorrow, as it carries the weight of difficult memories. The brightness of the life that she has created in Nelson is replaced by a solitary, murky, seemingly self-destructive darkness. Yet, paradoxically, the very permanence of death also marks the immutability of her sense of self—the "strange lullaby," she insists, is hers. Hence, in the last two scenes of the film, Ada appears to be closer to others and to the spectator than she has ever been before (through her middle-class lifestyle and her acquisition of spoken language), at the same time as she resolutely marks a literal, incompressible distantiation in her aquatic world.

Irigaray's conceptualization of space, in particular through her concept of the interval, can be used productively to analyze these scenes. She demonstrates in "Place, Interval" that the operation of phallocentrism is to constitute woman as a space from which man can elaborate his subjectivity. She develops her argument through an analysis of Aristotle's *Physics* and of the heterosexual relation,[6] and she notes that patriarchal sexuality negates woman's place and in fact makes her function as a place for man, for at its core lies the conviction that the vagina is a passive receptacle whose purpose is to welcome an active penis. She suggests, in a delightfully subversive interpretation of gender roles in straight coitus, that woman's purported passivity constitutes a disavowal of the vagina's actual activity, as it sculpts man's penis from the inside. Further, Irigaray notes that this disappearance of woman in and from the (hetero)sexual act is the result of a doubly impossible movement on man's part—formed by a piercing and destructive urge to appropriate her sex and a regressive, nostalgic, and inexorably failed attempt to be reintegrated within the womb. In this sad masquerade, woman is lost as she becomes territory for an other instead of enjoying the intensity of her own domain. Thus, Irigaray insists that it is crucial that woman forge a place for herself and create her own envelope.[7] However, having a place is not enough to meet the other, for two sealed-off containers would be unable to produce an encounter. Therefore, a threshold is necessary, and Irigaray calls it the interval.

In the sexual relation, the interval takes the shape of the mucus, a bodily fluid that marks the place where the two meet and the passage between the outside and the inside. Woman touches man through the mucus, which is still part of her since it emanates from her body, already producing an encounter with the other, at once espousing her boundaries and figuring her openness to the other. It is the mucus that enables a heterosexual relation in which woman's place is not destroyed, as is the case in phallocentric sex. Instead, the interval, as the creative operation of desire, enables the lovers to produce a place for each other at the same time as they enjoy their own respective places.

Beyond the mucus, Irigaray distinguishes two other forms of interval in "Place, Interval": 1) the placenta, that which comes between the mother and the child; and 2) the interval between matter and form that sustains her critical reading of Aristotle (Hill 2012, 58). Rebecca Hill notes, however, that Irigaray does not limit herself to these three categories (74). Elsewhere in her work, and in particular in *Sharing the World* (2008), Irigaray expands the concept of the interval to function for all types of relations between the sexes: since sexual difference exceeds carnal relations, all relationships between woman and man need to be reformulated.

The interval forms "the intermediary *between the boundaries*" (Irigaray 1993, 53; Irigaray's emphasis); it is the space between the two that enables their relation, the threshold between two envelopes. A close reading of "Place, Interval" reveals that Irigaray defines her concept through a series of oxymorons: the interval is at once undefinable and embodied, abstract and tangible; it is a distance that is both abolished to enable intimacy and maintained to guarantee integrity; it is present and yet to be realized; it is at once space and time. Further, the interval is not a static, motionless entity, but rather a radical openness engaged in a ceaseless movement (Hill 2008, 129). Hill suggests that the interval can be understood as the force of difference itself for it is through its activity that the two are constituted as subjects, as autonomous individuals that come in the place of the subject/object, master and slave dialectic of phallocentrism (2012, 155).

At first sight, the ending of *The Piano* would seem to suggest that Ada and Baines are enacting the Irigarayan interval by forging an amorous bond grounded in partnership. Campion presents us with the picture of marital bliss: Ada has deliberately thrown away her old piano and is starting afresh with a new instrument; Baines is lovingly devoted to her, and it seems that what he cherishes most about her is her strength and determination. Further, the penultimate scene appears to redeem him of his disturbing contract with Ada: whatever trace may have lingered on him from what he calls "the arrangement" seems to have been washed away as he unveils Ada, who is practicing speaking with a black scarf on her head, and kisses her passionately, holding her delicate face with his strong hands. His bodily vigor seems to serve as a token of the sincerity of his love as it demonstrates the force of his attachment to her.

But is this a new form of heterosexual alliance? This couple is far from undermining a fairly normative narrative: even though Ada and Baines are eccentrics by the standards of the Victorian era (they are in all likelihood unmarried, his face is covered in Maori tattoos, and Flora is not his daughter), they come across as rather traditional to the contemporary viewer for whom the film is intended. They have abandoned all the signs of marginality that they could leave behind: Ada is learning to speak, and Baines, now ensconced in a neat middle-class house, no longer enjoys a semi-Native lifestyle in the bush. They are more conventional in their new life together than either of them ever was. Most importantly, a closer look reveals that their sexual interaction remains in line with Baines's sexually abusive behavior earlier in the film: his vigor as he holds Ada's face maintains the enactment of a power play as her frailty contrasts with the grip of his robust hands; while she has a strong personality, she surrenders to his force with delight. This is an erotics that is endorsing, rather than challenging, the norms of phallocentrism. Ultimately, Ada is in love with a man who was sexually abusive to her earlier in the film, thereby subscribing to a (rather banal) patriarchal logic of male redemption and female self-elision. The Irigarayan interval is not to be found here.

But Ada does not surrender all of herself to her relationship with Baines, nor does she become entirely legible to the viewer. Instead, a part of her remains hidden, preciously protected in the dark, sublime world of her solitude. She is careful to keep her most intimate self shielded at a distance, at the bottom of the sea, tied to her old piano. Her last words are mysterious, widely open to interpretation, and it is telling that the movie ends with a movement of distantiation from her, as the camera tracks back to leave us with nothing but a dark spot. The piano remains a complicated symbol: it is linked to Europe and unknown trauma (the little we can fathom about her past life—muteness, an abusive father, a fatherless daughter—suggests grim circumstances), and it is evidently tied to death. But it does underscore Ada's sense of autonomy: she does not abandon her body and her soul to a romantic dream that *in fine* would mark her as place for Baines. Instead, she retains a measure of her identity without and beyond him.

The aquatic scene can thus be seen as the culmination of the movie's continual preoccupation with distance as Ada's propensity for withdrawal becomes literal. What she points to at the end of *The Piano* is a place of silence and independence that would exceed the limits of phallocentrism and from which a truly autonomous female subject *could* emerge.[8] This is, in fact, the space of the interval, as we, the spectators, are ceaselessly trying and always failing to reach Ada. The entire film is invested in this movement toward her, which begins with the near touch of her hands in the opening sequence, continues with Stewart's and Baines's courtships, and ends under water, in a scene that marks the incompressible nature of the distance that separates her most intimate self from the expectations of the world. At the very moment when we think that we have finally made sense of her, that a form of closure has been reached and that she is, after all, a very common woman, satisfied by the simple joys of married life, her true, mysterious depth comes forth one last time to defeat our delusional sense of conclusion. The interval remains in place.

This movement toward Ada is not limited to the final scene, but it is captured throughout the film in its dominant aesthetic motif, the close-up. The latter presents viewers with a constant "almost" that never finishes its curve, since the object to which the camera gets closer can never be touched. Although I can sense acutely what is represented on the screen, I can never actually touch it. The pictured object looks near enough that I can almost grab it; its sheer size, usually so much bigger than its actual referent, is overwhelming, and my desire for it can be as genuine as for a real body, but it remains eternally out of reach. Therefore, the close-up is about nonsatisfaction; it is an irrepressible sensual experience that remains slightly frustrating because it can never be consummated: the object can never be grasped; the moment can never be captured; one's amazement can only last as long as the shot lasts. Like the interval, this is a pleasure of the "almost."

In *The Piano*, the use of the close-up is intensely sensual and can only be adequately understood through references to its main character. Indeed, what better way than this "almost" of the close-up to represent a character such as the always elusive Ada? The close-up is, from the very beginning, intimately connected to her; the first two shots of the movie, which were famously analyzed by Vivian Sobchack (2004, 63), figure two hands shot from such proximity as to become almost spectral. A reverse shot in close-up reveals these to be Ada's own hands, looked at from her point of view. This short sequence captures some essential elements of the movie: an effect of her perspective, the close-up is attached to the character of Ada. We see the world of *The Piano* through her eyes; sometimes literally, through the numerous point-of-view shots, and sometimes in general because the whole world of the film is a function of her character. Indeed, her suppleness radiates everywhere: the harmonious tunes of the soundtrack, the eerie majesty of the bush, the perfection of every object. Even the abject is absorbed into beauty (recall, for instance, Flora being sick on the beach or Ada's greasy hair, neither of which is presented as repulsive). Ada is the force that sustains the movie and defines its aesthetics. The close-ups in *The Piano* reflect the way she goes about exploring the world—intimately and wordlessly. In other words, they form a way for the film to emulate Ada's largely tactile and intuitive mode of being and to let the spectator engage with the intimacy of her experience.[9] Since the close-up is bound up in an incompressible distance, it is, like the interval and like Ada, best captured by an oxymoron—an insuperable closeness.

Violent Spaces

The uninvasive wonderment that Ada's character invites, which, in tune with Irigaray's theory, allows her to develop a space of her own, contrasts with the pervasive intrusiveness of sexual violence, present everywhere in the movie, under the surface of things, ubiquitous yet unspoken, inflecting all relationships between men and women. It is there when Ada is married off to a man she does not know; it is there, if only potentially so, in her interactions with the sailors when she first arrives in New Zealand and in Stewart's insistence that he has rights over her body. And of course, it is everywhere in Baines's "arrangement." Thus, this movie is constituted on the basis of these two contradictory, irreconcilable tendencies: on the one hand, admiration at a distance, and on the other, constant threats of sexual invasion.

Campion sees sexual violence not only as ubiquitous, but also as that which gives its shape to the heterosexual relation, both in its passion and in its horror, as abuse morphs seamlessly into love through a complicated network of relationships. *The Piano* composes a play of connivances between heterosexual love and the trappings of phallocentrism; Ada is an ambivalent character who partakes not only of autonomy and the possibility of an actualization of the feminine, but also of a predilection for masochism and traditional patterns of desire, as she falls in love with a man whose courtship was fueled by the imposition of his material and phallic power on her. However, *The Piano* is more complex than most narratives of female degradation since it rests not on a straightforward imposition of phallic power, but on a bargain, which appears to endow Ada with a disturbing measure of agency. Bainbridge (2008) argues that Ada enters the agreement with Baines of her own will: "Ada is bargaining with her *own* body for her *own* right to her *own* desire by creating an economy of her *own*, which centers on the piano which has been unjustly removed by her new husband in exchange for some land" (157–58, emphasis in the text). But, in fact, Ada is trading something she cannot afford to lose (her dignity, her physical integrity) for an object without which she cannot survive (her piano, which is aligned with her most intimate self). To suggest that Ada has agency is to overlook the fact that trading sex in her case is not a deliberate choice. The bargain "offered" by Baines is imposed upon her since her social standing gives her no other option than to accept it or lose her piano: as a Victorian wife, she owns nothing and has only her own body to trade.

Sue Gillett (1995) has produced an influential account of sexual violence in *The Piano* based on Irigaray, in which she argues that *The Piano* forms an example of what Irigaray calls "women on the market" (a metaphor for the patriarchal economy of desire), since Ada functions as a commodity exchanged between men. However, Gillett contends that this economy breaks down when Baines realizes that he does not want to dominate Ada but rather wants her to desire him, and she sees *The Piano* as an "attempt to envision an economy of sexual difference in which a woman's desire is able to circulate" (Gillett 1995, 285). Therefore, she insists that Baines's behavior cannot be equated with rape or harassment. However, while I agree with her that Baines is not a rapist, the film does extensively blur the boundaries between consent and violation. Ada herself harbors a double nature, as both an autonomous woman and one who surrenders to another's coercive desire. Irigaray develops an astute theory of sexual violence that can help us make sense of Ada's complex characterization, in which she suggests that what constitutes rape and the absence of consent is much more comprehensive than the commonly accepted definition of these terms.

In "This Sex Which Is Not One," the title essay of the eponymous book (Irigaray 1985, 23–33), Irigaray argues that woman is unknown to herself because the specificity of her body has been ignored in phallocentrism; the feminine is a virtuality that remains to be actualized. But if a woman's body is conceived of in its singularity, if her vagina is not thought of as "a masculine organ turned back around itself" (23), then what are its traits? What is her pleasure when we look beyond the pervasive imperiousness of man's jouissance? Irigaray does not give a definite answer, but she notes that woman touches herself continually: the lips that constitute her sex are in constant contact, and the pleasure that she derives from this ceaseless self-affection happens without mediation, beyond activity and passivity. In contrast, "in order to touch himself, man needs an instrument: his hand, a woman's body, language" (24). Thus, what marks sexuate difference for Irigaray can be thought of spatially, in terms of nearness and distance; woman is morphologically closer to herself than man. Her lips' constant touching forms her autoeroticism, a mode of being in herself and to the world that diverges profoundly from phallocentric definitions of what constitutes sexuality and from the way a man may experience his own body. Instead of relying on a logic of penetration, the lips' perpetual embrace is marked by intimacy and nearness. Thus, Irigaray opens the way to a reconceptualization of sexuality, beyond a mythical and deceitful concept of complementarity between the bodies of men and women, against which she proposes difference as the foundational principle of any attempt to think the sexes.

Irigaray suggests that what woman could be, hopefully will become, will grow with and through her body from the sheltered, silent touching of her sex, just as man emerges from his own specific body. Woman's virtuality, however, is yet to be actualized as phallocentrism forces its violent logic upon her. Once again, Irigaray pursues her analysis in spatial terms: "This autoeroticism is disrupted by a violent break-in: the brutal separation of the two lips by a violating penis, an intrusion that distracts and deflects the woman from this 'self-caressing' she needs if she is not to incur the disappearance of her own pleasure in sexual relations" (24). The autoeroticism of woman is, metaphorically, constantly interrupted as phallocentrism, the force that estranges her from herself, functions like a "violating penis." Irigaray suggests implicitly that the intrusive operation of phallocentrism is isomorphic to rape since its engagement with women forms a series of variations on the fundamental estrangement that separates woman from herself through a violent moving apart of the lips. Thereby, Irigaray reveals the brutality that lies at the heart of all phallocentric heterosexual carnal relations. But she also redefines sexual violence: instead of being limited to forceful penetration and its avatars (such as sexual harassment, catcalls, and the standardization of female beauty), it comes to encompass the very obliteration of femininity in phallocentrism.

Irigaray does not consider all heterosexual relationships to be embedded in violence. As noted earlier, in "Place, Interval," she gives a different picture of what a heterosexual encounter could be: one that would be produced by the close distance of the interval and in which the vagina, far from being seen as a passive receptacle, would be recognized in its active nature. Thus, the alienating moving apart of the lips is not a mechanism of violation inherent to heterosexual sex, but one that is produced by phallocentrism. However, similarly to Campion, Irigaray shows sexual violence to be pervasive within a phallic economy of desire and to taint heterosexual relations, even consensual ones. For instance, Irigaray writes that "woman, in this sexual imaginary, is only a more or less obliging prop for the enactment of man's fantasies. That she may find pleasure there in that role, by proxy, is possible, even certain. But such pleasure is, above all a masochistic prostitution of her body to a desire that is not her own, and it leaves her in a familiar state of dependency upon man" (25). In this passage, Irigaray does not deny that women may find pleasure in their sexual relations with men within phallocentrism–indeed, she argues that they often do. But this pleasure is not a woman's own, only a parasitical engagement, in the passive mode, with another body's desire. *The Piano*'s initial portrayal of the romance between Baines and Ada is disturbing because it is his desire that shapes the relationship and his force that seduces her. Her pleasure is an offshoot of his.

Irigaray puts the very possibility of consent into question. Indeed, how could woman truly consent if she does not even know what she wants? *The Piano*, as we have seen, raises similar concerns. I agree with Gillett's astute observation that Baines ultimately realizes that "his desire is for her desire" (Gillett 1995, 282) and not for domination. Yet desire, regardless of how we choose to assess the male character, originates in Baines, not in Ada. It is not a spontaneous and independent expression of her erotic force but a deliberately submissive response to the violence of his. Further, it is impossible to tell at what point abuse turns into consent since we do not know exactly when Ada ceases to resent Baines's caresses. Certainly, Ada chooses Baines after he has put an end to the sordid arrangement. But she finds a form of pleasure in being demeaned and falls in love with him. However felicitous the outcome, Baines's deal with Ada remains profoundly uncomfortable; her ultimate pleasure only reveals that she does not know what *she* wants, beyond his overbearing desire.[10] Echoing Irigaray, Campion lets the shadow of violation hover above the affair.

In *The Piano*, the narrative tension revolves around threats to the heroine's physical integrity.[11] Spatiality becomes a field of usurping, conquering, penetrating forces, as Campion suggests that sexual violence is at the heart of heterosexual erotics, pervading as it does the two relationships of the movie, between Ada and her husband and between Ada and Baines. Indeed, even Ada's love for Baines finds its source in the demeaning, alienating nature of their arrangement. Similarly, Irigaray shows that, through the intrusive separation of the lips, the operation of phallocentrism is to estrange woman from herself and from the needs and interests of her body, thereby making of the feminine a virtuality whose actualization is ceaselessly postponed.

Conclusion

Campion and Irigaray develop two remarkably similar understandings of spatiality in relation both to sexual difference and to sexual violence. Distance and closeness, the fundamental qualities of space, find two corresponding modes of expression, one positive and one negative, in each project. As we have just seen, in the negative sense, distance manifests as alienation, and closeness as a form of intrusion. In their positive understanding, they are portrayed as a safe distance, on the one hand, and intimacy, on the other. Irigaray proposes the nearness of the lips as the core of an alternative sexuality to phallocentrism, one that would affirm, rather than ignore, the specificity of women's bodies. She further develops her spatial conceptualization of sexual difference with the interval, which refers to the intimate separation that ensures that the physical and emotional integrity of the two subjects is respected. The distance of the interval is thus a closeness; it is the force of desire—which is also the force of difference—that brings two subjects together without engulfing one in the other. The interval and the lips find a correspondence in the close-up: like the latter, they are invested in a nearness toward which they move but never capture. In *The Piano*, Ada's inner self is conveyed through the alternation between the intimacy of the close-up and the unattainable distance of her being that marks her autonomy and that becomes literalized in the very last, underwater scene. Further, her mysterious intent resonates with the open-ended nature of women, of whom Irigaray suggests that their unknown qualities remain to be actualized. In sum, both Campion and Irigaray, in their respective languages, propose a reflection on femininity (its current restrictions, what it could become) that relies on complex spatial compositions, the subtle alternation between closeness and distance, whose vibratory force, if attuned to the needs of women's bodies, could sketch the geography of a new world.

Notes

1. *The Dimensions of Difference: Space, Time, and Bodies in Women's Cinema and Continental Philosophy* (2015), which features a longer version of the argument presented in this chapter.

2. I am indebted to their pathbreaking scholarship, but I depart from their views in that I articulate my approach to Irigaray less around a theorization of the feminine in cinema (Bainbridge 2008) and the representation of female consciousness (Bolton 2011) than around space and its relation to sexual difference.

3. Kathryn Bigelow was the first woman to win the Academy Award for Best Director for *The Hurt Locker* (2008), and the film made more than $17 million in the United States.

4. *The Piano* was made for about $7 million and grossed more than $40 million in the United States alone.

5. This was in fact Campion's second Palme d'or, as she had already received the Short Film Golden Palm in 1986 for *Peel: An Exercise in Discipline.*

6. Irigaray limits her discussion of the interval to straight sexuality since what interests her is a reconfiguration of sexual difference. However, Hill suggests that the concept can be used productively to think about queer sex as well (2012, 73–74).

7. Irigaray understands the envelope to be the overlap of the actual borders of one's body (the skin) and the lived experience of one's boundaries.

8. I do not see Ada as an embodiment of the feminine; in her early works, Irigaray suggests that the feminine, in phallocentrism, is not actualized (and perhaps will never be) but remains a virtuality, a force that makes woman constantly overflow the contours that have been assigned to her by a model designed according to the interests of male bodies.

9. Similarly, the film's soundtrack draws us into Ada's aural relation to the world.

10. We see Ada exploring her own active desire on one occasion, when she caresses Stewart while he is asleep. Tellingly, he cannot stand it and pushes her away, which confirms that Ada's active desire cannot be contained by phallocentric norms.

11. It should be noted that these threats to Ada's body are echoed in the very context of the film—the colonization of New Zealand—as both evoke an invasive intrusion. However, properly accounting for Campion's very controversial treatment of racial and colonial relations would lead us too far away from the virtual dialogue between Campion and Irigaray that this article establishes. For further reflections, see, among others, Dyson 1995, Reid 2000, and McHugh 2007.

Works Cited

Bainbridge, Caroline. 2008. *A Feminine Cinematics: Luce Irigaray, Women and Film.* UK: Palgrave Macmillan.

Bigelow, Kathryn. 2008. *The Hurt Locker*. Seattle: First Light Productions.

Bolton, Lucy. 2011. *Film and Female Consciousness: Irigaray, Cinema and Thinking Women.* UK: Palgrave Macmillan.

Campion, Jane. 1993. *The Piano.* New Zealand: The Australian Film Commission.

Dyson, Lynda. 1995. "The Return of the Repressed? Whiteness, Femininity and Colonialism in *The Piano.*" *Screen* 36, no. 3: 267–76.

Gillett, Sue. 1995. "Lips and Fingers: Jane Campion's *The Piano.*" *Screen* 36, no. 3: 277–87.

Godart, Caroline. 2015. *The Dimensions of Difference: Space, Time, and Bodies in Women's Cinema and Continental Philosophy*. London: Rowman and Littlefield.

Hill, Rebecca. 2008. "Interval, Sexual Difference: Luce Irigaray and Henri Bergson." *Hypatia* 23, no. 1: 119–31.

———. 2012. *The Interval: Relation and Becoming in Irigaray, Aristotle, and Bergson.* New York: Fordham University Press.

Hood, Thomas. 2005. "Silence." In *The Poetical Works of Thomas Hood.* New York: A. L. Burt. http://www.gutenberg.org/files/15652/15652-h/15652-h.htm.

Irigaray, Luce. 1974. *Speculum, de l'autre femme.* Paris: Editions de Minuit. Translated by Gillian Gill as *Speculum of the Other Woman.* Ithaca: Cornell University Press, 1985.

———. 1977. *Ce Sexe qui n'en est pas un.* Paris: Editions de Minuit. Translated by Catherine Porter and Carolyn Burke as *This Sex Which Is Not One.* Ithaca: Cornell University Press, 1985.

———. 1984. *Ethique de la différence sexuelle.* Paris: Editions de Minuit. Translated by Carolyn Burke and Gillian Gill as *An Ethics of Sexual Difference.* Ithaca: Cornell University Press, 1993.

———. 2008. *Sharing the World.* London: Continuum.

Knight, Christine. 2006. "Ada's Piano-Playing in Jane Campion's *The Piano.*" *Australian Feminist Studies* 21: 23–34.

McHugh, Kathleen. 2007. *Jane Campion.* Urbana: University of Illinois Press.

Polan, Dana B. 2001. *Jane Campion.* London: British Film Institute.

Reid, Mark A. 2000. "A Few Black Keys and Maori Tattoos: Rereading Jane Campion's *The Piano* in Post-Negritude Time." *Quarterly Review of Film & Video* 17, no. 2: 107–16.

Sobchack, Vivian. 2004. *Carnal Thoughts.* Berkeley: University of California Press.

Contributors

Louise Burchill works mainly in contemporary French philosophy, feminist theory, and space studies. The translator of Alain Badiou's *Deleuze: The Clamor of Being*; *Second Manifesto for Philosophy*; and *Philosophy and the Event*, she has also published numerous texts on the respective work of Luce Irigaray and Badiou, among which the following figure most recently: "Reconsidering *chôra*, Architecture, and 'the Feminine,'" *Field Journal* 7, no. 1 (November 2017); "Woman's Adventures with/in the Universal," in *Badiou and His Interlocutors*, edited by Adam J. Bartlett (Bloomsbury 2018); and "Of a Universal No Longer Indifferent to Difference: Badiou (and Irigaray) on Woman, Truths, and Philosophy," *Philosophy Today* 62, no. 4 (Fall 2018).

Caroline Godart is an assistant professor of communication and cultural studies at the Institut des Hautes Études des Communications Sociales and a mentor at Advanced Performance and Scenography Studies, both in Brussels, Belgium. She is the author of *The Dimensions of Difference: Space, Time, and Bodies in Women's Cinema and Continental Philosophy* (Rowman and Littlefield 2015). Working on a new book addressing our relationship to nature, she has developed an unexpected interest in mitochondria and other organelles. Alongside her academic career, she is active as a dramaturg in the buoyant Brussels performing arts scene, where she collaborates with choreographers, stage directors, and visual/sound artists.

Rebecca Hill is a senior lecturer in literary studies at RMIT University in Melbourne (Eastern Kulin Nations), Australia. She is the author of *The Interval: Relation and Becoming in Irigaray, Aristotle, and Bergson* (Fordham University Press 2012) and the coeditor of *Philosophies of Difference: Nature, Racism, and Sexuate Difference* (Routledge 2018). Her research engages with the concepts of difference, time, place, and sexuate difference in continental philosophy and feminist theory. She is particularly concerned with elaborating her thought in relationship to Australian Indigenous ontology, and she acknowledges First Nations ancestors, elders, and leaders throughout Australia.

Emily A. Holmes is an associate professor in the Department of Religion and Philosophy at Christian Brothers University in Memphis, Tennessee. She is the author of *Flesh Made Word: Medieval Women Mystics, Writing, and the Incarnation* (Baylor University Press 2013) and the coeditor of *Women, Writing, Theology: Transforming a Tradition of Exclusion* (Baylor University Press 2011) and *Breathing with Luce Irigaray* (Bloomsbury 2013). Her teaching and research interests include women's writing practices in Christian history, feminist theology, religious pluralism, and the spirituality and ethics of eating.

Luce Irigaray is one of the greatest living philosophers writing in French or in English today. As Elena Tzelepis and Athena Athanasiou wrote in 2010 in *Rewriting Difference: Luce Irigaray and "the Greeks"* (State University of New York Press 2010), she is "director of research at the *Centre National de Recherches Scientifiques* (*CNRS* Philosophy Commission) in Paris, and she has held teaching positions in Paris and internationally, including positions at the University of Rotterdam, the University of Toronto," and various prominent institutions in the United Kingdom. "She has [also] been a grassroots activist and a practicing psychoanalyst" (275). Her body of work is vast and encyclopedic, comprising linguistics, sociology, and psychoanalysis; ancient, modern, and contemporary philosophy; feminist theory and politics; spirituality and the divine; art, architecture, and aesthetics; and life-thinking, nature, and sustainability.

Phyllis H. Kaminski is a professor emerita of religious studies at Saint Mary's College, Notre Dame, Indiana. She has taught undergraduate courses in religious studies; Catholic theology; and religion, sex, and gender. She studies the implications of Luce Irigaray's work for feminist spirituality. Among her publications are "Desire and Contemplative Silence: A Feminist Exploration of Transformation within and beyond Tradition," in *The Shaping of Tradition: Context and Normativity*, Annua Nuntia Lovanienses 70 (Peeters 2013); and "Holy Mary, Holy Desire: Luce Irigaray and Saintly Daughters," in *The Postmodern "Saints" of France*, edited by Colby Dickinson (T&T Clark 2013).

Erla Karlsdottir is a researcher engaged in a project entitled "Feminist Philosophy Transforming Philosophy" at the University of Iceland. She has translated texts by Irigaray into Icelandic and was coauthor of a *Calendar of Women Philosophers*, published by the University of Iceland Press in 2015. She teaches philosophy in a gymnasium.

Eva Maria Korsisaari is a researcher and activist concentrating on both combating violence and creating ethics. She has been a university lecturer in gender studies at the University of Helsinki and, within the institutional structures of Finnish NGOs, has worked against international human trafficking. Currently, she is managing a feminist publishing house and an autonomous research center.

Cheryl Lynch-Lawler is a training and supervising psychoanalyst on the faculty of the Saint Louis Psychoanalytic Institute where she also serves as Dean of Candidates. Her lens is transdisciplinary and includes psychoanalysis, feminist love studies, threshold hermeneutics, and feminist and pre-Socratic philosophy. She has presented and published papers on a range of interdisciplinary subjects, and her most recent publication, "Plato's Creative Imagination: (Re)Membering the *Chora*(l) Love that *We Are*," appears in the journal *Feminist Theology*. She is currently completing work on transmuting the concept of "womb envy."

Ellen Mortensen is a professor of comparative literature at the University of Bergen, Norway, and academic director of the Holberg Prize. She is author of *The Feminine and Nihilism: Luce Irigaray with Nietzsche and Heidegger* (Scandinavian University Press 1994) and *Touching Thought: Ontology and Sexual Difference* (Lexington Books 2002), as well as editor of, among others, *Sex, Breath and Force* (Lexington Books 2006). Mortensen has also published a number of articles on authors such as Baudelaire, Dickinson, Ibsen, Woolf, and Hamsun, to mention a few, and on feminist and queer theory.

Peg Rawes is a professor of architecture and philosophy and director of the master's program in architectural history at the Bartlett School of Architecture, University College, London, UK. Her research focuses on social and architectural histories of well-being, especially in contemporary housing, ecologies, and poetics. Her publications include "Housing Biopolitics and Care," in *Critical and Clinical Cartographies* (Edinburgh University Press

2017), and the edited collections *Poetic Biopolitics: Practices of Relation in Architecture and the Arts*, (with Timothy Mathews and Stephen Loo) (I. B. Tauris 2016) and *Relational Architectural Ecologies: Architecture, Subjectivity and Nature* (Routledge 2013). Her works have published architects alongside practitioners in the arts, specialists in environmental and human rights, and specialists in social and medical research.

Kristin Sampson is a professor of philosophy at the University of Bergen, Norway. She works mainly in the areas of ancient philosophy—primarily Plato and early Greek thought going back to Homer and Hesiod—and feminist philosophy, with a particular focus on the thought of Luce Irigaray. Her latest publications include "Hypatia: Famous and Forgotten" (2018), "Visible and Audible Movement in the *Protagoras*" (2017), and "The Temporality of Philosophy in the *Apology*" (2018).

Karen Schiler is an associate professor of English at Oklahoma City University, where she currently serves as chair of the department of English and modern languages. She teaches rhetorical and creative writing and some literature courses. Her work explores how we teach writing of all kinds and the composition of ethos and imaginaries in rhetorics of nonviolence and in literature for adolescents. She is the recipient of the Distinguished Faculty Award for the Oklahoma City University Honors Program and the Excellence in Teaching Award for Full-Time Faculty.

Britt-Marie Schiller is a professor emerita of philosophy at Webster University. She is also a training and supervising psychoanalyst at the St. Louis Psychoanalytic Institute and associate head of the Department of Psychoanalytic Education of the American Psychoanalytic Association. Her current research is in the intersections of psychoanalysis, philosophy, gender/sexuality, and art. Her most recent publications are "Disillusioning Gender" and "Hair, Threads, and Umbilical Cords: Louise Bourgeois's Dream of Connection."

Gail M. Schwab is a professor emerita of French at Hofstra University, Hempstead, New York. She is the translator of Luce Irigaray's *To Speak Is Never Neutral* (Continuum 2002) and of "Towards a Sharing of Speech" and "Spiritual Tasks for our Age" from *Key Writings* (Continuum 2004). She has published articles on many different aspects of Irigaray's work, including psychoanalysis, linguistics, law, relations between and among women, spirituality, Greek tragedy and mythology, pedagogy, and nature, agriculture, and sustainability. Her most recent publication, "Creating Inter-Sexuate Inter-Subjectivity in the Classroom?" appears in the collection *Engaging the World*, edited by Mary Rawlinson (State University of New York Press 2016).

Fanny Söderbäck is an associate professor of philosophy at DePaul University and cofounder and codirector of the Kristeva Circle. Her book *Revolutionary Time: On Time and Difference in Kristeva and Irigaray* is forthcoming with the State University of New York Press. Söderbäck edited *Feminist Readings of Antigone* (State University of New York Press 2010) and is a coeditor of the volume *Undutiful Daughters: New Directions in Feminist Thought and Practice* (Palgrave Macmillan 2012). She is also the editor of a special issue of *philoSOPHIA* on the topic of birth. Her current research includes a monograph on the Italian feminist thinker Adriana Cavarero and a project that puts into conversation Julia Kristeva and Gloria Anzaldúa around issues of foreignness and strangeness.

Alison Stone is a professor of European philosophy at Lancaster University in the United Kingdom. She has published widely on German idealism and romanticism, feminist philosophy, psychoanalysis, and, most recently, popular music. Her books include *Luce Irigaray and the Philosophy of Sexual Difference* (Cambridge University Press 2006) and *Feminism, Psychoanalysis, and Maternal Subjectivity* (Routledge 2011). Currently, she is completing her latest book, *Being Born: Birth and Philosophy.*

Sigridur Thorgeirsdottir is a professor of philosophy at the University of Iceland and principal investigator on the research projects "Feminist Philosophy Transforming Philosophy" and "Embodied Critical Thinking." She has published books on Nietzsche, feminist philosophy, Arendt and Beauvoir, and the philosophy of the body and nature, as well as on women in the history of philosophy. Thorgeirsdottir is chair of the Committee on Gender Issues of the International Federation of Philosophical Societies, a sponsor of the World Congress of Philosophy. She is also one of the founders of the United Nations University Gender and Equality Studies and Training Programme.

Tomoka Toraiwa is an associate professor in the Department of English Language and Culture at Keiwa College, Japan. Her major interests are the philosophy of education and gender and sexuality. She is currently a principal investigator on a comparative research project on the effects of governmentality on nonheterosexual women in Japan and Singapore. Her recent publications include "Coming Together in Difference: Democracy and Multiplicity in Dewey's *Democracy and Education*," *Bulletin of the John Dewey Society of Japan* 59 (2018) and "Enabling Education: Rethinking the Teacher-Student Relationship through Luce Irigaray's Ethics of Difference," in *Building a New World: Luce Irigaray: Teaching II*, edited by Luce Irigaray and Michael Marder (Palgrave Macmillan 2015).

Anne van Leeuwen is an assistant professor of philosophy and religion at James Madison University, Harrisonburg, Virginia. Her research is in twentieth-century French and German philosophy—from critical theory to psychoanalysis to structuralism and poststructuralism—and she is particularly interested in the relationship between feminist theory and materialist politics within this tradition. Van Leeuwen teaches a range of courses on twentieth-century French philosophy, critical theory, philosophy and film, and on philosophy, art, and literature; she also runs the Philosophy and Film Club.

Index

www.ingramcontent.com/pod-product-compliance
Lightning Source LLC
Chambersburg PA
CBHW020238290326
41929CB00044B/92

* 9 7 8 1 4 3 8 4 7 7 8 2 4 *